DICKENS'S IDIOMATIC IMAGINATION

DICKENS'S IDIOMATIC IMAGINATION

THE INIMITABLE AND VICTORIAN BODY LANGUAGE

PETER J. CAPUANO

CORNELL UNIVERSITY PRESS
Ithaca and London

Copyright © 2023 by Peter J. Capuano

All rights reserved. Except for brief quotations in a review, this book, or parts thereof, must not be reproduced in any form without permission in writing from the publisher. For information, address Cornell University Press, Sage House, 512 East State Street, Ithaca, New York 14850. Visit our website at cornellpress.cornell.edu.

First published 2023 by Cornell University Press

Library of Congress Cataloging-in-Publication Data

Names: Capuano, Peter J., author.
Title: Dickens's idiomatic imagination : the inimitable and
    Victorian body language / Peter J. Capuano.
Description: Ithaca [New York] : Cornell University Press,
    2023. | Includes bibliographical references and index.
Identifiers: LCCN 2023004248 (print) | LCCN 2023004249
    (ebook) | ISBN 9781501772856 (hardcover) |
    ISBN 9781501772863 (paperback) | ISBN
    9781501772870 (epub) | ISBN 9781501772887 (pdf)
Subjects: LCSH: Dickens, Charles, 1812-1870—Literary
    style. | Human body and language. | Human body in
    literature. | English language—Idioms.
Classification: LCC PR4594 .C37 2023 (print) | LCC
    PR4594 (ebook) | DDC 823 / .8—dc23 / eng / 20230208
LC record available at https://lccn.loc.gov/2023004248
LC ebook record available at https://lccn.loc.gov
    /2023004249

*For the Thomas family, who have for so long helped
make Nebraska (and Montana) home.*

What *is* present in the novel is an artistic *system* of languages . . . and the real task of stylistic analysis consists in uncovering all the available orchestrating languages in the composition of the novel, grasping the precise degree of distancing that separates each language from its most immediate semantic instantiation in the work as a whole, and the varying angles of refraction of intentions within it, understanding their dialogic interrelationships and—finally—if there *is* direct authorial discourse, determining the heteroglot background outside the work that dialogizes it.

Mikhail Bakhtin, "Discourse in the Novel" (1934–35)

Contents

Acknowledgments   ix

Introduction: Victorian Idiom and the
Dickensian "Toe in the Water"   1

1. The Beginnings of Dickens's Idiomatic
   Imagination: *Dombey and Son*'s
   "Right-Hand Man"   30

2. "Shouldering the Wheel" in
   Bleak House   80

3. "Brought Up by Hand": The Manual
   Outlay of *Great Expectations*   126

4. Sweat Work and Nose Grinding in
   Our Mutual Friend   171

Conclusion: The Afterlife of Idiomatic
Absorption Among Novelists and Critics   217

Appendix A: List of 100 Commonly Used Idioms   229

*Appendix B: Nineteenth-Century British Novel
Corpus for Idiom Usage Comparison*   233

*Appendix C: Full Code Used for Data
Comparisons*   239

Bibliography   243

Index   267

ACKNOWLEDGMENTS

This book's earliest iterations began at the National Humanities Center. There, I was fortunate enough to be involved in a two-year fellowship in Digital Textual Studies led by Willard McCarty and Matt Jockers. What I learned from these grant leaders and my cohort about text mining helped me to conceive of a project dealing with thousands of novels and hundreds of idiomatic expressions. During a research trip to the United Kingdom in the summer of 2016, I was lucky to meet with Michaela Mahlberg and her team at the University of Birmingham while they were developing the CLiC (Corpus Linguistics in Context) Dickens application. It was there that I first wondered how and why Dickens used certain idioms only in certain novels throughout his career. Later that summer, Jim Adams invited me to deliver a plenary talk at the Dickens Universe titled "Digital Dombey: The Computation of Dickensian Idioms," and I am indebted to the faculty, graduate students, and general audience for their engagement with my germinating ideas. I am similarly indebted to the University of Virginia's Department of English for an invitation to present an early version of my work at their Nineteenth-Century Workshop. The thoughts and questions I received there from Alison Booth, Andrew Stauffer, Chip Tucker, Karen Chase, and Steve Arata, among others, pushed me to think in new ways. Audiences at the following venues were also instrumental in this book's development: University of Colorado, Arizona State University, University of North Carolina, University of Wisconsin, Northern Illinois University, and Iowa State University's Digital Humanities Symposium. I am grateful, too, for the Dickens Society's invitations to speak at Modern Language Association conferences in Seattle, Vancouver, and San Francisco. A portion of chapter 1 appeared in *Dickens Quarterly*, copyright © 2022, The Dickens Society. This article first appeared in *Dickens Quarterly* 39, no. 4 (December 2022): 460–85. I thank General Editor Dominic Rainsford and the Johns Hopkins University Press for permission to republish this material in a revised and extended form here.

My home institution, the University of Nebraska–Lincoln, has provided support both large and small since I began this book as well. Early on, collaborations

x ACKNOWLEDGMENTS

with scholars in Nebraska's Literary Lab, the Center for Digital Research in the Humanities (CDRH), and the Interdisciplinary Nineteenth-Century Program have proven invaluable. I would like to thank particularly Marco Abel, Steve Behrendt, Michael Burton, Melissa Homestead, Guy Reynolds, Will Thomas, Stacey Waite, Laura White, and Adrian Wisnicki for their steadfast friendship and encouragement. My students at Nebraska, from the Dickens course to the Body Studies seminar, deserve applause, not only for humoring my growing obsession with idioms but also for constantly challenging my assumptions and offering me discerning pathways to think about the formation of vernacular body language in general. There is also no way I could be as confident about my word and idiom counts—particularly in the conclusion—without the superb work (counting and recounting, manually and by machine) of my graduate research assistants over the past several years: Caitlin Mathies, Luke Folk, Anne Nagel, Will Turner, Jonathan Cheng, and Trevor Bleick. In calmly helping me navigate through moments of desperation with interlibrary loans and maxed-out book limits, Brian O'Grady at Love Library deserves special thanks. This book would be far worse were it not for the following friends and colleagues who have read and commented on the project at various key stages: Barbara Black, Jay Clayton, Paul Fyfe, Peter Henry, Matt Jockers, Colin McLear, Daniel Pollack-Pelzner, Andrew Stauffer, Stacey Waite, and Adrian Wisnicki. I would know much less about Dickens's compositional processes without the generous access to the handwritten manuscripts offered to me by Douglas Dodds at the Victoria & Albert Museum and Philip Palmer at the Morgan Pierpont Library and Museum. Mahinder Kingra at Cornell University Press has been everything that an author could ever ask for since he assured me that he would be a "hands-on" (his idiom!) editor from the very start of the process; he patiently read and responded with wit and wisdom to every challenge and triumph along the way.

Last, I cannot fathom how this project could have been completed without the love and support of my family in Boston: Mom and Kenny, Dad and Janet, Missy and Jeff, Uncle Johnny and Auntie Carol, Auntie Neasie, Auntie Kate, and my four precious nieces, Parker, Sarah, Mia, and Mariah.

Introduction
Victorian Idiom and the Dickensian "Toe in the Water"

> There is a very deep material bond between language and the body, which communication theories that concentrate on the passing of messages typically miss: many poems, many kinds of writing, indeed a lot of everyday speech communicate what is in effect a life rhythm and the interaction of these life rhythms is probably a very important part of the material process of writing and reading.
>
> —Raymond Williams, *Politics and Letters* (1979)

This book argues that Charles Dickens develops a unique idiomatic style, deeply rooted in bodily expression, which eventually emerges as a fundamental dimension to the way he imagines his most mature and iconic fictional worlds. I did not originally set out to write a book about Dickens's use of idiomatic language, however. I began instead with an interest in researching how, when, and what it could mean that figurative expressions related to the body start to show up in Victorian novels. This broader interest took on more focus during a two-year grant in Digital Textual Studies from the National Humanities Center, where I assembled corpuses of nineteenth-century British novels and mined them for idiomatic body expressions. Surprisingly, Victorian authors, as it turns out, do not use idiomatic body expressions all that much and, when they do, the expressions are often literal or only partially idiomatic. In Charlotte Brontë's *Jane Eyre* (1847), for example, Jane's early experience of being "browbeaten" in her aunt's household is quite literally connected to the physical blows that John Reed delivers to her forehead in the novel's opening chapters (14). Her bullying cousin does not make "tongue-in-cheek" disparagements of Jane; he does so directly, "thrust[ing] his tongue into his cheek whenever he [sees]" her (26). If Brontë did not use many body idioms figuratively, however, I was almost certain that William Thackeray would. I expected to witness a myriad of "cold shoulders" turned by the prodigiously class-conscious

2   **INTRODUCTION**

characters in Thackeray's expansive and highly choreographed social satires. But instead, throughout his entire oeuvre, we get only a single (literal) description of "how the knife boy was caught stealing a cold shoulder of mutton" from the kitchen in *Vanity Fair* (1847–48) (49). This is not to imply that most Victorian novelists used idiomatic expressions only literally. What I encountered in the majority of cases in terms of idiomatic body expressions, though, was largely uninteresting and, worse yet, fairly predictable. Take the case of the body idioms that appear in George Eliot's major novels. It is hardly controversial to think of Eliot as a deeply cerebral and philosophical prose writer. It is not very remarkable, then, to discover that idioms involving the "mindsets" of her characters ("state of mind," "the same mind," "peace of mind," "on her/his mind," etc.) make up al-most half (44%) of all the body idioms Eliot uses in her major fiction.[1]

On the other hand, given what we know about Charles Dickens—his limited education, his time spent at Warren's Blacking Factory and Marshalsea debtor's prison, the intensely physical outlets he required for his astonishing energy (as an obsessive walker, passionate amateur actor, and exuberant public speaker), his attraction to "everyday" language (*Household Words*)—one might reasonably predict that Dickens would be a heavy user of body idioms in his work of all kinds. As impressive as it is, we may not be surprised to learn that the *Oxford Dictionary of English Idioms* (2009) lists Dickens among its most cited sources, alongside the Bible and Shakespeare. What is astonishing, however, is the *extent* to which Dickens is truly "inimitable" in comparison to his peers when it comes to his use of idiomatic language involving the body.

And it is not simply a matter of Dickens using a lot of body idioms either; it is that he uses, by far, the greatest variety of them as well. The tables below dem-onstrate how, when considering the unique body idioms used per novel, 12 of Dickens's novels hold the top 15 positions in my corpus of 124 novels by 11 dif-ferent Victorian authors (Table A). Dickens generally writes long novels, but so

---

1. In order to make comparisons between Victorian authors' use of idiomatic language, I as-sembled a corpus of 124 novels by 11 different authors and searched for the 100 most frequently used body idioms. This list of 100 idioms is derived from the "body" sections of volumes 1 and 2 of the *Oxford Dictionary of Current Idiomatic English* (1975, 1983). For a complete list of the body idioms as well as a list of the authors and novels used in my data, see appendixes A and B. Although it would certainly be possible to search for and count all occurrences of these idioms in every one of the 124 novels by hand, it would not be very practical. Instead of hand counting the body idioms in each novel, a simple looping script was developed that cycled through all of the novels, one at a time, test-ing for the presence of the idioms. When matches for a given idiom were found, the algorithm re-corded/counted the occurrences, and those data were then exported to an Excel file for easier review. See appendix C for both simplified and full versions of the code used in this process. I also recorded the total number of words in each novel so that the relative frequencies of each idiom (i.e., occur-rences per 100,000 words) could be calculated.

INTRODUCTION 3

Introduction Tables A and B

TABLE A	TABLE B
Unique Body Idioms Used per Novel	Body Idioms Used per 100,000 Words
1. *Bleak House* (45)	1. *Barnaby Rudge* (28.83)
2. *Martin Chuzzlewit* (41)	2. *The Old Curiosity Shop* (27.29)
3. *Dombey and Son* (41)	3. *Oliver Twist* (25.56)
4. *The Old Curiosity Shop* (39)	4. *A Christmas Carol* (23.80)
5. *Nicholas Nickleby* (38)	5. *Our Mutual Friend* (23.41)
6. *Barnaby Rudge* (38)	6. *Martin Chuzzlewit* (23.31)
7. *Our Mutual Friend* (37)	7. *Dombey and Son* (22.37)
8. *David Copperfield* (35)	8. *Bleak House* (22.13)
9. *Pickwick Papers* (33)	9. *Nicholas Nickleby* (21.07)
10. *Little Dorrit* (30)	10. *Tess of the D'Urbervilles* [Hardy] (20.41)
11. *Sketches by Boz* (29)	11. *Miss Marjoribanks* [Oliphant] (20.40)
12. *Vanity Fair* [Thackeray] (28)	12. *Romola* [Eliot] (19.69)
13. *Oliver Twist* (26)	13. *David Copperfield* (19.64)
14. *Hopes and Fears* [Yonge] (26)	14. *The Mayor of Casterbridge* [Hardy] (19.45)
15. *The Eustace Diamonds* [Trollope] (26)	15. *Pickwick Papers* (19.42)

do many of the authors in this corpus, including Charlotte Brontë, William Thackeray, George Eliot, Anthony Trollope, Margaret Oliphant, and Thomas Hardy. Nonetheless, to be sure that I was coming as close as I could to comparing apples to apples in my idiom measures, I tallied the total number of words in each novel so that the relative frequencies of each idiom (i.e., occurrences per 100,000 words) would be accurately recorded. What we see when adjusting for book length, therefore, is that Dickens's novels hold nine of the top ten positions and eleven of the top fifteen (Table B). I should also note that, for fear of unduly privileging Dickens, I do not include in these calculations the principal body idioms around which my main chapters take as their foci ("right-hand man," "shoulder to the wheel," "brought up by hand," "by the sweat of the brow," and "nose to the grindstone"). Had I included them, Dickens's novels would be even more prevalent in each table.

I begin by presenting the numerical comparisons above not because they "prove" anything definitive about Dickens but so that readers will have some context for my decision to write a book that sets out to analyze what such a seemingly minute lexical unit like body-derived idioms can tell us about the "Inimitable's" fictional imagination.

4   INTRODUCTION

Digital Methodologies

For good reason, literary scholars continue to wrestle with the place (even if it is to have one at all) of computer-assisted research in the humanities. "Traditional" critics justifiably object to the ways in which quantitative data often masquerade as a version of unquestioned and, ultimately, false objectivity.[2] As Lisa Gitleman makes explicit in the title of a book she edits, *"Raw Data" Is an Oxymoron*, numbers always come to the researcher "cooked" in one way or another simply because designing and implementing a text-analysis program is itself a necessarily interpretive act, not just a digital one.[3] This means I must acknowledge that the 124 novels by 11 different authors I use in my calculations constitutes *my* attempt to construct a representative sample—albeit a canonical one—of nineteenth-century British fiction against which to measure Dickens's idiom usage.[4] In later chapters, I draw on the Chadwyck-Healy database of 250 nineteenth-century English novels, another corpus of over 3,700 novels, as well as millions of pages of newspapers, journals, essays, and other periodical print material in an attempt to reach a point of what Andrew Piper (2022, 6) has called "evidentiary sufficiency" that far exceeds what we encounter in most traditional literary analyses. With this in mind, even bona fide skeptics of data mining and so-called distant reading practices like Johanna Drucker (2017, 631, 633) acknowledge that digital tools "can be helpful as departure points for research" because they "permi[t] the investigation of social and cultural issues in texts at a scale no representative single exegesis can produce."[5] Similarly, although Stephen Best and Sharon Marcus (2009, 17) correctly refer to computers as "weak interpreters but potent describers," they concede that machine reading "can help us to find features that texts have in common in ways that our brains alone cannot." Like me, Best and Marcus do

---

2. Early on, Gayatri Spivak (2003, 108) objected to digital methodologies' "claim to scopic vision" and this has remained a point of skepticism.

3. Katherine Bode makes a similarly valid point about the need for transparency in quantitative analyses. See *A World of Fiction: Digital Collections and the Future of Literary History* (2018). For the most sweeping, and controversial, critique of digital humanities research, see Nan Z. Da, "The Computational Case against Computational Criticism" (2019).

4. I maintain, however, that a digital approach that is open and forthright about where, how, and why it derives its data is a good deal more transparent than what we so often encounter in traditional analogue literary criticism where we almost never hear about the range of evidence that has been considered and what is considered as evidence. As Andrew Piper (2018, 11) has recently put it, "In traditional critical practices, we only ever hear about the passages and works that fit [the] thesis. . . . We almost *never* hear about the ones that did not, how many were considered, and how prevalent the phenomenon is that we are observing more generally."

5. See "Why Distant Reading Isn't" (Drucker 2017).

INTRODUCTION 5

not envision a world in which computers replace literary critics, but they are "curious about one in which we work with them to expand what we do" (17).[6]

Such is the spirit in which this project began. Dickens's extraordinarily high use of body idioms in comparison with his peers became an opportunity for provocation rather than simply proof; it was exploratory for me rather than strictly evidentiary. My interests lie in discovering what is distinctive but not necessarily definitive about Dickens's imagination as I analyze his imaginative processes through the alembic of his unique idiomatic propensities. Therefore, my predominant approach, even as it draws on numerical data, is not "truth" driven nor is it meant to be confirmational. I am far less interested in reaching interpretive closure, with proving or confirming anything about Dickens than I am with asking new questions about when, how, and why he came to rely so heavily on what I call his "idiomatic imagination."[7] Moreover, as my first footnote suggests, my ideas about Dickens's idiomatic imagination are not predicated on any elaborate or abstruse digital programming. The simple looping algorithm by which I identify bodily idioms in my corpora adheres in this sense to what Roopika Risam and others have begun to refer to as "minimal computing."[8] My practice aligns with a new generation of digital humanities practitioners whose relatively uncomplicated searches manage to provide the opportunity to ask complex and nuanced questions regarding what we thought we already knew about particular aspects of literary history. Daniel Shore advocates for *Cyberformalism*—a method of using simple search tools to radically expand as well as contextualize our understanding of what his colonic title calls *Histories of Linguistic Forms* (2018). Likewise, in *Reductive Reading*, Sarah Allison (2018, 30) contends that the major methodological contribution of computational analysis is the freedom it confers on us to read reductively, "through an aggressively simplistic lens" that paradoxically generates ways to

---

6. This openness to the interpretive possibilities that computer-assisted research can generate is shared even by corpus linguists like Michaela Malhberg (2013, 45, 46), who argue that algorithmically derived word clusters "can serve as starting points for further detailed analysis." In Mahlberg's view, like my own, the digital methodologies "do not replace other forms of stylistic analyses but complement them."

7. In this endeavor, I have been influenced by the orientation of digital humanists like Andrew Piper (2018, 6), who endorse the ways in which "computation, when applied critically and creatively, can confirm, revise, but also invent new narratives about literary history." Even so, Piper (2020, 6) acknowledges, and I concur, that no matter how exhaustive and transparent an algorithmically informed investigation of texts is, it will never "fully explicate once and for all the question of textual meaning."

8. See the 2022 special issue of *Digital Humanities Quarterly* (16, no. 2) dedicated to the practice of "Minimal Computing" in which the editors, Roopika Risam and Alex Gil, consider minimal or minimalist digital approaches undertaken either by choice or necessity. Though the data behind Mahlberg et al.'s (2020) CLiC applications are anything but simple, I would consider a user's interaction with the databases as a "minimal computing."

6   INTRODUCTION

open up new discussion by reducing literary problems to simpler terms. For me, ultimately, the power of minimal computing lies in its ability to show us how digital methods usually associated with distance and data crunching can direct us to a new kind of close reading often occluded because of our ordinary or traditional reading practices.

By identifying, comparing, and contextualizing the occurrences of certain uniquely Dickensian idioms, my book joins important conversations about the "scales" of reading—both digital and analogic. The search for body idioms at the center of this project actually makes the incorporation of several typically antithetical modes of reading—from Katherine Hayles's "hyper-reading" (2010) and Stephen Best and Sharon Marcus's "surface reading" (2009) to Alison Booth's "mid-range" reading (2017) and Jonathan Culler's "close reading" (2010)[9]—not only possible, but it also presents a rare opportunity to survey the benefits and limitations of purportedly "rival" interpretive practices. For example, many Victorian scholars in all likelihood have hyper- or surface read all 124 novels in my original corpus. Dickens specialists *may* and probably *have* performed traditional, "close," analogue readings (if not several directed but analogical rereadings) of every single one of Dickens's (seventeen)[10] novels at one time or another over the course of their careers. Thus, simply having read all of Dickens's fiction is a good example of what Booth has recently advocated in terms of a categorical "mid-range" reading. Having read a single author's entire oeuvre is not only possible but probable among specialists. Without digital tools (and unsophisticated ones at that), however, even the most earnest, perspicacious, and intellectually gifted Dickensian scholar will not notice, never mind consider, the importance of the fact that Dickens uses the idiom "right-hand man" only four times in his career but only in *Dombey and Son* (1846–48); "shoulder to the wheel" nineteen times but only in *Bleak House* (1852–53); "brought up by hand" more than thirty times but only in *Great Expectations* (1860–61); "by the sweat of the brow" and "nose to the grindstone" a combined forty-three times but only in *Our Mutual Friend* (1864–65).[11] From the departure point of this book, as Ted Underwood (2013, 9) has framed the

---

9. See Hayles, "How We Read: Close, Hyper, Machine" (2010); Marcus and Best, "Surface Reading: An Introduction" (2009); Booth, "Mid-range Reading: Not a Manifesto" (2017); and Culler, "The Closeness of Close Reading" (2010).

10. For the purposes of this study, the seventeen novels I refer to in Dickens's oeuvre are *Sketches by Boz, Pickwick Papers, Oliver Twist, Nicholas Nickleby, The Old Curiosity Shop, Barnaby Rudge, A Christmas Carol, Martin Chuzzlewit, Dombey and Son, David Copperfield, Bleak House, Hard Times, Little Dorrit, A Tale of Two Cities, Great Expectations, Our Mutual Friend*, and *The Mystery of Edwin Drood*.

11. Though Dickens never uses these idioms in any other novels, the numerical instances I cite here are approximate since I include collocations and variants of the expressions as well as the idioms as they are exactly worded here.

INTRODUCTION 7

case for digital methods in the humanities more generally, "we are probably overlooking important patterns because they happen to be invisible on the scale of reading we normally inhabit." But not all patterns are important, of course. The remainder of this introduction and, indeed, each detailed chapter that follows it will make the case for why bodily derived idiomatic expressions matter in Dickens's fiction as a vital but yet unremarked upon dimension of his imagination.[12]

Why Dickens? And Why Body Idioms?

I began by demonstrating the numerical extent to which Dickens surpassed his peers in his usage of idiomatic body language, and each of my upcoming chapters will incorporate digital search methods that consider his use of body idioms within his own fictional oeuvre, within his culture's broader lexical backdrop, and within nearly four thousand other nineteenth-century novels. But at its core, this book develops a literary-historical and at times even a philological argument—not a statistical one. By triangulating Dickens's idiomatic distinctiveness in relation to the social history of language alteration in nineteenth-century Britain more broadly and in relation to thousands of other novelists, I adopt a set of Bakhtinian methodologies where "the real task of stylistic analysis consists in uncovering all the available orchestrating languages in the composition of the novel . . . determining the heteroglot background outside the work that dialogizes it" (Bakhtin 1981, 416). I take seriously Bakhtin's belief that "historico-linguistic research into the language systems and styles available to a given era (social, professional, generic, tendentious) will aid powerfully in re-creating a third dimension for the language of the novel" (417). In Dickens's novels, this third dimension is often characterized by the "common" use bodily idioms in uncommon ways. It is for this reason that Dickens's unique penchant for body idioms forms a significant part of what the nineteenth-century critic David Masson (1859, 252) summed up as the "recoil" that often came early on from "cultivated and fastidious" circles. Contemporary criticisms of Dickens's idiomatic and generally more colloquial language had far deeper roots, of course. The *Oxford English Dictionary* cites a passage from Joseph Addison's *The Spectator* as the first published usage of the word *idiom*, wherein the following stylistic warning appears: "Since . . . Phrases . . . used in

---

12. That Dickens's use of idioms has gone unremarked upon is surprising when we take into account how many major critics—including Robert Alter (1996, 130)—consider him "above all the great master of figurative language in English after Shakespeare."

8   **INTRODUCTION**

ordinary Conversation . . . contract a kind of Meanness by passing through the Mouths of the Vulgar, a [writer] should take particular care to guard himself against Idiomatick ways of speaking" (1712, 9). A few decades later, Samuel Johnson enshrined similar interdictions to idiomatic phrasing while completing his *Dictionary of the English Language* (1755), acknowledging his "labou[r] to refine our language to grammatical purity, and to clear it from colloquial barbarisms, licentious idioms, and irregular combinations."[13]

The impact of Johnson's labor on this front was indeed long lasting. Even in the nineteenth century, the proscriptive Johnsonian style was still the benchmark for many early reviewers of Dickens. The *Quarterly Review*, for instance, objected to *Oliver Twist* (1837–39) by focusing on how "these Dodgers and Sikes break into our Johnsons, [and] rob the queen's lawful current English."[14] It goes on to say that Dickens is the "regius professor of slang, that expression of the mother wit, the low humour of the lower classes, their Sanscrit, their hitherto unknown tongue, which . . . seems likely to become the idiom of England" (92). In 1845, the *North British Review* specifically listed Dickens's use of idioms among the "gross offences against the English language."[15] It was not just the critics who singled Dickens out; his peers also lodged similar complaints. George Eliot's (1883, 145) appraisal of his characters' shallow psychological development was largely a matter of Dickens's supposedly outsized attention to their "idiom and manners." Anthony Trollope (1962, 200) claimed that Dickens's idiomatic voice—"created by himself in defiance of rules"—led to an "ungrammatical" style that was "impossible to praise." Others were quick to yoke this generally "lower" style to his relatively low educational attainment. Margaret Oliphant (1897, 305–6), commenting on the lack of allusions to classical literature, music, or painting in Dickens's writing, suggested that a want of literary education was to blame. George Henry Lewes (1872a, 152), even while attempting to praise Dickens for his instinctive talent, ended up patronizing him as an uneducated writer ("he never was and never would have been a student"), whose interests "remained completely outside philosophy, science, and the higher literature."

If early critics and higher-brow peers found Dickens's idiomatic leanings objectionable, however, the vast majority of his readers most certainly did not. Robert Patten (1978, 343) and others have shown how his soaring popularity, enabled in part by his enterprising publication schemes, essentially allowed

---

13. *Rambler* no. 208, in *Samuel Johnson* 2018, 413.
14. *Quarterly Review* 64 (1839): 92.
15. *North British Review* 3 (1845): 76.

Dickens to "democratiz[e] fiction."[16] Some lower-class readers could afford his novels in monthly numbers, and the literate among them often read aloud to larger groups of listeners with each new instalment.[17] Robert Forster (1892) describes a common occurrence where a landlord of a rooming house would, on the first Monday of every month, hold a communal tea. Those who could afford it purchased tea and cakes, but *all* lodgers were welcome to hear the landlord read the latest installment of Dickens's novel. Leslie Stephen (1988, 30) remarked on this phenomenon with typical combination of condescension and class snobbery in his entry on Dickens for the *Dictionary of National Biography*: "If literary fame could be safely measured by popularity with the half-educated, Dickens must claim the highest position among English novelists." Even so, George Ford (1955, 113) pointed out in the middle of the twentieth century that because of Dickens's popularity and what we know about the adoration that generations of readers (of all classes) have conferred on him, "we have lost a sense of how shockingly revolutionary Dickens's prose seemed to his contemporaries."[18] The *Quarterly Review* (1837, 507), for example, claimed it had never witnessed a novelist with Dickens's "felicity in working up the genuine mother-wit and unadulterated vernacular idioms of the lower classes of London."

Dickens's unique upbringing is one of the reasons that his prose style in general, and his heavy use of body idioms in particular, was revolutionary. Although his traditional education at Wellington House had been cut short, his early life experiences gave him direct access to a range of colloquial language that his peers simply did not possess. Working as a young boy at Warren's Blacking Factory, regularly visiting his father at Marshalsea debtor's prison, and later, spending time as a law clerk, a parliamentary stenographer, and a newspaper editor gave Dickens a broad spectrum of linguistic resources from which to build his fictional idiolect. Put simply and in conjunction with the topic of my study, Dickens had what Malcolm Andrews (2013, 29, 74) calls a "mind's ear" for the wide range of linguistic ingenuity he lived among, including as it

---

16. See also *Charles Dickens and "Boz": The Birth of the Industrial-Age Author* (Patten 2012a), especially chapter 3, "Writing Boz (1836–1837): *The Pickwick Papers.*"

17. As Ivan Kreilkamp (2009, 90–91) has argued, Dickens's ability "to transcribe and capture the energy of spoken language" helped him acquire a mass readership usually excluded from the literary field. See *Voice and the Victorian Storyteller* (Kreilkamp 2009).

18. Stewart (1974, 21) makes a similar point in *Dickens and the Trials of Imagination*: "Historical distance has . . . done some disservice to modern commentary on Dickens's style . . . as verbal adventure his style has left its context behind. We all too often take it merely, gratefully, as 'Dickensian.' We are not well equipped to judge its satire. Here the critics of Dickens's own time provide a welcome adjustment for our updated approaches."

10 INTRODUCTION

related to the body.[19] Better put, perhaps, by one of the finest career-long observers of Dickensian "mycrostylistics," Garrett Stewart (2001a, 136), "it often seems as if the untapped reserves of the English vernacular were simply lying in wait for Dickens to inherit them."

I take as my starting point Dickens's (numerically) unparalleled use of one very specific untapped reserve of the English vernacular: his usage of idiomatic body phrases, or what an early theorizer of idiomatic language, Logan Pearsall Smith (1925, 250), called "somatic idioms." Essentially, the story comes down to this: where Addison and Johnson warned, Dickens wallowed—as his semi-autobiographical character David says in *David Copperfield* (2004, 632): "I wallow in words." This wallowing was heavily imbricated with how he relished using common colloquialisms, idioms, and experimental combinations of both in *un*-common ways; how he delighted in the malleability of vernacular phrasing and the possibilities such language opened up for imaginative development in his novels. Instead of "guard[ing] himself against Idiomatick ways of speaking" because such language passed so easily through "the Mouths of the Vulgar," Dickens reveled in its use. I argue that his "bodily idiomatic style" is fundamental to the way in which Dickens approaches the world in language. Body idioms appear hundreds and sometimes thousands of times in each of his novels. *Bleak House* (1852–53), for example, contains nearly 1,100 usages of body-derived idioms.

It is important to note, though, that my central argument does not depend on the largeness of these numbers. Quite the opposite, in fact. I stake my biggest claims on analyzing how, and at times why, a conspicuous *deficit* of unique idiomatic expressions appears in Dickens's oeuvre. As we will see, the vast majority of his body idioms surface again and again in each one of his novels, cycling through in ebbs and flows of repetition. We will also see how and try to make sense of why, as Dickens matures as a writer, certain idioms appear uniquely and almost exclusively in specific novels. My argument rests not just on the surfeit of body idioms in Dickens's oeuvre, then, but also very much on the unique usage of only a small number of certain ones that subtend his more generally widespread employment of the idiomatic. Thus, one of my central contentions is that Dickens structures his most mature and iconic fiction—sometimes consciously, oftentimes not—by way of a distinctly idiomatic imaginative process that merges with, contributes to, and helps form the central themes of each successive novel.

My consideration of this process also offers an original analysis of a central paradox that helps explain the Inimitable's democratizing popularity with

---

19. This is a common but important observation often made about Dickens. Hugo Bowles (2019, 125), for instance, has recently commented on Dickens's exceptional "auditory memory."

INTRODUCTION 11

all classes of readers. That is, how Dickens's increasingly focused use of "low" and *slangular* (his neologism) idiomatic body language paradoxically allows him to construct some of the primary imaginative coordinates of his mature novels' most elevated and most sophisticated conceptual ideas—those enjoyed by the lowest scullery worker all the way up to the queen. Before Dickens, this unlikely alliance between weighty subject matter and low idiomatic tone had a long history of literary incompatibility. Samuel Johnson's *Dictionary* sought to "refine [the English] language to grammatical purity, and to clear it from colloquial barbarisms [and] licentious idioms" (Johnson 2018, 413) precisely because he saw "the laborious and mercantile part of the people['s]" diction as incapable of expressing elevated ideas and therefore deemed them "unworthy of preservation" (Johnson 1984b, 323) in his *Dictionary*: "Language is the dress of thought; and as the noblest mien or most graceful action would be degraded and obscured by a garb appropriated to the gross employments of rustics or mechanics, so the most heroic sentiments will lose their efficacy, and the most splendid ideas drop their magnificence, if they are conveyed by words used commonly upon low and trivial occasions, debased by vulgar mouths, and contaminated by inelegant applications" (Johnson 1984a, 695).

Johnson's late eighteenth-century belief in the incommensurability between low idiomatic diction and elevated ideas was pervasive. Even one of the earliest and most comprehensive idiom theorists, L. P. Smith (1925, 258), could not help but equate "the popular origin" of idiomatic expression with its supposed inability to convey intellectual sophistication and abstraction: "Since our idioms . . . are . . . so largely of popular origin, we should hardly expect to find abstract thought embodied in them, or scientific observation, or aesthetic appreciation, or psychological analysis of any subtle kind;—and these indeed are almost completely lacking. The subject matter of idiom is human life in its simpler aspects."

But Dickens had an unparalleled ability to connect the lowly with the lofty. One of my primary contentions is that readers really *should* expect to find abstract thought and sophisticated ideas constellating around Dickens's idiomatic language. To fulfill this expectation, I will track important moments in his career to demonstrate how Dickens came to relish using common, body-based idiomatic expressions in uncommon ways; how he began to delight in the malleability of idiomatic phrasing and the possibilities it opened up for imaginative development. I will trace how the young author grew to experiment with the ways in which idioms could be altered to fresh purposes, pressed into unanticipated service, and imported into different contexts that would confer novel associations on them. I am interested in tracking the process of how, after playfully tinkering with body idioms more and more steadily in his

12 INTRODUCTION

early fiction, Dickens began to see in them creative opportunities for combinatorial invention by abstracting, reliteralizing, and even violating some or all of their components, ultimately fashioning them (consciously or not) into new agents for major thematic innovation in his mature works.

The (In)visibility of Body Idioms

Although critics generally agree that Dickens shaped many of his era's most memorable characters by way of their fantastically embodied descriptions, and although there is certainly no shortage of scholarship dedicated to the analysis of uniquely Dickensian "styles" of writing,[20] the extent to which his imaginative craft is connected to constellations of body-derived idiomatic locutions has so far entirely eluded scholarly attention. The affordances of digital of methodologies aside, there are good reasons for this blind spot, and some of the reasons this elision exists are deeply infused with the larger arguments of my study. For one, I think that all professionally trained literary critics are—at least to some degree—inheritors of the Addisonian and Johnsonian tradition that leads us to privilege interpretations of what we would like to think of as complex and sophisticated ideas at the outset of our research. We tend to want to start projects with nuanced and intricate ideas. We are unlikely, as Sarah Allison so convincingly suggests in *Reductive Reading*, to begin research projects with simplistic ideas precisely because of their apparent reductiveness. More specifically for the topic of my study, it is almost certain that our own twentieth- and twenty-first-century associations with idiomatic expressions such as "right-hand man," "shoulder to the wheel," "nose to the grindstone," and so on, are purely figurative—always already evacuated of their literal, historical, and original contextual origins. Such idioms' figurative currency in our contemporary lexicon has had the effect of rendering them unobtrusive as we read and, hence, critically unremarkable.

My chapters will demonstrate, however, that Dickens was often using (and popularizing) these expressions at unique historical-linguistic moments when their very meanings teetered on the cusp of divergence from the literal to the

---

20. For only a partial list of scholarship concerned with Dickensian "style," see Mark Lambert's *Dickens and the Suspended Quotation* (1981), Robert Alter's "Reading Style in Dickens" (1996), Juliet John's *Dickens's Villains* (2001), Rosemarie Bodenheimer's *Knowing Dickens* (2007), Sally Ledger's *Dickens and the Popular Radical Imagination* (2007), Holly Furneaux's *Queer Dickens* (2009), Robert Douglas-Fairhurst's *Becoming Dickens* (2011), Daniel Tyler's *Dickens's Style* (2013), Michaela Mahlberg's *Corpus Linguistics and Dickens's Fiction* (2013), Garrett Stewart's *The One, Other, and Only Dickens* (2018) and "The Late Great Dickens: Style Distilled" (2022), and Hugo Bowles's *Dickens and the Stenographic Mind* (2019).

INTRODUCTION 13

figurative. For example, the transition from a strictly literal (military) sense of a "right-hand man" to the figuratively surrogate commercial and domestic contexts was just beginning to occur when Dickens was writing *Dombey and Son* (1846–48). People still put (or paid someone else to put) their actual shoulders to the wheel to free sunken carriages in the time of *Bleak House* (1852–53). Almost everyone knew that an infant "brought up by hand" was bottle rather than breast fed when *Great Expectations* (1860–61) appeared in *All the Year Round*, just as they were still aware of how perilously close a nose could come to one who lay on a body-length sharpening grindstone when reading *Our Mutual Friend* (1864–65). I also suspect that there is something to be said for the sheer fact that we are bombarded with bodily-derived idioms when we read Dickens; they appear at an average of around one per every two pages of his fiction.[21] This creates a situation where we fail to notice how Dickens isolates certain idioms for specialized treatment within a given fictionalized world where their use, combined with their figurative "ordinariness," have worn away their significance for contemporary audiences.

Perhaps most importantly, even if more paradoxically, critics consistently read past Dickens's seemingly ordinary idiomatic phrasings partly *because* of the way such phrasings become enmeshed in a novel's deepest structural and thematic concerns. They tend to hide in plain sight as figures in the narrative's lexical carpet because they fit in so well with many other thematic dimensions of a particular novel. Raymond Williams (1970, 81, 82) has noted, along these lines, how Dickensian social ideas may become "so deeply embodied that they are in effect . . . *dissolved* into a whole fictional world." The proliferation of Dickens's vernacular language has thus had the effect of camouflaging the important relationship between a given idiomatic expression and a novel's larger imaginative periphery. A significant portion of my method (both digital and analogue) is dedicated to bringing these camouflaged relationships into analytical focus so that we may see how a concentration on particular idiomatic expressions in Dickens's mature novels reveals an important dimension of *idiom absorption*—a process wherein the idiom, once articulated, begins, borrowing from Leo Spitzer's (1948, 27) formulation, to "soa[k] through and through . . . the atmosphere of the work" with such prevalence that its literalization, abstraction, and

---

21. This statistic applies for the four novels I treat in my chapters (all Penguin Classic editions): *Dombey and Son*, *Bleak House*, *Great Expectations*, and *Our Mutual Friend*. I arrived at the calculation by dividing the total number of body idioms in each text by the total number of their combined pages in the Penguin editions. A novel-by-novel breakdown would appear this way: *Dombey and Son* contains 410 body idioms in 937 pages of text; *Bleak House* contains 1,085 body idioms in 977 pages of text; *Great Expectations* contains 271 body idioms in 481 pages of text; and *Our Mutual Friend* contains 184 body idioms in 784 pages of text.

14   INTRODUCTION

even its explicit violation emerge as important new agents for imaginative innovation.

Philology and Intention

I am also guided by a broader philological concern for how Dickens came to construct some of his most mature and sophisticated novels beginning in the 1840s.[22] That is, I am interested in the intersections of Dickensian "style" and its philological underpinnings. If style may be described as the relationship between what a text says and how it expresses that saying, a philologically inflected analysis of style pays particular attention to the historical and linguistic record of a text and the extratextual material that helps inform its lexical horizon. It is no coincidence that the Philological Society of London was formed at about the same time (in 1842) Dickens began to press idiomatic expressions into more concentrated service in his novels and that the society's formation was driven by a growing interest in a democratic view of language where use and custom is decided by the majority—literate or not. Figures such as Benjamin Thorpe and John Mitchell Kemble had spent time in Germany studying with continental philologists, and they returned to England eager to chart a course where language could be studied as a product of usage by generation after generation of *speakers* rather than just its readers and writers.[23] For these thinkers and many later English philologists, a primary concern for their study of language became the ways in which words and phrases behaved in shifting contexts over time. The culminating achievement of this new, historical, and social orientation to language was the *Oxford English Dictionary* (OED, originally titled the *New English Dictionary on Historical Principles* in its early iterations) whose first edition was eventually published in 1884 after legions of people from the English-speaking world sent in "slips" documenting "the life-history" of every word and phrase (Mugglestone 2005, 5). This distinctly English strand of what might aptly be termed "participatory philology" also

---

22. Here, I join a steady drumbeat in literary studies that has signaled a renewed interest in philology. See Michael Holquist, "Why We Should Remember Philology" (2002); Geoffrey Harpham, "Roots, Races, and the Return to Philology" (2009); Frances Ferguson, "Philology, Literature, Style" (2013); James Turner, *Philology: The Forgotten Origins of Modern Humanities* (2014); Merve Emre, "The Return to Philology" (2023). Joshua Brorby has recently written about Victorian philology and its impact on *Our Mutual Friend*. See "Our Mutable Inheritance: Testing Victorian Philology in *Our Mutual Friend*" (2020).

23. For the best comprehensive study of the ways in which the "new" English philology emerged from debates about philosophy of mind and the German philological tradition, see Hans Aarsleff, *The Study of Language in England, 1780–1860* (1967), especially chapter 5, "Sir William Jones and the New Philology."

began to appeal to a far more popular audience in large part because of the well-attended lectures in the 1840s by Richard Chenevix Trench, Kemble's close friend and colleague at Cambridge. Newspapers and journals of the day steadily reported on the popularity of Trench's lectures, and they were subsequently published in 1851 as *On the Study of Words*—a text that went through nineteen editions by the time the OED's first edition appeared. In lectures and in print, Trench promised to uncover "riches . . . l[ying] hidden in the vulgar tongue of [the] poorest and most ignorant" principally by identifying the historical and social derivation of "daily words and phrases" (3).

Additionally, Friedrich Max Müller, a torchbearer of the German philological tradition, delivered a series of highly publicized lectures[24] at the Royal Institution in April, May, and June 1861 which, like Trench's, emphasized the benefits of a scientific, historical, and democratic orientation toward language study. Müller famously saw "the vulgar idiom of the peasant [as] no less than the refined dialect of the philosopher" (Cox 1862, 69). With the new philological orientation he espoused, Müller (1899, 79) predicted that "the popular, or, as they are called, the vulgar dialects, which had formed a kind of undercurrent, [would] rise beneath the crystal surface of literary language and sweep away, like the waters in spring, the cumbrous formations [of] . . . the more polite and cultivated speech."

Such a boldly democratized focus on the excavation of popular language hardly went uncontested, though. As Linda Dowling (1982, 170) has noted, this new approach "diametrically opposed established Victorian ideas of literature and literary decorum." The work of Trench and Müller, combined with the abolition of the paper tax and the subsequent flood of cheaper periodicals and newspapers, sparked a profound fear that the language of the uneducated would defile and overwhelm the purity of "correct" English usage. The publication of prescriptive books such as Henry Breen's *Modern English Literature: Its Blemishes and Defects* (1857) and Henry Alford's *The Queen's English* (1863) reflects the intensity of the debate on both sides.

The *Edinburgh Review* announced in January 1862 that it would "watch with keen interest the various influences which seem to be at work, whether to purify [the English language] or corrupt it" (Cox 1962, 68). Predictably, however, the journal was far from an impartial observer. It argued that "the speech of clowns and ploughmen can never deserve the patient attention of the scholar; the jargon of savages can never be worthy of comparison with the language of poets, orators, and philosophers" (68). But for all of its prejudice in favor

---

24. Müller's lectures were published in book form as *Lectures on the Science of Language* at the end of 1861.

16   INTRODUCTION

of elevated language "purity," the journal hinted at the "living force" Müller and others identified as operating within the lower linguistic registers. "To us," the *Edinburgh Review* wrote, dialects, idioms, and other common phrases "which come pouring in upon us may be simply ugly and repulsive, [but] our dislike may be quickened by *a secret feeling that there is a strange vitality* in the adversaries which we are striving to put down" (68; emphasis mine).

Dickens was not only aware of these philological developments; he made them his business—literally—both in what I contend is the idiomatic imagination of his novels and in the subject matter of the periodicals he owned and edited while he was composing them. It was Dickens, after all, who named his first weekly journal *Household Words* years before Trench (1852, 246; emphasis mine) urged "training and elevating an ever-increasing number of persons" to consider the history of word and phrasal meaning "till at length they have become truly a part of the nation's common stock, 'household words,' used easily and intelligently by nearly all." In terms of the subject matter of Dickens's journals, Dorothy Deering (1977, 12) has demonstrated how *Household Words* and *All the Year Round* contain a significantly larger portion of articles on the development of the English language, its usage trends, and its focus on the derivation of everyday diction than *Blackwood's*, *Fraser's*, the *Cornhill*, *Bentley's Miscellany*, and the *Edinburgh Review*. Although not the focus of Deering's study, it is noteworthy that a significant portion of the articles in Dickens's journals advocate for the depth of meaning that is socially and historically embedded in lower, colloquial, and idiomatic language. "Saxon-English," for example, justifies a democratic approach to writing based on contemporary philological exploration of "the History of the Language" which privileges common speech patterns: "If a man wishes to write for all," the *Household Words* piece avers, "he must know how to use the speech of all, and he will come nearest all hearts with words that are familiar in every home" (Morley and Rushton 1858, 89). Similarly, an article titled "Plain English" (1868, 205) attests that "all the words of everyday use, all the joints of the language, all that makes it an organism . . . are pure English." What is also at least as interesting for my specific concern is how many of the articles' titles in *Household Words* and *All the Year Round* are *themselves* body idioms: "If This Should Meet His Eye" (1852), "Foe under Foot" (1852), "The Gift of Tongues" (1857), "A Piece of Blood-Money" (1859), "A Stomach for Study" (1860), "At Your Fingers' Ends" (1863), "Skin Deep" (1863), "Noses out of Joint" (1864), "Out at Elbows" (1865), "Spirits on Their Last Legs" (1865), "Small Arms" (1866), "Skeleton in the Closet" (1867), "Touched to the Heart" (1867), and so on. These ideas about language fit Michel Foucault's (1973, 290) account of the philologic shift in the nineteenth century wherein "language [becomes] no longer

INTRODUCTION   17

linked to civilizations by the level of learning to which they have attained . . . but by the mind of the peoples who have given rise to it, animate it, and are recognizable in it."

Following this philological impulse to explore how texts are made based on the histories of their linguistic forms, I pay special attention to the various material and ideological conditions involved in Dickens's imaginative conception of his novels at the particular times of their composition. Here, it is helpful to draw on the sense of philological orientation Edward Said (2004) describes in the central chapter ("The Return to Philology") of his posthumous *Humanism and Democratic Criticism*. In order to evaluate the ideas that constitute the process of aesthetic creation, Said believes the critic must "put oneself in the position of the author, for whom writing is a series of decisions and choices expressed in words"—all of which "locate the text in its time as part of a whole network of relationships whose outlines and influence play an informing role *in* the text" (62; emphasis original). Said's aesthetic hypothesis also aligns with Bakhtin's *"sociological stylistics"* where "the novelistic word . . . registers with extreme subtlety the tiniest shifts and oscillations of the social atmosphere" (300; emphasis original). Each chapter of my study therefore responds to a version of the deceptively simple question that Robert Patten (2012a, xvi) sets forth in *Charles Dickens and "Boz"*: "When faced with a blank piece of paper and an urgent deadline, what prompted his imagination?"

As a result, my overarching argument that Dickens possesses an idiomatically oriented imagination necessarily intersects with vexed and thorny issues of intentionality which cannot and should not be sidestepped. What place, if any, does authorial intent have in explaining Dickens's usage of the phrase "right-hand man" in only a single novel (*Dombey*) which brings to life a character (Captain Cuttle) who has no right hand? The same question could be asked for the topics of my succeeding chapters: of the hundreds of body idioms that appear and reappear in almost all of his novels, did Dickens consciously intend to use the expression "shoulder to the wheel" only in *Bleak House*; "brought up by hand" only in *Great Expectations*; "sweat of the brow" and "nose to the grindstone" only in *Our Mutual Friend*?

These are important questions, and their "answers" contain the prospect of tipping the interpretational balance in multiple directions. Every major critic who sets as their task an assessment of the nature of Dickens's imagination—beginning with J. Hillis Miller's first book, *Charles Dickens: The World of His Novels* (1958), to Garrett Stewart's first book, *Dickens and the Trials of Imagination* (1974), to Rosemarie Bodenheimer's *Knowing Dickens* (2007)—grapples with the varying levels of intentionality we might ascribe to his prose. On this score, I tend to agree with Bodenheimer (2007, 19) that "the conscious and unconscious

18   INTRODUCTION

artfulness of Dickens's self-creation remains one of the most fascinating aspects of his writing." I agree, too, with Bodenheimer's sense that with Dickens, "conscious knowing sets off unconscious knowing" (20–21). Dickens undoubtedly knows *something* of his own isolated use of a particular idiom but how much? And how does the extent of that knowledge develop over the course of a novel's serial composition?

To these ends, I consider what some of Dickens's cross-outs and corrections in his handwritten manuscripts and planning documents can tell us about his imaginative process, his refinements in thinking, and how those refinements often become refinements of idiomatic expression. Amid all of these concerns, I maintain that the interplay between states of imaginative "knowing"—conscious or not—is important and relevant, though perhaps never conclusively determinate.[25] What is more, a novel can certainly fulfill an intention that its author was unaware of having, and I hope to demonstrate how both the fulfilled intention and the level of *un*awareness vis-à-vis Dickensian body idioms are objects of legitimate critical interest. Put somewhat differently, Dickens's furious imagination in all likelihood created elements that Dickens himself could never have fully known or articulated. A classic example of just such an instance comes from John Forster's (1892, 2:78) recollection that Dickens was "much startled" when he (Forster) pointed out that the initials created for his semi-autobiographical character, David Copperfield, "were his own reversed."[26] Insofar as some of these creative elements were distinctly idiomatic and bodily oriented, however conscious, we can learn something new from them about how Dickens's imagination worked at the height of his career.

The Body behind the Body Idioms

Dickens's penchant for body idioms is definitively and physiologically constitutional as well. What I mean by this is that his fascination with body idioms is not only a question of artistic expression or philological circumstance, but it is also an entailment of a lifelong fascination with the physicality of the

---

25. My thinking on this topic has been influenced by Charles Altieri's (2015) recent work *Reckoning with the Imagination*, where he maintains that "intentions have to be displayed—not explained": "There need not be any claim that in postulating an intention one also justifies something such as an explanation or a unified account of the text. For often the intention is not to mean but to display a relation of significant force fields within which tensions need not be reconciled or actions submitted to rational form" (35).

26. This particular example aligns with Immanuel Kant's (1950, 112) quintessential formulation that imagination is "a blind function of the soul, without which we would have no knowledge whatsoever, but of which we are scarcely ever conscious."

human body. Hillis Miller (1958, ix–x) persistently held to his phenomenological belief that the "imagining mind" is an "expression of the unique personality and vital spirit of its author" and, moreover, that an author's "style is his own way of living in the world given verbal form." Dickensian biographies have varied in their emphases over the years, but they all invariably agree that Dickens possessed an extraordinary and seemingly boundless physical energy.[27] Dickens's "way of living in the world" was, in a Husserlian sense,[28] bodily, and this physiological orientation manifested itself in at least two principal ways: (1) his attraction to the theater and (2) his compulsive walking. In terms of the former, Dickens's career-spanning love for acting and virtually anything having to do with the theater is well documented. The familiar story is that the world may have never known of Dickens the novelist had a terrible cold not prevented him from auditioning at Covent Garden in front of the stage manager George Barley and the actor Charles Kemble in 1832.[29] Of course, he eventually became a famous novelist, but he also managed and performed in amateur theatricals—a category that includes his exhaustively theatricalized staged novel readings—for the rest of his life. Beginning with Robert Garis's *The Dickens Theatre* (1965), a whole host of critical commentary has traced the ways that theatricality suffuses the worlds of his fiction.[30] Dickens was no doubt drawn to the theater because of its emphasis on the physicality of the body: the embodiedness of acting, the physicality of movement across the stage, the value and importance of physical gesture, projection of voice, manipulations of facial expression, and so forth.

There is also significant evidence that Dickens thought of his writing as *theatrical acting* in private, and to such an extent that bodily performance was often inseparable from his actual creative process. His daughter Mamie recounts how she once observed him in the process of composing one of his novels: "My father wrote busily and rapidly at his desk, when he suddenly jumped up from his chair and rushed to a mirror that hung near, and in which I could see the reflection of some extraordinary facial contortions which he was making. He returned rapidly to his desk, wrote furiously for a few moments, and then went back again to the mirror" (M. Dickens 1896, 49–50).

---

27. For only the most recent, see Tomalin 2011, 327–28; Douglas-Fairhurst 2011, 152–53; and Hartley 2016, 7–8, 36–37.

28. In both *Ideas Pertaining to a Pure Phenomenology* (1913) and *Experience and Judgement* (1939), Husserl finds that perception is shaped both by an embodied effort and activity and by a sediment or habitus, as he calls it, deriving from earlier experience—all of which constitutes an essentially embodied disposition.

29. "See how near I may have been, to another sort of life," Dickens wrote to Forster (December 30–31, 1844).

30. For a partial list, see Eigner 1989; MacKay 1989; Vlock 1998; and Andrews 2006.

20   INTRODUCTION

Similarly, the artist William Firth, who painted a portrait of Dickens in 1859, described "going to Dickens's study, where he was [writing], watch[ing] him from a corner as he muttered, grimaced, and walked about the room, pulling his beard" (C. Tomalin 2011, 305). This thoroughly embodied method of composition apparently applied even early on, in the rare instances when Dickens wrote outside of his study. His brother-in-law Henry Burnett, for instance, recalled an evening spent at the Doughty Street residence when Dickens came into the drawing room carrying his work for the monthly installment of *Oliver Twist* (1837–39):

> In a few minutes he returned, manuscript in hand, and while he was pleasantly discoursing he employed himself in carrying to a corner of the room a little table, at which he seated himself and re-commenced his writing. We, at his bidding, went on talking our little nothings,—he every now and then (the feather of his pen still moving rapidly from side to side), put in a cheerful interlude. It was interesting to watch, upon the sly, the mind and the muscles working (or, if you please, *playing*) in company as new thoughts were being dropped upon the paper. And to note the working brow, the set mouth, with the tongue slightly pressed against the closed lips, as was his habit. (Kitton 1890, 1:13; emphasis original)

Robert Douglas-Fairhurst (2011, 263) correctly surmises that this recollection provides us with a privileged glimpse into how Dickens "drew his characters out of himself and then channeled these physical tics and grimaces into the rhythmic movements of his hand traveling across the page." Not only did Dickens think of writing as acting in private—or semiprivate in the case above—but he also believed that organizing his many amateur theatricals was "like writing a book in company" (Hartley 2016, 37). In fact, the embodied theatricality of Dickens's writing has become so apodictic in twentieth- and twenty-first-century critical assessments that Nicholas Dames (2007, 13), in his pathbreaking study *The Physiology of the Novel*, chooses to pass on Dickens for "its literary evidence" specifically because of its obviousness.[31]

Physiologically speaking, perhaps only Dickens's dedication to compulsive exercise rivaled his attraction to the theatrical: his ten- to fifteen-mile daily walks through London have become the stuff of legend for biographers. As Claire Tomalin (2011, 257) has noted, the sedentary, quiet concentration that other authors required to write was simply not a feature of Dickens's working life. He once told John Forster that "if I couldn't walk fast and far, I should

---

31. Beyond scholarship on the theater, Kaplan (1975) inaugurated a host of studies on Dickens's relationship to the physical body.

INTRODUCTION 21

just explode and perish."[32] George Lakoff and Mark Johnson (1980) have made convincing arguments that our language is structured by the physicality of our bodily orientations and that, in particular, our imaginative capabilities are rooted in the bodily experiences of our physical environments.[33] My association of these physiological theories of language with Dickens is threefold. First, it helps explain why the human body itself is so often the basis of the idiomatic expressions we all use so unwittingly. Second, if everyone—sedentary or not—experiences imagination and language in a bodily way as Mark Johnson (1987) in *The Body in the Mind: The Bodily Basis of Meaning, Imagination, and Reasoning* and Kathleen Wider (1997) in *The Bodily Nature of Consciousness* so convincingly argue,[34] how much more is this the case for someone like Dickens whose experience with the world was so decidedly embodied? Third, the intensity and the regularity of Dickens's walking was not just a matter of blowing off steam; it was a primary way by which he accumulated the broad array of idiomatic expressions that pervade his writing. The compulsive walking and the vernacular noticing was a ceaselessly converging activity—what Foucault (1973, 290) calls *energeia*—involving both body and language.

One of Dickens's early pieces of nonfiction for *Bentley's Miscellany*, "The Pantomime of Life" (1837), is representative of his tendency to experience the theatrical, the idiomatic, and walking as converging parts of a single enterprise. Not only does this article contain twenty-three body idioms in fewer than seven pages of text, but it begins with a distinctly bodily and theatrical set of idiomatic expressions. The first clause "plunge[s] [us] headlong" into "the scene [of] a street" where walking "in the open street" is essentially "the drawing up of a curtain for a grand comic pantomime" that "occurs in real life day after day" (291, 292, 296, 294).

It is no secret that Dickens's experiences of walking provided him with a great deal of fodder for his fiction. Part of what Dickens loved about his walks through virtually every section of London was the variousness of the language employed by the people he encountered. An article titled "Slang," which appeared early on in *Household Words*, encourages a prospective author to "take advantage of what he hears and sees in his own days and under his own eyes,

---

32. September 29, 1854.

33. See M. Johnson 1987. Lakoff and Johnson (1980) draw on a history of language going at least as far back as John Locke's view in his *Essay Concerning Human Understanding* (1690) that all awareness is experientially embodied through the senses. For a study of the primacy of the body in the idea of the human during the Victorian period, see W. Cohen 2009.

34. Turner (2014, xiv; emphasis original) is particularly interested in what he contends has been missing or undervalued in objectivist accounts of meaning and rationality: namely, "the *human body*, and especially those structures of imagination and understanding that emerge from our embodied experience."

22   INTRODUCTION

and *incorporate into his language those idiomatic words and expressions* he gathers from the daily affairs of his life and the daily conversations of his fellow men" (Sala 1853b, 73; emphasis mine). Therefore, it is not just that Dickens's truncated education or upbringing around the Marshalsea debtor's prison and Warren's Blacking Factory inclined him to colloquial language and idiomatic speech patterns. There is also every reason to believe that he sought out such language by immersing himself among the people who spoke with what Bakhtin (1981, 297) would later call "speech diversity." To take only one example, Dickens claimed that he composed *A Christmas Carol* (1843)—a novel containing a high incidence of body idioms—in a series of walks through "the black streets of London, fifteen and twenty miles, [on] many a night."[35] London's streets are famous for their variety. In her essay "Street Haunting," Virginia Woolf (1930, 165) describes her walks through the city as a kind of escape from the self where "one is not tethered to a single mind, but can put on briefly for a few minutes the bodies and minds of others." Dickens was apparently so good at doing precisely this, and for many hours (not minutes), that Douglas-Fairhurst (2011, 153) has appositely described him as "less a human being than [London's] conscience given legs and a voice." This description is no doubt accurate as well as appropriate given my interest in bodily orientation and idiomatic phrasing, but it is missing a body part that was crucial for establishing Dickens's authorial "voice": his ear.[36] Dickens's fictional voice is so distinctive in large part because of his ear's ability to take in and mimic what it heard on the London streets. Steven Marcus (1972,192) has attested to the unusual quality of Dickens's "ear" probably most succinctly: "For a number of important formative years [Dickens] had worked as a kind of written recording device for the human voice, for speech, for the English language." In this way, he becomes, as Dennis Walder (1995, xxi) has cleverly dubbed him, the ultimate "metropolitan wanderer, and wonderer." Although there is nothing particularly theoretical about this part of my argument, it is worth noting that theorists of walking have lent a certain credence to my observations about the relationship between Dickens's walking and his vernacular language. Michel de Certeau (1984, 100), for instance, discusses a "rhetoric of walking" wherein "a series of turns . . . can be compared to 'turns of phrase.'" De Certeau goes on to say that "the art of 'turning' phrases finds an equivalent in an art of composing a path" and that walking through an urban environment composed of differing lexical registers is akin to "the drifting of

---

35. Dickens to Cornelius Felton, January 2, 1844.
36. Robert Douglas-Fairhurst (2022, 278) has even more recently noted that, while walking, Dickens's "ear [was] permanently cocked for oddities he could use in his fiction."

INTRODUCTION   23

'figurative' language" itself. I stress these ideas because of my belief that not only did the aleatory circumstances of Dickens's life and upbringing make him more idiomatically inclined than his peers; his own bodily propensity for walking and listening made him so as well.

The Idiom Embryonic: Early Dickensian Body Language

As we have seen, it is widely accepted that the origins of idiomatic phrasing come to us from the illiterate and colorfully *spoken* worlds of the lower classes that Dickens would have encountered time and time again during his legendary walks.[37] L. P. Smith (1925, 212) puts it this way: "Our figurative and idiomatic phrases are of popular origin, are drawn from the interests and occupations of humble life. The phrase-making, like the word-making, faculty belongs pre-eminently to the unlettered classes, and our best idioms, like our most vivid and living words, come to us, not from the library or the drawing-room or the 'gay parterre,' but from the workshop, the kitchen and the farm-yard."

The everyday "familiar style"[38] of lower-class language users had, of course, become part of a seismic poetic shift espoused by William Blake, Samuel Taylor Coleridge, and William Wordsworth well before Dickens began to write fiction. Wordsworth famously wrote in his 1802 preface to *Lyrical Ballads* of his desire to keep the "reader in the company of flesh and blood"—what Paul Younquist calls his "physiological aesthetics" (1999, 152)—by using "the real language of men in a state of vivid sensation" (1991, 250, 241).[39] Wordsworth (1991, 244) also sought "to render the plainest common sense interesting . . . by throw[ing] over them a certain colouring of the imagination, whereby ordinary things should be presented to the mind in an unusual way." Indeed, even the work of England's best early nineteenth-century essayists began to reflect how far grammatical strictures had gradually changed since the days of Addison and Johnson. William Hazlitt's *New and Improved Grammar of the English Tongue* (1810), for example, not only refrained from disparaging the use of idioms, but it went so far as to isolate them as a vital form of expression. "The

---

37. For one of the more recent explications of this view, see Fernando and Flavell 1981.

38. This phrase comes from the title of one of William Hazlitt's essays, "On Familiar Style," in *Table-Talk* (1905, 1821–22).

39. As Shelley argues in "A Defence of Poetry" (1821), the unacknowledged legislators of the world are those who are endowed with and who express a heightened sensitivity toward or awareness of the senses—those who possess what James Allard (2007, 143) calls the "hypersensible body."

24   INTRODUCTION

idioms of every language," writes Hazlitt, "are in general the most valuable parts of it, because they express ideas which cannot be expressed *so well* in any other way" (124; emphasis original).

It is thus also important to trace the ways in which Dickens's own lexical and phrasal use of idiomatic expression derives from his early reporting and writing about the discourses of everyday life he encountered in and around London—what Catherine Robson (2006, 7) has described as his "rapturous immersion in the quotidian." The full title of Dickens's first fictional work could not be more indicative of the important relationship between familiar people and familiar idiom: *Sketches by Boz, Illustrative of Every-day Life and Every-day People* (1836).[40] Overall, this set of stories contains more than three hundred body-derived idioms—many of which eventually get recycled throughout Dickens's later career as a novelist. They include idioms such as "on first blush," "by main force," "open-mouthed," "skin and bone," "cold-blooded," "a deaf ear," "in everybody's mouth," "looking with a jaundiced eye on," "purple in the face," "a matter of neck or nothing," and "on the tiptoe of expectation." The opening story, "The Beadle—The Parish Engine—The Schoolmaster," uses a body idiom ("from hand to mouth") in just its second sentence[41] and then goes on to incorporate seven more in its barely five pages of prose. Forster's (1892, 30; emphasis mine) appraisal of *Sketches by Boz* thirty years after its appearance is therefore accurate both in general and in terms of the young author's predilection for bodily language: "[Dickens] gave, in subsequent writings, so much more perfect form and fulness to everything [*Sketches*] contained. . . . But the first *sprightly runnings* of his genius are undoubtedly here." Once such instance occurs in a tightly controlled paragraph that Dickens ([1836] 1995, 106) wrote in "Hackney-Coach Stands." Here, the narrator begins the paragraph with a humorously concise assertion that "our acquaintance with hackney coach stands is of long standing." After describing the many other means of conveyance available to Londoners, the narrator concludes the paragraph with a playfully witty idiomatic expression of support for hackney coach travelers: "Leaving these fleeter means of getting over the ground, or of depositing oneself upon it, to those who like them, by hackney-coach stands we take our stand" (106).

So far as bodily idioms are concerned, Dickens's early fiction shimmers with many of these brilliant but generally unrelated occurrences of what Daniel Tyler (2013, 22) has called the felicitous "twinning of literal and figurative sig-

---

40. Dennis Walder (1995) uses the term *"everyday"* eleven times in his introduction to *Sketches by Boz*.

41. "A poor man, with small earnings, and a large family, just manages to live on from hand to mouth . . ." (Dickens [1836] 1995, 17).

nifiers." There is therefore likely a connection between the picaresque dimension of Dickens's first novel, *Pickwick Papers* (1836–37), and its smattering of foot-related idioms. The driving plot of the novel, if there is one, revolves around the group's peregrinations and, more specifically, Mr. Pickwick's repeated question to his circle: "Where shall we go next?" ([1836–37] 2003, 440). The Pickwickians' "goings" involve a fair amount of walking. Hence, it should not be surprising that there are many foot-related idioms in the novel. Several that surface at times throughout the novel include "continuing closely upon each other's heels," "following at his heels," "turned on his heel," "set my heel," "equal footing," "to set foot in," and so forth. But although *Pickwick* contains more body idioms than most novels written by other novelists at this time, within Dickens's oeuvre, it has the lowest incidence of body idioms of per page (168 body idioms in 740 pages; 11.7 body idioms per 100,000 words). So rather than a more definitive coherence between the novel's themes and its idioms, what we witness in *Pickwick* is a kind of fleeting inventiveness of active, spontaneous imaginative creativity where, as Steven Marcus (1972, 193) famously describes it, we see "the best parliamentary reporter of his time spitballing away in . . . free, wild, inventive doodling language."[42]

Often, this inventive spitballing involves idiomatic experimentation. For example, Dickens plays with the idiomatic senses of "facing" an uncomfortable circumstance and "looking someone in the face" during a humorous interaction between the lawyers Dodson and Fogg, Mr. Perker, and Pickwick. The narrator comments on Pickwick's belief that "Messrs. Dodson and Fogg ought to be ashamed *to look him in the face*, instead of his being ashamed to see them" (671; emphasis mine). Mr. Perker then assures Pickwick that the lawyers would never "exhibit any symptom of shame or confusion at having *to look [him], or anybody else, in the face*." When the lawyers enter the room and come "face to face" with Pickwick for the first time in their long, drawn-out suit, however, Mr. Fogg is taken aback at discovering that Pickwick is the defendant: "Dear me . . . how do you do, Mr. Pickwick? I hope you are well, Sir. I thought I knew the *face*" (emphasis mine). In another instance, Pickwick's genial gullibility is set against the experienced card playing of the dowager Lady Snuphanuph, Mrs. Colonel Wugsby, and Miss Bolo. Here, too, we can witness Dickens beginning to play with the variability of meanings embedded in idiomatic language.

---

42. I am drawing here on Steven Marcus's (1972, 201) still-famous essay on Dickens's "first and freest novel": "Language into Structure: Pickwick Revisited." This fits the more general consensus in which John Butt and Kathleen Tillotson (1957, 67) refer to Dickens's more spontaneous composition practice in *Pickwick Papers* as "hand-to-mouth writing." Jenny Hartley (2016, 64) more recently notes, "improvisation [not planning] was the spur" for the novels of the 1830s and early 1840s which "can seem as if they might sprawl indefinitely with weak and implausible plotlines."

26   INTRODUCTION

Recognizing him as an easy mark, the women "no sooner set eyes upon Mr. Pickwick . . . than they exchanged glances with each other, seeing that he was precisely the very person they wanted" to round out their table (452). No match for the ladies' skills, Pickwick is carved up almost as quickly as he sits down to the table. What is much more notable than Pickwick's poor gaming skills, though, is the masterful play with idiomatic language through which Dickens renders the scene: "Poor Mr. Pickwick! he had never played with three thorough-paced female card-players before. They were so desperately *sharp* that they quite frightened him. If he played a wrong card, Miss Bolo *looked a small armoury of daggers*" (452; emphasis mine). Although these instances do not yet begin to cohere with the themes or structures of the early novels, they nonetheless offer early glimpses of Dickens's penchant for figurative expression and preoccupation with phrasing that will eventually lead to his more fully fledged idiomatic imagination.

Garrett Stewart (1974, 14) has long maintained that the Inimitable's "borrowed figures and idioms" constitute "a sheer gymnastics of words on vacation from the chore of meaning." This assessment fits my sense of how Dickens's idiomatic imagination works early on where we encounter these verbal calisthenics and doubling (if not tripling) of language's expected form in the bodily idioms employed throughout nearly all of the early novels. Examples of this in *Oliver Twist* (1837–39) include the narrator's description of Oliver's starvation during his journey to London: "If he begged at a farmer's house, ten to one they threatened to set the dog on him; and when *he showed his nose* in a shop, they talked about the beadle, which brought Oliver's *heart up into his mouth*,—very often the only thing he had there" ([1837–39] 2003, 59; emphasis mine). The narrator's comical account of Barney, the waiter with the perpetually stuffed-up nose at the Three Cripples, offers another example when Fagin nervously inquires if there is anybody else at the establishment: "'Dot a shoul,' replied Barney, whose words, whether they *came from the heart* or not, made their way through the nose" (119; emphasis mine).

The Old Curiosity Shop (1840–41) is interesting in that we start to witness Dickens extend some of the conceits of his idiomatic expressions beyond individual instances or immediately consecutive sentences. At the outset of the novel, for instance, the grandfather begins a paragraph by asking to speak privately with Master Humphrey (still the narrator at this point). "A word in your ear, sir," the old man requests ([1840–41] 2000, 34). Humphrey then begins the next few paragraphs by referring to "the eagerness with which all this was poured into my ear" (34). It is in this sense that we see Dickens taking more delight in the ways idiomatic constructions allow him to press multiple senses into punning phrases with adjacently extended figurative and literal meanings. When Quilp is attempting to enlist Nell's brother, Frederick, in his villainous plans to siphon money from their grandfather, he connivingly insists on a nonexistent friendship by saying, "Frederick . . . I have always *stood* your friend" (183; emphasis mine). The first sentence of the next paragraph farcically literalizes the idiom: "With his head sunk between his shoulders, and a hideous grin overspreading his face, the dwarf *stood up* and stretched his short arm across the table" (183; emphasis mine). The remainder of the scene alternates between Quilp's sitting and rising from the table—as if to dramatize the absurdity of the selfish villain's idea that to "stand by" someone means simply to "stand up" and shake hands while conducting nefarious business. A similar extension of idiomatic expression occurs in the comic section where Sampson Brass enlists Dick Swiveller to help gather information about the mysterious lodger who has come to let a floor in the lawyer's building. Dick suggests setting up a ladder to gain access, but Brass objects, saying, "The neighborhood would be *up in arms*" (268; emphasis mine). A few paragraphs later, after they decide to make a racket at the lodger's door, we learn that Dick has "*armed* himself with his stool and [a] large ruler" and that Brass comes "*armed* with a poker or other offensive weapon" (268–69; emphasis mine).

I have been tracing these various instances of Dickens's affinity for idiomatic phrasing not because they are the *only* places where they exist in his early work but more so to consider the extent to which his budding experiments with such language help create a relational basis for assessing how some of the deepest pools of his mature imaginative genius took shape. My much closer analysis of individual novels begins with *Dombey and Son* (1846–48) in chapter 1 partly because critics widely agree that it represents the gateway to Dickens's mature, "planned" fiction. This does not mean that Dickens all of a sudden—shazam—starts using body idioms in an iron-clad, fully fledged way even in *Dombey*, however. Instead, my first chapter seeks to evaluate the personal, social, historical, and philological conditions that contribute to the novel's inception of what we may consider the beginnings of a definitively more sustained dimension of Dickens's idiomatic imagination. My other chapters demonstrate how this dimension then becomes more and more embedded in the compositional processes of each successive novel—to such an extent that Dickens's idiomatic imagination shifts from the realm of the experimental to one of formal necessity by the time of *Our Mutual Friend*. In my conclusion, we will see how the bodily-oriented idiomatic dimension to Dickens's imagination eventually proves so generative and pervasive that it ends up affecting not only the prose of the modern novelists who come after him but also (uncannily) the criticism of those who continue to analyze his life and work today.

28   INTRODUCTION

Idiomatic Shortcomings

For all of the dazzling dimensions of Dickens's idiomatic imagination, I would be remiss not to acknowledge its limitations, too. One of the most serious, to my mind, is the assumption of male normativity that we see reflected in the explicit usage of the body idioms I discuss in Dickens's work. Despite my belief that a powerful sense of "right-hand womanness" emerges alongside the "right-hand man" idiom in *Dombey and Son*, for instance, Dickens never actually uses the expression "right-hand woman" in the text. The same could be said with varying degrees of the mostly masculine subjectivity regarding other body idioms as well. Esther Summerson and Charley Neckett undeniably exhibit a "shoulder to the wheel" orientation toward labor in *Bleak House*, but it is never explicitly acknowledged as such.[43] Similarly, the "sweat of the brow" idiom is associated—albeit sardonically—with Rogue Riderhood, Mortimer Lightwood, Eugene Wrayburn, and Silas Wegg rather than to the far more deserving female laboring characters like Lizzie Hexam, Betty Higden, and Jenny Wren. The reasons for the gendered nature of these idioms range from the fairly straightforward to the biographically complex. Dickens's language may be seen as a product of the gendered conventions of the society in which he was writing. Victorians in the 1840s were just barely beginning to use the "right-hand man" idiom outside of military contexts, and so the idea of a "right-hand woman" may have been unthinkable this early on in the expression's movement from the literal to the figurative. But there is also something more deeply concerning about the relationship between Dickens's masculinized idiomaticity and his particular views of women. Put differently, I think Dickens's well-known inability to understand women[44] is part and parcel of his often disembodied idealizations of them. To borrow a term from Mary Ann O'Farrell (1997, 68, 84), so many of Dickens's domestic heroines lack "somatic legibility" because of his real-life preference for virtuously etherealized[45] rather than "real women" (C. Tomalin 2011, 194). Dickens's reaction to the early and sudden death of his sister-in-law, Mary Hogarth, at seventeen, starkly manifests this tendency to, as Lillian Nayder (2012, xiv) and many others have shown, "idealize" women. He told a close friend that this sweet-natured but quite ordinary young woman was an angelic paragon: "So perfect a creature never breathed. I knew her inmost heart, and her

---

43. The "brought up by hand" idiom in *Great Expectations*, by virtue of its original association with breastfeeding, is always already feminized to a certain extent. For better or for worse, Biddy, Molly, Estella, and even Miss Havisham *are* explicitly designated as having been "brought up by hand."

44. "My father did not understand women," Dickens's daughter Kate famously said. See Storey 1939, 100.

45. See Knoepflmacher 1988, 79.

INTRODUCTION   29

real worth and values. She had not a fault" (quoted in C. Tomalin, 2011, 79). Dickens removed a ring from her finger on her deathbed and wore it perpetually on one of his own for the rest of his life in which he was periodically visited by Mary in "Madonna-like" dream visions. This is not the only case where Dickens maintained disembodied fantasies of feminine virtue and desirability. For example, since Maria Beadnell had jilted him very early on, he also built up an edifice of her in his own mind through many years of separation only to be shocked upon arranging a meeting with her later in life where he saw "an overweight woman, no longer pretty, who talked foolishly and too much" (C. Tomalin 2011, 286).

It is important that Dickens's personal shortcomings, along with his more generalized artistic male subjectivity, not go unremarked in a book dedicated to the inner workings of his imaginative life. That said, however, I leave the far more contextualized close readings of my individual chapters to make the case that the worlds generated by his idiomatic imagination are powerfully inclusive with respect to how each idiom applies to its novel's wider thematic concerns—even if Dickens himself is at times incapable or unaware of creating such an applicability. It is also worth noting that I am not alone in sensing these wider, thematically oriented idiomatic applications irrespective of gender, though. As we shall see, critics routinely and themselves unconsciously— thus all the more remarkably—write about *both* male and female characters with rhetorical variations of the idioms that I maintain are so crucial for our understanding the imaginative conception and development of Dickens's mature novels.

CHAPTER 1

The Beginnings of Dickens's Idiomatic Imagination

Dombey and Son's "Right-Hand Man"

> In a novel what is said two or more times may not be true, but the reader is fairly safe in assuming that it is significant.
>
> —J. Hillis Miller, *Fiction and Repetition* (1982)

Rarity, Idiomatic Provenance, and the "Planning" of *Dombey*

We have seen in the introduction how Dickens not only uses far more body idioms in his novels than his peers but also how he playfully experiments with embodied idiomatic language throughout his early fiction. But his experimental use of body idioms does not start to intersect with his compositional methods nor his fiction's deepest thematic concerns until about midway through his career. Because of this, *Dombey and Son* (1846–48) constitutes a decisive moment in Dickens's career for a particular set of reasons. We know from the overall numerical comparisons and from the brief analyses of his early fiction that Dickens does not suddenly start using bodily derived idiomatic expressions only with this novel. Quite the contrary: he uses hundreds of them in each of his previous novels. The point of this chapter is to demonstrate how he starts pressing certain idioms into a more unified thematic service with *Dombey and Son*. In other words, although the sheer number of idiomatic expressions Dickens uses in each of his novels is sui generis among major Victorian novelists—and therefore noteworthy itself in terms of authorial "style"—this is not nearly as interesting as the *way* he begins emphasizing certain expressions for isolated repetition midway through his career. What I mean by isolated repetition is this: the vast majority of the hundreds of body

THE BEGINNINGS OF DICKENS'S IDIOMATIC IMAGINATION 31

idioms Dickens uses in any given novel are ones that he typically recycles throughout all or many of his other works. For instance, the expression "hold your tongue" appears over and over again in fourteen novels, "at arm's length" in fifteen novels, "from head to foot" in all seventeen novels, and so on.[1] Only in *Dombey and Son*, though, the seemingly obscure idiomatic expression "right-hand man" occurs four times.[2]

Despite what Hillis Miller (1982, 2) says about the significance of that which is said two or more times in a novel, the "right-hand man" idiom's unique usage has probably escaped critical attention for good reason. Most of us now probably use it unwittingly in our contemporary speech and because, after all, it appears only four times in *Dombey and Son*—Dickens's longest novel at 356,610 words. But unlike virtually every other bodily derived idiom that repeatedly turns up in Dickens's work throughout his career ("at arm's length," "hold your tongue," "head to foot," etc.), this figurative sense of "right-hand man" appears *only* these four times in *Dombey*; never before or again in his entire fictional oeuvre. I concede that viewed solely in this numerical context, such rarity of phrasing four times in such a lengthy novel still does not amount to much. Over the course of this chapter and throughout this book, however, we will see how its rarity inaugurates a process of idiom generativity that offers us a new way to frame and interpret Dickens's mature imaginative development.

Assessing how and why Dickens's unique usage of the "right-hand man" idiom in *Dombey* matters for the imaginative process which unfolds throughout the novel first requires some additional and more general contextualization. Twenty-first-century readers have most likely assimilated a pervasive and always-already figurative sense of what a "right-hand man" signifies in our contemporary lexicon. Indeed, its figurative embeddedness in our everyday vocabulary is one reason why we read right past it even when it does appear in *Dombey*.

The wider idiomatic usage of a "right-hand man" was still relatively rare from a philological perspective in the 1840s, however. As Frances Ferguson (2013, 328) reminds us, philology attends to the histories of words and phrases so as to establish not just the variety of things one might say with a particular word or phrase but also to mark the changes in what one might say with that

---

1. The following seventeen works are the texts in which I searched and which, for the purposes of this book, I consider his "fictional oeuvre": *Sketches by Boz, The Pickwick Papers, Oliver Twist, Nicholas Nickleby, The Old Curiosity Shop, Barnaby Rudge, A Christmas Carol, Martin Chuzzlewit, Dombey and Son, David Copperfield, Bleak House, Hard Times, Little Dorrit, A Tale of Two Cities, Great Expectations, Our Mutual Friend, The Mystery of Edwin Drood.*

2. These four instances represent the places where the idiom is explicit. It is directly implied in at least two other places in *Dombey*.

32   **CHAPTER 1**

word or phrase at various historical moments. It is therefore important to understand how and when the idiosyncratic uniqueness of the "right-hand man" expression achieved its idiomaticity—that is, the historical, cultural, and linguistic processes by which the expression moves from the literal to the figurative within the language's vernacular.

According to the *Oxford English Dictionary* (OED), the first use of the phrase "right-hand man" occurs in a military context in 1626 describing the literal placement of "a soldier holding a position of responsibility or command on the right hand of a troop of [cavalry] horses."[3] It is not until more than one hundred years later, in 1739, that the phrase began to acquire the figurative meaning we are familiar with today: as "a person (esp. a man) who serves as a chief assistant or indispensable helper to another." We will see how the idiom expands even more later on in its life cycle from "chief assistant or indispensable helper" to broader forms of surrogacy and factotum (as in Dombey sends his "right-hand man," Carker, to broker his second marriage). Even so, it still remains difficult to gauge how the phrase moves from its first instantiations to its more common usage in the second half of the nineteenth century. For example, the *Hansard Corpus*, which is made up of over seven million parliamentary speeches by some forty thousand speakers, turns up only two instances of the idiom from 1800 to 1850. It stands to reason, though, that even if MPs at this time were becoming familiar with the idiom, they would be unlikely to dip into the colloquial register while trying to impress and persuade their mostly aristocratic peers in professional settings for fear of using what was common and, in Addisonian terms, "vulgar" language. Olivia Smith (1986, 30) has pointed out that between 1797 and 1845, Parliament dismissively refused to admit petitions from certain sectors of the public simply because of the colloquial language in which they were written.

Newspapers, given the explosive expansion of their distribution and readership in the first half of the nineteenth century, provide a far more accurate picture of how the idiom increased in popular usage. Manfred Görlach's influential study, *English in Nineteenth-Century England* (1999) has convincingly established that journalism, combined with the exponential rise of literacy after 1840, had significant and more or less immediate effects on the spread of the vernacular in

---

3. "right-hand man, n. 1," http://www.oed.com/viewdictionary/entry/165885 (accessed July 24, 2016). There is also a powerful and lasting influence from the multiple "right hand" anthropomorphic phrasings in the Judeo-Christian tradition where Christ appears *dextera domini*, at the right hand of the Lord. For only few biblical examples, see Colossians 3:1, Romans 8:34, Hebrews 8:1 and 12:2, Acts 2:33, Matthew 22:64, Mark 16:19, and Luke 22:69. Dickens was no doubt aware of this biblical inflection, as he weaves it into the comic preposterousness of Dombey's myopically selfish worldview presented in chapter 1: "Common abbreviations took new meanings in his eyes, and had sole reference to them. A. D. had no concern with anno Domini, but stood for anno Dombei—and Son" (12).

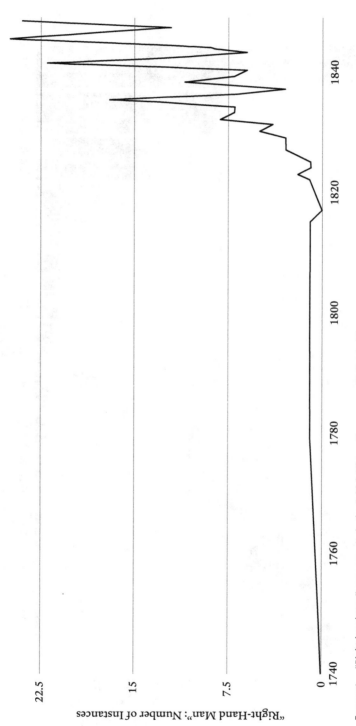

FIGURE 1. "Right-hand man" appearances in the *British Library Newspapers Digital Archive*

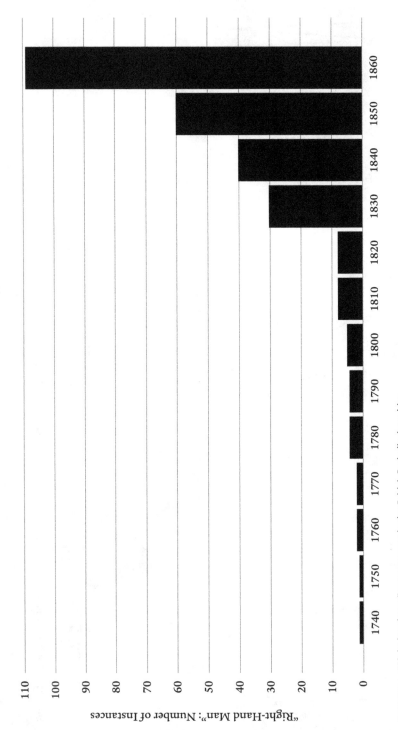

FIGURE 2. "Right-hand man" appearances in the *British Periodicals* archive

THE BEGINNINGS OF DICKENS'S IDIOMATIC IMAGINATION   35

standard English (13). Searches through the *British Library Newspapers Digital Archive* and the *British Periodicals* database corroborate Görlach's claim. The Newspapers archive contains over two million pages from forty-eight daily and weekly papers in Britain, while the *British Periodicals* database contains over six million pages from 460 magazines and journals. The sheer breadth of these resources therefore provides a more comprehensive sense of how and when the phrase "right-hand man" gained traction in contemporary popular usage.[4] The following graphs provide visualizations of the phrase's traction and rising popularity in the newspaper and periodical presses, respectively, in the time before and during when Dickens was composing *Dombey and Son*.

These visualizations reveal that the idiom first appears in 1740—consistent with the year the OED dates its first figurative appearance—and its use in newspapers and periodicals rises very slowly until about 1835, when its usage then begins to spike. Although the graphs demonstrate actual occurrences in 1845 (about twenty-five occurrences in figure 1, forty occurrences in figure 2) and show that usage is still *relatively* rare, they nonetheless demonstrate that the phrase was becoming much more widely used in newspapers and periodicals around the time that Dickens began to compose *Dombey* in 1845. Moreover, a closer look at each of these occurrences shows an increasing elasticity of the phrase in its figurative usages as it spreads from strictly military contexts to religious, political, juridical, and eventually, to commercial ones as it becomes more popular.[5] It is also very likely that Dickens was aware of these developments considering that he maintained a keen interest in journalism (editing the *Daily News*—if only for a matter of months—in 1846) and in the periodical press (editing *Bentley's Miscellany* for three years).[6] Dickens's identification of the expanding applicability of the idiom—however he comes by it—reflects what Mikhail Bakhtin (1981, 259) would later discuss in terms of "the fundamentally social modes in which discourse lives" in the novel more generally. For Bakhtin, every

---

4. Even so, no collection of texts, no matter how vast, can ever hope to represent anything close to the totality of social, linguistic, or literary history. See Gailey 2016 and Katherine Bode 2018.

5. I feel confident making this statement because the relative rarity of the idiom into the middle of the nineteenth century allowed me to "hand sift" the digital results analogically. My protocol was the following: I wrote a script to return all instances of the phrase "right-hand man" from 1733 to 1846 in the *British Library Newspapers Digital Archive* and the *British Periodicals* databases. I then manually sorted through the 324 returns from in the *British Library Newspapers Digital Archive* and the 532 returns from the *British Periodicals* database, sorting (and counting) each of the returns into military, religious, political, juridical, and commercial categories.

6. Dickens would have been aware of the idiom's published usage no later than 1837, when an article he edited in *Bentley's Miscellany*, "A Visit to the Madrigal Society," used the phrase in its description of the society's organization hierarchy (Hullah 1837, 466). The idiom also appears in an 1842 article in *The Examiner*—a weekly edited by John Forster, Dickens's closest confidant and eventual biographer—wherein William Gladstone is referred to as Robert Peel's "right-hand man." See Hunt 1842, 753.

36   **CHAPTER 1**

word, phrase, and idiom of a novel "tastes of the context and contexts in which it has lived its socially charged life" (293). We shall see how the socially charged life of the "right-hand man" idiom does just this in *Dombey*; it moves from what Bakhtin describes as "familiar zones of contact with still-evolving contemporaneity . . . from professional jargon into more general use" (395, 418).

On a more personal level, one of the very few fictional authors who *did* employ the "right-hand man" idiom before *Dombey and Son*, Frederick Marryat, lived in close proximity to Dickens in Lausanne, Switzerland during the mid-1840s. The two were close friends who socialized and discussed their fictional crafts regularly while Dickens was in the process of developing his ideas for *Dombey and Son*. In a germane and idiomatically framed observation, Angus Wilson (1961, 379) long ago claimed that Dickens's "greatest natural gift was his ear," and so it is entirely possible that Dickens picked up the "right-hand man" expression from Marryat, a former Royal Navy officer who was conversant in both military jargon and nautical injuries. It is worth noting, too, that Dickens's library at Gad's Hill contained a full set of Marryat's thirteen novels (see Stonehouse 1935). Although there is no way nor any essential necessity to confirm whether Dickens read the several Marryat novels that featured the (still relatively) rare idiom, the friendship with the popular and successful nautical novelist clearly informed *Dombey*'s maritime themes more generally as well as the novel's representations of ocean commerce and seafaring characters such as Jack Bunsby, Solomon Gills, Walter Gay, and especially, the hook-handed Captain Edward Cuttle.[7] Not only did Marryat use the "right-hand man" idiom in his own novels, but he also employed several hook-handed characters within them.[8]

Frederick Marryat, of course, was no Charles Dickens. Where Marryat just happens to feature the "right-hand man" expression in his nautical novels, I think Dickens, perhaps unconsciously at first, saw thematic potential for the new novel he was writing—one that was to explore the possibilities and limitations of a distinctly "right-hand" sense of surrogacy (filial, commercial, gendered, and otherwise).[9] Moreover, it fits Dickens's brilliantly grotesque sensibilities to build into his finest fictional exploration of substitution and proxy a character—

---

7. Counterintuitively, *Dombey* is the one early Dickens novel that Donald Hawes (1972) does not analyze in connection with the two authors' personal and literary relationship.

8. The actual Marryat novels containing the idiom before *Dombey* are *Peter Simple* (1834), *Rattlin the Reefer* (1836), *Joseph Rushbrook* (1841), and *Percival Keene* (1842).

9. Criticism of the novel in the last twenty-five years has focused on this theme of surrogacy and substitution. Waters (1997, 56) correctly notes "the prominence given to surrogate and substitute relationships of various kinds in the novel." "The prevalence of surrogate family relationships," Waters asserts, "is truly remarkable" (56). Andrew Miller (2008, 164) traces Dickens's "well-nigh structuralist penchant for substitution" in *Dombey*. Armstrong (2005, 90) explores "the figure of the go-between,

THE BEGINNINGS OF DICKENS'S IDIOMATIC IMAGINATION 37

Captain Cuttle—who comically but compellingly *embodies* all the characteristics of a "right-hand man" without actually possessing a right hand.[10]

I grant that despite the historical data and personal anecdotes, the fact that Dickens uses the phrase "right-hand man" only in *Dombey* when he recycles many of the hundreds of other body idioms throughout his oeuvre may still seem rather unremarkable. It becomes more interesting and provocative, however, when we consider this anomaly in conjunction with the long-established consensus that *Dombey* stands out among Dickens's fiction as the earliest example of deliberate and successful planning. This consensus stretches at least as far back as John Butt and Kathleen Tillotson's (1957) pioneering book, *Dickens at Work*, where their chapter on *Dombey* is appositely titled "Design and Execution" (90).[11] Hillary Schor (1999, 49) has described this now twenty-first-century critical consensus perhaps most succinctly: "*Dombey and Son* marked a new beginning for Dickens in many ways: it was the first of his novels for which he wrote number plans in advance; the first to use complicated and involved metaphors for itself; the first he spoke of 'branching' off in ways we [now] think of his novels developing . . . with newly plotted tightness."

But my sense of how a rare idiomatic expression operates in the world of the novel pushes Schor's idea of "complicated and involved metaphor" further to locate the beginning of an imaginative process in *Dombey* that has so far gone entirely unnoticed. I contend that Dickens anchors the composition of *Dombey* around a pervading sense of "right-hand manness" *and* "right-hand womanness" in such a way that it becomes the founding (though still somewhat fledgling) instance of what will become standard imaginative procedure for much of his later and most sophisticated work. This particular idiomatic expression operates as a varied but surprisingly cohesive unifying force in *Dombey*—a force that radiates outward to how Dickens imagines characterization, narrative voice, plotting, and most importantly, thematic schema. In terms of the last of these, the multiple meanings bound up in this bodily idiom influence the subtle ways in which *Dombey and Son* forges the exploration

---

who substitutes" for a myriad of *Dombey*'s characters. Law (2010, 35) reads *Dombey*'s "relay of substitutions" in terms of as "[breast]milk kinship."

10. The influence of Marryat on Dickens as he began his new novel in Switzerland may also be seen in the choice of another important fictional character. Dickens gives his *Dombey* daughter the name of "Florence," the same name as Marryat's oldest and most precociously literary daughter, who was often among them at their gatherings in Lausanne during the mid-1840s. Florence Marryat went on to become a prolific novelist and her father's biographer; she dedicated her novel *Véronique* (1869) to Dickens.

11. J. Hillis Miller (1958, 143) maintains that *Dombey and Son* has a "coherence which was entirely lacking in *Pickwick Papers.*" For just a partial list of others who contribute to this critical consensus, see Williams (1970, 221), Hardy (1970, 60) and (2008, 88), Stone (1987, 56–57), Schlicke (1999, 183), Philpotts (2014, 24), Stewart (2015, 161), Adams (2012, 113), Hartley (2016, 64), and Douglas-Fairhurst (2011, 272).

38   **CHAPTER 1**

of its deepest and most interrelated themes: surrogacy and succession, commerce and commitment, care and neglect, ability and disability.

This rare but unusually prominent idiom, in other words, offers us not only an as-yet-unacknowledged pathway to meaning in *Dombey* but also a new and alternative way of thinking about the relationship between bodies, language, and the wider imaginative structures that begin to characterize Dickens's mature fiction. Indeed, his felicitous ability to integrate and elevate idioms of popular origin—ones that an early theorist of figurative language assert "fly at no high pitch of thought"—into the grandest structural and aesthetic achievements of his most mature fiction should be considered a major component of Dickens's appeal to readers of all classes (L. Smith 1925, 269). It is also important to recognize that the integration and elevation of this particular body idiom in *Dombey* need not be entirely conscious to be meaningful.

The Embodied Rhetoric of *Dombey*'s "Right-Hand Man"

Dickens, no doubt, had been considered a virtuoso wordsmith since he burst onto the scene with *Pickwick Papers* (1836–37), but what we could call his "idiomatic inventiveness" begins to develop in new ways as he experiments with the boundaries of ordinary vernacular language—bringing dormant connotations to literal, figurative, *and* thematic life after the successes of *Oliver Twist* (1837–39), *Nicholas Nickleby* (1838–39), and *The Old Curiosity Shop* (1840–41).[12] By the time Dickens starts composing *Dombey and Son* in early 1846, he begins using idiomatic expressions in systematic ways that analogically stretch and even violate their accepted meanings. The choice to introduce the character of Captain Cuttle in conjunction with the phrase "right-hand man" in his first "planned" novel is exemplary in this regard. It is part of a multifaceted, embodied playfulness that perhaps only Dickens could pull off—where idiomatic expressions both *do* and *do not* have the meanings generically ascribed to them. In his only novel to incorporate the phrase "right-hand man," for instance, one of the originally planned characters is conspicuously presented in prose and illustration as having no right hand; Cuttle has a hook and various other attachments that he uses *as* a right hand. Dickens's single page of notes outlining the major events of the novel include the identification of the following characters, in this order: Mr. Dombey, Paul Dombey ("born to die"), Florence, Captain Cuttle, Mrs. Chick, Polly Toodle,

---

12. See the introduction for an analysis of what I call Dickens's "idiomatic embryonic" as it surfaces sporadically in these early novels.

THE BEGINNINGS OF DICKENS'S IDIOMATIC IMAGINATION   39

Miss Tox, Solomon Gills, Walter Gay, and Major Bagstock—a list that interestingly does not include the novel's most ostensibly obvious and explicit "right-hand man," James Carker (Stone 1987, 56–57). Of course, we may read nothing whatsoever into the fact that Captain Cuttle appears as the first non-Dombeyan character listed in Dickens's first planned notes. But I hope to demonstrate how Cuttle's centrality from the very start helps open up generative possibilities for other, extra filial characters to operate within modes of proxy, substitution, and surrogacy that extend and even transcend what it means to be a "right-hand man" in this novel. "Some of the most effective embodiments of an idea in fiction," writes Raymond Williams (1970, 80), "create so immediate and convincing a reality that it is only by analysis . . . that the shaping idea can be separated out." This is what I aim to do; to analyze how, by way of an ironic idiomatic association of the "right-hand man" with Captain Cuttle, Dickens creates one of his first and most effective embodiments of both character *and* shaping idea.

As one of the originally planned characters, Major Bagstock also plays a central role in establishing the multiple ways that the idiom works its way into the novel. Since, as Miss Tox says, there is "'something so truly military'" in the man, it is fitting that Bagstock is the one who eventually uses the "right-hand man" idiom first and most explicitly later on in reference to Carker (Dickens [1848] 2002, 102). This confirms an important part of Bakhtin's (1981, 302) theory of how heteroglossic discourse enters fiction—notably, where "common language" aligns with "the verbal approach to people and things normal for a given sphere of society." Bagstock's sphere of society is military oriented, and thus it is fitting that it is he who first introduces the idiom into the text. But Bagstock comes to embody nearly all of the phrase's literal and figurative connotations beforehand. He proposes "to be [Dombey's] guest and guide at Leamington," encouraging Dombey to "command him in any way [he] please[s]" (Dickens [1848] 2002, 306). Their relationship gets to this point because, as the narrator tells us early on, "Dombey observed of the Major . . . that besides being quite a military man he was really something more, as he had a very admirable idea of the importance of things unconnected with his own profession" (148). One of these "things unconnected with his own profession" at which Bagstock excels (and which Dombey most certainly does not) is romantic sociability. When all is said and done, it is Bagstock who suggests the trip to Leamington and who sets up the particulars of where they will stay, what they will eat, where they will visit, and whom they will see there. Thus compacted within Bagstock is the military-historical provenance of the idiom but also some of its expansive future potential beyond.

The assistance that the major offers is hardly handled by Bagstock alone, however. Even as he becomes the "right-hand man" for Dombey's social excursion, he himself employs his own "right-hand man": "the dark servant" known

CHAPTER 1

FIGURE 3. Major Bagstock is delighted to have that opportunity

only as "the Native" (102, 303). Because it is the Native who assembles the luggage, arranges the transportation, does the cooking, and even carries messages around to Mrs. Skewton and Edith Granger at Leamington, there is undoubtedly a troubling social and racial power dynamic underwriting Bagstock's ability to *be* a "right-hand man" for Dombey. Perhaps nowhere is this cascading dynamic of hierarchical "right-hand" power more apparent than in the illustration depicting the scene where Bagstock formally introduces Dombey to his future (second) wife and mother-in-law (figure 3). Here, the subordinate hierarchy repeatedly embedded in the idiom could not be more visually explicit in the positioning of the characters. The "right-hand man," Bagstock, stands di-

THE BEGINNINGS OF DICKENS'S IDIOMATIC IMAGINATION 41

rectly to the right of Dombey, while Bagstock's "right-hand man," the Native, appears directly to his right.

Even Major Bagstock, though, is not at the top of Dombey's hierarchy of right-hand men—and his position as such is crucial for when and how the idiom enters the text. Bagstock, along with the Native, orchestrate and set in motion all of the various courting campaigns at Leamington that make Dombey's romantic affiliation with Edith possible, yet it is "the [business] Manager," Carker, who swoops in to sanction the relationship (399). The irony of this unmilitary, untrustworthy, and "sly" character supplanting the major's role as Dombey's "right-hand man" is not lost on Bagstock (399). He cannot resist a hearty "chuckle" when he sees how Dombey blindly considers his firm's "second-in-command" as his right-hand man (399).

This ironic perspective is also an important element in the idiom's first explicit appearances in the novel. Attempting to convince Mrs. Skewton that Dombey "is in earnest" about a prospective match with Edith, Bagstock points to the arrival of Carker in Leamington—who is dispatched there presumably to assess the situation in (right-hand man) proxy for the exceedingly proud "Colossus of commerce" (407, 398). The major again chuckles at his own use of the idiom before becoming serious:

> "Dombey's *right-hand man*, Ma'am," said the Major, stopping abruptly in a chuckle, and becoming serious, "has arrived."
>
> "This morning?" said Cleopatra. . . .
>
> "Well, Ma'am," said the Major. "I have thrown out hints already, and the *right-hand man* understands 'em; and I'll throw out more, before the day is done." (407; emphasis mine)

Consultation with Dickens's handwritten manuscript from the Victoria & Albert Museum reveals something very interesting—perhaps crucial—here in this first usage of the idiom. His handwriting in the manuscript flows cleanly up until "Dombey's . . . ," and then several undecipherable cross-outs show Dickens struggling indecisively with how he wants (Bagstock) to describe Carker, until he eventually settles on labeling him "Dombey's right-hand man." Could these cross-outs and insertions provide a glimpse into Dickens's thinking about how to reconcile the ways in which the novel's most "official" but officially negligent right-hand man is known for his teeth while the most capable but unofficial one (Cuttle) is known for his hooked right hand? Whatever the case may be, Dickens appears pleased with the applicability of Bagstock's label because he applies it without hesitation in each subsequent reference to Carker as the "right-hand man"—that is, the idiomatic adjective appears without any cross-outs hereafter. These important textual details occur in conjunction with

42 **CHAPTER 1**

what happens so often and so seamlessly in Dickens's work: the ironic diction of his characters begins to blend with the diction of his narrators. This phenomenon, which Patricia Ingham (2008, 128) has appropriately termed "the listening narrator," occurs when the narrator hears and amplifies a characters' idiosyncratic—and, in this case, idiomatic—ways of speaking.[13]

In fact, the scene at Leamington is a quintessential example of Dickens's listening narrator. Just a few pages after Major Bagstock dubs "the man with the teeth" Dombey's "right-hand man," for example, the narrator recounts how Bagstock leaves Mrs. Skewton upstairs while he descends to rejoin Dombey "and his right-hand man," Carker. Here is how the narrator describes the scenario just moments after Bagstock's original introduction of the idiom: "At length, the Major . . . went down stairs to enliven 'Dombey' and his *right-hand man*. Dombey was not yet in the room, but the *right-hand man* was there, and his dental treasures were, as usual, ready for the Major" (410; emphasis mine). Although this scene appears twenty-six chapters into the novel, I concur with Alan Horsman's (1974, xxxi) belief that Major Bagstock's part in the second marriage "seems to be among the very earliest plans for the novel, judging by the presence of the military witness at the marriage ceremony in the [monthly number] cover design." Moreover, in the moments before the wedding (in the presence of Carker), it seems as if Bagstock wants to set the record straight about who is the more worthy "right-hand man" by comically and self-indulgently demonstrating his loyalty in terms of his own literal right hand: "'Dombey,' says the Major, with appropriate action, 'that is the hand of Joseph Bagstock; of plain old Joey B., Sir, if you like that better! That is the hand, of which His Royal Highness the late Duke of York, did me the honour to observe, Sir, to his Royal Highness the late Duke of Kent, that it was the hand of Josh; a rough and tough, and possibly up-to-snuff, old vagabond" (Dickens [1848] 2002, 481). This, combined with how the idiom appears in the original handwritten manuscript, what we know about the military provenance of the idiom, and its concentrated use in the Leamington scene, informs my sense that Dickens, at some level, was able to register the idiom's literal but multiply valenced applicability for the themes of service, surrogacy, and substitution that he was already exploring from the novel's opening pages when he

---

13. Hardy (2008, 79) has also referred to this phenomenon as "rhetorical miming." Ingham's "listening narrator" and Hardy's "rhetorical miming" reflect Bakhtin's (1981, 415–16; emphasis original) earlier analysis: "authorial language itself still remains a stylistic system of languages: large portions of this speech will take their style (directly, parodically, or ironically) from the languages of others, and this stylistic system is sprinkled with others' words, words not enclosed in quotation marks, *formally* belonging to authorial speech but clearly distanced from the mouth of the author by ironic, parodic, or polemical or some other pre-existing 'qualified' intonation."

THE BEGINNINGS OF DICKENS'S IDIOMATIC IMAGINATION   43

thought of his principal characters, including Captain Cuttle—the disabled character who, for hundreds of pages, has already performed the role of the text's most effective "right-hand man."

Bakhtin's understanding of how speech operates in the novel genre may help explain the "intentional" complexities involved in this seemingly straightforward scene of dialogue. The listening narrator's commentary with Major Bagstock's dialogue partakes of Bakhtin's (1981, 324; emphasis original) formulation that such speech constitutes a special type of "double-voiced discourse":

> Heteroglossia, once incorporated into the novel (whatever the forms of its incorporation), is *another's speech in another's language*, serving to express authorial intentions but in a refracted way. Such speech constitutes a special type of *double-voiced* discourse. It serves two speakers at the same time and expresses simultaneously two intentions: the direct intention of the character who is speaking, and the refracted intention of the author. . . . And all the while these two voices are dialogically interrelated, they—as it were—know about each other . . . it is as though they actually hold a conversation with each other.

If the closely related scenes do constitute a conversation, in the Bakhtinian sense, between Major Bagstock and the narrator, they allow Dickens to compact, reiterate, and transfer the meanings of a heteroglossic and increasingly popularized idiom within a single important though otherwise unremarkable scene where "the refracted intention of the author" may or may not be wholly conscious.

As I have stressed, though, conscious or not, part of what makes Dickens's idiomatic imagination so remarkable is the way he delights in exploiting the idiomaticity of an expression by continually alternating between—and even violating—its figurative and literal dimensions. We see this, for instance, in the dining room illustration (figure 4) which appears more or less immediately after Carker supposedly takes over from Bagstock as Dombey's "right-hand man." The inverted positioning of the characters in the illustrated dinner show Carker at Dombey's left hand, not his right. Such positioning only pages after Carker has been labeled Dombey's "right-hand man" perhaps suggests (as well as predicts) the treacherousness of Carker's true orientation toward Dombey.[14]

Something similar is implied on a far bigger stage later in the novel when Dombey hosts a "housewarming" dinner party for his business associates. In this instance, the narrator recounts in considerable detail how and where the guests, including Carker, Cousin Feenix, Edith Dombey, Major Bagstock, and

---

14. I am indebted to one of Cornell University Press's anonymous readers for this valuable suggestion.

44   CHAPTER 1

Figure 4.   Joe B is sly, sir, devilishly sly

Mrs. Skewton, arrive at their seats during the elaborately choreographed dinner. The description of the seating's specificity is inversely proportionate to one errant guest's obscurity: "When all the rest were got in and were seated, one of these mild men still appeared, in smiling confusion, totally destitute and unprovided for, and, escorted by the butler, made the complete circuit of the table twice before his chair could be found, which it finally was, *on Mr. Dombey's left hand* (Dickens [1848] 2002, 556; emphasis mine). Although it is comical that Dombey's frozen demeanor even at what is billed as a "housewarming" event causes a seat to be left open on one side of him, it is conspicuously a seat on his left hand because his now publicly declared and professionally

THE BEGINNINGS OF DICKENS'S IDIOMATIC IMAGINATION 45

instituted "right-hand man," Carker, is this time seated directly to his right (62).

These kinds of failed applications and reliteralizations of the idiom will become more interesting as they relate to other characters and larger themes in subsequent novels, but for now, it is important to mention briefly the two other (for a total of six) instantiations of the idiom in *Dombey*. One occurs when Mr. Morfin pays a visit to the home of Carker's disgraced older brother, John, and his sister, Harriet. Morfin is an underling assistant manager in the commercial hierarchy of Dombey's firm. He is deeply concerned for Harriet Carker's well-being (a concern that will develop into romantic interest), and so he offers his services should she ever decide to terminate her resolution to live in isolation with her brother, saying, "If you should see cause to change your resolution, you will suffer me to be as your right hand. My name shall then be at your service" (521). Morfin's steadfast promise to act as Harriet's "faithful steward"— another figurative collocation of the "right-hand man" idiom—culminates in his marriage to Harriet at the end of the novel (885). The sixth explicit instantiation of the idiom occurs when Solomon Gills leaves the Wooden Midshipman to search for the presumably drowned Walter Gay—an event that causes a realignment of the shop's "management." The narrator informs us that Captain Cuttle, unaware of Rob's treachery, installs "the Grinder" to be the second in "command" of shop: "[Cuttle] had believed in the false Rob. . . . He had made a companion of him as the last of the old ship's company; he had taken command of the little Midshipman with him a[s] his right-hand" (597). And it should be noted, here, that my stance regarding the essential idiomaticity of the expression despite its exact phrasing is bolstered by overwhelming textual evidence culled from Dickens's entire oeuvre: every other of the 224 instances where the adjectival phrase "right hand" appears in his novels, unlike the two examples above, delineates either literal proprioception (something in the environment's or a character's kinesthesiastic place to the right of) or a literal action of a character's right hand ("holding out a clenched right hand," etc.).[15]

Even so, these occurrences of the expression in *Dombey* also need to be additionally contextualized in terms of their rarity both in Dickens's fiction and in that of other contemporary novelists. Despite the bourgeoning use of the "right-hand man" idiom in newspapers, magazines, and journals, novelists still hardly ever employed it in their fictional prose. Dickens does not use the idiom even a single time outside of *Dombey* in the entirety of his career, and a

---

15. The sole possible exception to these 224 instances could be the scene in *Little Dorrit* ([1855–57] 2003, 284) when Mr. Meagles arranges for Daniel Doyce and Arthur Clenham to form a joint business venture, saying that "each of you will be a right hand to the other."

46   **CHAPTER 1**

search through the Chadwyck-Healey database Nineteenth-Century Fiction, made up of 250 novels by more than 100 different British and Irish authors, reveals that the phrase is used in only four other instances—once in a military context in William Thackeray's *Vanity Fair* (1848), once in Anthony Trollope's much later *Phineas Redux* (1873), and twice in Dickens's friend Frederick Marryat's pre-Dombeyan *Percival Keene* (1842). In my much larger corpus of 3,719 nineteenth-century novels, the idiom appears in only ninety-seven other books—and even then, it occurs a maximum of twice in only four of the nearly four thousand texts.[16] Such rarity provides additional context for thinking about the idiom's relatively dense concentration in *Dombey and Son*. Its extreme rarity (inside and outside of *Dombey*) is itself a provocation to explore a more specific question about the idiom's isolated concentration in only this particular novel.[17] Dickens's concentrated use of the idiom multiple times only in a single novel, especially considering that it was virtually unused in thousands of other nineteenth-century novels, fulfills the definition of what the digital humanities scholar Judith Flanders (2013, 24) calls a true "phraseological peculiarity."[18] Making sense of this phraseological peculiarity remains the central task of this chapter. As we shall see, what might be called "right-hand manness" (and eventually "right-hand womanness") supersedes the rarity of its numerical instantiation as it comes to pervade almost every aspect of *Dombey*. So much so, in fact, that it becomes pivotal for how the text represents its most salient themes in various but related ways.

Of course, linguistic usage outside of print is difficult to quantify precisely because of its tendency to proliferate through the unseen (and unverifiable) substrata of a culture. But *Dombey* is nonetheless one place where I think we can identify Dickens operating at the forefront of such a subterranean linguistic root system. We know from the content of his own later periodicals *Household Words* (1850–59) and *All the Year Round* (1859–70) that Dickens was deeply curious about philology, the derivation of everyday phrases, and the social history of language alteration more generally.[19] Even before his insistence on the usage

---

16. This larger corpus is comprised of a combination of the following databases: Chadwyck-Healey's Nineteenth-Century Fiction, Project Gutenberg, the Internet Archive, and the Nebraska Literary Lab.

17. The fact that the idiom appears very rarely in a corpus spanning one hundred years, of course, does not prove that it was actually rare at that time. Rather, it demonstrates that it is rarely present in the novel types which exist in that particular corpus. But it is a corpus that is far more representative of the expansive number of Victorian novels than we typically are asked to consider as evidence in a strictly "analogue" argument.

18. For a discussion of how data mining that "brings forth idiosyncratic uniqueness" still requires close contextual interpretation and analysis, see Rockwell and Sinclair 2016.

19. Dorothy Deering (1977, 12) has demonstrated how *Household Words* and *All the Year Round* contained a significantly larger portion of articles on the English language and its usage patterns than in *Blackwood's*, *Fraser's*, the *Cornhill*, *Bentley's*, and the *Edinburgh Review*.

THE BEGINNINGS OF DICKENS'S IDIOMATIC IMAGINATION   47

"plain English" ("household words") in his periodicals, however, at this point in his career Dickens seems to possess the ability to predict how idiomatic expressions, carried into new lexical and thematic relationships, act like linguistic burrs that stick and retain some of their original (literal) meaning even as they enter the realm of the figurative. He was fascinated by the ways past meanings could illuminate new but related meanings of a current (or emerging) phrase—what Bakhtin (1981, 288) referred to as "the uninterrupted process of historical becoming that is characteristic of all living language." The way the "right-hand man" idiom originates in *Dombey* with Major Bagstock is exemplary in this regard. By virtue of his career in the British army, Major Bagstock has spent his entire life in the profession from which the idiom literally emerged. And as English commerce greatly expanded in the 1840s, the idiom becomes transferable from Bagstock's "regimental stories" to other nonmilitary contexts. This is precisely what we see in Bagstock's use of the phrase to introduce Carker to Edith and Mrs. Skewton in Leamington; he transfers it from the "regimental" to Dombey's commercial and marriage-brokering contexts with Carker operating as "second-in-command," "go-between," and "medium of communication" (399, 681, 709). Transferences such as these help account for the spike in usages of the phrase that we see in the graphed figures from the *British Library* Newspapers and *British Periodicals* archives. It is a testament to Dickens's acute awareness of emerging linguistic trends and his mastery of vernacular speech that the phrase emerges in *Dombey* almost simultaneously and in the same categorical contexts with which it surfaces in much more expansive popular discourse.[20]

Idiomatic Malleability and Dickensian "Style"

Although critics have yet to recognize how specific bodily derived idioms function in the worlds of Dickens's novels, I am in good company when it comes to their acknowledgment of his more general ability to connect seemingly insignificant details to his larger artistic aims. Some forty-five years ago, Garrett Stewart (1974, xv–xvi) convincingly argued that Dickens's "style" often consists of "small moments of almost impossible insight and rightness . . . sudden illuminations that take our breath away [and] frequently collapse into a single disclosure the largest themes of their books." More recently, Daniel Tyler (2013, 11) has argued that "Dickens often marshals attributes of his style—his figurative

---

20. This process operates on the threshold of what Bakhtin (1981, 363) calls "stylization" and "variation": "Variation freely incorporates material from alien languages into contemporary topics, joins the stylized world with the world of contemporary consciousness, projects the stylized language into new scenarios, testing it in situations that would have been impossible for it on its own."

48   **CHAPTER 1**

language, his wordplay, his sound effects—to the immediate thematic ends of each fiction." Tyler's edited collection, entitled *Dickens's Style* (2013), contains eleven articles ranging from Robert Douglas-Fairhurst's assessment of "Dickens's Rhythms" (2013) to Jennifer Gribbles's exploration of "Dickens's Figurative Style" (2013).

My contribution to these discussions of Dickens's style is to point out that the most exceptional of Dickens's thematic wordplay is often directly related to his unique constructions of idiomatic embodiment—a dimension of Dickensian style that none of Tyler's contributors mention. Dickens's penchant for idioms involving the body also fits with what we know of his performative personality: he loved bodily performance as much as he loved phrasal virtuosity, and he especially delighted in combining the two. As John Bowen and Robert Patten (2006, 5) have suggested, bodily performance "structured [his] creative process itself, which for him sometimes involved a physical process of embodiment and acting-out, even before a mirror whose reflections of his impersonated characters he could study and transcribe." Indeed, what we might call Dickens's use of a *bodily vernacular* is sometimes hard to detect precisely because of the way it blends in so organically to wider issues of characterization or thematic plotting. His verbal bravura often resides in those moments that participate in the surrounding themes which they so unsuspectingly parallel—a participation so imbricated with the novel's themes that it sometimes becomes a condition of its own invisibility. In *Dombey*, the text's abiding concern for what I have been calling a kind of "right-hand" surrogacy acts in organic concert with the ways in which individual characters occupy positions "as deputy and proxy for some one else," to use the novel's own language (Dickens [1848] 2002, 60). Catherine Waters's (1997, 56) listing of the various relationships suggests just how dominant this theme is in *Dombey*: "Polly Toodle acts as surrogate mother to Florence and Paul, Sol Gills and Captain Cuttle act as surrogate fathers to Walter and Florence respectively, Florence is a surrogate mother for Paul, Walter is a surrogate brother for Florence, Edith is a surrogate mother for Florence (for a time), Miss Tox becomes a surrogate aunt to the Toodle family." Andrew Miller (2008, 164) casts *Dombey*'s "well-nigh structuralist penchant for substitution" in terms of a "particularly fluid interchange" of surrogate replacements.[21]

---

21. Andrew Miller (2008, 164) writes, "Mr. Dombey imagines his son to be an extension of himself, and understands that, in the future, he will be replaced by his son in the family business. . . . But, in the event, the son dies and is replaced by Dombey's daughter. Similarly, Dombey's first wife in the novel, Fanny, is replaced by a second, Edith—who in turn replaces Dombey with the perfidious Mr. Carker. But in Carker's company, Edith herself is only a replacement for the woman Carker long ago deserted, the outcast Alice."

THE BEGINNINGS OF DICKENS'S IDIOMATIC IMAGINATION   49

Another prominent and post-Dombeyan example of this organic process of idiom pertinence (and prevalence) occurs a few years later in *Hard Times* (1854) with the connection between Mrs. Sparsit's "Coriolanian nose" and the inherent "nosiness" of her persona (Dickens [1854] 2003, 48). Not only does Dickens identify her nose over twenty times in this short novel, but more importantly for the process of idiomatic extension and expansion that I am analyzing, he has Josiah Bounderby repeatedly refer to Sparsit with a conspicuously nasal idiomaticity, such as when the Bully of humility talks of "hav[ing] the skin off her nose" because of his annoyance at the housekeeper's tendency of "pok[ing] her officious nose into [his] family affairs" (251). This more refined and sustained ability to oscillate between the literal and the figurative in various narrative voices—what Peter Brooks (2005, 44) has aptly called Dickens's "quicksilver agility of [his] narrator's styles"—is certainly of a piece with how "right-hand manness" operates almost ten years earlier in *Dombey*. Thus, the scene at Leamington where the narrator "listens in" on and repeats Bagstock's own repeated appellation of Carker as Dombey's "right-hand man" is an as-yet-unremarked-upon instance of Dickens's linguistic inventiveness that becomes interwoven with the novel's larger themes in a process of *idiom absorption*. The idiom, once articulated and repeated, becomes absorbed into the text whole cloth in such a way that its literalization, abstraction, or even its explicit violation emerges as new agents for thematic innovation, "soak[ing] through and through" as Leo Spitzer (1948, 27) held, into "the atmosphere of the work."

One of the principal ways that "right-hand manness" becomes absorbed into *Dombey* is paradoxically through the continued presence (in prose and illustration) of the character who has no right hand. The novel's first monthly installment, at the start of October 1846, introduced readers to Captain Cuttle with an unequivocal "hook-first" description. We learn that he is "a former pilot, skipper, or privateersman . . . with a hook instead of a hand attached to *his right wrist*" (Dickens [1848] 2002, 55; emphasis mine). Here, the narrator's important first description includes Cuttle's most distinguishing feature. Moreover, this description parallels his first illustrated appearance (figure 5), where his right-hand hook appears almost levitating at the very center of the sketch—its centrality to his characterization mirroring its central location in the illustration.

The narrator also consistently emphasizes the specific placement of Cuttle's hook on his right hand. To cite just a couple of instances that span the text, Cuttle "re-attache[s] the hook to his right wrist" after he had "screwed a knife into its wooden socket" during an early dinner scene (139, 138). Later, we are reminded that Cuttle cannot write with his (right) hook and so applies "his own left-handed signature" to a set of documents for Jack Bunsby (601).

50   CHAPTER 1

FIGURE 5.   Captain Cuttle consoles his friend

None of this "handed" specificity would matter very much, of course, were it not for my argument that it works in close conjunction with how Dickens imagines idiomatic surrogacy in *Dombey*. Part of this conjunction also involves thinking about Cuttle's appearance in an outsized share of the novel's illustrations. He shows up in better than a quarter of the novel's total illustrations—more than any other character besides Florence Dombey (Carker, the supposedly explicit "right-hand man," appears in only four illustrations).[22] This is significant in terms of the novel's planning because Dickens worked closely with Hablôt K. Browne ("Phiz") to ensure that the coordination of his prose

---

22. The theatergoing public similarly acknowledged Cuttle's centrality to the novel. As Kreilkamp (2009, 101) points out, one of the more famous and long-running stage adaptations of the novel was John Brougham's, which ran at the Burton Theater under the title not of *Dombey and Son*, but of *Captain Cuttle*.

THE BEGINNINGS OF DICKENS'S IDIOMATIC IMAGINATION   51

and illustrations matched the spirit of his imaginative outlay. Doing so was no easy task, especially at the start of the novel when Dickens was writing from Lausanne and Browne was illustrating from London.[23] Perhaps the most important point here is that the spirit of Captain Cuttle's representation—both in illustration and in prose—is unilaterally one of warm and genial capability and almost always associated with the use of his right hook: the use of "his one hand and his hook with the greatest dexterity . . . overflow[s] with compassion and gentleness" (725). Because of this, I wish to consider Cuttle's characterization not only in terms of an idiomatic interplay between the literal and the figurative but also in its association with important notions of how his surrogacy operates in the context of ability and disability. One of the central themes in *Dombey* revolves around the embodied relationship between physically abled but emotionally limited characters and those that are physically disabled but emotionally competent. Moreover, there is a crucial interrelationship between the wider idiomaticity of the "right-hand man" expression and the text's concern for surrogate affiliations that become defined amid a backdrop of ability and disability, competence and incompetence.

Dombey and (Dis)ability

More than sixty years ago, Kathleen Tillotson was among the first critics to comment on the difference in Dickens's large-scale planning and organization, which began with *Dombey and Son's* overall and monthly-number plans. Although this view has now reached near total critical consensus, I return to Tillotson's formulation because her specific choice of diction in presenting Dickens's new approach is particularly germane for the line of inquiry that I am tracing in this section. She maintained that "with *Dombey* [Dickens] began to write novels founded on a theme, *embodied* in a relation between characters" (Tillotson 1956, 159; emphasis mine). Tillotson does not pursue material embodiment in her analysis, but the sense of an embodied relation between Mr. Dombey and Captain Cuttle is pivotal precisely because of what its stark inversion reveals about how the novel's themes manifest themselves through the interplay between bodily and characterological dispositions (see Gitter 2004). For instance, if Dombey is the chief embodiment of selfish pride and emotional frigidity, Cuttle is the fullest embodiment of generous humility and tender care. But these thematic embodiments are also literal embodiments as the narrator insists again and again on the radical contrast between these two

---

23. For a more detailed account on this complicated process, see J. Cohen 1980, 90.

52   CHAPTER 1

characters' physical and dispositional representations. Where Dombey appears "hard, inflexible, unyielding" (Dickens [1848] 2002, 655), "stiff with starch and arrogance" (110), and "unbending [in] form" (469), Cuttle appears with "impenetrable equanimity" (259), with "a lively sense upon him" (265), with "a manner that [is] at once comfortable, easy, and expressive" (260).[24]

There is little question that Dickens, especially in his early fiction, either sentimentally objectifies or bluntly villainizes characters with disabilities. As Julia Miele Rodas (2006, 373) notes, though, "disability in Victorian fiction [also] indicates . . . a desire to experiment with places and roles."[25] The opposing descriptions of Dombey and Cuttle, like those cited above, might be a place where this sort of experimentation emerges in Dickens's more mature work. Rodas (2004, 79–80) maintains that the disabled in such cases can "seem to exist, not apart from, but along a continuum with other ostensibly nondisabled characters." In the general descriptions of Dombey and Cuttle, however, the continuum appears less homogenous than directly reversed. Dombey's unfeeling bodily demeanor of inflexibility and stiffness, in comparison with Cuttle's empathetic liveliness and comfort, complicates the question of what it means to be abled or disabled in the world of this novel. We know from Dickens's letters that he was keenly interested in conflated notions of able- and disable-bodiedness elsewhere in *Dombey*. He wrote to Browne, for example, that Mrs. Skewton should be shown "shoved about in a Bath chair" by an assistant "even though nothing [is] the matter with her to prevent her from walking" (March 10, 1847). The spirit of Mrs. Skewton's feigned disability matches almost exactly the narrator's prose description of her meeting with Major Bagstock: "The beauty and the barouche had both passed away, but she still preserved the attitude, and for this reason expressly maintained the wheeled chair and the butting page: there being nothing whatever, except the attitude, to prevent her from walking" (Dickens [1848] 2002, 319).

Dickens extends (and reverses) this kind of able-bodied conflation most specifically to Dombey and Cuttle. Where Dombey's bodily inclination is to coldness—bearing a "cold, hard armour of pride" (608), Cuttle's is to warmth—offering a "manner of warm approval" to all he encounters (260). Perhaps Dickens's most revealing and embodied juxtaposition of these opposing dispositions appropriately comes with the first narrated meeting between the two characters, which occurs when Cuttle goes to Brighton as Walter Gay's "right-

---

24. See Bourrier (2015), where she argues that disabled male characters in Victorian novels are often used to fill out the interiority of strong, taciturn male heroines, especially in cases where the disabled character is able to articulate feelings for the taciturn man of business.

25. According to Rodas (2004), it is in *David Copperfield* (1849–50) that Dickens begins to experiment with and to widen his views of disability.

THE BEGINNINGS OF DICKENS'S IDIOMATIC IMAGINATION   53

hand man" in an attempt to secure a loan from Dombey for the struggling Wooden Midshipman. Cuttle's role as an effective "right-hand man" to Walter in this scene is thus paradoxically but powerfully underscored by his repeated "waving his hook" and "kiss[ing] his hook" throughout the negotiations (150, 155). The emphasis becomes most intensely focused on the actions of Cuttle's hook and hand, though, once the loan is secured and preparations are made to leave: "[Cuttle] could not refrain from seizing [Dombey's] right hand in his own solitary left, and while he held it open with his powerful fingers, bringing the hook down upon its palm in a transport of admiration. At this touch of warm feeling on cold iron, Mr Dombey shivered all over" (155).

At least a part of the effectiveness of this arresting handshake tableau is the way in which it formally, and physically, establishes the inverted relationship between what counts as ability and disability by reversing expectations. Cuttle's "touch of warm feeling" emanates from the way he uses his left hand in tandem with his prosthetic hook, while Dombey "shiver[s] all over" because he senses only cold iron in the touch. Dombey does not yet possess the (cap) ability for "warm feeling" that characterizes the entirety of Cuttle's physical and temperamental disposition from the start.

Writing about touch in the context of disability, Janet Price and Margrit Shildrick (2002, 69; emphasis original) argue that "touch *frustrates* hierarchy" because it "has the power to disrupt devaluing fantasies of autonomy, superiority, and normalcy." Dombey certainly wields fantasies of extreme autonomy and superiority over the one-handed sea captain whom he has just met, and these feelings culminate in his frustration that his daughter Florence—following "the earnestness of her heart"—attempts to leave this scene in the "low" company of Cuttle and Walter rather than stay with her father and the household servants: "Mr Dombey called her back, and made her stay where she was" (Dickens [1848] 2002, 155). As Dombey is emotionally incapacitated, and therefore inclined to coldness, he is incapable of registering the "earnestness of [his daughter's] heart" and the "warm feeling" emanating from the captain's entire disposition; instead, he sees and senses only the irregularity of Cuttle's body and, as a result, feels only the "cold iron" of the prosthetic touch. However, Cuttle's use of his prosthetic device as if it is endowed with the capabilities of a fully functioning hand importantly reflects his *own* sense of capability which, as we will see, forecasts his ability to continue acting as a far better "right-hand man" than the technically abled but emotionally deficient Carker with whom the idiomatic phrase originates.[26]

---

26. The early work of Davis first historicized how concepts of "normalcy" in relation to "disability" are themselves constructions that arose out of and were confirmed by the radically changing

54   CHAPTER 1

Lennard Davis (2012, x) has recently argued that the problem with "metamorphiz[ing] disability" is that it creates a process that is "a substitutive one in which you say something is something else"—where "the effect is to distract, to disengage from the original [disabled] subject." Davis's sense of "metaphorizing," no doubt, obtains similarly to "idiomatizing" disability in the way that I am construing it here with Cuttle. Referring to someone as a "right-hand man"—and associating the idiom with a character not possessing a right hand— necessarily, and perhaps unfairly, abstracts meaning *away* from the actual body; it avoids, elides, or even erases "seeing the object as in itself it really is," to use Davis's terms (x). At times in *Dombey*, this is quite obviously the case. In the same scene from above where Dombey "shivers" at the sight and touch of Cuttle's hook, for example, Miss Tox stumbles over how to describe Cuttle to Dombey just prior to their introductory handshake. She eventually settles on an all-too-familiar ableist description which reduces Cuttle to his physical "irregularity." Unable to introduce Cuttle with a description that recognizes him beyond the visual horizon of his impairment, she stammers through her introduction and, finally, cannot refrain from making it the focal point of her announcement: "'The gentleman with the . . . —Instrument,' pursued Miss Tox, *glancing* at Captain Cuttle,'" as she introduces him to Dombey (Dickens [1848] 2002, 154; emphasis mine). Reactions such as Miss Tox's to Cuttle's prosthetic hook encourage the pitiable spectacles of readerly stare that Rosemarie Garland-Thomson (2002, 59) has attributed to the harmful visual rhetoric of nineteenth-century conceptions of bodily "irregularity."[27]

Moreover, critics correctly note that Dickens has a tendency to use disability and disfigurement as a visual shorthand for varying levels of villainy, incompetence, or pity throughout his entire career (see Holmes 2004 and Janecheck 2015). Little Nell, Tiny Tim, Daniel Quilp, Mr. Dick, and Silas Wegg are just a sampling of the iconic characters Dickens has generated in this regard. And yet, as the representation of Cuttle's capability may indicate, it is every bit as problematic to emphasize the "saintliness" of disabled characters who heroically manage to overcome their disabilities. Lennard Davis, Martha Stoddard Holmes, and others have pointed out how damaging "supercrip" narratives can be because their stereotypical focus on overcoming, heroism, and the extraordinary all too often "erases" impairment (see especially Davis 1995, 106 and Holmes 2004, 194). Other disability scholars have analyzed how these supercrip representations focus on individual attitude, work, and perseverance rather

---

industrial conditions of the mid-nineteenth century. *Enforcing Normalcy* (1995, 24) demonstrates how "the word 'normal' as 'constituting, conforming to, not deviating or differing from, the common type or standard, regular, usual' only enter[ed] the English language around 1840."

27. For Garland-Thomson's book-length study of this phenomenon, see *Staring: How We Look* (2009).

THE BEGINNINGS OF DICKENS'S IDIOMATIC IMAGINATION   55

than on social barriers, making it seem as if all effects of disability can be erased
if only one works hard enough (see Schalk 2016, 73). More specifically, Vivian
Sobchak (2006, 24) has expressed concern about the overuse of the metaphor
of prosthesis and its ramifications—namely, the forgetting of the material reality of prosthesis and the lived experience of those with prosthetic body parts.

I am in no position, nor do I desire for the purposes of this chapter, to adju-
dicate Cuttle's supercrip status. Instead, I want to focus on how Cuttle, as the
text's most effective "right-hand man," (literally and idiomatically) embodies
how Dickens imagines his first planned novel's central concern for the possibilities of surrogate care. My sense is that Cuttle's very real disability, beyond functioning as a simple trope, metaphor, or idiomatic emblem, compounds his
importance and complexity in framing the deepest themes of *Dombey* insofar as
it is a novel about what it means to live ably—fully, generously—even if by surrogate relations—in a world where too many have gravely limiting emotional
and moral deficiencies. Captain Cuttle is easily one of the most generous and
decent characters in the cruel world of this novel, and it is worth considering
further how he most often expresses his generosity and decency through the
actions of his iron-hooked "hand."[28] This point deserves emphasis because during the nineteenth century, it was widely assumed that the physically disabled
required rather than dispensed assistance. With Cuttle, Dickens simultaneously
imagines and tests how alternate forms of surrogacy may be successfully
achieved—how one may be a viable and genuine "right-hand man" even without possessing a right hand and, as we shall see, even without being a man.

Situating Victorian disability as a relational category, Holmes (2004, 29) argues that some novels "posit an emotional exchange system in which cur-
rents of feeling, stimulated by the presence of a corporeally 'different' body,
connect people who are not disabled to people who are." It is in this way that
Captain Cuttle operates as a fulcrum of filial surrogacy—a kind of parental
"right-hand man"—to those like Walter Gay and Florence Dombey who have
lost the "blood" element of direct family relation.[29] We witness this acutely in
Cuttle's deft preparation of meals for both of these surrogate children. Early in
the novel, Cuttle prepares a dinner for Walter Gay consisting of "loin of mutton, porter, and some smoking hot potatoes, which he had cooked himself."

---

28. Davis uses as his literary example a scene from Conrad's *The Secret Agent* (1907) where coachman
with "a prosthetic hook for an arm" maintains a bearing far different than Cuttle's. The one-armed man
exclaims, "'This ain't an easy world. . . .'Ard on 'osses, but dam' sight 'arder on poor chaps like me'"
(quoted in Davis 1995, 47).

29. Waters (1997, 56) maintains that "the ties of blood are shown to matter much less [in *Dombey*]
than the affective bonds of the middle-class family, which have been naturalised as universal human
values."

56   **CHAPTER 1**

The narrator tells us matter-of-factly that "he unscrewed his hook at dinnertime, and screwed a knife into its wooden socket, instead, with which he had already begun to peel one of these potatoes for Walter" (Dickens [1848] 2002, 138). Cuttle's resourcefulness reaches even greater heights while cooking for Florence at the Wooden Midshipman—her surrogate home—after she has been brutally disowned by her father and cast out of his house:

> The Captain spread the cloth with great care, and was making some egg-sauce in a little saucepan: basting the fowl from time to time . . . as it turned and browned on a string before the fire. Having propped Florence up with cushions on the sofa . . . the Captain pursued his cooking with extraordinary skill, making hot gravy in a second little saucepan, boiling a handful of potatoes in a third, never forgetting the egg-sauce in the first, and making an impartial round of basting and stirring with the most useful of spoons every minute. . . . The dinner being at length quite ready, Captain Cuttle dished and served it up, with no less dexterity than he had cooked it. . . . He wheeled the table close upon Florence on the sofa, said grace, unscrewed his hook, screwed his fork into its place, and did the honours of the table. (737)

These passages remind the reader that Cuttle accomplishes an elaborate set of culinary tasks with one hand and a set of prosthetics, but they do so without isolating this aspect. The change from hook to fork occurs not in isolation but right alongside wheeling the meal closer to Florence, saying grace, and doing the honors of the table. This swift and matter-of-fact description endows Cuttle with a practicality, warmth, and general demeanor that focuses *on*, rather than erases or diminishes, his competencies. In other words, the narrator does not elide but, in fact, merely includes Cuttle's prosthetics in his meal preparation for Walter and Florence as one aspect of his surrogate competency, which is both practical *and* emotional. This makes space for an idea that highlights the possibilities of an alternative relationship between physicality and inner character—one where the "regular" or "irregular" features of the body simply and without fanfare take their place alongside other aspects in the spectrum of identity.

Such a presentation nonetheless ironically situates Cuttle in striking contrast to the able-bodied characters like Dombey who need all manner of "right-hand men" or those operating *as* supposed "right-hand men," like Carker, who have such egregious emotional and ethical shortcomings. In characteristically Dickensian wordplay, this thematic irony is also embedded in the referential rhetoric attached to his characters' names, with which we know Dickens famously experimented (see Hardy 2016, 43). Thus, D-o-m-b-e-y—an anagram of "embody"—may be the "Head of the Firm," but he has no heart and fails

THE BEGINNINGS OF DICKENS'S IDIOMATIC IMAGINATION   57

miserably as the "Head of the Home Department";[30] Captain "Cut-tle" may have a hand "cut off" from his body, but he manages his role as a "right-hand man" (to Florence, Solomon, Walter) far more competently than "Carker the [actual] *Manager*"—who, as we have seen, is supposed to be the novel's explicit and official "right-hand man" to Dombey. According to Derek Attridge (1989, 193), in an effective and well-crafted pun "two similar sounding but distinct signifiers are brought together, and the surface relationship between them is invested with meaning through the inventiveness and rhetorical skill of the writer." The "Cuttle / cut-off" pun thus raises the possibility that Dickens conceived of his name not in terms of lack but rather in terms of overabundant competence. After all, a cuttlefish is an *eight*-limbed mollusk, and it is hard to fathom that this punning association would have been lost on Dickens.

Herbert Sussman and Gerhard Joseph (2004, 620), in "Prefiguring the Posthuman: Dickens and Prosthesis," come closest to my view of Cuttle's amplified but unsensationalized capability when they assert that his hook is "both 'iron' and 'hand' . . . a synecdochic 'helping hand,' however mechanical." It is worth recalling that the sense of a "helping hand" as Sussman and Joseph use it (whether synecdochic, metonymic, or metaphoric) is embedded in the OED's definition of the idiomatic "right-hand man" that was beginning to take root just as Dickens was starting to compose the novel: "an indispensable helper to another." But there was also a historical "prosthetic precedent" for Cuttle's singular optimism and for his varied use of multiple appendages. After losing his right arm in the Battle of Vittoria (1813), Captain George Webb Derenzy published *Enchiridion: or A Hand for the One-Handed* (1822)—a text that was well circulated in England through the 1830s as the nation confronted waves of disabled veterans returning home from the Napoleonic Wars. Frederick Marryat, Dickens's Royal Navy friend in Lausanne when he was beginning *Dombey*, owned a copy of *Enchiridion*, and the many corresponding prosthetic attachments shared between the real-life Derenzy and fictional Cuttle suggest that Dickens may have modeled the one on the other. Derenzy's litany of missing hand attachments prefigure several of those used by Cuttle: a "regular" hook, boot hook, nail file, syringe, egg holders, penknife, quill holder, ruler, cardholder, nutcracker, knife, fork, and (one of Cuttle's favorites) a toasting fork. The fictional Cuttle and the historical Derenzy also share similar aspects of personality. As Sue Zemka (2015, 4) has observed, Derenzy's book is "a testimony to his adaptation." Derenzy (1822, iv) states only once (and in no detail) in the opening dedication to his book that he lost most of his right arm at war, but his brief "confession of helplessness prefaces

---

30. For a general discussion of the intentionality of anagrams, see Ahl 1985.

58   CHAPTER 1

FIGURE 6. The shadow in the little parlor

a manual replete with [a] description" of the multiple ways in which he successfully and without alarum *uses* his right limb (Zemka 2015, 3). Zemka maintains that Derenzy's sanguine characterization of his use of the multiple attachments ensures that "the overall tone [of the book] is one of satisfaction with the can-do ingenuity of the devices" (3).

If anything, Dickens perhaps outdoes Derenzy with his frequent depictions—in both illustrations (figure 6) and prose—of Cuttle's unconscious physical capability.

THE BEGINNINGS OF DICKENS'S IDIOMATIC IMAGINATION   59

This particular illustration (figure 6) depicting Cuttle using his prosthesis as a toasting fork is preceded by the following prose description: "The Captain, *without knowing what he did*, had cut a slice of bread from the loaf, and put it on his hook (which was his usual toasting-fork), on which he now held it to the fire" (Dickens [1848] 2002, 748; emphasis mine). Cuttle reveals a similar degree of matter-of-fact substitution between his hand and his hook as he describes life at sea to Florence: "'Think on it when the stormy nights is so pitch dark,' said the Captain, solemnly holding up his hook, 'as you can't see your hand afore you, excepting when the wiwid lightning reveals the same'" (745). Cuttle even "put[s] his iron hook between his teeth" to, as he says, "'bite his nails a bit'" when cogitating upon difficult situations (238). Comical though they may be, such descriptions of Cuttle's prosthetic hook (or knife or fork) are decidedly not pitiable spectacles of readerly stare or objectification of the kind we saw associated with Miss Tox's stammering reference to Cuttle as "the gentleman with the . . . —Instrument" (154). Instead, they focus on an unconscious and prosthetically symmetrical body that does not need or require "repair."[31]

Insofar as Captain Cuttle displays an unconscious but practical competence— cheerfully "arrang[ing] his hair with his hook" (259), regularly "flourish[ing]" it to embellish his conversation (255), earnestly "wav[ing] it in token of welcome and encouragement" (482), and "kiss[ing]" it "with great elegance and gallantry" (155), nervously "bit[ing]" it instead of phantom fingernails (238)— the injury becomes depathologized and, consequently, begins to merge with what Tobin Siebers (2008, 8) calls an "ideology of ability." If this is true, Cuttle's eminently practical and even comfortable proficiency in all sorts of settings begins to align with disability studies' seminal notion that impairment is a process dependent on the social (constructed) hierarchization of bodies rather than something inherent in the body itself (Garland-Thomson 1997, 7). And ultimately, my point is that this kind of portrayal serves as an alternate but important vector in the novel's larger thematic paradigm: Cuttle's surrogate ability to *be* a right-hand man to so many different people in the novel despite not *having* a right hand emphasizes a sense of competence that depends not on the binary limitations of ability and disability but rather on the way we experience our bodies as both features and extensions of our deeper selves.

That deeper, surrogate self for Cuttle involves his acting not just as a practical (food-preparing) "right-hand man" but also, importantly, as an emotional "right-hand man" in the world of *Dombey*. Indeed, we witness Cuttle's deepest

---

31. These manual substitutions reveal Cuttle's capacity to live in way that echoes Merleau-Ponty's (1962, 234) phenomenological notion of *motility*, where objects attached to the body may transform into more capable extensions of the limbs themselves.

60   **CHAPTER 1**

and most generously proficient self when he attends to the physically and emotionally scarred Florence at the Wooden Midshipman after she has been mercilessly cast out of her father's house. Dickens's description of Cuttle's actions at this pivotal stage in the novel "overflo[w] with compassion and gentleness," which underwrite his practical physical competence: "Finding [Florence] insensible . . . Captain Cuttle snatched from his breakfast-table, a basin of cold water, and sprinkled some upon her face" (Dickens [1848] 2002, 724). Even more impressive is how Cuttle merges the practical with the emotional so that his physical practicality and emotional care become indistinguishable. The narrator describes Cuttle's use of "his one hand and his hook with the greatest dexterity" as he transforms the upper chamber of the Wooden Midshipman into a surrogate home of emotional refuge:

> The Captain . . . converted the bed into a couch, by covering it all over with a clean white drapery. By a similar contrivance, the Captain converted the little dressing-table into a species of altar . . . that made a choice appearance. Having darkened the window, and straightened the pieces of carpet on the floor, the Captain surveyed these preparations with great delight, and descended to the little parlour again, to bring Florence to her bower . . . and the Captain *carried her up out of hand*, laid her down, and covered her with a great watch-coat. (728; emphasis mine)

The point is not that Cuttle performs all of these tasks with only one hand and his hook, though. Rather, it is that Dickens repeatedly emphasizes Cuttle's loving and emotional ability to be so much more than a fragmented body.

This is significant because a legacy of *Dombey* criticism has treated Cuttle as fragmented, "fractured," and fundamentally lacking many qualities, especially normative masculinity. Robert Newsom (1989, 210) considers whether Cuttle's fractured body makes him a "model androgyne," and Gillian Gane (1996) in "The Hat, the Hook, the Eyes, the Teeth: Captain Cuttle, Mr. Carker, and Literacy," as her title suggests, analyzes prosthetic masculinity through the lens of reading proficiency, a capacity that Cuttle quite obviously lacks in comparison to Carker who can read and write in several languages. More recently, Rosemary Coleman (2014, 126–27; italics original), in "How *Dombey and Son* Thinks about Masculinities," sees the text as laboratory "to solve the enigma of masculinity" and, in so doing, concludes that the novel "is unable to conceive of [even] . . . *one whole* man." But if we think of Cuttle's deep concern for Florence's well-being as situated at the intersection of questions about gender and disability, it becomes possible to recognize how "disabled" men may successfully access alternative notions of masculinity and embodiment. For example, Russell Shuttleworth (2004, 175) identifies disability as an opportu-

THE BEGINNINGS OF DICKENS'S IDIOMATIC IMAGINATION   61

nity to expand a "masculine repertoire" that can more flexibly accommodate so-called feminine roles. Thomas Gerschick and Adam Miller (1995, 265) likewise interpret the fragmented male body as offering a unique chance for men to recraft their masculine identity "along the lines of their own abilities, perceptions, and strengths"—all of which help to inaugurate positive and diversified categories of disabled masculinities. It is hard to imagine Captain Cuttle as ever being less than an earnest, cheerful, and caring person, but it *is* possible that the loss of his hand at sea heightens, rather than diminishes, these qualities. So Dickens does not so much soften Cuttle's disability with a fragmented feminization of it; he exalts it in a way related to what Holly Furneaux (2009, 214) has called "reparative masculinity." Indeed, with Cuttle's impairment, Dickens has created a most unexpected aberration: "the seamless fusion of hard metal and soft flesh . . . as the instrument of love and nurturing care" (Sussman and Joseph 2004, 620).

Dickens ([1848] 2002, 728; emphasis mine) acknowledges this prospect in the decidedly manual rhetoric he uses to describe how the one-handed "Captain carried [Florence] up *out of hand*, laid her down, and covered her with a great watch-coat" as he makes a new home for her at the Wooden Midshipman. Knowing what we do about Dickens's unrivaled penchant for crossphrase puns and aural syncopations, it also seems likely that Dickens aims to draw the reader's attention in this crucial scene to the relationship between acts performed *"out of hand"* and Cuttle's performance of these very same acts *"without a hand."* Such a tight pun would certainly seem to qualify as one of Dickens's "small moments of almost impossible insight and rightness" (Stewart 1974, xv) because, in Jonathan Culler's (1985, 2) formulation, it reveals "unexpected connections, whose suggestiveness shimmers on the borders of concepts."[32] The idiomatic blending of the figurative with the literal which we witness here, where auricular wit manifests itself as the phonematic partaking in the semantic, will come to characterize the Dickensian imagination more and more definitively in later novels.[33]

---

32. Culler is building on Roman Jakobson's (1987, 60) analysis of "sound texture," where "punlike, pseudo-etymological figures, by involving words similar in sound, stress their semantic affinity."

33. As Jonathan Culler (1985, 9) further notes, "The most general claim for puns as the foundation of letters would doubtless come from focusing on what Roman Jakobson called the poetic function of language: the projection of the principle of equivalence from the axis of selection onto the axis of combination, so that similarity becomes the constitutive device of the sequence." Culler himself is no doubt referring to Jakobson's famous reading of the word *nevermore* in Poe's "The Raven." "However great the variety of contextual meanings, the word *nevermore*, like any other word," writes Jakobson (1987, 58–59; emphasis original), "retains the same general meaning through all its varied applications. The tension between this intrinsic unity and the diversity of contextual or situational meanings is the pivotal problem of the linguistic discipline labeled *semantics*, while the discipline termed *phonemics* is primarily concerned with the tension between identity and variation on the level of language."

62   CHAPTER 1

Davis and others have long maintained that an accurate understanding of disability requires a recognition that seemingly neutral norms exist only in contrast to forms of deviance and disfiguration—in this case, of one-handedness. Just such a crucial component of contrast exists in *Dombey*, even if in reverse order. Whereas Dombey uses his ableism to strike his daughter with such force that "on her breast there was [a] darkening mark of an angry hand," Captain Cuttle uses his prosthetic hook to minister to Florence's pain and grief with the sensitivity and sympathy of genuine human touch (Dickens [1848] 2002, 736, 734). The brilliant Dickensian thematic irony is that the prideful Dombey requires a retinue of "right-hand men" (Carker, Morfin, Bagstock, Blimber, etc.) and "right-hand women" (Polly Toodle, Mrs. Skewton, Edith Granger, eventually Florence) while Cuttle, the character with no right hand, becomes a "right-hand man" for the novel's most fellow-feeling characters. In this sense, Cuttle is a case study in contrast to Dombey, and the contrast may be observed most starkly in the discrepancy between their participation in and reliance on the idiomatic valences of "right-hand manness." Dombey's body, an "unbending form" of "cold, hard armour," mirrors his emotional rigidity in a way that limits his able-bodiedness and requires other seemingly-abled characters to act as his appendages in a surrogate process of emotional and literal fragmentation (469, 608). The captain, with his "cut off" (Cut-tled) body, operates oppositely as a *consolidator* of the novel's disparate characters, feelings, and plots. It is an important paradox that the physically fragmented Cuttle acts as a bodily (and emotional) consolidator in a novel that has traditionally been interpreted as being preoccupied with a "particular [masculine] anxiety about going to pieces or being torn to pieces," as Carker is by the train in one of its most famous scenes (Newsom 1989, 204). But if we focus more on Cuttle, the particular coalescence of such opposing forces within his character provides a striking exemplar of Stewart's (2001a, 137) general contention that "characters in Dickens appear as embodied rhetorical strategies." Cuttle's ability to act as a right-hand man is not just an embodied rhetorical strategy, however; he is the central figure and catalyst for an embodied and variously refracted thematic strategy which registers the novel's deepest concerns for alternate forms of care and surrogacy.

Dombey's "Right-Hand (Wo)men"

The thematic strategies that surround the idiomatic and literal senses of "right-hand manness" in *Dombey* also reverberate far beyond Captain Cuttle's dynamic presence, and they, too, emerge from deviations, failed applications, or ironic

THE BEGINNINGS OF DICKENS'S IDIOMATIC IMAGINATION   63

violations of the original idiom. These wider reverberations help confirm what Douglas-Fairhurst (2006, xiii) has noted in a different context: "the contagiousness of [Dickens's] vocabulary, the way in which [his] prose often takes up its own earlier terms." In this vein, the earlier terms of Carker's explicit role as Dombey's "right-hand man" and Cuttle's more successful capabilities as a genuine "right-hand man" contagiously redound to other characters and additional scenarios but crucially to ones that continue to highlight idiom's generative relationship to the novel's dominant thematics of surrogacy and substitution. Hence, the novel's invocation of and preoccupation with "right-hand manness" is not restricted to the masculinist contexts of the military and commercial worlds despite the idiom's almost exclusively gendered orientation within those nineteenth-century worlds. Just as the novel's most adept "right-hand man" does not possess a right hand, attaining a level of competent surrogacy designated by the idiom does not require one to be a man. There are many important "right-hand women" in *Dombey*, and they, too, play pivotal roles in establishing the larger imaginative structure of the narrative. As Andrew Elfenbein (1995, 366) observes, "*Dombey and Son* is never more a business novel than when it concentrates on the home" where "the magic of analogy allows the good woman [Florence] to supplant the bad manager [Carker]."

Unfortunately, though, since Victorian women lived within a cultural system that granted them power only as auxiliary subordinates of men, the possibilities of what a "right-hand woman" might be—both in the wider world of mid-nineteenth-century Britain and within this novel—are considerably more vexed. Their gender alone already conferred many women "right hand" status in the sense of the idiom's definition as an "indispensable *helper* [to a man]."[34] Dickens himself certainly maintained this view. For example, he often referred to his sister-in-law, lifelong house manager, and unwavering adviser, Georgina Hogarth, as his "little right hand" (Dickens to W. H. Wills, October 21, 1855). But because of the spectacular failures of seemingly important men, "right hand" (Carker) and otherwise (Dombey Senior and Junior), an anxiety of feminine competence nonetheless pervades *Dombey*. This anxiety stems from the various ways in which women assume (in the singular), execute (in solidarity), and even refuse their status as traditionally inferior "right-hand women" in relation to men.

---

34. Think, for instance, of the nearly simultaneous scenario Brontë (2019, 439) describes at the end of *Jane Eyre* (1847) where Jane acts a traditionally construed "right hand woman" for Rochester: "Mr. Rochester continued blind the first two years of our union: perhaps it was that circumstance that drew us so very close; for I was then his vision, as I am still his right hand." This is all the more interesting if we consider how Brontë must mean this idiomatically because it is Rochester's *left* hand and arm that are maimed in the fire at Thornfield Hall.

64   CHAPTER 1

In fact, it is precisely the awareness of a decidedly competent female network of surrogacy and the accrual of significant and powerful "right-hand women" that fuels the elder Dombey's anxious and growing indignation toward women as the plot unfolds. At the very outset of the novel, for instance, Dombey is thoroughly humiliated—and embittered with "angry sorrow"—that the future of his all-male firm is so entirely dependent on Polly Toodle's surrogate function as a wet nurse to the newborn Paul:[35] "That the life and progress on which he built such hopes, should be endangered in the outset by so mean a want; that Dombey and Son should be tottering for a nurse, was a sore humiliation. And yet in his pride and jealousy, he viewed with so much bitterness the thought of being dependent for the very first steps towards the accomplishment of his soul's desire, on a hired serving-woman" (Dickens [1848] 2002, 27). In this early scene, the death of Mrs. Dombey imperils the sustenance necessary to sustain the family heir. Her premature death ensures that it is the woman's breast, not her hand, that makes her an indispensable surrogate that no traditional "right-hand man" could fulfill at the outset of the novel.

There is also evidence that Mr. Dombey prefers his "right-hand women," if forced by necessity to employ them in such stark dependence for the future of the firm, to be considered as nearly as possible "right-hand *men*." We see this in the fact that Polly Toodle may only enter the Dombey household under the masculine pseudonym "Richards" to perform her surrogate function as the family's wet nurse.[36] Such a curious arrangement reflects the lengths to which Dombey will go to recast his humiliating dependence on women as an unfeeling business transaction wherein he may recuperate masculine dominance and control. "It is not at all in this bargain," he assures the newly named Richards, "that you need become attached to my child, or that my child become attached to you. I don't expect or desire anything of the kind. Quite the reverse. When you go away from here, you will have concluded what is a mere matter of bargain and sale, hiring and letting" (28–29).

Jules Law (2010, 36) has emphasized how the "milk kinship that Dombey abhors becomes in fact the guiding principle of sociality for the remainder of the novel."[37] It does so because it forces Dombey to recognize his dependence on a

---

35. Claire Tomalin (2011, 192) is certainly correct to think about this in terms of Dickens's own life: "Reading the Polly Toodle chapter makes you wonder about the wet nurses who came to work for the Dickens family year after year, and what sort of conversations Dickens may have held with them."

36. It is true that servants were often called by their surnames at this time (and in Dickens's other novels). However, Dombey's insistence on calling Polly by the invented and masculinized name "Richards" is considerably different than if Dickens had chosen to have Dombey call her by her actual surname, "Toodle."

37. For an earlier treatment of the novel's gendered binary oppositions in terms of the "nurturing female breast," see Houston 1994, 90–122.

THE BEGINNINGS OF DICKENS'S IDIOMATIC IMAGINATION   65

kind of feminine capability that threatens his exclusively masculine view of the world. Law is correct that we witness this early in the novel in Dombey's insistence on a thorough inspection of the domestic and the feminine: Miss Tox has to testify to the hygienic conditions of the Toodle household and Miss Chick must examine Polly, her children, her marriage certificate, and so forth—all steps that lead the narrator to comically but accurately refer to Dombey as "the beadle of our business and our bosoms" (71). Yet, in contrast, the "business" that the recreant, Carker, will assume receives not even the slightest of professional vetting.

These gendered assumptions sharpen, as Hilary Schor (1999, 58) notes, into "anxiety that women can do quite well without the firmness of Mr. Dombey" and the other normative genteel men connected to him in surrogate mercantile associations. Throughout the novel's middle sections, there is a tragic lopsidedness in the relationship between Dombey's unexamined acceptance of the baleful "management" activities of his "right-hand man," Carker, in comparison to his deep and explicit mistrust of those who become "right-hand women" in his life. Where Dombey takes for granted the success of Carker's management of the firm's day-to-day activities, he appears "almost foaming" with anger at what he perceives to be the mismanagement of his household by his female staff (668). One particular outburst directed at Mrs. Pipchin is representative of Dombey's escalating misogyny. "Do you call it managing this establishment, Madam," an excoriating Dombey says, "to leave a person like this [Susan Nipper] at liberty to come and talk to *me!* A gentleman—in his own house—in his own room—assailed with the impertinencies of women servants!" (668; emphasis original). He is here referring to how Susan Nipper, acting in the capacity of a "right-hand woman" to Florence, takes it upon herself to berate her longtime employer for the "sinful" mistreatment of his daughter (668). Dombey's eruption at Mrs. Pipchin is also likely affected by his indignation and utter disbelief that his second wife, Edith, has by this point in the plot bluntly refused to assume her expected position as a subservient "right hand woman" of her husband and their new domestic sphere. Dombey no doubt sees these relationships as simple questions of "management": the "right-hand man," Carker, is the manager of the firm while Edith's "right-hand" role is supposed to be to manage the "home Department." Instead, Edith is "imperious to all the house but [Florence]" and this flabbergasts the "Colossus of commerce" whose entire life had, until his second marriage, been spent in "magnificent supremacy" (553, 610).

Because he is accustomed to "duty and submission" everywhere, Dombey appears unproblematically reliant on the "right-hand men" in his life, and yet he exhibits a marked anger with and distrust of women acting in similar surrogate

66   **CHAPTER 1**

capacities who operate independent of his authority. This misogyny is heightened by Dombey's selfish and mounting recognition that Edith Dombey acts unequivocally more as a "right-hand woman" to his daughter, Florence, than she does for him as a dutiful (submissively normative) Victorian wife. Here, as in the case of Susan Nipper's defense of Florence, "right-hand" surrogacy built on feminine allegiance is unfathomable to Dombey. However, the strength, depth, and emotional connection between Florence and her stepmother is forged in contradistinction to the cold, proud aloofness that Edith maintains in the company of her new husband. While she maintains an "indomitable haughtiness of soul" toward her husband, Edith "entreat[s] [Florence] to love and trust her . . . and would have laid down life to shield [Florence] from wrong or harm" (462, 463). The love and trust between stepmother and stepdaughter is mutual. After Florence confides in Edith about her dire concern for the banished Walter Gay, Edith responds with an emotional ardency and warmth which surfaces only in her relationship with her stepdaughter. She assures the lonely and scorned Florence, "I will be your true friend always. I will cherish you, as much, if not as well as any one in this world. You may trust in me . . . with the whole confidence even of your pure heart" (551).

This compassionate interaction with Florence, and the feminine solidarity it reflects, becomes additionally conspicuous because it appears in the chapter immediately preceding the one in which Edith "disdain[fully] and defiant[ly]" spurns the entire collection of East India Company brass, its directors, and "chairmen of public companies" that Dombey automatically expects her to entertain with subservience at his "housewarming" party (555–56). The fact that Edith "receives [these businessmen] with proud coldness, [and] show[s] no interest or wish to please" infuriates Dombey, who believes that it is her wifely "duty . . . to have received [his] friends with a little more deference" (560, 564). Dombey becomes even more thoroughly nonplussed by her outspoken refusal of his direct and "sovereign command . . . to be deferred to and obeyed" (613). Surely, his disbelief is exacerbated by the "bare ceremony of reception" Edith maintains at the housewarming party in comparison to the "loving consideration" he sees her cultivating in the relationship with her stepdaughter (560). It is clear that Dombey senses and despises the growing bond between his new wife and his daughter, telling Carker in no uncertain terms that he "do[es] not approve of Mrs. Dombey's behaviour towards [his] daughter" (647). These two aspects of Edith's refractory imperiousness culminate in her early exit from Dombey's housewarming party, as she abruptly terminates her participation in the event—"swe[eping] past [Dombey] with his daughter on her arm" (559). Since Edith is "imperious and proud to all the house but [her stepdaughter]," Dombey's physical striking of Florence may also be seen as an expression—and

THE BEGINNINGS OF DICKENS'S IDIOMATIC IMAGINATION 67

extension—of his feckless resentment that he possesses so little power over a defiant woman who refuses to be the "right-hand woman" of his elaborately renovated domestic sphere. Rather than hazard any further direct encounters with "this rebellious woman" whom he senses is "powerful where he [is] powerless," Dombey enlists Carker, his "second in command," to be his "go-between" and "medium of communication" (711, 399, 681, 709).

Perhaps Edith Dombey's most symbolic act of rebellion in her refusal to be a normative ("right-hand") wife, though, comes from what she does literally to her *left* hand—the hand that Helena Michie's (1987, 98) work has demonstrated to be a powerfully synechdocal representation of the female married heart and its sexual organs. At the moment she realizes that both Dombey and Carker desire to claim her hand, as it were, Edith "str[ikes] it on the marble chimney-shelf, so that, at one blow, it was bruised, and bled" (655). This act of "dark retaliation" is as brutal and ruthless as it is discreet and discerning, however (698). The maiming of her left hand symbolically breaks "the manacle that . . . fetter[s]" her married life to Dombey via her ring finger, but it also erases (or at least mitigates) the kiss Carker adulterously applies to her same left hand and, in so doing, simultaneously ensures her refusal to be neither a "right-hand wife" nor a "right-hand" mistress (699). In terms of the latter, Edith's decision to damage, and hence disable, her ring-bearing hand is a gorgeously conceived preemptive maneuver. When Carker pruriently attempts to kiss her hand again, assuming that she has decided on a path of infidelity, it is prophylactically bandaged and gloved (684).

Edith's endurance of such a violent self-inflicted wound also reveals the ways in which Carker overplays his own hand—both professionally and romantically. Instead of procuring what he thought he was (carnally) with the unsolicited kiss to Edith's hand and the subsequent fleeing to Dijon, Carker gets a "resolute," "steadfast," and "undauntable" woman "with no more fear of him, than of a worm" (823). This is appropriately rendered, especially since Dickens extends the saurian characterization only a few pages later when the narrator tells us that Carker becomes "trodden down by the proud woman" and "spurned like any reptile" (829).[38] Furthermore, the dramatic shift in gendered power is reinforced by the accompanying illustration (figure 7), which is sarcastically titled "Mr Carker in His Hour of Triumph."

The shifting power in what Michael Steig has appropriately called "the theme of male-female conflict" in this illustration is multiply valenced: the

---

38. These reptilian characterizations of Carker are interesting as well for the way they reverse contemporary male representations of "slithering" female heroines. Think, for instance, of Thackeray's infamous depiction of Becky Sharp in his concurrently running *Vanity Fair* ([1847–48] 1963, 617) as a "fiendish marine cannibal." The best analysis of this phenomenon is still Auerbach 1982.

FIGURE 7. Mr. Carker in his hour of triumph

THE BEGINNINGS OF DICKENS'S IDIOMATIC IMAGINATION   69

erectly standing Edith offers her left hand to the sitting and slouched Carker while her right hand remains concealed behind her body (94).[39] Even the blocked hand positioning in the illustration registers Edith's refusal to be Carker's "right-hand mistress," though. This is at least in part because the right hands of the women whom we *can* see in the illustration—Judith slaying Holofernes in a painting above and a warring Amazon woman on horseback in a statuette below—are facing Carker's open legs and poised in positions of fierce bellicosity. Although no one could ever (correctly) identify Dickens as a reliable advocate for feminine autonomy, these refusals of traditionally gendered, subservient "right-hand womanness" lend an idiomatic context to what Nancy Armstrong (2005, 89) and Barbara Hardy (2008, 102) have recently discussed as the "spectacularly scandalous" and "radically feminist" dimensions of Edith's character.[40]

Dombey and Daughter

If Edith's most powerful role in Dickens's idiomatic imagination resides in her steadfast resistance to becoming a submissive "right-hand woman" for any male character, Florence's development offers a striking contrast but one no less important in terms of the idiom's centrality to the novel's themes. Put simply, though for a myriad of reasons, Florence is the text's most earnest and capable "right-hand woman"; and because of this, she matches Captain Cuttle, as she eventually transforms her surrogate, substitutional, and subordinated status to one of exceedingly competent and even lifesaving primacy. Florence assumes this kind "right-hand" capacity in relation to her brother early on when she takes up the young Paul's studies adjacent to him at Doctor Blimber's forcing school so that she might "track Paul's footsteps through the thorny ways of learning" (187). The books, travel, and tutoring required for her to support Paul's learning are certainly not easy to arrange, but Susan Nipper—whom we

---

39. Steig (1978, 94) also says the following regarding this illustration: "Since much of the novel is devoted to Dombey's attempt to crush his second wife's spirit, our sympathies do tend to rest with Edith, but this illustration (along with subsequent plates) helps to state the theme of male-female conflict, with the woman a match for the man." For a more detailed use of the biblical story of Judith slaying Holofernes, see Philpotts 2014, 470.

40. Hartley (2016, 55–57) has even more recently noted that although Dickens often fails to convincingly construct adult women, he sometimes "does give us complex female characters, often with elements of sexuality" with whom he fashions "heroine material" out of "potential victims." See also Hager's (2010, 91) argument that Edith Dombey's spectacular defiance of and flight from her husband "makes available a feminist Dickens, or, at the very least, Dickensian heroine who looks more like a New Woman than an Angel in the House."

70 **CHAPTER 1**

have already seen in the role of "right-hand woman" to Florence—"is not easily baffled in the enterprise" (187). Paradoxically, this feminine partnership is precisely what allows the young Paul to make "great progress" at Doctor Blimber's (all-male) school: "Regularly . . . Florence was prepared to sit down with Paul on a Saturday night, and patiently assist him through so much as they could anticipate together, of his next week's work" (189). We learn that "it was not long before she gained upon Paul's heels, and caught and passed him" (187). Florence's indispensable role in Paul's education also importantly predicts the ways in which she will transcend her subservient "right-hand" status in relation to the novel's other male characters.

It is in this sense that Florence importantly eclipses her status as a normative "right-hand woman" in her assertive romantic courtship of Walter Gay. Where her stepmother disables her hand in a prophylactic maneuver to retain agency, Florence uses hers to secure marriage to the man she desires. The narrator tells us that she "put[s] her trembling hand in [Walter's]" as *she proposes marriage to him* in an extremely rare Victorian inversion of the traditional, heteronormative, gendered construction of female passivity that her own father so desperately prizes: "If you will take me for your wife, Walter," she says while taking Walter's hand, "I will love you dearly" (770). Most importantly, the union she initiates and the home it provides for the ruined and bankrupt Dombey makes Florence a remarkably forgiving and effective "right-hand woman" to her father after the novel's explicit but deprecating "right-hand man," Carker, conspires to have the firm's riches to "mel[t] away" (906). Elfenbein (1995, 378) correctly observes that "Carker is foiled by two women who prove better managers than he." And since Elfenbein correctly uses the terms "manager," "second-in-command," and "surrogate" more or less interchangeably, it is hardly a stretch to say that Edith and Florence are better "right-hand women" than the novel's definitively labeled "right-hand man." By the late stage in the novel where this poetic irony comes to pass, Dombey's cold inability to feel has transformed itself into a physical incapacity with grave tangible consequences. The loss of his business, his associates, his home, and all his belongings threatens to leave "the white-haired gentleman" etiolated and alone to perish in his old age.

But Florence transcends the idiom's gendered and necessarily subservient connotations as she fulfills the place that each and every one of Dombey's "right-hand men" could not by rescuing him from desuetude and immanent suicide, making him a part of her family. In doing so, she operates as what disability theorists call a "satellite" (Rodas 2004, 51). Florence "orbits" for the entire novel with a seemingly endless desire to rehabilitate her father's disabled emotions. This is not to suggest that Florence's orbiting makes her a perpetual caretaker for the disabled. Her rotation through important parts of the

THE BEGINNINGS OF DICKENS'S IDIOMATIC IMAGINATION   71

novel, as we have seen, benefits from Cuttle's and Edith's care and empathic rehabilitation when she needed it.[41] The reception of such care affords Florence the endurance to maintain her own unflagging concern for her father's emotional (and later, physical) deficiencies. After a painful duration that lasts most of the novel, this eventually pays off for both Dombey and daughter. Florence so effectively rehabilitates her father's emotional incompetency and physical infirmity to the (almost miraculous) extent that by the novel's final pages, "he hoards her in his heart," "cannot bear to see a cloud upon her face," and "cannot bear to see him sit apart" from her (Dickens [1848] 2002, 947). Dickens specifically anchors this rehabilitation in Dombey's emerging ability to *feel*—that emotion he so conspicuously lacked in his physical interactions with others, as we saw reflected so early on in his introductory "handshake" with Cuttle. Note, for example, the narrator's quintupled emphasis on Dombey's new sense of physical and emotional feeling as he embraces his daughter for the first time in a brief paragraph 910 pages into the novel: "He *felt* her draw his arms about her neck; he *felt* her put her own round his; he *felt* her kisses on his face; he *felt* her wet cheek laid against his own; he *felt*—oh, how deeply!" (910; emphasis mine). Such a conversion to expansive feeling, though its swiftness has often been criticized as too pat, is consistent with disability theorists' commitment to a relational ethics of limitation and care. Davis (2013, 275), for example, calls for understanding of *all* humans as disabled, as "partial, incomplete subjects whose realization is not autonomy and independence but dependency and interdependence." Similarly, Talia Schaffer (2021, 6) has emphasized what is at stake in acknowledging the realities of interdependence and the value of depending on others and being depended on in what she terms "communities of care": the fluid "care dynamic is a complicated, flexible set of actions" where "the carer and cared-for roles slip around." "For if 'being human' is defined as 'that which needs help,'" Schaffer (2016, 167–68) writes, "then the disabled become the clearest type of humanness. They are not the exception; they are the exemplar."

Dombey's movement from "domineering coldness" to "deep affection"—from being humiliated by dependence (particularly dependence on women) to accepting it—helps him become fully human for the first time. His disabilities enable him to become a person who needs and appreciates care, and perhaps most crucially, one who can finally dispense it as well. This process is also one that other recent critics have identified as a situation uniquely fitted to plots featuring prominent disabilities. David Mitchell and Sharon Snyder (2000, 53)

---

41. Schaffer (2021, 15) identifies the ways in which Florence, "an iconic 'angel in the house' . . . in the heyday of the feminized ideal," benefits from the care of many characters, both male and female.

72   **CHAPTER 1**

argue that "the concept of narrative prosthesis evolves out of [the following] specific recognition: a narrative issues to resolve or correct . . . a deviance marked as abnormal or improper in a social context." Mitchell and Snyder further outline the schematic of the "prosthetic narrative structure" that could easily serve as a blueprint for *Dombey*:

> First, a deviance or marked difference is exposed to the reader; second, a narrative consolidates the need for its own existence by calling for an explanation of the deviation's origins and formative consequences; third, the deviance is brought from the periphery of concerns to the center stage of the story to come; and fourth, the remainder of the story seeks to rehabilitate or fix the deviance in some manner, shape, or form. This fourth move toward the repair of deviance may involve an obliteration of the difference through a cure, [or] the rescue of the despised object from social censure. (53–54)

The irony, of course, is that it is Dombey—the seemingly able-bodied character—and not Cuttle—the one with the prosthetic hand—who most requires care, rehabilitation, and rescue from social censure in the end. It is Dombey toward which the plot moves for a "repair of [emotional] deviance" and an "obliteration of difference through a cure." Meanwhile, far from requiring repair or cure of any kind, Cuttle proudly transcends the role of Solomon Gills's "right-hand man" at the Wooden Midshipman as he becomes a full and equal partner in the newly named business, "GILLS AND CUTTLE" on *Dombey*'s final pages (Dickens [1848] 2002, 943).

The multiple collisions between what constitutes a "right-hand man" and a "right-hand woman," what counts as ability and disability are, in this regard, part and parcel of how the novel imagines the importance of surrogate relationships. The narrator tells us at the relative outset that "Florence had tried so hard to be a substitute for the one small [Paul] Dombey, that her fortitude and perseverance might have almost won her a free right to bear the name herself" (187). Thus there is undeniably a sense of poetic justice linking Florence's ascension as her father's most genuine and capable "right-hand woman" and Miss Tox's prescient idea after little Paul's death "that Dombey and Son should be a Daughter after all!" (253). It is worth noting as well that Dickens may have had this in mind for Florence all along; he ends his first installment (chapter 4) with Walter Gay's prescient toast: "Here's to Dombey—and Son—and Daughter" (58).

There is also a paradoxically reversed but apposite reciprocity at work here in the novel's conclusion where Dombey's refocused filial pride and feeling actually makes *him* his daughter's "right-hand man." We learn that Dickens's most prideful character's "only pride is in his daughter and her husband. He

THE BEGINNINGS OF DICKENS'S IDIOMATIC IMAGINATION   73

has a silent, thoughtful, quiet manner, and is always with his daughter" (942–43). Andrew Miller (2008, 174) suggests that Florence's child allows her to become "a model for Dombey to follow": "she has learned what parental love is, and is now displaying for [her father] what he could never display for her." This would help explain how Dombey's new devotion extends to the proud, active relationship he takes in the lives of his grandchildren: he "talks" with them, "walks" with them, "attends" on them, and "watches" them "as if they were the object of his life" (Dickens [1848] 2002, 947). This kind of extended family cohesion, as those fortunate enough to have it know, is one of the finest examples of a practical and loving surrogacy where a grandparent may assume the status of a "right hand" to the parents.

Viewed from the perspective achieved at the novel's close, then, even the realigned title predicted by Miss Tox and Walter Gay, *Dombey and Daughter*, contains a kind of embodied, filial, and (properly) "right-handed" surrogacy without subordination that would have been unthinkable at the outset of the story when Florence is ignored precisely *because* of her gender. Its full realization by the conclusion registers the extent to which Dickens's idiomatic imagination pervades the ways in which this sprawling novel treats characterization, plot, theme, and meaning. The singular numerical use of the idiom "right-hand man" in *only* this novel—containing a prominent character with no right hand—reflects perhaps an early characterological and conceptual manifestation of Dickens's imaginative planning. This is not a novel that simply deploys the idiom on multiple occasions. Instead, it explores what it means and does not mean to be a "right-hand man" at the very time when the phrase was entering the era's popular lexicon. This exploration of the idiom throughout *Dombey* allows us to see in new ways how Dickens explores the interrelationships between substitution and service, pride and impairment, kindheartedness and competence.

The Idiomatic Beginning in *Dombey*'s Ending

It is crucial to emphasize my sense that the "right-hand man/woman" expression and all of its attendant collocations does not come prior to meaning, as a mere and fleeting idiomatic flourish in this first "planned" Dickens novel. I have argued that the idiom's extreme rarity—both inside and outside of Dickens's work—provides the provocation to look more closely at how the multiple associations that abide in the vernacular expression soak into the fabric of *Dombey*'s imaginative world in a process of idiom absorption. Raymond Williams (1970, 81, 82; emphasis original) identifies something of this process

74   **CHAPTER 1**

when he discusses how the "fictional world of the novelist is directed by an idea, or a complex of ideas . . . [that] are so deeply embodied that they are in effect . . . *dissolved* into a whole fictional world." Following his logic, we see tangible evidence of this kind of dissolved absorption even at the very "end" of Dickens's compositional process in *Dombey*. The cover design illustration (figure 8), which appeared on the first number in October 1846 and repeated through to the final installment in March 1848, allegorically portrays the "pride goeth before the fall" moral of the narrative.

Without explicitly giving the plot away, the original cover design illustration charts a line of prosperity and promise that runs upward (clockwise) from the left, through precariously balanced ledger books, to the top center where Mr. Dombey sits enthroned on an office chair mounted on an enormous cash box, and down through a tumbling house of cards on the right, finally resting on the slumped shoulders of a physically disabled Dombey who uses crutches to hold himself upright. As all novelists did in the process of moving from wrapper illustrations to the title pages in bound volume editions of their work, Dickens settled on a new cover page illustration when the novel was issued in book form by Bradbury and Evans in April 1848. And germane for my wider argument, he replaced it with a title page illustration (figure 9) that features Captain Cuttle pointing his hooked hand across a table at Rob the Grinder—a character who himself is a "right-hand man" to both Carker as a spy and to Cuttle when he takes over the Wooden Midshipman in the absence of Solomon Gills. The decision to have only Cuttle, of all the novel's major characters, on this title page vignette may also reveal the growing prominence that Dickens saw Cuttle fulfilling as the novel developed. The only problem is that the illustration reveals an obvious mistake: Cuttle's hook appears on his *left* hand.

There are several possible explanations for what has happened here. Most commentators, if they notice the issue at all, chalk it up to the complications related to the procedures of nineteenth-century book illustration, where artists created their work, hired engravers to etch the work onto copperplate quarto, which then appeared "reversed" from the original in the actual printed illustration. In this scenario, Phiz would have drawn the illustration "correctly" with the hook on Cuttle's right hand (as it always appears in the text and other illustrations), showed it to Dickens, only to have the engraver, Robert Young, etch it into the copperplate incorrectly (reversed). We know for a fact that this kind of mistake sometimes caused errors to make it all the way through the proof stage and, in other illustrations in *Dombey*, even to the final printing. Incongruent details that appear in figure 3 (Miss Skewton in her wheelchair) reveal as much.

Note that in the top right portion of the illustration, there is a sign with a pointing finger that reads (correctly): "TO THE PUMP ROOM." But in the top

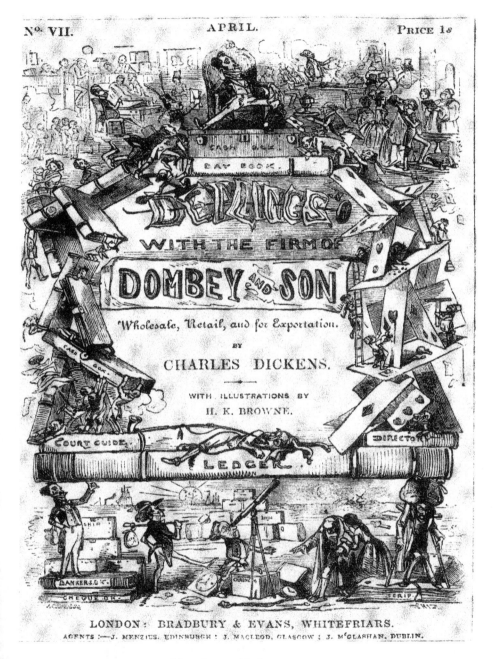

FIGURE 8. *Dombey and Son* serial number cover design

DEALINGS WITH THE FIRM OF DOMBEY AND SON,

Wholesale, Retail and for Exportation,

BY

Charles Dickens.

FIGURE 9. New title-page vignette for *Dombey and Son* book edition

THE BEGINNINGS OF DICKENS'S IDIOMATIC IMAGINATION 77

FIGURE 3. Major Bagstock is delighted to have that opportunity

middle of the illustration, the sign above the hotel reads (incorrectly, reversed): "LETOH." This means that multiple errors in orientation could occur even in a single illustration as the drawing went from the author's directive to the artist's rendition and finally to the engraver's etching. This is the conclusion reached in 1884 by David Croal Thomson in the *Life and Labours of Hablot Knight Browne, "Phiz"* (233–35), in 1899 by Frederic Kitton in *Dickens and His Illustrators* (90–101), in 1906 by Alex Philip in the "Blunders of Dickens and His Illustrators" (294–96), and in 1980 by Sarah Solberg in "Dickens and Illustration: A Matter of Perspective" (128–37). Even so, once we enter the world of nineteenth-century engraved illustration, we are entering a hall of mirrors

78   **CHAPTER 1**

where the multiple levels of intentional (in)distinguishability become infinitely precarious. It still remains a possibility—however far-fetched—that there was no mistake: that Dickens thought so much of Cuttle as a "right-hand man" that he, perhaps, wanted to show the utter transformation of Cuttle in that role by giving him a "real" right hand in the end. None of these scenarios necessarily proves anything about my argument—nor do I desire any of them to do so. Thankfully, we will never know for certain what Dickens was thinking. But the central placement of Cuttle on the title page should provoke us to ask new questions about how and why Dickens made—consciously or not—the decisions he did in his first novel that showed a new and increased level of planning. As I have maintained throughout this chapter, I think it is unlikely that mere coincidence could explain Dickens's first and only use of the "right-hand man" idiom in conjunction with the imaginative invention of a major character[42] who has no right hand; he is just too fastidiously punning an artist for this to be the case. Beyond this, though, I do not make the facile claim that Dickens consciously intended or consciously designed every thematic instantiation of the idiom that I have analyzed simply because critics agree on *Dombey*'s status as his first "planned" novel. What is more likely the (aleatory) case is that Dickens began the imaginative work of the novel with an interest in how substitution, surrogacy, and proxy operate in business and domestic contexts at just the time when an idiomatic phrase that "embodied" these concepts was emerging in the English vernacular. Thus, his rare but sustained literal and figurative employment of it throughout the novel may be seen as both creatively opportunistic and structurally dynamic regardless of any specifically conscious or unconscious design. In the end, language endlessly frustrates intention because, as David Bromwich (2019, 1) has recently argued, "no conceptual category, no enforceable distinction can seal off language from its effects . . . whatever an author might have meant, the consequences of language are not controlled by the author."[43]

---

42. I am aware that claiming Cuttle as a major character is a contested topic. Most recently, Clare Walker Gore (2021, 22; emphasis original) claims that "a crucial feature of Dickens's minor characters" is that "they are all to some extent marginalised within the novels they enliven by their failure as realist characters, more or less disabled in narrative terms by their embodiment. We know upon meeting a minor character in Dickens that they *are* minor because their [disabled] bodies betray them as such." This may be the case for other minor characters in Dickens, but it hardly applies to Cuttle. In the case of Cuttle, I am more inclined to think, like Alex Woloch (2003, 130) that a "Dickensian minor character can pull the narrative focus away from a more important character, reconfiguring the contours of the novel."

43. Garrett Stewart (2015, 31) puts it similarly well in describing his own questions about authorial meaning as a young adult reading poetry: "What if I didn't know what meaning held the poet in its slippery grip? Here I sensed . . . what I've made methodological since: that it doesn't matter, doesn't matter ultimately, what the writer had in mind, because the only mind in which those thoughts are now to be had, in which they happen, is the reader's own, guyed and guided by the filaments of a written syntax."

THE BEGINNINGS OF DICKENS'S IDIOMATIC IMAGINATION 79

One of the most illuminating recent literary biographers of Dickens, Rosemarie Bodenheimer (2007, 36), shrewdly claims that none of his fiction could be made "without a mysterious interplay between conscious and unconscious energies." I agree and think that the "mysterious interplay" involving Dickens's idiomatic energies in *Dombey* is far more interesting than any attempt to pin down exact areas or instances of linguistic intentionality. Perhaps the case that Harry Stone (1985, 191) discusses in relation to Dickens's readers—that "hindsight [and] wisdom . . . comes only after we have been made privy to the grand design of the novel"—turns out (and why would it not?) to be true of the author/artist himself.[44] Maybe only after the book's completion was Dickens himself convinced of the extent to which "the grand design of the novel" involved a kind of right-handed surrogacy that Cuttle paradoxically but compellingly embodies better than any other character. These are creative circumstances that gladly cannot be solved definitively, and this chapter about the *beginnings* of Dickens's idiomatic imagination is meant to be suggestive rather than prescriptive. I simply submit that *one* of the generative components of *Dombey and Son* involves the emerging idiomaticity of a newly circulating expression that caught Dickens's attention because of its unique and expansive thematic elasticity. Just how generative and consequential this particular idiom is in *Dombey* must be evaluated alongside the ways Dickens uses other individual body idioms in the processes through which he imagines several of his major post-Dombeyan novels. It is likely that the best measure of the "mysterious interplay between conscious and unconscious energies" at work in the process by which I am arguing Dickens "began" to idiomatically imagine and compose his most sophisticated novels starting with *Dombey* may only be seen in retrospect, as Harry Stone suggests. But to look back and assess the right-handed idiomaticity of *Dombey* is only to begin a discussion of Dickens's penchant for idiomatic inventiveness, not to end it. That is, we must start that retrospection by assessing how much Dickens relies on what I am calling his idiomatic imagination in generatively accretive ways with his other major novels, beginning with *Dombey* but continuing in the four subsequent years with *David Copperfield* (1849–50) and *Bleak House* (1852–53), which are the subjects of the next chapter.

---

44. Apropos of Dickens's sometimes obliviousness to seemingly obvious (conscious) intentions, we should recall how he was apparently "much startled" when Forster pointed out that the initials of his eponymous character in *David Copperfield* (1849–50) were "but his own reversed." "Why else," he mused about his semiautobiographical novel, "should I so obstinately have kept to that name once it turned up?" (Forster 1892, 2:84).

CHAPTER 2

"Shouldering the Wheel" in *Bleak House*

> As we stand and look back at . . . Dickens's developed
> fiction . . . there is at first an absence of ordinary
> connection and development. . . . But then as the
> action develops, unknown and unacknowledged
> relationships, profound and decisive connections,
> definite and committing recognitions and avowals are
> as it were forced into consciousness.
>
> —Raymond Williams, *The Country and the City* (1973)

Stuck in the Idiom of Circularity

The critical consensus regarding Dickens's longer-term planning that we saw in *Dombey and Son* (1846–48) intensifies in the novel T. S. Eliot (1927, 525) famously praised as "his finest piece of construction": *Bleak House* (1852–53). John Butt and Kathleen Tillotson (1957, 178–79) saw for the first time in *Bleak House* Dickens's ability to organize an immense "diversity of detail into a single view of society." J. Hillis Miller (1971, 15), in his prominent introduction to an early Penguin edition of *Bleak House*, noted the ways in which Dickens's planning may be seen in the novel's "complex fabric of recurrences"—where "scenes, themes and metaphors return in proliferating resemblances." Similarly but more recently, Kate Flint (2018, 230) has seen Dickens's heightened planning reflected in the recurring "resonances of the denotative language and the rich proliferation of metaphors" that cycle through the text and "reinforce some of its major tenets, such as the importance of responsibility."[1] These influential assessments are important for thinking about the refinement of Dickens's organizational processes as he composed what might very well be his most sophisticated novel. But they do not account for the multiple ways in which crucial developments in his idiomatic imagination inform how *Bleak*

---

1. For an alternate reading of responsibility, see Robbins 1990.

"SHOULDERING THE WHEEL" IN *BLEAK HOUSE*

House achieves some of its most salient and thematically cohesive effects. This chapter begins by arguing that in the process of constructing what is undoubtedly the most powerful beginning to any of his novels,[2] Dickens gradually hits on and then develops this sprawling text's most central imaginative body idiom in conjunction with of some its deepest themes.

Although it is difficult to pin down decisively, the graduality of this process during the composition of *Bleak House* is important. Dickens in all likelihood began the novel with little idea of how central a role the idiom would eventually come to play in his developing novel. But what is clear is that his earliest thinking about *Bleak House* began with an emphasis on circularity in general and on wheels in particular. My sense is that this emphasis on circularity and wheels at the novel's outset prompts in Dickens himself the very process that Raymond Williams (1973, 155) attributes to those who read him: "as the action develops, unknown and unacknowledged relationships, profound and decisive connections, definite and committing recognitions and avowals are as it were forced into consciousness." The only difference in my interpretation is that these relationships, connections, and recognitions are also forced into *the author's* consciousness by way of another never-used-before-or-again idiom: "shoulder to the wheel."

Of the several possibilities Dickens considered for prospective titles before settling on *Bleak House*, four include variations on "The Ruined *Mill* House" (Stone 1987, 185–285; my emphasis). This is important because wheels of all kinds spin and have great difficulty gaining traction throughout the text. As Steven Connor (2000, 4) has pointed out, the novel begins by "collating different modes of ineffectual motion, of goings-on that never get anywhere." Amid the fog of *Bleak House*'s famous opening paragraphs, pedestrians, ploughboys, and horse carts appear "slipping and sliding" through the "spongey fields" and soot-blackened streets, just as the tractionlessness of the High Court of Chancery spins endlessly in a "groping and floundering condition" in "mud and mire too deep"—a condition of endless futility that extends to the members of the bar who appear "tripping one another up on slippery precedents, groping knee-deep in technicalities" (Dickens [1852–53] 2003, 14).

This aspect of circular and "miry" futility, once established, pervades the novel in a torrent of literal and figurative associations (20). The name of the main Chancery case, Jarndyce and Jarndyce, is in itself of course tautologically circular, and we learn early on—via the words of Tom Jarndyce—how perilous it is to be caught up in Chancery's centripetal force: "it's being ground to bits in a slow mill" (71). Connor (2000, 4) remarks that "Jarndyce and Jarndyce does

---

2. See C. Tomalin (2011, 240), Bradbury (2003, xxxvii), and Altick (1980).

82   **CHAPTER 2**

not progress, but just continues starting and stopping," which creates a "strong sense that the suit is more of a mill or roundabout than a conveyance." As if to hint at the impossibility of gaining traction amid its circular pull, even the generally sunny carriage ride that Esther, Ada, and Richard take to John Jarndyce's cozy home in the country near Saint Albans has ominous stops and muddy slippages. The group has to get out of the carriage to "wal[k] up all the hills," and watching the wheels spin into the mud, Esther remarks on how they "cut up the gravel so terribly" that they "sent the road-drift flying about [their] heads like spray from a water-mill" (Dickens [1852–53] 2003, 81, 115, 82). This rhetoric of tractionlessness also envelops the streetsweeper, Jo, who confronts the "daily spin and whirl" in Tom-all-Alone's where he perpetually "fights it out, at his crossing, among the mud and wheels" (258, 259). I focus on these early sections of the novel because of what they may be able to reveal about how and when the "shoulder to the [stuck] wheel" idiom eventually emerges as one of the text's most dynamic imaginative catalysts.

With *Bleak House*'s sprawling canvas, Dickens no doubt wants not just to critique the failure of Britain's heaving and wildly ineffectual public institutions at mid-century, but he also wants to celebrate the importance of individual and collective "shoulder to the wheel" effort, earnest duty, and responsibility—the only kind that has any chance of gaining traction amid the muddy bureaucracy, selfishness, and chaos of mid-century London life. This celebration of successful, gritty effort in the face of inert bureaucratic failure is almost certainly a residual effect stemming from the triumph of the hardworking individual displayed in *David Copperfield* (1849–50), Dickens's semi-autobiographical novel that sits directly between *Dombey* and *Bleak House*. In this sense, *Bleak House* expresses an unmistakable indignance with the evils of the unfeeling state of England it describes, but it also focuses in equal measure on the lives of people who strive to improve themselves and those around them through sheer hard work, personal responsibility, and generous fellow feeling—the traits that eventually make David Copperfield successful and happy. Herein lies the tension at the heart of mid-Victorian debates about liberalism that Kate Flint, Hilary Schor, Lauren Goodlad, Jim Buzard, and others have identified.[3] It is no secret that Dickens is far better at diagnosing and critiquing social problems at the granular level than he is at providing larger workable solutions. *Bleak House* is no exception. Instead of systemic solutions to societal problems in *Bleak House*, we get a Copperfieldian triumph of those who offer active resistance and subscribe to the Victorian "Gospel of

---

3. See Flint (2018), Buzard (2005), Schor (2006), Goodlad (2003), Pykett (2000), Robbins (1990), and J. H. Miller (1971).

Work."[4] The most sanguine (and ultimately triumphant) characters in this bleak novel—Esther Summerson, John Jarndyce, Allan Woodcourt, Charley Neckett, the Rouncewells, and Phil Squod—all exhibit a "shoulder to the wheel" earnestness, industriousness, and sense of responsibility that separates them from both the public systems they run up against and the other characters who represent such countervailing indolent, uncaring, and avaricious values.

Dickens's configuration of hard work and responsibility in terms of a strenuous body idiom fits not only his general obsession with physical activity but also his distinctly embodied representations of David Copperfield's (read his own) path to economic self-sufficiency in the novel immediately preceding *Bleak House*. Realizing that he would have to make his own way to support himself and Dora after his aunt Betsey's financial ruin, David makes the decision "to work with a resolute and steady heart" at Dr. Strong's both before and after his regular occupation as a clerk with Spenlow and Jorkins: "up at five in the morning, and home at nine or ten at night" (Dickens [1849–50] 2004, 526, 532). Despite the fact that he works with nothing heavier than a pen in each of his occupations, David repeatedly describes his "perseverance at this time in [his] life" with the rhetoric of intense physical labor: "What I had to do," the young Copperfield remarks, "was to take my woodman's axe in my hand, and *clear my own way* through the forest of difficulty, by cutting down trees" (526; emphasis mine). If nothing else, it is worth recalling that Dickens had this model—his own model—of embodied self-sufficiency swirling in his head just before he embarked on *Bleak House* where he would eventually settle on another, more repetitively embodied articulation of self-sufficient labor. Thus, David's industriousness in forging an independent life for himself and Dora stands in stark contrast to the one he would invent just two years later for Richard Carstone, whose early and sustained reliance on a Chancery decision for himself and Ada is what leads to his demise.

We have seen in the introduction and in the previous chapter how Dickens tends to recycle hundreds of body idioms throughout his novels. In the case of *Bleak House*, this tendency swells to the point where he uses over one thousand body idioms (in a novel of similar length to *Dombey*). Partly because of this, *Bleak House* holds the overall number one position in its usage of unique body idioms (table A) in the 124-novel corpus. As with the *Dombey* chapter, though, my larger argument here rests on Dickens's unique use of only one

---

4. The best discussion of the conceptual roots of this phenomenon is still Houghton 1957, 242–51. See also Danahay (2011), Pettitt (2004), Hack (2005, esp. chap. 3), Purton (2000), and Bradshaw and Ozment (2000).

84   **CHAPTER 2**

particular idiom amidst all the others that rotate through the text. He invokes the idiomatic phrase "to put one's shoulder to the wheel" (or its variants) nineteen times in *Bleak House* and *only* in *Bleak House*—never in any of his novels before or after. This level of repetition inevitably raises even more complex questions of intentionality than we encountered in *Dombey*'s explicit usages of the "right-hand man" idiom. Surely at some point in the composition of *Bleak House* Dickens *must* have been aware of his repeated use of the shoulder idiom, but *when*? And what would that tell us (if such a precise determination were possible) about how the novel generates structure, characterization, and ultimately, meaning? The scale and rarity of the expression in Dickens's oeuvre suggest that somewhere in the process of using these nineteen invocations, the idiom was—pace Williams—forced into his own consciousness. At some point or points, Dickens realized that the "shoulder to the wheel" idiom worked as a wonderfully germane and imaginatively generative counterweight to the circular flounderings and slippages that literally and figuratively pervade so many of the novel's themes. My aim, however, is less to identify exactly where this occurs and more to explore how and why it matters for our interpretation of the text—and Dickens's construction of it—that it happens *at all*.

Context and Intertext

As with *Dombey*'s "right-hand man," it is important to start with a consideration of this new idiom's context both outside and inside *Bleak House*. There is no question that the "shoulder to the wheel" idiom was better known to people of all classes by the middle of the nineteenth century than was the case for "the right-hand man." This is likely because the former idiom originated from one of Aesop's fables as part of a popular oral tradition dating back to antiquity (around 600 B.C.). People were using it, saying it, understanding it in its literal and figurative contexts long before it ever appeared in print. Even with the arrival of printing, collections of Aesop's fables were among the earliest books to appear in a variety of languages, and English translations date to the sixteenth century. The opening lines of Aesop's (1926, 13) myth of "Hercules and the Wagoner" reveal the fable's apposite connections to the "slipping and sliding" of *Bleak House*'s opening chapters: "A waggoner [*sic*] was once driving a heavy load along a very muddy way. At last he came to a part of the road where the wheels sank halfway into the *mire*, and the more the horses pulled, the deeper sank the wheels" (145; emphasis mine). As the fable continues, the wagoner falls to his knees and prays to Hercules for help. The actual idiom is derived from Hercules's response, which reproaches the wagoner for relying on an interventionist deity rather than on his (the wagoner's) own efforts: "'Tut, man,'" says Hercules, "'don't sprawl there. Get up and put your shoulder to the wheel'" (145). The *Oxford English Dictionary* also quotes "the mire," a particular form of heightened muddiness that reappears throughout the opening of *Bleak House*, in its definition of the idiom: "To put (occasionally lay, set) one's shoulder to the wheel; (literally) so as to extricate the vehicle from *the mire*; hence the figurative to set to work vigorously" (emphasis mine).

Although the British public's general awareness of the Aesopian "shoulder to the wheel" was more widespread than what we saw with the previous chapter's "right-hand man," it was still rare to encounter it in print until well into the nineteenth century. Here again, we see the accuracy of Manfred Görlach's (1999, 13) findings that journalism, combined with the exponential rise of literacy after 1840, had immediate effects on the spread of vernacular expression in standard English. Similarly modeled searches through the *British Library Newspapers* (figure 10) and *British Periodicals* (figure 11) archives give an indication of when the "shoulder to the wheel" idiom became more prominent in contemporary printed usage.

Figure 10 shows that the idiom makes its first substantial spike in the years immediately preceding *Bleak House*; from 1849 to 1850, the expression jumps by 40 percent (38–95 appearances). The data from figure 11 show the idiom spiking in 1844 and then again in 1852—the year *Bleak House* began its serialization (March 1852). I will attempt to make no grand causal claims here beyond the fact that according to data pertaining to millions of words in hundreds of newspapers and journals, the "shoulder to the wheel" idiom was becoming increasingly popular around the middle of the nineteenth century. Sally Ledger (2011, 3) has connected Dickens's cultural positioning in Victorian England, for better or for worse, with "what some regarded as his vulgar embrace of the popular" precisely because of his association with everyday newspaper rhetoric. "An anonymous reviewer for the *Saturday Review* derided Dickens's determined engagement with contemporary social and political concerns, remarking that 'Mr Dickens's writings are the apotheosis of what has been called newspaper English'" (quoted in Ledger 2011, 3). Dickens *was* close to this kind of writing. Not only was he a one-time editor of the *Daily News*, his closest friend, confidant, and future biographer, John Forster, was an editor of *The Examiner*, which used the idiom on multiple occasions in the years just before Dickens began writing *Bleak House*. Forster's publication, for instance, reported on Sir Robert Peel's failure "to set his shoulder to the wheel" in the Carlew Bill (Hunt 1846, 257), landlords "with no great aptitude" for "putting the shoulder to the wheel" in Lord George Bentinck's Irish Railway Bill ("The Bentinck Bubble" 1847, 97), MP Daniel O'Connell's inability "to pu[t] his shoulder to the wheel" for Catholic

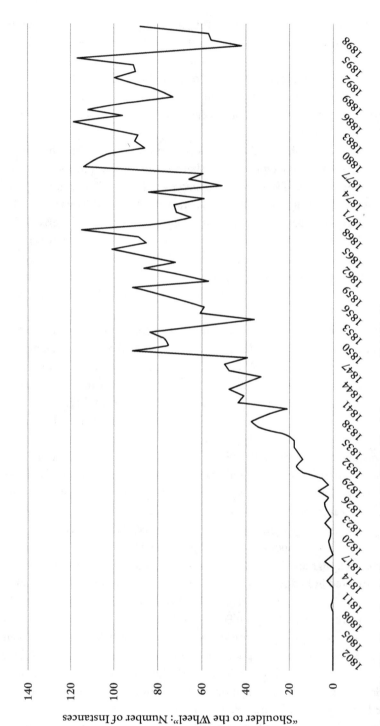

FIGURE 10. "Shoulder to the wheel" appearances in the *British Library Newspapers Digital Archive*

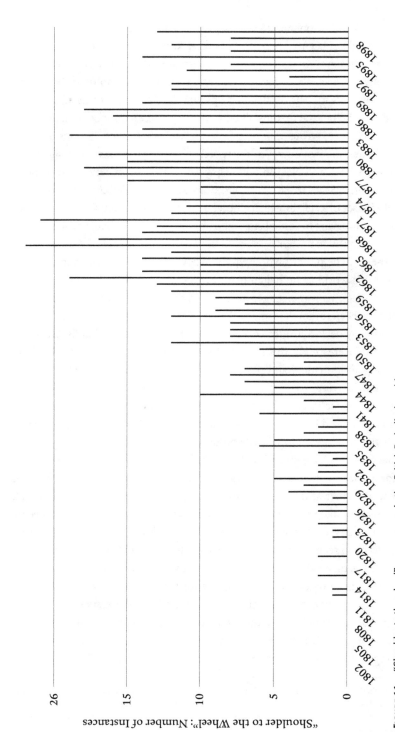

FIGURE 11. "Shoulder to the wheel" appearances in the *British Periodicals* archive

88 **CHAPTER 2**

emancipation ("O'Connell" 1847, 337), and Dr. Thomas Thomson's "shoulder to the wheel" effort to bring new medical knowledge to the Bengal Army (*"Western Himalaya"* 1852, 548). Beyond these instances, Dickens, in his role as editor of *Household Words*, himself oversaw contributors who used the expression prominently in their articles. Perhaps most interesting in terms of its timing just one day before the first installment of *Bleak House*'s miry opening, Richard Horne (1852, 538) wrote an article for *Household Words* titled "Strings of Proverbs" wherein the first entry (of thirty-six) is "'Goad your oxen, set your shoulder to the wheel, and Heaven will help you!'" Then, in an eerie echo of *Bleak House*, George Sala (1853a, 253) wrote an article for *Household Words* called "Legal Houses of Call" in which a hotel owner "manfully put[s] his shoulder to the wheel" in saving his establishment from the ruins of a Chancery suit.

There are still yet other reasons to believe that the moral of Aesop's fable, that "the gods help them who help themselves," occupied a prominent place in Dickens's world as he began planning *Bleak House* in November 1851. By this time, Dickens was an eager disciple and dutiful reader of the secular high priest of the Victorian "Gospel of Work," Thomas Carlyle (1919, 147), who had famously declared eight years earlier in *Past and Present* that "work alone is noble."[5] Interestingly, this nobility for Carlyle was also a matter of explicitly Aesopian individual and physical triumph: "Show me a People energetically busy; heaving, struggling, *all shoulders at the wheel*; their heart pulsing, every muscle swelling, with man's energy and will;—I show you a People of whom great good is already predictable; to whom all manner of good is certain, if their energy endure" (200; emphasis mine).

One other instance involving the idiom from Dickens's own life is noteworthy for its timing as well as its content. Dickens had long been scheduled to serve as the chair at the sixth annual dinner of the General Theatrical Fund, which was to take place on April 14, 1851. We know, too, that several events earlier in that year had stretched Dickens quite thin. His ailing wife, Catherine, had been recuperating at the spa at Malvern, and Dickens was spending much of his time with her there. But he was also deeply involved in the rehearsals of his amateur acting company for the first performance of *Not So Bad as We Seem*, which carried the enormous additional pressure of its scheduled performance before the queen. At the same time, he was in the middle of publishing *David Copperfield* in book form and helping Angela Burdett Coutts with the administration of her Home for Fallen Women. Then Dickens's father

---

5. Dickens dedicated *Hard Times* to Carlyle—the novel that immediately followed *David Copperfield* and *Bleak House*. The standard view of Dickens's "discipleship" comes largely from House (1941), Tillotson (1856), and Ford (1958). For more on the literary relationship between Carlyle and Dickens, see Goldberg 1972.

"SHOULDERING THE WHEEL" IN *BLEAK HOUSE*   89

died on March 31. Consequently, he and others went to great lengths to release him from his promise to chair the General Theatrical Fund dinner when it rolled around in April. But when no one else of similar stature could be found on such short notice, Dickens consented to preside at the event anyway (Fielding 1858, 118). What is interesting for the purposes of this chapter is how Dickens rhetorically channels his personal resolve in agreeing to honor his engagement into his *actual* speech. "If you help this Fund," Dickens declared in the keynote toast, "you will not be performing an act of charity, but you will be helping those who help themselves, and you will be coming to the aid of men who *put their own shoulders to the wheel of their sunken carriage*, and do not stand idly by while it sank deeper in the mire" (122; emphasis mine).

I do not cite these scenarios from Dickens's life because I seek to endorse a facile "smoking gun" sense of one-directional artistic causality in the composition of *Bleak House*. Instead, I wish to follow such critics as Lillian Nayder, John Bowen, Rosemarie Bodenheimer, Robert Douglas-Fairhurst, and John O. Jordan in considering Dickens's "life" as a series of texts to be interpreted themselves rather than a "real" that precedes, and so dictates, the grounds of his fiction.[6] For this reason, my central claim that Dickens's mature fictional imagination is idiomatically oriented does not mean that he approached the composition of each mature novel in the same way. The idiomatic orientation of a "right-hand man" in *Dombey* has similar but also different connections to what it means to "put a shoulder to the wheel" in *Bleak House*. Dickens grows into his own unconscious and conscious imaginative relationship with a given idiomatic expression as the novel itself develops—in a manner I suggest we see from the end of the previous chapter where Dickens chooses to put the hook-handed right-hand man, Captain Cuttle, on *Dombey*'s vignette title page in the Bradbury and Evans book edition.

Not only is it interesting that Dickens, despite the idiom's relative popularity and his multiple associations with it, uses the expression *only* in *Bleak House* in all of his fiction, but its extreme rarity among other contemporary novelists is also noteworthy. For example, in my corpus of 3,719 nineteenth-century novels, the idiom appears a single time in only 82 novels, appears on two occasions in only 7 novels, and it never occurs three or more times.[7] Although I

---

6. I am borrowing language here from John Jordan's "Response" to Deirdre David's review of Jordan's *Supposing Bleak House* (2010), which was published at www.review19.org on September 17, 2011.

7. This larger corpus is comprised of a combination of the following databases: Chadwyck-Healey's Nineteenth-Century Fiction, Project Gutenberg, the Internet Archive, and the Nebraska Literary Lab. Searching for usages of "shoulder to the wheel" and its cognates in a corpus of this size required new code to extract not only the phrases but also the number of instances in each of the 3,719 novels. See appendix C to the introduction.

90   CHAPTER 2

stand by my guiding methodological premise that numerical instantiation does not matter much for literary analysis without careful and rigorous textual interpretation, these data nonetheless give some indication of how anomalous it was for Dickens to employ variations of "shoulder to the wheel" idiom nineteen times even in a novel as lengthy as *Bleak House*.

Given *Bleak House*'s status as one of Dickens's most critically acclaimed works, it is surprising that critics have yet to detect any relationship between the multiple occurrences of "shoulder to the wheel" idiom and the novel's larger imaginative and thematic concerns. Simon Joyce (2002, 130) has fittingly described this novel's particular lure for Victorian literary scholars: "[*Bleak House*] is perhaps best seen as the Victorianists' white whale, the one text that we are all destined to take a shot at." Part of *my* shot at interpreting this novel involves an assessment of some major critics who have overlooked Aesop's "shoulder to the wheel" idiom in favor of other fable-based interpretations. For example, Butt and Tillotson (1957, 176–200) refer to *Bleak House* several times as a "fable" of contemporary London topicality.[8] Alice Benston (2002), and more recently, Robert Lougy (2018) have made compelling cases for the strains of *Oedipus Rex* that run through the novel. Barry Qualls (1992) has compared *Bleak House*'s characters' preoccupation with inheritance with Christian's quest in Bunyan's *Pilgrim's Progress*. George Ford (1958, 98), more than sixty years ago, came so close as to note "the *almost* Aesopian scheme of the novel," not in terms of the wagoner's tale, but where characters like Skimpole are likened to insects in a way that echoes Aesop's ant and the grasshopper fable. Indeed, these formidable critics and many others who have "taken a shot at" interpreting the forces (and intertextual sources) that possibly lie behind *Bleak House* have done so with a methodology more recently articulated by Patricia Yaeger in the editor's column of a *PMLA* issue dedicated to "Polyphony." Yaeger (2007, 436; emphasis mine) emphasizes the discovery of "new categories for thinking about mixed-up works of art and intermingled texts," encouraging critics to "investigate polyphonies that *are almost not there*: the creased, corner-hugging rubrics of *ghostly and unread citation.*"

Although I acknowledge the power and efficacy of tracing such fleeting intertextual components in any work of art, my interest in how the "shoulder to the wheel" idiom operates in *Bleak House* is most certainly not an interest in "almost not there . . . ghostly and unread citation[s]." Quite the contrary, in fact. I contend that it is voiced almost everywhere in the text—in a Bakhtinian polyphonic manner—and yet generations of critics have read right over it or past it.

---

8. Butt and Tillotson refer to the novel as a "fable" on multiple occasions in their chapter (7) titled "The Topicality of *Bleak House*" but never connect it to Aesop's fable of the wagoner.

But this may not be so surprising if we think, as Garrett Stewart (1974, 21) has, that "as verbal adventure [Dickens's] style has left its context behind." Assuming a twentieth- or twenty-first-century orientation, we are all relatively far away from the time when wagon or carriage wheels needed actual shouldering. Additionally, without computational search methods, one would be hard-pressed to notice Dickens's isolated use of this particular idiom, among the thousands of others, only in *Bleak House* of all his works. Even using traditional methods— that is, reading analogically—as we saw in *Dombey*, we are likely to miss important dimensions Dickens's idiomatic imagination precisely because of how seemingly organic its suffusion is within a given novel's thematic architecture. This process, which I have termed *idiom absorption*, soaks into the novel's imaginative atmosphere so fully that it paradoxically becomes a condition of its own invisibility. As proof of concept, I want to note an example par excellence of how the idiom has become unwittingly absorbed, beyond the text, into a scholar of the highest caliber's critical vocabulary. Terry Eagleton (2003, ix), a critic who by my lights does not miss very much, writes in his preface to *Bleak House* that this is a novel about survival and persistence. Fair enough. He then notes that one of *Bleak House*'s main focal points rests on "prematurely aged children who have been forced *to shoulder the responsibility* that their elders have selfishly disowned" (x; emphasis mine). Such wording represents a process of rhetorical mimesis wherein the critic's language partakes of the larger themes of the text that the Geneva school adherent Georges Poulet (1969, 61) called "transposition." "On the level of indistinct thought, of sensations, emotions, images, and obsessions of preconscious life, it is possible for the critic to repeat, within himself, that life of which the work affords a first version, inexhaustibly revealing and suggestive," writes Poulet. As we shall see, Eagleton is not the only critic whose rhetoric absorbs and transposes *Bleak House*'s guiding idiom.

Eagleton also writes in his preface to *Bleak House* that "artists can reveal forces and processes invisible to the naked eye" and that these forces can have "an autonomous existence beyond the control of any one individual" (x). The forces and processes behind this element of creativity may be ironically invisible even to the artist him- or herself, as Dickens marveled about his unconscious "seeing" in a letter to Forster while composing *Barnaby Rudge* (1841). "When I sit down to my book," Dickens writes, "some beneficent power shows it all to me, & tempts me to be interested, & I don't invent it—I really do not— *but see it*, and write it down" (House et al. 1965–2002, ii, 411; emphasis original). He responded similarly to a question from George Henry Lewes, who had inquired about how Dickens thought up an episode in *Oliver Twist* (1837–39): "how it *came*, I can't tell. It came, like all my other ideas . . . readymade to the point of the pen—and down it went" (House et al. 1965–2002, ii, 403; emphasis

92   CHAPTER 2

original). In terms of Dickens's obliviousness to seemingly obvious (conscious) intentions, we should also again recall how he was apparently "much startled" when Forster pointed out that the initials of his eponymous character in *David Copperfield* (were "but his own reversed." "Why else," Dickens mused about his semiautobiographical novel, "should I so obstinately have kept to that name once it turned up"? (v, 518). I do not entirely mistrust Dickens's depiction of his unconscious creative process—especially in his early fiction—but I would like my analysis of the "shoulder to the wheel" idiom in *Bleak House* to demonstrate that there is something of a chiastic *both/and* rather than *either/or* dimension to his more mature, "planned" fiction. Dickens could have *both* had the idea of "shoulder to the wheel idiom" on his mind (from its appearances in journalism he was close to, Aesop, Carlyle, his Theatrical Fund speech) *and* not yet been conscious of how well it would fit the overarching atmosphere of *Bleak House*'s mud and mire until the novel was under way.

A Class-Defining Idiom

Goodlad and Flint have noted how *Bleak House*'s strong emphasis on what I contend is a "shoulder to the wheel" need for personal responsibility locates a tension that lies at the heart of mid-Victorian debates about liberalism. On the one hand, Dickens implicitly suggests the necessity for the state to act in ways that will improve the lives of individuals—especially those living in the noxious conditions of such appalling slums as Tom-all-Alone's. On the other hand, there is a conspicuous demand for personal responsibility of a kind that is aligned, in Flint's (2018, 224) relevant articulation, with useful social activity and caregiving that begins at home. As in so many of his novels, Dickens does not so much as present an answer to these ideological conflicts as he points the way to a multiplicity of behaviors and actions that make living in a world with such conflicts more bearable. What makes such imperfect Dickensian worlds bearable, though, is often a matter of bearing down. Nicola Bradbury (2003, xxi), following Eagleton's preface, maintains in her Penguin introduction that "the real issue in [*Bleak House*] emerges as survival, the value of going on." And as we shall see, those who "keep their shoulders to the wheel" (in every sense of the idiom) not only survive but also flourish in the world of *Bleak House*. This, after all, is Carlyle's (1919, 200) prediction from *Past and Present*: for "People energetically busy; heaving, struggling, all shoulders to the wheel . . . great good is already predictable . . . if their energy endure."

Despite the fact that Dickens's plans for *Bleak House* reveal a "precise imaginative command," critics correctly assert that such precision is sometimes hidden or misleading at the outset (Bradbury 2003, xix, xxiii). This is how the first explicit instantiation of *Bleak House*'s controlling idiom appears—as kind of non sequitur that will make more sense later. As we have seen, the "miry" environment that opens the novel is replete with a sense of circularity and immobility that restricts movement of all kinds: pedestrian, carriage, legal, and so forth. In the second number (chapter 6), however, Dickens sets up a scene where the entrenched aristocratic immobilization of the Dedlock family is briefly compared to their housekeeper Mrs. Rouncewell's son's desire to alter his life's circumstances—to move beyond the inertia and fixity built into the aristocratic social order. The narrator reports that "her second son would have been provided for at Chesney Wold, and would have made steward in due season; but he took, when he was a schoolboy, to constructing steam engines with saucepans, and setting birds to draw their own water . . . so assisting them with artful contrivance of hydraulic pressure, that a thirsty canary had only, in a literal sense, *to put his shoulder to the wheel*, and the job was done" (106–7; emphasis mine). The handwritten manuscript from the Victoria & Albert Museum reveals that Dickens was quite certain in his decision to use the idiom at this point in the text; there are no cross-outs or other insertions in or around the phrase here. I raise this point not to suggest that Dickens was entirely conscious of his reliance on the idiom from this relatively early stage in the novel on. He still may not have registered how well the idiom fit with the novel's famously slippery and mud-laden opening, despite the fact that he had used it in a speech at the General Theatrical Fund only months before composing those sections of the novel. All the state of the original manuscript in this section tells us with certainty is that Dickens used the "shoulder to the wheel" idiom without hesitation at this relatively early point in *Bleak House*'s composition. The fact that he does so here will help later on in the assessment of some critical junctures where the idiom appears in altered states in the manuscript.

Nonetheless, this first explicit instantiation of the idiom in *Bleak House* is unmistakably Aesopian in its association with hard work and dependence on the self—even if it is the canary's shoulder that is put to the wheel. It still captures the early inklings of the young Rouncewell's individual determination to free himself from a life of aristocratic servitude. His "very persevering" efforts as he grows older lead to "constructing a model of a power-loom" and eventually to forging his own life in "the iron country father north" (Dickens [1852–53] 2003, 107). Interestingly, Sir Leicester's assessment of this perseverance reduces Rouncewell's individual determination to nothing more than a set of inborn "tendencies" (107). But we learn in later chapters of the hard individual work involved in making the "the Ironmaster's" career successful. For example, when Mr. Rouncewell returns to Chesney Wold to inform the

94   **CHAPTER 2**

Dedlocks of his own son's desire to marry Mrs. Rouncewell's maid, Rosa, he is unequivocal about the individual effort he has exerted to reach his position of professional distinction.

This is where the idiom begins to make sense (Williams's [1975, 155] "profound and decisive connections") in its transference from the young boy's construction of his mechanical canary to his professional ambitions. "I made my way," says Rouncewell, "I have been an apprentice, and a workman. I have lived on workman's wages, years and years, and beyond a certain point have had to educate myself" (Dickens [1852–53] 2003, 452–53). What is more, Rouncewell's "shoulder to the wheel" determination—evident in his boyhood experiments with hydraulic engineering and then later in his professional life—appears in great relief compared to Dedlock's self-centered wallowing in his own aristocratic inertia. The narrator sarcastically reports just pages after the description of the persevering, "shoulder to the wheel" young Rouncewell that the Dedlock "family greatness" consists "in their never having done anything to distinguish themselves, for seven hundred years" (110). The sarcasm only deepens when we learn that Sir Leicester is "rarely bored" because "when he has nothing else to do, he can always contemplate his own greatness" and "generally revie[w] his importance to society" (183).

The extended idiomatic contrast between the rising middle classes who "put their shoulders to the wheel" and the aristocrats who (proudly) do not culminates in chapter 28, titled "The Ironmaster." Here, the idiomatic and the ideological appear—according to Sir Leicester's formulation, "diametrically opposed"—in body as well as belief (455). Reminiscent of the novel's mud-laden opening paragraphs, "the waters are out again on the low-lying grounds" of Chesney Wold, but it does not matter because Sir Leicester could not gain a "foothold" even if he tried, immobilized as he is by "the family gout" (446, 445). The chapter's first sentence informs us that he is "in a literal no less than figurative point of view, upon his legs" (445). Mr. Rouncewell, in comparison, enters as a "responsible-looking gentleman . . . of a good figure . . . strong and active" (451). This bodily contrast between Sir Leicester's immobility and Mr. Rouncewell's exertive mobility neatly reflects the growing frustration Dedlock harbors toward the alteration of rigid social frameworks in existence from "time out of mind" (17). Learning that his housekeeper's son has been invited to become an MP (because of the success of his individual efforts) sends Sir Leicester into an anxious meditation on the economic change and social movement where such a previously unthinkable scenario could occur: "From the village school of Chesney Wold, intact as it is this minute, to the whole framework of society, to the aforesaid framework receiving tremendous cracks in consequence of people (ironmasters, lead-mistresses, and what not) not minding their catechism, and getting out of the station unto which they are called . . . the first station in which they happen to find themselves; and from that, to their educating other people out of *their* stations, and so obliterating the landmarks, and opening the floodgates, and all the rest of it" (455; emphasis original). The contrast between aristocratic inertia and middle-class mobility also extends to the treatment of time in this important chapter. Although the two men are "diametrically opposed" in "*all* [their] views," Sir Leicester invites (and even expects) Rouncewell to stay the night at Chesney Wold "where the sun-dial on the terrace has dumbly recorded [time] for centuries" (455, 451; emphasis original). Rouncewell declines the offer on account of professional (temporal) necessity: "I am much obliged to you, but I have to travel all night, in order to reach a distant part of the country, punctually at an appointed hour in the morning" (456). The diametric opposition manifested by Mr. Rouncewell's visit in this chapter makes Sir Leicester "actually sti[r] with indignation" as the baronet contemplates "his repose and that of Chesney Wold to the restless flights of ironmasters" (452, 451). The young Rouncewell's is not a capricious or "restless flight," though. He has exhibited this desire (and its required work ethic) to transcend his lower-class upbringing from his earliest days putting the canary's shoulder to the wheel in his hydraulic experimentation.

Relatively early in the novel, Dickens also establishes a series of more equitable comparisons (i.e., not servants turned ironmasters) between those who industriously "put their shoulder to the wheel" and those who do not by focusing principally on the "vocationlessness," as Goodlad (2003, 527) euphemistically terms it, of Richard Carstone. One of the wards in Jarndyce and Jarndyce, Richard starts life in a distinctly different class position from Mr. Rouncewell, but because of the perpetually stalled nature of the case, it is clear (at least to those around him) that, in the words of his guardian, John Jarndyce, he "must have a profession; he must make some choice for himself" (Dickens [1852–53] 2003, 121). Unlike the case with the young ironmaster, Richard never settles on a profession *for himself* despite the fact that Jarndyce calls in a series of favors to help him get started in at least three prospective vocations.[9] The first of these, a nautical profession aided by Sir Leicester, is

---

9. There are interesting connections between Richard Carstone's predilections toward idleness and Dickens's feelings about his son, Charley. In the winter of 1851–52, for instance, Dickens was dissatisfied with his son's haphazard progress at Eton and eventually decided to remove him from the school and, despite the fact that Charley was only sixteen, asked him to decide on a career. In a letter to Miss Burdett Coutts, Dickens speaks of Charley in ways that seem eerily familiar to his depiction of Richard Carstone: "His inclinations are all good; but I think he has less fixed purpose and energy than I could have supposed possible in my son. He is not aspiring, or imaginative on his own behalf. With all the tenderer and better qualities which he inherits from his mother, he inherits an indescribable lassitude of character—a very serious thing in a man" (House et al. 1965–2002, vii, 244–46).

96   CHAPTER 2

meant to align with Richard's childhood inclination for the sea. Perhaps more importantly for Richard's eventual fate, he exhibits an early aversion for the kind of earnest work and industry required to advance in any profession, whether he possesses Sir Leicester's sense of inborn tendencies or not. Richard's description of "harum-scarum" days "grinding away at those [nautical] books and instruments" reveals his disappointment that he does not enter the profession by starting out as a commander of a ship at sea (138). The insouciant tone of Richard's discussion with Esther regarding this professional foray could not be further from what we know of Rouncewell's earnest willingness to "make [his] way" by first working as an apprentice "for years and years" in pursuit of professional advancement: "'So I apprehend it's pretty clear . . . that I shall have to work my own way. Never mind! Plenty of people have had to do that before now, and have done it. I only wish I had the command of a clipping privateer, to begin with, and could carry off the Chancellor and keep him on short allowance until he gave judgment in our cause'" (138). Esther presciently gleans from Richard's quixotic wish to enter his nautical work as the captain of a swift armed vessel that he "had a carelessness in his character" which is perilous because of the way he mistakes "buoyancy and hopefulness and gaiety . . . for prudence" (138). We see her concern extended shortly hereafter when Richard and Ada announce their love for each other. Although she is clearly happy for them, Esther's immediate reaction is to advise the couple that their "early love could [only] come to anything" if they maintained "a steady resolution" to "duty . . . constancy . . . fortitude, and perseverance" (211).

John Jarndyce also notices the carelessness in Richard's character early on, but as Richard's elder (male) ward and distant kinsman, he is in a more favorable position than Esther to voice such concerns. Initially, Jarndyce expresses his reservations as a practical matter that could apply to any young couple declaring their love for the first time: "you don't know your own minds yet; that a thousand things may happen to divert you from one another" (212). But then he specifically focuses his admonition on Richard and particularly on the exigency of the young man's comprehension of the crucial relationship between dedication ("constancy") in romance and in other (professional) aspects of life. Jarndyce's advice, connecting as it does individual effort and Aesop's wagoner, appears in this instance as a not-so-subtle directive for Richard to "put his shoulder to the wheel" on the final page of the fourth monthly installment of *Bleak House*:

> Trust in nothing but Providence and your own efforts. Never separate the two, like the heathen wagoner. Constancy in love is a good thing; but it means nothing, and is nothing, without constancy in every other kind of

effort. If you had the abilities of all the great men, past and present, you could do nothing well, without sincerely meaning it, and setting about it. If you entertain the supposition that any real success, in great things or in small, ever was or could be, ever will or can be, wrested from Fortune by fits and starts, leave that wrong idea here, or leave your cousin Ada here. (213)

So although Richard is still very early in his pursuit of his first professional path, this solemn advice simultaneously predicts the "fits and starts" that will imperil Richard's life and idiomatically invokes its corrective of keeping his "shoulder to the wheel." Even though Richard is quick to promise his guardian that he "will work [his] way on," he fails to comprehend the importance of the Aesopian edict to take personal responsibility and to rely on his own efforts rather than on divine intervention—which, in this novel, is tantamount to "being provided for" through a seemingly miraculous judgment in Chancery's Jarndyce suit.[10] It is Richard's conspicuous inability to keep his shoulder to the wheel, his *inconstancy in every kind of effort, that ultimately leads to his failing health and premature death.

Indeed, it is because Jarndyce's advice, here, so appositely and presciently pinpoints Richard's flaw in contrast to the earnest efforts of the thriving young Rouncewell that we may see Dickens relatively early in the text consciously alighting on what will become the novel's most generative idiom. His handwriting from this section of the original manuscript may be helpful in determining the level of his conscious intention. Dickens's writes out clearly and without corrections Jarndyce's injunction to "Trust in nothing but Providence and your own efforts. Never separate the two." But then there are several undecipherable cross-outs before he extends the sentence after a comma to include "like the heathen waggoner." Although we will never know definitively what was going through Dickens's mind as he added this additional clause after crossing out several other possibilities, it seems reasonable to surmise that he began to register how well the "shoulder to the wheel" idiom fit the crucial (and ultimately fatal) flaw in Richard's character. Moreover, it should not be underestimated (or, better put, left unconsidered) that Dickens chose to end a relatively early monthly serial number with this scene. Throughout his career, and especially after he began maintaining number plans for his novels, Dickens often ended serial numbers with punctuated developments that he meant to leave his readers thinking about for the month until the next number arrived. As Anna Gibson and Adam Grener (2022a) have most recently articulated in

---

10. See Keatley (2017) for a recent analysis linking the Jarndyce will to religious will.

98   **CHAPTER 2**

their *Digital Dickens Notes Project*, it is "difficult for [contemporary readers] to imagine how seriality shaped Dickens's creative practice, as he conceived, composed, and published his novels in these installments." Just as Gibson and Grener (2022b, emphasis original) have set as the goal for their project a better understanding of "the iterative development of a serial novel's form over time" by "foregrounding *process* in reading and analyzing Dickens's novels," I am interested in the process by which certain idiomatic expressions enter Dickens's imagination over the course of a novel's composition.

With this in mind, it is worth noting that Richard Carstone's inability to persevere in the novel's early numbers is rendered in a manner that we have seen previously spur Dickens's idiomatic imagination. That is, the concept develops thematically—at least at the start of *Bleak House*—as both a confirmation *and* a violation of the idiom: the young Rouncewell's drive to put his shoulder to the wheel in his profession appears in contradistinction to Richard's unwillingness or inability to do the same. This is similar to what we witnessed in Captain Cuttle's ability to be a right-hand man amid Carker's spectacular failure to live up to his own explicit idiomatic label in *Dombey*.

Bleak House's Idiomatic Humor

Dickens's violation of the "shoulder to the wheel" idiom as a guiding principle in *Bleak House* is not all doom and despondency, though. After all, we are dealing with an author whose stock in trade is humor of nearly every stripe. Dickensian humor has been the subject of admiring critics from U. C. Knoepflmacher to James Kincaid, John Cary to Deborah Vlock, Malcom Andrews to Claire Tomalin.[11] Even George Henry Lewes (1872b, 146), a contemporary critic long skeptical of Dickens's craft, had to acknowledge that his "popular" success was directly connected to a sense of "overflowing fun" where "laughter is irresistible." This is surely the case in Dickens's portrayal of the elder Turveydrop in *Bleak House*, to whom the narrator introduces us in the chapter immediately following the one in which Jarndyce implicitly urges Richard to keep his shoulder to the wheel through his explicit invocation of "the heathen wagoner" (the first chapter of serial number five). Here, we quickly learn that a significant part of what makes the comical Turveydrop "a model of Deportment" is his absurdly affected physical demeanor (Dickens [1852–53] 2003, 225). This is how Caddy Jellyby, now engaged to the son, Prince Turveydrop,

---

11. See Knoepflmacher (1971), Kincaid (1971), Carey (1973), Vlock (1998), Andrews (2006, 2013), and C. Tomalin (2011).

introduces Esther to her future father-in-law "in the full lustre of his Deportment": "He was a fat old gentleman with a false complexion, false teeth, false whiskers, and a wig. . . . He had, under his arm, a hat of great size and weight, shelving downward from the crown to the brim; and in his hand a pair of white gloves, with which he flapped it, as he stood poised on one leg, in *a highshouldered* round-elbowed state of elegance not to be surpassed. . . . He was like nothing in the world but a model of Deportment" (225; emphasis mine). Caddy matter-of-factly recounts how the "high shouldered" Mr. Turveydrop does "nothing whatever, but stand before the fire, a model of Deportment" at the Dancing Academy while the younger (Prince) Turveydrop "work[s] for his father twelve hours a-day" (226–27). Furthermore, we learn, as Esther does, of Mr. Turveydrop's long and tragicomical history of foisting the labor of the dancing school off on others: "He had married a meek little dancing-mistress . . . and had worked her to death, or had, at best, suffered her to work herself to death, to maintain him in those expenses which were indispensable to his position" (226). His blind and appallingly blatant hypocrisy culminates in his edict to his son to "work, be industrious, earn money" (379). The kind of blunt, unmitigated hypocrisy we see in Mr. Turveydrop creates a comic dimension that in Kincaid's (1971, 1) words, can "cement our involvement in the novel's themes and events."

One of the ways that the novel cements our involvement in its themes is by the comically (but physically) failed application of the "shoulder to the wheel" idiom in Mr. Turveydrop. We have seen in *Dombey* how Dickens began to exploit the malleability of idiomatic expressions by analogically stretching and reversing their accepted meanings (physiologically with Cuttle, figuratively with Carker, femininely with Edith and Florence) in ways that opened new paths for thematic innovation. Perhaps because of an increased level of consciousness, he becomes even better at manipulating this dimension of the failed idiom application in *Bleak House*—both in the nuance of the idiomatic failures and in the multiplicity of characters enlisted to perform the idiom's reversals and violations. Dickens's characterization of the elder Turveydrop is exemplary in this regard. With him, we have a character who has a long and perilously distinguished history of putting no shoulder to *any* kind of professional wheel whatsoever, and yet the single most defining feature of his ridiculous "Deportment" is his "high-shouldered bow" (Dickens [1852–53] 2003, 228)! In the two pages immediately following the story of Mr. Turveydrop's appalling professional negligence, for instance, Esther describes how he uses his "high shoulders" five times in tandem with what he says: "'To polish—polish—polish!' he repeated . . . with the high-shouldered bow"; "'Where what is left among us of Deportment,' he added . . . with the high-shouldered bow"; "'You are very

100   **CHAPTER 2**

good,' he smiled, with the high-shouldered bow again"; "he took another pinch of snuff and made the [high-shouldered] bow again"; "'Yes, my dear . . .' said Mr Turveydrop . . . lifting up his shoulders" (228–29).[12]

Malcolm Andrews (2013, 149) has commented recently that "when Dickens sniffed comic prey his nose wrinkled up and his eyes glittered with anticipation." This sense of comic anticipation is, I think, what occurs in the closing moments of Mr. Turveydrop's first introduction to the reader. As if the presentation of a "high-shouldered" character who shirks individual responsibility in the chapter directly following Jarndyce's Aesopian admonishment were not enough satiric humor for one section, Dickens presents us with one more shoulder-oriented pun to round out our comic introduction to the master of deportment. In the midst of all of his high-shouldered bowing, Mr. Turveydrop not so subtly reminds his son that he (Prince) barely has time to eat during his twelve-hour days working for the Dancing Academy:

> "My son," said he, "it's two o'clock. Recollect your school at Kensington at three."
>
> "That's time enough for me, father," said Prince. "I can take a morsel of dinner, standing, and be off."
>
> "My dear boy," returned his father, "you must be very quick. You will find *the cold mutton* on the table."
>
> "Thank you, father. Are *you* off now, father?"
>
> "Yes, my dear. I suppose," said Mr Turveydrop, shutting his eyes and *lifting up his shoulders*, with modest consciousness, "that I must show myself, as usual, about town." (229; emphasis mine)

This seemingly quotidian interaction between father and son during a normal "work" day (at least for the younger Turveydrop) contains something quite extraordinary: a "high-shouldered" father who refuses to put his own shoulder to the wheel gives his hardworking son "the cold shoulder"—both literally and figuratively. The multiplicity of the punning here is as dizzying as it is brilliant. But it has almost certainly been lost on contemporary readers because most people today assume "the cold shoulder" idiom derives its meaning from the act of physically turning one's shoulder away from another in an act of social repudiation. In fact, though, it emerged from a second-rate culinary option like the one Turveydrop offers to his son in between his work as a dancing master. The *Oxford English Dictionary* lists serving a leftover "cold shoulder of mutton" (as opposed to the warm dish first served to the original diners)

---

12. For an extremely original interpretation of the thematic potential embedded in suspended quotations, see Lambert 1981.

as the origin for "the cold shoulder" idiom which expresses "intentional and marked coldness, or studied indifference" toward another. This interpolation of the two shoulder idioms here confirms Jenny Hartley's (2016, 42–43) recent observation that "Dickens never does just one thing" with his comic "suggestiveness from heaviest to lightest." And perhaps only Dickens could incorporate such elaborately and grotesquely punning humor by fathoming a father whose "absorbing selfishness" makes him utterly indifferent to working his own family to death (first wife) and physical incapacitation (Prince) (Dickens [1952–53] 2003, 227). Because these descriptions appear at the start of *Bleak House*'s fifth installment, just after John Jarndyce sternly exhorts Richard Carstone to learn from the heathen wagoner's misguided reliance on others, it is probably not wrong to surmise that Dickens was aware—at *some* level—of the "shoulder to the wheel" idiom's capacity for sustained, humorous, and generative thematic potentiality—where it becomes both an object of parody and preoccupation. But exactly what that level might be remains to be seen as it continues to surface throughout the novel.

Idiomatic Seriousness

The only other character who can match Mr. Turveydrop for deleteriously *not* working, for *not* putting a shoulder to the wheel, is Harold Skimpole—the father of three who nonetheless remains, as he himself repeatedly says, "a perfect child" for the entire novel (87). The difference between these two iconic shirkers of work and responsibility lies in Dickens's presentation of their idleness. Where Turveydrop quite literally poses and performs idleness in his physical and sartorial demeanor, Skimpole unabashedly theorizes (and, in his own mind, justifies) his indolence. One of the earliest and most salient examples of his theorizing occurs (ventriloquized through the narrator) during a breakfast discussion following the scene in which Esther, Ada, and Richard pool their money together to release Skimpole from the debt collector, Coavinses (Neckett).

> He had no objection to honey . . . but he protested against the overweening assumptions of Bees. He didn't see at all why the busy Bee should be proposed as a model to him; he supposed the Bee liked to make honey, or he wouldn't do it—nobody asked him. It was not necessary for the Bee to make such a merit of his tastes. . . . He must say he thought the Drone the embodiment of a pleasanter and wiser idea [than professional work]. The Drone said, unaffectedly, "You will excuse me; I really cannot attend the shop! I find myself in a world in which there is so much

102   CHAPTER 2

to see, and such a short time to see it in, that I must take the liberty of looking about me, and begging to be provided for by somebody who doesn't want to look about him." This appeared to Mr Skimpole to be the Drone philosophy, and he thought it a very good philosophy. (116)

Of course it is Skimpole's putting of this philosophy into everyday action that indirectly leads to the orphaning of Neckett's three young children. While the group travels to Bell Yard to check in on Neckett's newly orphaned young children, Jarndyce asks a question that could be considered a governing trope of the novel's preoccupation with the Aesopian idiom: "'Was he [Neckett]—I don't know how to shape the question . . . *industrious?*'" asks Jarndyce (243; emphasis mine). And the neighborhood boy's response places Neckett unequivocally among those in the novel who put their shoulders to their professional wheels: "'Yes, wery much so. He was never tired of watching. He'd set upon a post at a street corner, eight or ten hours at a stretch, if he undertook to do it'" (243). This industriousness exacts such a dire physical toll on Neckett (as it does to a slightly lesser degree on the eventually disabled Prince Turveydrop) that, in Esther's hindsight, is apparent on the night Coavinses tracks down Skimpole for debt payment: "I had already recalled, with anything but a serious association, the image of a man sitting on the sofa that night, wiping his head" in physical exhaustion (242).

Unlike the scenario at the Turveydrop Dancing Academy where fatherly idleness forces the son's work, in Bell Yard, fatherly earnestness begets daughterly industriousness. Here, we witness the elder Neckett child, Charley, subduing the sorrow of losing mother and father "by the necessity of taking courage, and by her childish importance in being able to work, and by her bustling, busy way" as she goes about her washing (247). The stark necessity of having to muster this kind of courage and industriousness at such a young age is as terrifically appalling as it is extraordinary, and the situation is captured best in Jarndyce's reaction to the dawning realization of what has come to pass as a result of Neckett's death: "'Is it possible,' whispered my Guardian, as we put a chair for the little creature, and got her to sit down with her load: the boy keeping close to her, holding her apron, 'that this child works for the rest? Look at this! For God's sake look at this!'" (245). Esther's reaction indexes a similar awe: "It was a thing to look at. The three children close together, and two of them relying solely on the third, and the third so young and yet with an air of age and steadiness that sat so strangely on the childish figure" (246).

Dickens's emphasis on Charley's practical responsibility and industry despite her age surely elevates the preposterousness of Skimpole's repeated self-description of himself as a "child" (92). The latter is an educated adult and father of three and yet proudly professes to have "no idea of time" and "no idea of money" (90). Charley, uneducated and just thirteen years old, has no choice but to manage both time and money as she works and cares for her five-year-old brother and infant sister. Richard Altick (1980, 73) maintains that *Bleak House's* "manifold strains of imagery and theme, its very language, induce echoes that are repeatedly heard, often elaborated or modified." Such elaborated and modified thematic echoes certainly reverberate in Dickens's treatment of Charley's earnestness. Her actions, in the sense that she relies entirely on her own effort in her washing work, echo, elaborate, and modify the advice Jarndyce gives to Richard to put his shoulder to the wheel "in every kind of effort"—in contrast to the Aesopian wagoner who appeals for divine intervention (Dickens [1852–53] 2003, 213). Charley's "shoulder to the wheel" approach to taking up washing when her father dies dramatizes Richard's failure to do the same, even in something as light and simple as his promise to write letters for Ada every week (265). To borrow a phrase from Judith Butler (1993, 2), which takes Altick's observation concerning the "very language" of *Bleak House* to new heights, discourse in Dickens—in this case, the discourse surrounding Charley's efforts—often rhetorically "produces the [embodied] effects [that] it names." Butler's insight into the workings of language also applies to critical discourse outside the text. It is principally Charley to whom Eagleton (2003, x; emphasis mine) is referring when he asserts in his preface to the novel that a recurring theme in *Bleak House* involves "precocious, prematurely aged children who have been forced *to shoulder* . . . responsibility."

This uncanny, and who knows how conscious, critical language is an important extension of the "listening narrator" which informs Dickens's idiomatic imagination more broadly. When such idiomatic rhetoric enters the language of influential Dickensian critics, though, it adds a third integer into the calculus of Bakhtinian (1981, 324; emphasis original) dialogic heteroglossia where "*double-voiced discourse* . . . serves two speakers at the same time." As we saw in Bagstock's "right-hand man" appellation and the narrator's adoption of it in *Dombey*, Bakhtin develops this point further by adding that "all the while these two voices are dialogically interrelated, they—as it were—know about each other. . . . It is as if they actually hold a conversation with each other" (324). My argument up to now has been that this kind of dialogic interrelation becomes idiomatically refracted in Dickens's novels to such a degree that it could be said to scaffold some of their most imaginative and structural thematics. But when I and other critics (as with Eagleton's above-cited phrase) use bodily idioms in our own assessments of Dickens's language, we are participating in a kind of

104   **CHAPTER 2**

extra-dialogical interrelation that adds a compelling new dimension to Dickens's "idiom absorption."[13] Not only is the dominant idiom of the author absorbed into the novel at the levels of narrative voice, characterization, and theme, but it is also heteroglossically absorbed into the language of the critics who read and write about the novel.

The rhetoric used by Karen Chase and Michael Levenson in their recent work on *Bleak House* provides another striking example of this unique extra-dialogic interrelation between author, character, and critics. After their appraisal of Esther Summerson as "a tireless laborer," they write that "she finds herself in, and *gives her shoulder to*, the realm of filth" and "relentless housekeeping" (Chase and Levenson 2017, 210; emphasis mine). Here, again, Georges Poulet's (1969, 63; emphasis original) theoretical work on the transposition between artist and critic anticipates the ways in which Chase and Levenson's "criticism achieves a remarkable *complicity*" with the text—where "a verbal mimesis which transposes into the critic's language the sensuous themes of the work" itself.

This is fitting in terms of my argument because Esther's individual effort and work ethic in her housekeeping profession and beyond make her—with the possible exception of Phil Squod (whom I address later)—the finest example of a character "putting her shoulder to the wheel." She is an "unfortunate girl, orphaned and degraded from the first" as her godmother tells her on an early birthday that "'it would have been far better . . . that [she] had had no birthday; that [she] had never been born!'" (Dickens [1852–53] 2003, 30). Her godmother follows up this fantastically bleak assessment with one even more damning but equally as cryptic: "'Your mother, Esther, is your disgrace, and you were hers'" (30). "Diligent work," she is told, offers her one of the only "preparations for a life begun with such a shadow on it" (30). Unlike Richard, who fails to heed Jarndyce's solemn advice in relation to the Aesopian wagoner, Esther tells us very early on that she "would strive as [she] grew up to be industrious, contented and kind-hearted" (31, 563). And once she reaches Bleak House, she seemingly does nothing but deliver on this kind of striving. Soon after her arrival, she reports having "made up [her] mind to be so dreadfully industrious that [she] would leave [herself] not a moment's leisure to be low-spirited" (274). Gail Turley Houston (1994, 123) marvels that Esther's hard work allows her to achieve "a kind of cosmic good housekeeping." Indeed, the narrative is spangled with accounts of her "great determination" (Dickens [1852–53] 2003, 274) and industriousness: "I sat up working . . . late to-night (273–74); "I could go, please God, my lowly way along the path of duty" (570);

---

13. I offer a much more detailed analysis of this element of "critical" idiom absorption in my conclusion.

"SHOULDERING THE WHEEL" IN *BLEAK HOUSE* 105

"still my present duty appeared to be plain" (589); "'Once more, duty, duty, Esther,' said I" (609); "I had considered within myself that the deep traces of my illness, and the circumstances of my birth, were only new reasons why I should be busy, busy, busy" (693); "I resolved to be doubly diligent" (775).

Despite this emphasis on Esther's earnest and hardworking qualities, however, it must be acknowledged that Dickens does not ever explicitly use the "shoulder to the wheel" idiom in direct connection with either her or Charley. Its connotation and, as I have argued, is pervasive enough that critics like Eagleton, Chase, and Levenson themselves apply it to female characters. But Dickens conspicuously does not. The fact that critics do so while Dickens does not simultaneously reflects the expression's diffusive presence and also its troubling absence, which is both propitious and problematic. As we saw with the kinds of "right-hand" feminine solidarity that emerge in *Dombey and Son*, Dickens's idiomatic imagination can be expansively positive but still problematically gendered. It is clear that Dickens imagines characters like Charley Neckett and Esther Summerson with "shoulder to the wheel" determination but not clear why he does not explicitly characterize them with direct invocations of the idiom—as he does with the younger Rouncewell and, as we will see later, with Phil Squod. One could reasonably argue that many of Dickens's other invocations of the idiom represent failed applications; that is, they apply in an unequivocally *negative* way to male characters such as Richard Carstone, the Elder Turveydrop, the lawyer Vholes, and grandfather Smallweed who conspicuously do *not* put their shoulders to the wheel. But we are still left with Dickens's failure to use the expression in association with women who so clearly do live up to its positive connotations. Pointing out the failure of male characters to live by the maxims of the idiom still obscures the point that Dickens often tends to have a troublingly disembodied imagination when it comes to female characters.

It is likely that Dickens's imagination in this regard was shaped by the mid-nineteenth-century gendered subjectivity that, as Nancy Armstrong (1987, 20) has demonstrated, constructed ideal "femaleness" along the lines of moral "depth" rather than physical "surface." This differentiation between inner morality and physical embodiment is a major factor in what Schor (1999, 1) and many others have perceived as "the flatness and unrealistic nature of Dickens's treatment of women." In her first narrated section of *Bleak House*, for example, Esther tells the reader that her "little body will soon fall into the background now" (Dickens [1852–53] 2003, 40). And she follows through on this; her physicality rarely surfaces in the novel. She consistently avoids discussing her own appearance, even after her face is scarred by smallpox. The conspicuous deficit of attention to her body led George Orwell (1965, 131) to include Esther at the top of his list of Dickens's so-called "legless angels." As I discuss

106   **CHAPTER 2**

from a more biographical perspective in the introduction, it is likely that Dickens simply could not move past his tendencies to "angelicize"—and thus disembody—his notions of woman in ways that accord with important analyses of disembodied feminine representation in wider Victorian contexts by Sally Mitchell, Helena Michie, Marlene Tromp, and others.[14]

Expansions of the Idiom

Despite Dickens's tendency toward elision with Esther's body, it is curious, and probably not purely coincidence, that Esther's relentless work ethic is juxtaposed with Richard's wayward inability to keep his shoulder to a whole host of professional wheels. In the same chapter (17) that Esther tells us of her unwavering decision to be "dreadfully industrious," we learn not only of Richard's failure in the simple task of letter-writing to Ada but also of his displeasure with yet another profession that Jarndyce has arranged, this time medicine via Bayham Badger. We witness Richard's continued reliance on eventually "[being] provided for" by the Chancery suit in the way he nonchalantly exchanges what he calls the "harum-scarum" of nautical work for the "jog-trotty and hum-drum" of studying medicine (Dickens [1852–53] 2003, 269). His primary (but vague) complaint about studying medicine is its monotony: "'to-day is too like yesterday, and to-morrow is too like today'" (270). To this, Esther shrewdly responds, "'I am afraid . . . this is an objection to all kinds of application—to life itself, except under very uncommon circumstances'" (270). The exchange reveals Richard's inability or, perhaps better put, his unwillingness to recognize the work behind any professional application—the kind of "persevering" we have seen Rouncewell describe in conversation with Sir Leicester (107). Richard thinks that to "take to" a profession is tantamount to automatically arriving at its pinnacle, as when he expresses his desire to command a ship at the outset of his nautical studies (270). And perhaps most importantly for the argument I have been pursuing in this chapter, Dickens characterizes Richard's lack of industriousness in rhetoric that reverberates with the shoulder idiom. He admits to Esther and Ada that he does not "settle down to constancy" in medicine because "it's such *uphill*

---

14. Sally Mitchell (1981, xii) suggests that materiality itself belonged to the workplace and that middle-class women thus lacked this embodiment. Helena Michie argues that "the distance between the heroine's body and the words used to describe it are not simply *différance*, but an intervening between a subject and its representation." See Michie 1987, 84. Tromp (2000, 23) focuses on the character of Nancy in *Oliver Twist* to explore "the ways that a middle-class woman's body served as a counterpoint to the working woman's physicality, providing instead a means of social embodiment that denied the physical body and therefore made it seem impervious to violence."

work, and [because] it takes such time!" (270; emphasis mine). This rhetoric of "uphill work" contains echoes of the wagoner's shoulder to the mired wheel and also of the Sisyphean shoulder put to the enormous rock that must be pushed perpetually up a hill. Moreover, the fact that Sisyphus is futilely destined to repeat this action simultaneously points up Richard's past (nautical), present (medical), and future (military and legal) professional failures.

And as is typical of the contrasting nature of Dickens's representation of work in *Bleak House*, characters who do not shoulder responsibility often appear in tandem with those who do. For example, Mrs. Badger, speaking in the context of Richard's careless approach to medical study discussed above, emphasizes Allan Woodcourt's earnest industriousness in the same professional sphere (as a medical doctor). "Young men, like Mr Allan Woodcourt, who take it from a strong interest in all that it can do," says Mrs. Badger, "will find some reward in it through a great deal of work for a very little money, and through years of considerable endurance and disappointment" (267). Here, Mrs. Badger's description of Woodcourt's commitment to working for gradual success resonates with what we know of the ironmaster Rouncewell's similar commitment.

Without a question, though, the most thematically condensed and rhetorically explicit way that wheels and shoulders enter *Bleak House* is through the lawyer Mr. Vholes. It is fitting that a lawyer who repeatedly circles around the statement of his need to provide for his three daughters and father ("in the Vale of Taunton") articulates this need by way of a professional mantra where "the mill should always be going" (607). Richard's downfall becomes more precipitous once he aligns himself with Vholes, who insists on his ability to turn the wheels of the miry Jarndyce case in the young ward's favor. Eager for and, as we have seen, inclined toward outside intervention rather than individual effort, Richard fatally misjudges Vholes's "energy and determination" in relation to the Jarndyce suit, telling Esther, "We are beginning to spin along with that old suit at last. . . . We don't do things in the old slow way now. We spin along, now!" (592, 594). Richard's tragic miscalculation is abetted by Vholes's hollow idiomatic reassurances: "We have put our shoulders to the wheel, Mr Carstone, and the wheel is going round" (623).

With this phrasing, even in reverse order, Dickens explicitly links two of the novel's master tropes. The devil is in the details of the linkage, though. Vholes's phrasing channels John Jarndyce's early advice in terms of Aesop's (1926, 13, 623) wagoner, but as the notoriously "slipping and sliding" opening chapters should remind us, because "the wheel is going round" does not necessarily mean that it is gaining any traction. Mistaking "spinning one's wheels" for "putting one's shoulder to the wheel" eventually has fatal implications for Richard, and Dickens repeatedly emphasizes these phrases' tragic conjunction

108   **CHAPTER 2**

until they eventually come to fruition near the end of the novel. The effect essentially produces an extended series of brilliant rhetorical puns reminiscent of the kind and caliber we saw in the paronomasiac *out of hand/without a hand* example in *Dombey*.[15] As a result of its repeated piggybacked emphasis throughout *Bleak House*, though, the "wheeled" pun begins to partake of what the "ordinary language" philosopher, Ludwig Wittgenstein (1997, 7), would later consider an evolving "language game." The invocation of "spinning one's wheels" in idiomatic terms tangentially but still relationally connected to the original formulation of "putting one's shoulder to the wheel" reveals Wittgenstein's notion of how the demarcated "rules" of language are contextual rules, always awaiting possibility-enhancing creative reformulation. Stewart (2015, 132) has referred to this mode of Dickensian creative play as a "vocabular twofer," but it appears here in an even more specific sense as an "*idiomatic* twofer"—all the more impressive because of its imbrication with the theme of circularity in the novel. Even Richard's other rhetoric identifies—but crucially ignores—all others ("it has been death to many") who have attempted to move the case out of the wheel-spinning mud and mire and into the traction of judgment and conclusion (Dickens [1852–53] 2003, 17). "Others," he tells Esther, "have only half thrown themselves into it. I devote myself to it. I make it the object of my life" (599). Fatally, Richard confuses "throw[ing] himself [wholly] *into* the object" with throwing money *at* the object in the form of Vholes's legal shoulder to the wheel (601; emphasis mine).

Part of the point is to highlight the unfathomable futility of any endeavor attempting to supply traction to the wheels of Jarndyce and Jarndyce, which the novel's opening chapter makes clear have been spinning without traction for generations. But it is also to emphasize Richard's selfishly quixotic belief that the wheels would gain traction once *he* puts his shoulder (or his lawyer's) to it. The first exchange between Richard and Vholes on the hiring of the latter reflects the young client's despondency that traction could not be gained more or less immediately, echoing Richard's naive belief that he could command a gun boat on first entering the nautical profession:

> [Richard] throws his hat and gloves upon the ground . . . flings himself into a chair, half sighing and half groaning; rests his aching head upon his hand, and looks the portrait of Young Despair.

---

15. It is difficult to locate the pleasures of encountering this kind of inventive strain ("the glory of the quotidian") in Dickens any better than Garrett Stewart (1974, xxiii, 14) put it: "the sheer verbal gymnastics of words on vacation from meaning, the stylistic fun of language at play." For a discussion of how the trope of syllepsis operates as "a kind of distended pun," see Stewart (2015), especially "The Sylleptic Turn" section of chapter 4.

"SHOULDERING THE WHEEL" IN *BLEAK HOUSE*   109

"Again nothing done!" says Richard. "Nothing, nothing done!"

"Don't say nothing done, sir" returns the placid Vholes. "That is scarcely fair, sir, scarcely fair!"

"Why what *is* done?" says Richard, turning gloomily upon him.

"That may not be the whole question," returns Vholes. "The question may be a branch of what is doing, what is doing?"

"And what is doing?" asks the moody client. . . .

"A good deal is doing, sir. We have *put our shoulder to the wheel*, Mr Carstone, and the wheel is going round."

"Yes, with Ixion on it. How am I to get through the next four or five accursed months?" exclaims the young man, rising from his chair and walking about the room. (623–24; emphasis mine)

Richard's additional reference to Ixion in this extended "shoulder to the wheel" sequence recalls the "uphill" work of Sisyphus and implies a different kind of polyphonic futility by way of another closely associated Greek myth. Zeus orders Hermes to bind Ixion to a winged and fiery wheel that is "to spin in perpetuity." The fact that Dickens inserted the Ixion comment very late (in the final proof stage) suggests a connection may have emerged in his imagination between the explicit idiom of "putting one's shoulder to the wheel" and the implicit one of "spinning one's wheels."[16] Thus Richard's impetuous sarcasm in *Bleak House* contains a deeper and darker irony than he can possibly know at this early stage of his so-called dedication to the suit. Like Ixion, all his efforts will be maddeningly futile as he "throw[s] himself into" the hell of torment that is the Jarndyce case—one that is fittingly described by Tom Jarndyce, the ward who "in despair blew his brains out at a coffee-house in Chancery Lane," as "being ground to bits in a slow mill" (16, 71).

This tragic element is particularly cruel because Richard's early clear-eyed sarcasm is momentary and fleeting. Since, as we have seen, he knows nothing of personal or professional perseverance, he is easily convinced of such professionalism's effectiveness in others—most disastrously in the blind assurances of his lawyer that the case can and will be "prosperously ended" through the nebulously described application of shoulders to wheels (629). Paradoxically

---

16. Parts of my formulation here are indebted to H. P. Sucksmith (1970, 66–67) who notes the following: "Vholes's remark about putting one's shoulder to the wheel suggests Sisyphus as well as Ixion; the two damned and tortured souls were always closely associated and represented side by side in Tartarus. The momentary sarcasm of Richard has a deeper irony than he knows; his case is to be an exact parallel to that of Ixion and Sisyphus. All his schemes are to come to nothing, he is to be involved in an impossible punitive task and his life will become a hell of endless torment. Moreover, the classical reference is perfectly natural in Richard's mouth since his exclusively classical education at a public school has been insisted upon early in the novel."

110   **CHAPTER 2**

for Richard but now almost certainly consciously for Dickens at this point in the novel, the empty repetition of this idiom *about* the effectiveness of practical work suffices for *actual* work in the novel's middle sections. The idiom's appearances in all of the following instances appear in the original manuscript with no hesitation or cross-outs:

> Mr Vholes, who never gives up hopes, lays his palm upon the client's shoulder, and answers with a smile, "Always here, sir. Personally, or by letter, you will always find me here, sir, *with my shoulder to the wheel.*" (629–30; emphasis mine)
>
> "We whose ambition is to be looked upon in the light of respectable practitioners, sir, can but *put our shoulders to the wheel*. We do *it*, sir. At least I do *it* myself." (698; emphasis mine)
>
> "But it is some satisfaction, in the midst of my troubles and perplexities, to know that I am pressing Ada's interests in pressing my own. *Vholes has his shoulder to the wheel*, and he cannot help urging it on as much for her as for me, thank God!" (703; emphasis mine)
>
> "I wish, sir," said Mr Vholes, "to leave a good name behind me. Therefore, I take every opportunity of openly stating to a friend of Mr C, how Mr C is situated. As to myself, sir, the labourer is worthy of his hire. If I undertake *to put my shoulder to the wheel*, I do it, and I earn what I get. I am here for that purpose." (780; emphasis mine)
>
> The money Ada brought [Richard] was melting away . . . and I could not fail to understand, by this time, what was meant by *Mr Vholes's shoulder being at the wheel*—as I still heard it was . . . I knew they were getting poorer and poorer every day. (921; emphasis mine)

I have proposed that an unnoticed dimension of Dickens's "inimitability" lies in his penchant for and felicity in deploying idiomatic language in ways that ingeniously stretch and refract an idiom's rhetorical application to additional characters and thematically connected scenarios. An example in connection with one of the idiomatic scenarios listed above demonstrates this stretching and refracting quite poignantly in terms of Dickens's listening narrator. It occurs as Vholes attempts to assure Jarndyce and Esther that despite not making any tangible progress, he and Richard should remain positive simply because they "put [their] shoulders to the wheel" (698). The sense of its effectiveness wanes with Vholes's clipped description, though: "We do it [put our shoulders to the wheel], sir. At least *I* do *it* [put my shoulder to the wheel] myself" (698; emphasis mine). The fact that Richard is not included in Vholes's last formulation of wheel shouldering causes Esther—on the very next page—to present her conflicted musings in definitively circular, wheeled rhetoric: "At one while, my journey looked hopeful, and at another hopeless. . . . In what state should I find Richard, what I should say to him, and what he would say to me, occupied my mind *by turns* with these two states of feeling; and *the wheels* seemed to play one tune with these two states of feeling; and *the wheels* seemed to play one tune . . . over and over again all night" (699; emphasis mine). Rhetorical linkages by narrators such as this one with Esther make it seem at times as if Dickens is not only conscious of the idiomatic energy running through his prose but that he also wants to flaunt its sustained performative and linguistic exploration of the ways in which vernacular expressions both do and do not have the meanings popularly ascribed to them.[17]

In this sense, *Bleak House* offers us one of the finest examples of Dickens's development in alternating between, and also meshing, the hypocritically figurative and the admirably literal. We have seen how characters such as Mr. Turveydrop, with his "high-shouldered" bowing and "cold-shouldered" treatment of his family, fit into what I am referring to as the "hypocritically figurative" camp. We have also seen how characters like Mr. Rouncewell, Charley Neckett, and Esther fit into the "admirably literal" designation. But in terms of the former category, Dickens almost outdoes even his own finely tuned sense of humor. It is hard to believe that Dickens did not relish depicting the illustrations (figure 12) of a character, like Vholes, who claims to have his shoulder constantly to the wheel, with very little in the area of *actual* shoulders.

Here, I am extending Robert Patten's (2002, 123) notion that illustrations in Dickens's serialized novels "can expound, elaborate, and enlighten the text." As with his (vole) namesake—a rodent whose miniscule shoulder vertebrae are precisely what allow it to burrow through the smallest of spaces—Vholes is repeatedly illustrated and described as being so "narrow and stooping" (Dickens [1852–53] 2003, 606, 695) that his "thin shadow" (695, 698) announces his macabre comings and goings.

We see Dickens at the height of his (probably now conscious) imaginative flair in this regard as he cleverly extends the association of Vholes and voles in his chapter-opening description of the "nook in the dark" from which the

---

17. Philip Horne (2013, 160) makes a similar point: "The style of speech of a character can extend beyond the sphere of direct quotation and seep into the narration at times so that the prose of the quasi-omniscient narrator takes on local colour from words characteristic of the figures and texts—and places—in the vicinity."

112   CHAPTER 2

FIGURE 12.   Attorney and client, fortitude and impatience

lawyer—with the "hole" hiding in his name—comes and goes (789).[18] The passage is worth citing extensively:

> The name of MR VHOLES, preceded by the legend GROUND FLOOR, is inscribed upon a doorpost in Symond's Inn, Chancery Lane: a little, pale, wall-eyed, woe-begone inn, like a large dustbin of two compartments and a sifter. It looks as if Symond were a sparing man in his day, and constructed his inn of old building materials, which took kindly to the dry rot and dirt and all things decaying and dismal, and perpetuated Symond's memory with congenial shabbiness. Quartered in this dingy hatchment commemorative of Symond, are the legal bearings of Mr Vholes.
>   Mr Vholes's office, in disposition and in situation retired, is squeezed up in a corner, and blinks at a dead wall. Three feet of knotty floored dark passage bring the client to Mr Vholes's jet black door, in an angle pro-

---

18. I am indebted to Garrett Stewart for this formulation. Stewart (1974, 135) remarks that Vholes "is hideously 'inward' and without surface, a devouring void like the 'hole' hiding in his name."

> foundly dark on the brightest mid-summer morning, and encumbered by
> a black bulk-head of cellarage staircase, against which belated civilians
> generally strike their brows. Mr Vholes's chambers are on so small a scale,
> that one clerk can open the door without getting off his stool, while the
> other who elbows him at the same desk has equal facilities for poking the
> fire. . . . The atmosphere is otherwise stale and close. (620–21)

The narrator seems to delight in drawing our attention to the incommensurability of Vholes's professional mantra and the space where he ostensibly practices it. The "squeezed up" subterranean office is on the "GROUND FLOOR" of a building comprised of "dry rot and dirt." Moreover, its extreme compactness is matched only by its profound darkness—a combination that causes civilians (non v(h)oleses) to strike their heads as they descend the cellarage staircase to meet with him. (Actual voles live subterraneously and thrive in darkness.) This elaborate and ingenious punning reaches its apex in the supreme irony that to be able to get to the place where Vholes puts his professional shoulder to the wheel, he must possess a cylindrical, vole-like body known *not* for "shouldering" but for *shoulderless* burrowing and tunneling into the smallest of places—as do the "vermin parasites" that "craw[l] in an out of gaps in walls and boards" at Tom-all-Alone's (256–57).

Like we see in relation to Richard's death later in the novel, the comic absurdity of a nearly shoulderless Vholes also takes on a decidedly more predatory valence. The narrator makes an explicit reference to cannibalism, for example, within the same chapter we learn about Vholes's subterranean office: "As though, Mr Vholes and his relations being minor cannibal chiefs, and it being proposed to abolish cannibalism, indignant champions were to put the case thus: Make man-eating unlawful, and you starve the Vholeses!" (622–23).[19] Such untoward associations appear even more sinister if we consider their tangential relationship to Dickens's contemporaneous editorial work outside the novel. During the late summer of 1853, as Dickens was chronicling Richard Carstone's demise at the hands of Chancery and, by extension, at the shoulder of Vholes, *Household Words* ran a piece titled "The Mind of Brutes" wherein the object was "to find in ['various beasts'] analogies with corresponding characters and classes of mankind" (Dixon 1853, 565). The article devoted to "Brutes" does not discuss the dangerousness of larger animals of prey as we might expect but instead focuses on the brutality of rodents—beginning with the biological and homonymical relation to the vole, "The Mole" (565). The article establishes "true brutality" in an animal's cannibalistic eating of its own kind: "The Bengal

---

19. For another view of Vholes's cannibalism see Stone 1994, 139–41.

114   **CHAPTER 2**

tiger is a lizard of sobriety and a lamb of gentleness, when considered side by side with the mole; for the Bengal tiger has never turned the point of its canines against its own flesh and blood. Send your friend a present of a couple of tigers shut up in a box; they will reach their address without accident or injury. Place two moles in the same position, and they will have swallowed each other completely up, before they get to the first baiting-place" (566). The timing and content of this article are provocative considering that it ran during the very month (August 1853) that Dickens was completing the final double number of *Bleak House* (September 1853). It is in the final pages of this final number that Esther makes the observation that Vholes harbors "a devouring look . . . as if he had swallowed the last morsel of this client" (Dickens [1852–53] 2003, 976). This devouring look, of course, applies as much to Vholes's vampiric relationship with Richard as it does to the long-awaited judgment in the Jarndyce suit, which is consumed—"eaten up" as it were—by legal costs. Moreover, according to the *Household Words* article, the "muscular superiority of the mole" resides in its minute shoulder vertebrae which give it the ability to flourish "fifty feet underground" (Dixon 1853, 566). This rodent affiliation is further emphasized in what little we learn of Vholes's private living arrangements: so vole-/mole-like is Vholes, in fact, that he even "dwells . . . in *an earthy cottage* situated in a damp garden at Kennington" (Dickens [1852–53] 2003, 630; emphasis mine).

Vholes is hardly the only shoulderless burrowing figure in the novel, but as I have surmised from the start, a whole cast of them have escaped critical interpretation partly because of their organic absorption into the novel's wider thematic concerns. The various "shoulderless" motifs (and characters) become so reticulated with some of the innermost themes and structures of the novel, so infused and shaped by Dickens's idiomatic imagination, that it is easy not to register their significance. Dickens invokes other animals of various kinds lacking pronounced shoulders often throughout *Bleak House* and always in a negative light. Early on, for example, when John Jarndyce learns of his failure to warn his innocent wards of Skimpole's free-loading ways, he exclaims, "'Why, what a cod's head and shoulders I am . . . to require reminding of it!'" (101). This "boneheaded" idiom works, according to the *Oxford English Dictionary* because of its implication that a cod's "head" (brain) is as small as its "shoulders"—which, of course, as a fish, it completely lacks. Skimpole, in turn, brags about his ability to "roll [him]self up like a hedgehog" to avoid responsibility on various occasions (293, 678). Tom-all-Alone's is "a swarm of misery" in part because of the legion of "vermin parasites" that "craw[l] in and out of gaps in the walls and boards" (256–57). Furthermore, Guppy "ferret[s] out evidence" in part by devising a plan to embed (weevil-like) his friend, Tony Jobling-turned-Mr. Weevle, at Krook's (152, 329). The larger point is that all

Figure 13. The Smallweed family

of these associations contribute to the arc of Dickens's idiomatic imagination where, as we have seen, those who try to short-circuit earnest industry for the prospect of quick financial gain literally and figuratively have no shoulders to put to the wheel.

Beyond Vholes, the characterization of the Smallweed family is the most prominent and sustained example of the extended idiomatic emphasis on shoulders or lack thereof. The chapter immediately following the one where Weevle digs in as Krook's boarder serves as an introduction to the Smallweed family lineage, which is encapsulated in similarly burrowing and parasitic language: Smallweed is "a grub at first, and . . . a grub at last" in the narrator's estimation (332). The Smallweed family's "little narrow pinched ways" become embodied in Mr. Smallweed's perpetual "sliding down in his chair" and illustrated (figure 13) in his "dark little parlour certain feet below the level of the street" (342, 346, 333).

116   **CHAPTER 2**

Like Vholes, Mr. Smallweed appears virtually shoulderless, and this grub-like attribute indeed serves his "Druidical" clan well as they descend on Krook's en masse, "digging, delving, and diving" among the ruins (633). The multivalenced association that this particular kind of "grubbing" had begun to accrue in the 1800s was also likely not lost on Dickens. The *Oxford English Dictionary* lists the verb "to grub" as already beginning to assume its colloquial connotation of groveling meanness by the middle of the century. It makes sense, then, that Krook refers to the Chancery lawyers' parasitic moneymaking as "grub[bing] on in a muddle" (70). This is exactly what the Smallweeds do as they "retire into holes" and make their money not by earnest industriousness but by grubbing for it upon the laws of "compound interest" (332–33).

The trope of shouldering is also refracted in compelling ways to *Bleak House*'s earnestly industrious minor characters who *do* possess the literal and figurative abilities to shoulder responsibilities small and large throughout the novel. The hardworking Chesney Wold housekeeper, for instance, Mrs. Rounce-well, is "broad across the shoulders," and her self-made ironmaster son has the same broad-shouldered "good figure, like his mother" (451). Mrs. Rounce-well's other son, Trooper George, is often depicted "squaring" these same "broad square shoulders" to the most venal elements and characters he en-counters in the novel's corrupt landscape (722, 544). Indeed, "the special con-trast Mr George makes to the Smallweed family" is rendered in decisively physical, shouldered terminology (341). Where Smallweed (as figure 13) is a shoulderless "clothes-bag with a black skull-cap on top of it," Trooper George always maintains a "broad-shouldered," "squared," and "developed figure" (334, 342). Perhaps most telling in this respect, though, Dickens renders the physical contrast between George and Smallweed as "a broadsword to an oyster-knife" (342). This small but striking comparison is not insignificant for the argument that I have been pursuing: a broadsword's most defining feature is its oversized "shoulder hilt," which stops an opposing sword from traveling down the blade to harm the bearer's hand in combat; by contrast, a narrow oyster knife's lack of a shoulder hilt is precisely what allows it to run the length of the oyster's shell and pry it open. Thus, even the smallest of comparative metaphors in this novel carry shouldered implications.

Fittingly, the colloquial expressions other characters use to describe Trooper George's determination are also shoulder oriented. For instance, when Jarn-dyce inquires about changing George's mind to hire a lawyer after he is falsely imprisoned for murder, Mrs. Bagnet responds that "you could as soon take up and shoulder and eight-and-forty pounder by your own strength, as turn that man" (799). George's "habitual manner . . . of carrying himself" takes on "an extraordinary contrast" on reuniting with his mother during this prison scene

(845). He falls to his knees and sobs, repenting for what he calls a life of "incumbrance and . . . discredit" to the Rouncewell family reputation (846). The narrator, ever playful and punning with the elasticity of these recurring idiomatic orientations, has Mrs. Bagnet's shoulder-poking umbrella punctuate the cadences of George's self-deprecating conversation with his mother. On five different occasions in this scene, George slouches in despair as he recounts what he takes to be his various shortcomings, and each time, Mrs. Bagnet's umbrella forces him to square his shoulders and reassume the "broad-chested upright attitude" for which he has become known: "[Mrs. Bagnet] relieves her feelings, and testifies her interest in the conversation, by giving the trooper a great poke between the shoulders with her umbrella; this action she afterwards repeats, at intervals, in a species of affectionate lunacy" (543, 846, 847, 848). Because of Dickens's emphasis on all kinds of shoulders throughout the novel, though, Mrs. Bagnet's literally pointed remonstrances are *not* "affectionate lunacy"; they are small but fitting integers in *Bleak House*'s more general calculus of thematic structure.[20] Her umbrella's correcting pokes also reflect the Bagnet family's larger imperative that "discipline must be maintained" (441, 544, 802, 983). Their discipline, unlike the Jellyby family, represents another example of how personal and collective responsibility, along with productive labor, emerges as the best way of coping with the entropic forces that appear elsewhere in the novel.[21]

The Capability of Disabled Shoulders

The most admirably literal instantiation of Dickens's idiomatic theme of shouldering work, responsibility, and duty, however, comes from the most unlikely of characters: Phil Squod. He is the "little grotesque man" who loyally and ably assumes the position of custodian at Trooper George's shooting gallery despite being severely scorched and lamed in a gasworks accident (350). The initial description of Phil as he shuts up the gallery is an exquisite study in perseverance:

> As Phil moves about to execute this order [to "shut up shop"], it appears that he is lame, though able to move very quickly. On the speckled side

---

20. Mrs. Bagnet's umbrella pokes offer a far more effective—not to mention more positive—analogy to Judy's constant "upshaking" of the ever-slouching Smallweed. For a brilliant assessment of Dickens's "style" by way of his umbrellas, see Bowen 2013.

21. My reading here differs significantly from D. A. Miller, who maintains the Bagnets and their repeated motto exemplify the practice of self-policing that, according to Foucault, characterizes bourgeois society. See D. A. Miller 1988, 105.

118   **CHAPTER 2**

of his face he has no eyebrow, and on the other side he has a bushy black one, which want of uniformity gives him a very singular and rather sinister appearance. Everything seems to have happened to his hands that could possibly take place, consistently with the retention of all the fingers; for they are notched, and seamed, and crumpled all over. He appears very strong, and lifts heavy benches about as if he had no idea what weight was. He has a curious way of limping round the gallery *with his shoulder against the wall*, and tacking off at objects he wants to lay hold of, instead of going straight to them, which has left a smear all round the four walls, conventionally called "Phil's mark." (350–51; emphasis mine)

As if to demonstrate how "Phil's mark" could become so recognizable, the narrator continues on to detail the frequency with which the custodian displays his most "curious" attribute: "Phil cannot even go straight to bed, but finds it necessary to shoulder round two sides of the gallery, and then tack off at his mattress" (351); "the dirty little man was shuffling about with his shoulder against the wall" (401); "shouldering his way around the gallery in the act of sweeping it" (418); "Phil Squod shoulders his way round three sides of the gallery" (422).

This emphasis on Phil's literal use of his shoulders is even more conspicuous in the narrative given the placement of its initial description just after Richard's able-bodied failure to put his shoulder to a profession, and after Mr. Turveydrop's similarly able-bodied and "high-shouldered" refusal even to *consider* a profession. In stark contrast, the repeated descriptions of how Phil makes his shoulder "mark" listed above appear almost immediately before he alone carries "the shapeless bundle" of Grandfather Smallweed (in his chair) up the stairs and into the Shooting Gallery—a feat that prompts Smallweed to remark that "your workman is very strong" despite the attendant observation that "he seems to have hurt himself a good deal" (427, 425, 426).

The narrator also gives us a privileged glimpse into the first meeting between Trooper George and Phil Squod, which explicitly emphasizes the latter's most conspicuous and yet most paradoxically capable feature:

"It was after the case-filling blow up, when I first see you, commander. You remember?"
    "I remember, Phil. You were walking along in the sun."
    "Crawling, guv'ner, again a wall—"
    "True, Phil—*shouldering your way on*—" (421; emphasis mine)

Here, George's observation that Phil was "shouldering [his] way on" may be seen as a distillation of Dickens's wider imaginative structure for some of the

"SHOULDERING THE WHEEL" IN *BLEAK HOUSE*

novel's deepest preoccupations with work, responsibility, and as Bradbury (2003, xxi) has put it, "the value of going on." It illuminates the latent "shoulder to the wheel" idiom by the invocation of an otherwise literal description of Phil's physical bearing when George meets him. Rather than shirk responsibility as so many of *Bleak House*'s able-bodied do, the lamed Phil who refers to himself as "a limping bag of bones" actively invites it: "'If a mark's wanted, or if it will improve the business, let the customers take aim at me. They can't spoil *my* beauty. *I*'m all right. . . . They won't hurt *me*. I have been throwed, all sorts of styles, all my life!'" (422; emphasis original). The punning on two senses of "mark" here is also telling. Phil offers himself up as a mark, and yet such dedication to his profession is marked—at shoulder height—all over the walls of George's shooting gallery. Through sheer perseverance and sense of duty, Phil puts his shoulder to the wheel by putting it to the wall. What we get, then, is another brilliant instantiation of Dickensian paronomasia: the literal "shoulder to the wall" calls forth the idiomatic "shoulder to the wheel" in a cross-phrase association where auricular wit manifests itself as the phonematic partaking in the semantic. Thus, it is not surprising that Dickens represents Mr. Jellyby's frustration with his wife's "telescopic philanthropy" among their pressing domestic affairs in similar terms of walls and "marks." Throughout the novel, Mr. Jellyby uses the wall behind his sitting position to compensate for the inability of his shoulders to hold his head upright so often that Esther "plainly perceive[s] the mark of Mr. Jellyby's head against the wall" each time she visits the Jellyby household (611).[22] The contrast between Phil Squod's active perseverance and Mr. Jellyby's passive futility, like so many other dimensions of this novel, is shoulder oriented. Where the able-bodied but feckless Mr. Jellyby finds "consolation in walls," Phil Squod shoulders them in order to carry out his professional duties (774).

I have discussed at considerable length Dickens's tendency to conflate ability and disability in my first two chapters. I draw attention to this because one of the larger aims of my book is to demonstrate how Dickens's imagination of disability often operates within the framework of his wider idiomatic imagination.

---

22. Here are the other instances where Dickens presents Mr. Jellyby's passive reliance on walls: "During the whole evening, Mr Jellyby sat in a corner with his head against the wall" (57); "Poor Mr Jellyby . . . very seldom spoke, and almost always sat when he was at home with his head against the wall" (479); "he came in regularly every evening, and sat without his coat, with his head against the wall; as though he would have helped us, if he had known how" (480); "Mr Jellyby groaned, and laid his head against the wall again" (481); he "sat down on the stairs with his head against the wall. I hope he found some *consolation in walls*. I almost think he did" (484; emphasis mine); he "then sit down, with his head against the wall, and make no attempt to say anything more" (774); "His *sole occupation* was to sit with his head against the wall" (774; emphasis mine); "Mr Jellyby spends his evenings at [Caddy's] new house with his head against the wall, as he used to do in her old one" (987).

120   **CHAPTER 2**

I hope it is obvious that my interpretations of his tendencies to render disability idiomatically are certainly not meant to invalidate or sidestep disability itself; but they *are* meant to offer a set of alternative explanations for how disability in (some) Dickens can operate "positively"—similar to the manner in which Bakhtin conceives of the grotesque body in *Rabelais*.[23] The case of Phil Squod in *Bleak House* is exemplary in this regard. Many critics, for example, have noted the legion of Dickens's disabled "grotesqueries."[24] Talia Schaffer has emphasized the connection between the Dickensian grotesque and entertainment. "This is especially evident in the case of Dickens's 'grotesques,'" Schaffer (2016, 164) writes, because they are "descended from the carnival or the freak show, in which the disabled individual proudly displays the body for others' enjoyment. Although today we would deplore this kind of voyeuristic gaze, disabled subjects like Phil Squod in *Bleak House* relish attention."[25] Such a position is difficult to contest, especially when the novel's narrator first describes Phil as "a little *grotesque* man, with a large head" (Dickens [1952–53] 2003, 350; emphasis mine). My point here is not to contest that this is true. However, I want to suggest that something additional is also true: that Phil Squod's disability—his reliance on his shoulders to move about George's shooting gallery in performing his professional duties—is an extended dimension of Dickens's idiomatic imagination in *Bleak House* where the linguistic and thematic energies of the text so often merge with the putting (or not) one's shoulder to the wheel.[26] As is the case with Captain Cuttle's hook-handed contribution to *Dombey*'s "right-hand man" theme of surrogacy, Phil Squod's decisively shouldered descriptions extend *Bleak House*'s emphasis on a "shoulder to the wheel/wall" type of earnest industry, toughness, and responsibility.

The novel's most egregious and heartbreaking examples of disowning such responsibility occur with society's failure to find a place for the streetsweeper, Jo—who "fights it out, at his crossing, among the mud and the wheels" (259).

---

23. Bakhtin (1968, 303) states that "exaggeration, hyperbolism, excessiveness are generally considered fundamental attributes of the grotesque style." These attributes so often part of Dickens's characterization, but it is also worth noting Bakhtin's belief that "in grotesque realism . . . the bodily element is deeply positive" (19).

24. See, for instance, only one recent example from Stewart (2015, 157): "Edgeworth pushes the trope further toward Dickensian grotesquerie in insisting 'that 'tis better for a lady to lose her leg than her reputation.'"

25. For an interpretation arguing that the disabled in Dickens function to facilitate the heteronormative marriage plot from which they themselves are disbarred, see Free 2008.

26. It is worth noting that most critics who discuss Phil Squod do so by locating his disfigurement in his face. See, for example, Scarry (1994, 56), who maintains that Phil "has a physical countenance in which every millimeter of its damaged surface maps the complexities and vagaries of the industrial revolution." More recently, Breton (2005, 73) explains that "the sympathetic Phil Squod has been physically deformed by capitalism, by a life of labour. But . . . if labour creates an identity, the apparatus to identify character (physiognomy) is nonetheless upheld."

"SHOULDERING THE WHEEL" IN *BLEAK HOUSE*   121

He is told by nearly every person and entity he encounters to "move on." Chapter 19, titled "Moving On," features a constable who claims to have told Jo to "move on" "five hundred times" (308). And Jo has no choice but to comply, saying, "'I have been moved on, and moved on . . . and they're all a watching and a driving of me . . . from the time when I don't get up, to the time when I don't go to bed'" (491). The fact that Jo—nicknamed "toughy" because he is such a "Tough Subject"—does so often "move on," "with his bare feet, over hard stones, and through the mud and mire," invokes yet another dimension of setting one's shoulder to the wheel (359, 261). Seldom appealing for assistance and laboring nonstop in this manner without sleep naturally makes him susceptible to sickness. When Liz attempts to secure help in Tom-all-Alone's, society's bureaucratic failure begins to resemble the futile, wheel-like circularity of the suit in Chancery: "At first it was too early for the boy to be received into the proper refuge, and at last it was too late. One official sent her to another, and the other sent her back again to the first, and so backward and forward; until it appeared . . . as if both must have been appointed for their skill in evading their duties, instead of performing them" (491–92). Despite receiving no (medical) care aside from a brief stay at the Bleak House property, Jo "moves on" until Allan Woodcourt tracks him down in Tom-all-Alone's and his death becomes imminent.

But it is important that Dickens infuses the description of the events leading up to Jo's death with several of the literal and figurative senses of the central idiom I have been tracing in this chapter. When Woodcourt first glimpses Jo, for instance, "he sees a ragged figure coming very cautiously along, crouching close to the soiled walls" (713). And later, we learn that "Jo, shaking and chattering, slowly rises, and stands, after the manner of his tribe in a difficulty, sideways against the hoarding, resting one of his *high shoulders* against it" (716; emphasis mine). So unlike the elder Turveydrop, Jo's high shoulders are put to (good) use. The descriptions of them in this way reveal that Jo, even at the end of his life, not only "moves on" but "shoulders on" in a manner distinctly reminiscent of "Phil's mark." It is appropriate, then, that Jo is taken to the shooting gallery in a chapter titled "Jo's Will"—where Phil prepares the streetsweeper's deathbed by "bear[ing] down upon them, according to his usual [wall-shouldering] tactics" (725). Jo and Phil appear to be members of the same "tribe" not because of their orphaned, outcast, or grotesquely disabled status but because of their "will" to shoulder on and ahead amid the most difficult of circumstances. We witness Phil, for instance, at one point "shouldering his way round the gallery in the act of *sweeping*" (418; emphasis mine). In Jo's actual death scene, Dickens brings the guiding idiom that we have been tracing full circle, so to speak, as he transfers the focus from the streetsweeper's

122   CHAPTER 2

literal shoulders to his figurative "cart." He has had his shoulder to the wheel of this cart for his whole life and only physical disintegration slows this. But he still "labours up" and "labours on" to his very last breath:

> That cart of his is heavier to draw, and draws with a hollower sound . . . as the cart seems to be breaking down. (728)
>
> For the cart so hard to draw, is near its journey's end. . . . All around the clock, it labours up the broken steps, shattered and worn. (731)
>
> The cart had very nearly given up, but labours on a little more. (732)
>
> The cart is shaken all to pieces, and the rugged road is very near its end. (733)

Although the metaphor figures Jo's life as the cart, it is clear that road he has had to traverse has been mercilessly arduous in terms of "work."[27] We have been aware since the outset of the novel that "Jo fights it out, at his crossing, among the mud and wheels" for "a scanty sum to pay for the unsavoury shelter of Tom-all-Alone's" (259).

This orients, even as it contrasts, Jo's struggle and his "will" to keep the cart "moving on" with the Aesopian wagoner who gives up so easily and pleads for divine assistance. Jo's around-the-clock "labours," laboring to move his cart on "a little more" through the "stagnant channels of mud," recalls the easily defeated wagoner but also more specifically Richard—the person for whom Dickens principally invokes the idiom and for whom, by this point in the narrative, is already "broken, heart and soul, upon the wheel of Chancery" (711, 559). As we have seen, Jarndyce alludes to Aesop's idiomatic fable in order to stress the importance of trusting to constancy and individual effort instead of what he senses is Richard's budding tendency to rely (Skimpole style) on others. One of the great tragedies of the novel, though, is that for Richard, his guardian's advice—to use terminology germane to *Bleak House*'s wheeled atmosphere—has no traction. Richard's early "habit of putting off—and trusting to this, that, and the other chance" only becomes more deeply entrenched as he flounders in his military endeavors but "beseeches Mr Vholes, for Heaven's sake and Earth's sake, to do his utmost, to 'pull him through' the Court of Chancery" (197, 629).

This failure to put his shoulder to the wheel, in the end figured by a reliance on Vholes to *pull* him through, also has consequences for how Dickens treats the respective deaths of Jo and Richard. Put plainly, the constancy of Jo's cart-figured struggle with his broom and his sickness embodies what Bradbury (2003, xxi)

---

27. In *David Copperfield*, the novel Dickens ([1849–50] 2004, 553) had most recently finished, David remarks on his various labors with similar rhetoric: "I was always punctual at the office; at the Doctor's too: and I really did work, as the common expression is, like a cart-horse."

and others have described as "the real issue" of survival in the novel. Richard's death, on the other hand, is narrated with a conspicuous deficit of what we witness in Jo's almost miraculous "will" to shoulder his life's cart until its collapse; Richard seems simply to be "wasting away beneath the eyes of [his] adviser" as he ineffectively "haunts the Court" for hundreds of pages of the novel (924). Even his dying words that he will "begin the world" but not "in the old way now" echo with the empty rhetoric of perseverance which characterized the beginnings of each previous failed attempt put his shoulder to the wheel (977–78).

The Idiom at Full Circle

Critics have long marveled at the intricate connections and reconnections woven throughout *Bleak House*. J. Hillis Miller (1971, 17) has made an influential assertion that "a complex fabric of recurrences" circle around in such a way that "characters, scenes, themes and metaphors return in proliferating resemblances." In a similar observation on the circularity of the novel's language, Altick (1980, 73) has pointed out how "manifold strains of imagery and theme, its very language, induce echoes that are repeatedly heard, often elaborated or modified, down to the very last chapters." Schor (2006, 96) has more recently argued that it is "impossible to make real sense of *Bleak House*" without accounting for the buried and revolving "connections between one set of images, one set of characters, one set of social crises, and another." No one would quibble with the validity of these observations. I return to them here because of their common emphasis on the generally circular movement of the novel at a myriad of levels. For my part, I have sought to add a new and very specific argument about the central place of literal and figurative wheels in Dickens's idiomatic imagination as he composed this intensely complex novel.

We have seen how Dickens's imaginative course began by seriously considering several variations on "The Ruined Mill" as the title for the book. And clearly, the sense of chaos and futility bound up in the thematic rhetoric of broken or slipping wheels continues to proliferate until very late in the narrative. In her fevered chase with Inspector Bucket to locate Lady Dedlock, for example, Esther reports after each unproductive search that "we were again upon the melancholy road by which we had come; tearing up the miry sleet and thawing snow, as if they wore torn up by a waterwheel" (Dickens [1852–53] 2003, 885). Here, the mud and "mire" of Aesop's "shoulder to the wheel" fable converges with the image of a water mill. Indeed, the most melancholy and futile of the Bucket/Esther searches in these final chapters are shot through

124   **CHAPTER 2**

with hopeless, wheel-oriented imagery. Think, for instance, of the narrator's description of their stop among the "waste[d]" and "wretched" brickmaking section near Tom-all-Alone's: "where the clay and water are hard frozen, and the mill in which the gaunt blind horse goes round all day, looks like an instrument of human torture" (864). This particular formulation echoes Richard's fateful comment regarding Ixion's torturous bondage on the wheel to which Vholes so often claims to have put his shoulder.

Although Dickens characteristically does not set forth any programmatic solutions to the heaving failures of mid-Victorian society, hope does (predictably) emerge in the comingling of individual effort and domestic harmony. In the novel's final chapters, those who truly put their shoulders to the wheel are rewarded—but crucially for my argument, they are rewarded in an abruptly positive atmosphere where wheels finally *do* gain traction and *do* turn productively. Gone are the many debilitating slippages among the fog and mire of the opening's setting amid the "implacable November weather" (13). At the end, Esther takes possession, on "a beautiful summer morning," of her very own Bleak House which is set in "such a lovely place, so tranquil and so beautiful, with such a rich and smiling country spread around it; with *water sparkling away* in the distance, here all overhung with summer-growth, there *turning a humming mill*" (962; emphasis mine). Water finally takes a sparkling, not miry, form. It seems hardly coincidental, then, that the industrious Charley Neckett is married to a prosperous miller and that Esther can observe, from the desk at her window, "the very mill beginning to go round" (986). Moreover, her hardworking brother Tom's apprenticeship to the miller recalls the earnest ironmaster who apprenticed and worked his way to a fulfilling life. Even Caddy, as Esther tells us, "works very hard" to support her disabled husband and their child, but "she is more than contented, and does all she has to do with all her heart" (987). This rhetoric aligns Caddy with a "double" diligence that Dickens so highly prized both in and outside the worlds of his novels. First, it reveals Caddy's achievement of what Esther, perhaps the novel's hardest-working "shoulder to the wheel" character, set out for herself very early on in terms of "striv[ing] . . . to be industrious, contented and kind-hearted" (31). Second, it connects Caddy to the exalted sense of industriousness that Dickens had identified in his previous novel regarding David Copperfield (and by proxy, himself). David's professional maturation occurs in conjunction with his "golden rule" realization that "whatever I have tried to do in life, I have tried with all my heart to do well . . . and there is no substitute for a thorough-going, ardent, and sincere earnestness. Never to put one hand to anything, on which I could throw my whole self" (Dickens [1849–50] 2004, 613).

By the time he starts his next novel, *Bleak House*, the amalgam of "heart," "hand," and "whole self" reaches a new idiomatic configuration in shoulders and wheels—and more specifically, the putting of the former to the latter.

It is worth recalling that Dickens uses the "shoulder to the wheel" idiom or its variants nineteen times in his fictional career, all of which appear in *Bleak House*. The exclusivity of this finite number provides, if nothing else, I hope, a useful provocation for us to think more broadly and holistically about the mysterious workings of Dickens's idiomatic imagination in this extraordinary novel. It turns out that *Bleak House*'s expanding and multiply-valenced reiteration of the shoulder idiom resembles Esther's moral resolution to combat the inadequacies of "telescopic" work. "I thought it best," she concludes, "to be as useful as I could, and to render what services I could, to those immediately about me; and to try to let that *circle of duty* gradually and naturally expand itself (Dickens [1852–53] 2003, 128; emphasis mine). To embrace circles of duty (Esther, Charley Neckett, Caddy Jellyby, Trooper George, Phil Squod, Allan Woodcourt, etc.), to misjudge the reach of those circles (Mrs. Jellyby and Mrs. Pardiggle), to focus on too-narrow circles (Richard and his Chancery suit, Vholes and his "Vale of Taunton"), to renounce circles of duty altogether (Mr. Turveydrop and Harold Skimpole)—these are all expressions of the novel's concern for circularity and the need for ethical traction. G. K. Chesterton's (1911, 152) now-classic contention, therefore, that in "the story['s] circl[ing] round . . . itself," Dickens sees "the conclusion and the whole" of *Bleak House* seems not only like a viable general claim but one that may be bolstered by specific analysis from an as-yet-unremarked-on, idiomatically oriented perspective. This allows us to see how Dickens draws attention to the crucial ways in which *Bleak House* is, among other things, an imaginative and thematic exploration of work and responsibility—how we shoulder (or do not) important duties in a far more complex and socially expansive world than the one in which *David Copperfield* ends. In the next chapter, we will see how Dickens squares his depiction of a similarly complex world with a compacted (weekly) publication schedule in what I call the "manual outlay" of his first post-Darwinian novel.

CHAPTER 3

"Brought Up by Hand"

The Manual Outlay of *Great Expectations*

> It is not easy to be done with a civilization of the hand.
>
> —Roland Barthes, "The Plates of the *Encyclopedia*"
> (1982)

Forcing Dickens's Idiomatic Hand

There is a good reason why John Butt and Kathleen Tillotson (1957) did not include a chapter on *Great Expectations* (1860–61) within their pioneering study of Dickens's compositional practices in *Dickens at Work*.[1] Simply put, there has never been much to analyze in the way of planning documents for this novel. Dickens, uncharacteristically for this late period in his career, maintained no working notes, no number plans, no "memoranda."[2] As Edgar Rosenberg (1999, 477) has framed it, "compared with the ample documentation we have for Dickens's other works, the pickings are slim." The only notes Dickens made while composing *Great Expectations* consist of but three individual sheets, and even these pertain solely to the novel's final episodes.[3] It has

---

1. Butt and Tillotson's book contains chapters on *Sketches by Boz*, *Pickwick Papers*, *Barnaby Rudge*, *Dombey and Son*, *David Copperfield*, *Bleak House*, *Hard Times*, and *Little Dorrit*.

2. Dickens's *Book of Memoranda* (begun in 1855) includes a list of more than 125 possible names for fictional characters. Eleven of these names do eventually appear in *Great Expectations*: Magwitch, Provis, Clarriker, Compey (Compeyson), Pumblechook, Horlick (Orlick), Doolge (Dolge), Gannery-Gargery, Wopsell (Wopsle), Hubble, and Skiffins.

3. Stone (1987, 318) describes these three sheets as follows: "one sheet of notes (begun after the last stage had been written) reviews the central, already established chronologies in the novel and the consequent ages of the chief characters as the resolution starts to unfold; a second sheet of succinct memos (written . . . about halfway through the last stage) sets for the chief events and developments to be de-

126

"BROUGHT UP BY HAND"   127

never been quite clear why Dickens forwent the planning stages of *Great Expectations* when such documented planning had been his practice since *Dombey and Son*. Of course, it is well known that the slumping sales of *All the Year Round* (due to Charles Lever's poorly performing novel *A Day's Ride*) prompted Dickens "to strike in"[4] personally—altering the time frame for his "new book" from an originally intended monthly format to a weekly serialization in his own journal. What is not well known and what has not been posited until now is that Dickens had learned from his experiences with *Dombey* and *Bleak House* that he could organize a novel around a governing idiom relatively quickly—especially if he started with the idiom itself.

This may partially explain Dickens's confidence that he could "strike in" with a novel of his own for his magazine with very little time for preparation. Once the decision was made to intervene, he moved quickly. He had to. There were less than eight weeks from the time of his decision to the projected debut of the novel in the December 1, 1860 installment of *All the Year Round*. Sometime in mid-September, he wrote to John Forster that "a very fine, new, and grotesque idea has opened upon me. . . . It so opens out before *me* that I can see the whole of a serial revolving on it, in a most singular and comic manner."[5] By October 4, he assured Forster that he would be finished with "the first two or three weekly parts to-morrow" and that "the name is GREAT EXPECTATIONS." Dickens's swift and resolute determination of the title is another factor that reflects the unusual rapidity and confidence with which his new story materialized. This was not at all typical for an author who had found it difficult to begin many of his most famous works and, once he did, often vacillated for months between as many as twelve titles for those same novels.[6] Then, a mere twenty days after the original letter to Forster, on October 24, Dickens reported to Wilkie Collins that "four weekly numbers have been ground off the wheel, and that at least another must be turned before [they] meet" on November 1. By the end of October, Dickens had exceeded his goal: he had finished the first eight chapters of *Great Expectations*—up to Pip's first visit to Satis House where he meets Miss Havisham and Estella.

---

tailed in the remainder of the unfolding; and a third sheet of notes concerns the Thames tides—for use in constructing the episodes surrounding Magwitch's attempted river escape."

4. Dickens to Forster, in House et al. 1965–2002, ix, 319.

5. House et al. 1965–2002, ix, 310; emphasis original.

6. We know from Dickens's notes that he used up fully ten half sheets on working titles for *Bleak House* and seventeen for what eventually becomes *David Copperfield*. Many are also familiar with how close *Little Dorrit* came to being titled *Nobody's Fault*. The most detailed and fascinating analysis of Dickens's process in this last example is still chapter 9 of Butt and Tillotson (1957), which is titled "From 'Nobody's Fault' to *Little Dorrit*."

128   **CHAPTER 3**

Such unparalleled production in so short a time has subsequently inclined critics to view the novel's genesis in terms of economic exigency.[7] J. Hillis Miller (1958, 250), for example, initiated this line of inquiry when he wrote that "never, perhaps, was the form of a great novel conceived as the response to so practical a concern." Rosenberg (1972, 308) observed "from a strictly commercial point of view . . . necessity, it would appear, was never more pressingly the mother of invention than in producing Pip and Magwitch and Joe: their incubation period seems to have been uniquely brief." Robert Patten (1978, 287) has more recently asserted that "both the timing and the form of the story were . . . determined by economic considerations." I wholeheartedly agree with these long-standing and generally uncontested assessments, but I will argue that a crucial and, indeed, a guiding idiomatic dimension to *Great Expectations* also emerges out of Dickens's formal and economic requirements to move the novel so quickly from its imaginative beginnings to its weekly publication. My aim is to follow the arc of this early imaginative activity, starting with its germinating idiom, which I maintain not only establishes the parameters of the novel's narrative and thematic development but also reflects its very specific sociohistoric moment.[8]

Great Expectations is as complex as any of Dickens's best fiction, but its complexity is heightened by a retrospective first-person narrative viewpoint that necessarily constrains the manner in which he could present an "end-directed" fictional piece via weekly installments. After all, Pip (and presumably Dickens) knows from the opening pages how things will generally turn out in the end for the major characters. Dickens had already told John Forster before he started writing that he had alighted on the central "pivot on which the story will turn" (House et al. 1965–2002, x, 325). Daniel Tyler (2011) maintains that "one of the novel's great accomplishments" is Dickens's "ability to wrest a sense of devastating unknowability of the future from a narrative that he knew, in its larger and smaller structures, its story and its sentences." A principal reason Dickens was able to accomplish this so successfully in *Great Expectations*, and to accomplish it in an expedited compositional time frame with almost no planning, is because he organizes the novel—especially in its early stages— around a probing exploration of the relationship between nature and nurture which reaches its crystallization in the idiomatic phrase of being "brought up by hand." Unlike the idioms that I contend shape Dickens's imaginative processes in earlier novels, an overwhelming majority of readers are likely to re-

---

7. See also Fielding 1961.

8. For an alternate interpretation of the novel in terms of its lack of "planning" notes, see Stone 1970. Herein Stone contends that Dickens had met an "eccentric and wealthy lady" in boyhood and is therefore able to build his story around that haunting memory.

"BROUGHT UP BY HAND"   129

call this expression's prevalence in *Great Expectations*. It is genuinely hard to miss because of its repetition in the mouths of nearly every major character: Pip, Mrs. Joe, Joe, Pumblechook, Estella, Miss Havisham, and so on. As such, this obviousness marks a new stage in Dickens's growing tendency to "imagine" idiomatically. In the earlier novels, Dickens seems to write his way into what eventually becomes their guiding idioms. We shall see, however, as Dickens's conscious tendency to rely on unique idiomatic expressions grows, so too does the subtlety, depth, and even indispensability of his reliance on them.

There is also an important aberration embedded within the uniqueness of the "brought up by hand" idiom that has salient implications for the early stages of *Great Expectations'* composition. Dickens invokes the idiom or a derivation of it more than thirty times in Pip's story, though he *does* use it previously in his oeuvre but only on a single occasion and only in one other novel. That single instance outside of *Great Expectations* occurs in the first sentence of the second chapter of *Oliver Twist* (1837–39) where the narrator tells us, "For the next eight or ten months, Oliver was the victim of a systemic course of treachery and deception—he was brought up by hand" (Dickens [1837–39] 2003, 6). This anomaly is interesting because at the end of the same letter in which Dickens informed Forster that he had arrived at "the pivot on which [*Great Expectations*] will turn," he also wrote, "To be quite sure I had fallen into no unconscious repetitions, I read *David Copperfield* again the other day, and was affected by it to a degree you would hardly believe" (House et al. 1965–2002, ix, 325). The young David Copperfield, like the young Oliver Twist, is also "brought up by hand" in the idiom's sense of physical abuse. At the outset of *David Copperfield*, it is primarily Mr. Murdstone's violent hand that quite literally delivers the euphemistic "firmness" that comes to define his time as David's new stepfather (Dickens [1837–39] 2003, 56). Murdstone frequently hurls books at David, violently clutches his arm, and boxes his ears before the culminating moment at the end of chapter 4 where David reports that Mr. Murdstone "beat me then, as if he would have beaten me to death" (56, 57, 65, 69). Once he is sent away to school at Salem House, of course, it is the cruel hand of Mr. Creakle that continues to make David "flinc[h] with pain" (94). So Dickens uses the idiom once at the outset of *Oliver Twist* and then, ten years later, begins his only other first-person novel by describing in considerable detail how another unfortunate child is figuratively brought up by hand through physical abuse.

At the phrase "no unconscious repetitions," the editors of the *Letters of Charles Dickens*—Madeline House, Graham Storey, Kathleen Tillotson, and Margaret Brown (1965–2002, ix, 325)—attach a footnote that reads, "There are no repetitions of *Copperfield* in Pip's story." I disagree with this dream team of Dickensian scholars but only on the narrow grounds of their footnote's categorical

130   **CHAPTER 3**

certainty. Does not Dickens's act of rereading the physically abusive *David Copperfield* as he starts his only other first-person novel all but guarantee that there will be at least a few unconscious repetitions? This vexing question aside, what, almost more importantly, of its inverse corollary? Are we to take his letter to Forster to mean that there are no unconscious repetitions but that there are *conscious* repetitions in *Great Expectations*? The answers to these important questions are impossible to solve definitively because Dickens left no planning documents for *Great Expectations*. Nonetheless, I argue that the sheer number of times Dickens uses the "brought up by hand" idiom—especially, as we will see, in the opening chapters of the novel—make it almost certain that Dickens identified it early on as a central imaginative conceit, one strong enough to bear the narrative and thematic weight of a new fictional work requiring weekly publication.[9] That said, through the process of idiom absorption we have encountered in other novels, the idiom then soaks into the text in ways that Dickens may or may not have been fully aware. His conscious idiomatic intentions, in other words, do not exhaust the significance of what the idiom *may* mean in many other, perhaps unintentional, contexts. The larger point is that we can learn from these various idiomatic extensions important new things about Dickens's creative process and about this famous novel's historical complexities as well as its thematic anxieties.

The expressions I treat in previous chapters on *Dombey* and *Bleak House* are integral to the way those novels create theme and meaning, but the case with the "brought up by hand" idiom in *Great Expectations* is of an altogether different order. Here, it is the sine qua non of the novel because of its particular narratological and historical indispensability. Pip, Joe, Biddy, Miss Havisham, Estella, Molly, and finally, Magwitch *must* be "brought up by hand" (lacking certain kinds of biological parental care) for the narrative to unfurl the way it does. Moreover, each character's literal hands become potential sites of the utmost importance in connection with the idiom because of the novel's historical timing. This ratcheted-up reliance on the figurative idiom and its literal embodiments thus emerges in lockstep with the exigencies of the novel's publication history and from the evolutionary preoccupations of the cultural moment in which the text was composed week to week. This part of my argument is informed by Mikhail Bakhtin's (1981, 356) notion that "language in its historical life, in its heteroglot development, is full of such potential dialects" that "intersect with one another in a multitude of ways." Even so, un-

---

9. Although my sense is that Dickens was intentional in his choice of the "brought up by hand" idiom to begin the novel, and I agree with Stone (1987, 317) that "Dickens planned the book with great art and subtlety," I disagree with Stone that Dickens "calculated every effect and nuance." Instead, I think that at least some of the idiom's refractions are organically and therefore somewhat unconsciously extended.

"BROUGHT UP BY HAND" 131

like the idioms I treat in other chapters, I am far from the first critic to notice Dickens's repeated use of this idiom (and the general preponderance of "hands") in *Great Expectations*.[10]

But my interest in hands, idiomatic and literal, differs significantly from that of other critics in its historical specificity. I trace how Dickens's sense of being "brought up by hand" affects virtually every dimension of the novel's formal and thematic features but with an emphasis on what Bakhtin (1981, 362, 346; emphasis original) calls the historical contemporaneity of "a specific linguistic consciousness"—against whose common, everyday phrases "reveal even newer *ways to mean.*" We shall see the ways in which the "socioverbal intelligibility" of the idiom in Dickens's first post-Darwinian novel is of a piece with the cultural moment of evolutionary anxiety that riled up so many readers in the 1850s and 1860s. This will allow us to reassess not only how Britons perceived the anxious relationship of nature to nurture via newly popularized evolutionary theories but also how Dickens's own views about such a fundamental relationship informed his changing ideas about religion, class, gender, labor, and race over the course of his career.

Handling Idiomatic Narrative Contingency

As I have posited, there are good reasons to speculate that Dickens knew very early on that he had seized on an idiomatic expression that would prove extremely versatile for the thematic and narratological purposes of a new novel which required accelerated imaginative development. In the twenty days (between October 4 and 24) that Dickens had "push[ed] himself hard" writing the first four weekly numbers (chapters 1–8), he employs variations of the "brought up by hand" idiom fifteen times (out of about thirty more generalized usages in the novel as a whole).[11] It first surfaces—and resurfaces—in

---

10. For a history of criticism focused on hands in *Great Expectations*, if not the actual "brought up by hand" idiom, see Forker (1961–62), Parish (1962), Moore (1965), Stone (1979), W. Cohen (1993), Macleod (2002), and Woloch (2003, 201). I have also contributed to this body critical work on hands in the novel. See Capuano 2015.

11. It is interesting to consider this in conjunction with the letter Dickens wrote to Charles Lever on October 6, 1860 explaining why Lever's work was not performing well in *All the Year Round*: "Whether it is too detached and discursive in its interest for the audience and the form of publication, I can not say positively; but it does not *take hold*" (House et al. 1965–2002, ix, 321–22; emphasis original). Then, a week later (October 15), Dickens followed up: "*For such a purpose,* it does not do what you and I would have it do. I suppose the cause to be, that it does not lay some one strong ground of suspended interest. . . . Some of the best books ever written would not bear the mode of publication; and one of its most

132   **CHAPTER 3**

the opening paragraph of chapter 2, which ran in the first weekly installment of the novel in *All the Year Round* (December 1, 1860):

> My sister, Mrs. Joe Gargery, was more than twenty years older than I, and had established a great reputation with herself and the neighbours because she had *brought me up "by hand."* Having at that time to find out for myself what the expression meant, and knowing her to have a hard and heavy hand, and to be much in the habit of laying it upon her husband as well as upon me, I supposed that Joe Gargery and I were both *brought up by hand.*
>
> She was not a good-looking woman, my sister; and I had a general impression that she must have made Joe Gargery marry her *by hand.* (7–8; emphases mine)

Here, we see, from the idiom's earliest instantiation in the novel, Pip comically but cruelly assigning a figurative, and also quite literal, meaning to his being "brought up by hand." The literal sense of the expression—to be manually spoon- or bottle- as opposed to breastfed—had been known in the British lexicon since at least the mid-eighteenth century when several medical treatises included it in their titles. For example, Michael Underwood's 1784 *A Treatise on the Diseases of Children* was subtitled *"With Directions for the Management of Infants from the Birth; Especially Such as Are Brought Up by Hand."* Charlotte Mitchell (1996) points out that the phrase was used much more widely, however, during the time of *Great Expectations'* publication. Isabella Beeton's (1861, 486) best-selling *Book of Household Management* bears this out. Beeton's popular text contains an entire chapter on nonbreast infant feeding titled, "Rearing by Hand" (1040–44). The following visualizations (figures 14 and 15) provide some additional context for the idiom's growing prevalence in British newspapers and journals at roughly the time Dickens was publishing *Great Expectations.* The spikes that occur in the expression during this time (1859–64) reveal even more of what we already know about Dickens's tendency to anticipate (and participate in) his culture's changing idiomatic lexicon.

However, it is still important to point out that despite the idiom's growing circulation in various contemporary Victorian contexts, it was extremely rare to encounter it in a nineteenth-century British novel. The rarity in this case is actually quite staggering. In my corpus of 3,719 novels, the idiom is used in a *single instance* only twelve times by ten novelists. This underscores two interrelated points. First, Dickens employs the "brought up by hand" idiom more

---

remarkable and aggravating features is, that if you do not fix [affix] the people in the beginning, it is almost impossible to fix them afterwards" (ix, 327–28).

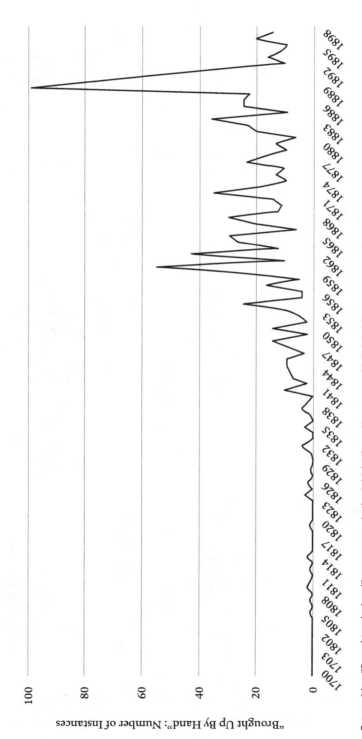

FIGURE 14. "Brought up by hand" appearances in the *British Library Newspapers Digital Archive*

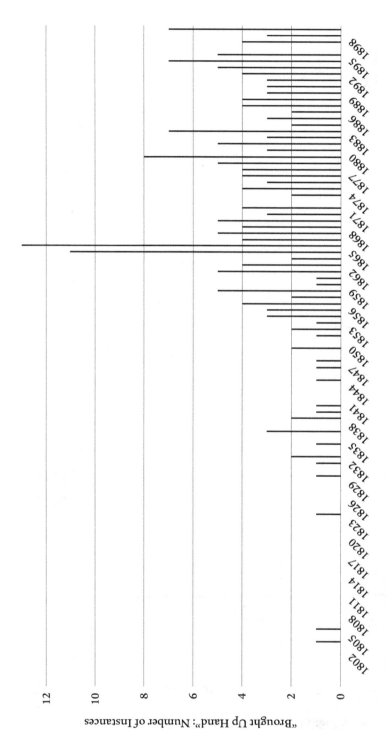

FIGURE 15. "Brought up by hand" appearances in the *British Periodicals* archive

times (15) in *Great Expectations'* first eight chapters than we encounter throughout an entire corpus of 3,700 novels. Second, for every other nineteenth-century novelist in the corpus, the expression is a one-off snippet, a dash of contemporary parlance of the kind Dickens himself first employed it in *Oliver Twist*. This demonstrates what we saw in the introduction's data: that Dickens is in the vanguard of his profession in terms of his use of idiomatic language in his novels. Even as these idiomatic expressions become more and more prevalent (at least in millions of pages of British newspapers and journals), other nineteenth-century novelists do not include them in their fictional discourse. But more important than simply the mere absence of idiomatic language in the case of other novelists is Dickens's ability to imagine idiomatically as he singles out particular workaday body idioms and elevates them to inform—and in the case of *Great Expectations*, to give actual thematic and narrative form—to his most sophisticated novels.

The malleability of the "brought up by hand" idiom serves many purposes for Dickens, all of which lie at the core of *Great Expectations'* earliest and most urgent concerns. To be "brought up by hand" in the sense that Pip assigns it to Mrs. Joe is, of course, to be subject to all manner of violent physical abuse of the kind we witness at the outset of *David Copperfield*. However, the idiom also probes more generally the relationship between nature and culture (nature and nurture) that develops into one of this novel's central preoccupations. As the *British Newspaper* and *British Periodical* data suggest generally—and as Isabella Beeton's best-selling chapter on "Rearing by Hand" reveals more specifically—Victorians were becoming increasingly fascinated by the differences between the "natural" and the "artificial" and particularly by the consequences in terms of the predictability of characterological traits contained therein. These anxieties surrounding the distinctions between the "natural" and the "artificial" may be traced in both the tone and the content of Beeton's (1861, 1040–41; emphasis original) opening sentence, for example: "As we do not for a moment wish to be thought an advocate for an artificial, in preference to the natural course of rearing children, we beg our readers to understand us perfectly on this head; all we desire to prove is the fact that a child *can* be brought up as well on a spoon dietary as the best example to be found of those reared in the breast." Whereas Beeton's focus is clearly with the narrow *physical* ramifications (and possibilities) pertaining to an infant's mode of "natural" or "artificial" feeding, Dickens widens the idiom's scope to explore the relationships between his characters' natures (in the dispositional sense) and their various upbringings to the extent that none of his other novels can match. Simply put, *Great Expectations* is a novel fixated on how the nurture of

136   **CHAPTER 3**

virtually every character relates—both positively and negatively—to her or his dispositional (and eventually biological) "nature."

The most immediate and influential exploration of the relationship between one's disposition and one's upbringing occurs, unquestionably, with Pip. Upon the conclusion of his first devastating visit to Satis House (a scene still a part of Dickens's first twenty-day burst of composition), the adult Pip retrospectively reflects on the cruelties and consequences of what U. C. Knoepflmacher (1988, 83) aptly calls his much older sister's "non-nurturant" upbringing:

> My sister's bringing up had made me sensitive. In the little world in which children have their existence whosoever brings them up, there is nothing so finely perceived and so finely felt, as injustice. It may be only small injustice that the child can be exposed to; but the child is small, and its world is small, and its rocking-horse stands as many hands high, according to scale, as a big-boned Irish hunter. Within myself, I had sustained, from my babyhood, a perpetual conflict with injustice. I had known, from the time when I could speak, that my sister, in her capricious and violent coercion, was unjust to me. I had cherished a profound conviction that her *bringing me up by hand*, gave her no right to bring me up by jerks. Through all my punishments, disgraces, fasts and vigils, and other penitential performances, I had nursed this assurance, and to my communing so much with it, in a solitary and unprotected way, I in a great part refer to the fact that I was morally timid and very sensitive. (Dickens [1860–61] 2003, 63; emphasis mine)

This hindsight reflection on the experience of being "brought up by hand" is not only discerning, pellucid, and heartfelt, but its conclusions are absolutely necessary for the structural and thematic outlay of the entire novel. Specifically, the final sentence where Pip refers to how his bringing up "by hand" made him "morally timid" and "very sensitive" identifies the two major—and eventually converging—strands of narrative tension that must be established from the start in order for the novel to unfold the way it does. His moral timidity prevents him from doing "what [he] knew to be right" as he steals provisions from his house for the escaped convict in the novel's opening scene, thereby tying Pip to a pervasive sense of criminality and guilt that surfaces throughout the novel. Next, Pip's extreme sensitivity blindly rivets him to Estella despite her own heartless "nature" and her repeated warnings for him stay away. Perhaps Herbert Pocket captures the disastrous implications of this sensitive but blind attraction most succinctly when he predicts that the collision of Estella, made hard-hearted by her "bringing-up," with Pip, "whom nature and circumstances made so romantic," will "lead to miserable things" (250). Thus the moral timidity and extreme

"BROUGHT UP BY HAND"   137

sensitivity which Pip directly attributes to his sister's "bringing him up by hand" in the novel's early sections operate as complementary parts of the narrative's most essential machinery.

Dickens's conception of Estella is also refracted, although through a slightly different prism, by the idiom of "being raised by hand." We know, for instance, that Estella comes to Miss Havisham as a "mere baby" and, as such, may have been reared by hand in Beeton's literal sense—a possibility that Estella often reinforces on several important occasions by addressing Havisham coldly as her "Mother by adoption" (304, 364).[12] As is the case with Pip, Dickens makes sure to emphasize with Estella those elements of her rearing that are figuratively more important than the possibility of Miss Havisham's literal feeding by hand rather than by breast. Bringing Estella up "by hand" means to Havisham that she will be able "to mould [Estella] into the form that her wild resentment, spurned affection, and wounded pride, found vengeance in" (399).[13] In an attempt to "save [Estella] from a misery like [her] own," Havisham unabashedly tells Pip, "I adopted her to be loved. I bred her and educated her, to be loved. I developed her into what she is, that she might be loved" and to "wreak revenge on all the male sex" (399, 240, 177). We know, in Estella's own words, that such an upbringing "in that strange house from a mere baby" deprives her of the ability to feel or to dispense feeling in return (267). She has been brought up instead knowing only how "to deceive and entrap" (311).

The important point here is to recognize the extent to which Estella's "bringing up by hand" works to establish and fulfill narratological imperatives—even if we learn of them later in the novel. Just as in the case with the sensitivity and moral timidity that develops in Pip as a result of being "brought up by hand," it is necessary that Estella's upbringing (by hand) makes her haughty and unfeeling. For it is precisely this aspect of her "nature" (which is really the product of her nurture) that establishes one of the novel's principal vectors of narrative tension after Pip's first visit to Satis House. And there is an important symmetry in Dickens's invocation of literal hands in his deployment of the figurative idiom. Mrs. Joe's abusive hand prompts Pip's moral timidity and emotional sensitivity in ways that allow the plot to be intertwined with early

---

12. Estella says that she was "brought up in [Satis] house from a mere baby" (267). Many influential critics assume that Estella was indeed "brought up by hand." See, for example, Peter Brooks's (1984, 134) claim that "Estella's story in fact eventually links all the plots of the novel: Satis House, the aspiration to gentility, the convict identity, . . . bringing up by hand, the law."

13. It is worth noting the cyclical dimension to the Havisham-Estella relationship. There is evidence that the young Havisham was also literally also brought up by hand. Herbert Pocket reveals that the young Havisham was "a spoilt child" because "Her mother died when she was a baby and her father denied her nothing" (180). This spoiling also leaves her completely unprepared to deal with her marital jilting—and so the cycle continues.

138   **CHAPTER 3**

taints of criminality and unrequited love. Similarly, Estella's willfully dismissive behavior toward Pip during their first meeting at Satis House results from "the days when [Estella's] baby intelligence was receiving its first distortions *from Miss Havisham's wasting hands*" (312; emphasis mine).

Even the originating decision that lands the baby Estella in Miss Havisham's wasting hands is predicated on a belief about the ways nurture affects nature. Jaggers tells Pip (in the hypothetical "put the case") that he "held a trust to find a child for an eccentric rich lady to adopt and bring up" (413). He then justifies his decision to have Estella "brought up by hand" in a virtuoso summation of experiential knowledge regarding how profoundly nurture can affect nature:

> Put the case that he [Jaggers] lived in an atmosphere of evil, and that all he saw of children, was, their being generated in great numbers for certain destruction. Put the case that he often saw children solemnly tried at the criminal bar, where they were held up to be seen; put the case that he habitually knew of their being imprisoned, whipped, transported, neglected, cast out, qualified in all ways for the hangman, and growing up to be hanged. Put the case that pretty nigh all the children he saw in his daily business life, he had reason to look upon as so much spawn, to develop into the fish that were to come to his net—to be prosecuted, defended, forsworn, made orphans, be-devilled somehow. . . . Put the case, Pip, that here was one pretty child out of the heap, who could be saved. (413)

As if to corroborate the accuracy of what we might call Jaggers's avant la lettre, thoroughly Foucauldian[14] sociodemographic assessment of Estella's optative fate[15] had he allowed her to be brought up by her mother's instead of "by [Havisham's] hand," the chapter containing this quotation ends with Jaggers's hypothetical come alive in a client's desperate visit to his office. Pip tells us that "Mike, . . . the client whom [he] had seen on the very first day [in Jaggers's office] . . . who, either in his own person or in that of some member of his family, seemed to be always in trouble (which in that place meant Newgate), called to announce that his eldest daughter was taken up on suspicion of shoplifting" (415). Nurtured in such an "atmosphere of evil," the text implies, would have made Mike's daughter's fate and Estella's interchangeable: "both [would]

---

14. Foucault (1977, 255, 297) famously claims that "the delinquent is an institutional product" wherein "the prison fabricates delinquents" by repeatedly "bringing them back, almost inevitably" to its "carceral archipelago," its "carceral net."

15. I am using this phrase in the sense that Andrew Miller (2008) has developed. See, especially, chapter 7, "On Lives Unled." For an analysis of counterfactuals and "the optative mood" in *Great Expectations* (in connection to moral reflection and realism), see A. Miller (2012).

"BROUGHT UP BY HAND"   139

develop into the fish" that would become caught up in what Foucault calls prison's "carceral net" (297). Later in this chapter, we will reassess the extent to which parts of Estella's and other characters' "natures" remain fixed despite various nurturing elements that would seem to make them otherwise.

For now, though, I would like to continue focusing on how the "brought up by hand" idiom helped Dickens imagine and compose *Great Expectations* with uncharacteristic speed and decisiveness from the time of its early conception in October 1860. As Schlicke (1999, 252) and others have observed, "Dickens appears to have proceeded with [this novel] with untroubled confidence." He notes more specifically that "the months during which *Great Expectations* was in progress are singularly free of the cries of anguish which punctuated his composition of other novels" (253). Schlicke arrives at essentially the same conclusion as Rosenberg (1999, 469), who writes that "Dickens seems to have had the main action of *Great Expectations* fairly well mapped out from the early stages of composition and could dispense with most of the working plans as he went along, nor did he bother with the incidental reminders and queries—names, sequence of action, problems of 'tone'—that we find in other *Mem[oranda]*."

I maintain that this is the case in part because Dickens was able to depend so heavily on the deep wells of imaginative possibility that the "brought up by hand" idiom made possible—especially in terms of the novel's abiding interest in the relationships between nature and nurture. So dynamic is the idiom as an originating principle in *Great Expectations* that the expression even has important narratological implications for the conception of those who manage to break the abusive cycle which is so often attendant on it. Joe Gargery, for instance, is without a doubt the best example of a character, conceived of very early on, who manages to resist the cyclical pattern of abusive behavior which governs much of the interaction among characters.[16] In chapter 7, one of the chapters that Dickens composed in his original burst of writing to stay ahead of what he called the "story-demand" of the weekly publication format, Joe tells Pip of how he, too, was "brought up by hand": "My father, Pip. He were given to drink, and when he were overtook with drink, he hammered away at my mother most onmerciful. It were a'most the only hammering he did, indeed, 'xcepting at myself. And he hammered at me with a wigour only to be equaled by the wigour with which he didn't hammer at his anwil" (46).

Unlike Mrs. Joe's conspicuously disdainful association with the idiom, though, Joe believes his father is "good in his hart" and for that reason Joe

---

16. Maya Angelou's twentieth-century formulation that "hurt people hurt people" accurately describes many of the cycles of abuse we encounter in *Great Expectations*, and it is one that emphasizes the role of nurture in peoples' "nature." Joe is an exception as a hurt person who hurts no one.

140   **CHAPTER 3**

works "tolerable hard" (without complaint) to support him until his death (47). Here, Dickens emphasizes the difference between Pip's parental figures by interpolating the story of Joe's upbringing with "the muscular blacksmith's" admission that his marriage to Mrs. Joe has been characterized by the same abusive dimension of the "brought up by hand" expression as Pip: "'A little redness, or a little matter of Bone, here or there, what does it signify to Me?'" (142, 48). The only cycle that Joe repeats, though, is one of protection; he makes clear that he only wishes he could protect Pip and absorb all of Mrs. Joe's physical abuse the way he did for his mother.

And this is crucial for the outlay of the novel because it galvanizes the bond between Joe and Pip as fellow sufferers who both endure being brought up by hand. It also cements a major component of the narrative arc to end where Joe eventually *does* bring Pip up by hand, literally, but in nearly all the positive nurturing senses of the idiom. After Pip falls into a prolonged and delirious state of depressive illness near the end of the novel, it is Joe who nurses (nurtures) Pip back to health—a *re*nurturing that is as definitively restorative as it is decidedly manual:

> I asked for a cooling drink, and the dear hand that gave it to me was Joe's. (463)
>
> I was slow to gain strength, but I did slowly and surely become less weak, and Joe stayed with me, and I fancied I was little Pip again. (466)
>
> In the old unassertive protecting way . . . Joe wrapped me up . . . carried me down to [the carriage], and put me in, as if I were still the small helpless creature to whom he had so abundantly given the wealth of his great *nature*. (466–67; emphasis mine)
>
> For, the tenderness of Joe was so beautifully proportioned to my need, that I was a little child in his hands. (466)
>
> Joe patted the coverlet on my shoulder with his great good hand. (471)
>
> Joe's restoring touch was on my shoulder. (475)

Holly Furneaux (2009, 222) has noted how the "tactile language" of Joe's nursing in this scene "atones for Pip's suffering at the hands of the other members of the forge household" because "it comprises belated reparation for the child Pip's abuse by Mrs. Joe that Joe had felt powerless to prevent." Furthermore, Pip's emphasis on the ways in which Joe's restorative touch induces a return to a childlike state suggests that natures are not immutably defined by the originating acts of nurture. That is, one may be renurtured by people or events that can alter one's supposedly unchanging nature. There's no doubt, for example, that Pip becomes a better person after acknowledging these and other

"BROUGHT UP BY HAND" 141

salutary interactions with Joe's "great nature" throughout the novel (Dickens [1860–61] 2003, 467).

Somewhat paradoxically but no less integral for the novel's larger narrative demands, Magwitch is also a character for whom being "brought up by hand" has important implications. When we meet him just two pages into the opening chapter, his "savage" demeanor and violent behavior—not to mention his escape from the prison ship—ostensibly link him to untold levels of depraved criminality. This is just the point, though; his crimes are as yet untold, and the reader (along with Pip) need to assume the worst in order for the taint of his presence to haunt the text the way it does until he returns from New South Wales later in the novel. Since Dickens availed himself of no working notes, it is of course impossible to know for sure what he had in mind for Magwitch as he composed the first eight chapters in the burst of writing he completed in October 1860. There are clues, however, such as when Pip meets the stranger in the Jolly Bargemen who stares at Pip while stirring his drink "not with a spoon that was brought to him, but *with a file*" (77; emphasis original). This, along with the stranger's gift of "two fat sweltering one-pound notes," renews in Pip the feeling that he is "on secret terms of conspiracy with convicts" (78–79). Other clues from early on are perhaps deliberately misleading. For example, Magwitch's brutal seizure of the "other [escaped] convict" would seem to implicate him in the most vicious and violent criminal activity. Despite this, Joe exhibits his almost to-good-to-be-true humaneness when he says, "God knows you're welcome to it [the stolen pork pie]. . . . We don't know what you have done, but we wouldn't have you starved to death for it, poor miserable fellow-creatur" (40). These lines, and their sentiment, are more important than they might seem because they predict how Magwitch's own experience of being brought up by hand affects his nature and, hence, the true makeup of his nonviolent (bank-note forging) criminality. The unsolicited lie Magwitch offers the constables about stealing food from the Gargerys is certainly, therefore, meant to protect the young Pip in the near term, but it is also an acknowledgment of Pip's help that establishes the longer arc of connection between them at the novel's outset.

Furthermore, Magwitch's lie also aligns with what we eventually learn later regarding the primary motivation for his criminality and, crucially for the argument I am tracing, how he came to be a criminal in the first place—that is, how he was *nurtured* into a life of criminality like the one Jaggers predicts for an orphaned Estella and like the one we witness in his client Mike's eldest daughter. Essentially, Magwitch tells Pip that he steals to eat and to keep himself alive:

142   **CHAPTER 3**

> I've no more notion where I was born, than you have—if so much. I first became aware of myself, down in Essex, a thieving turnips for my living. Summun had run away from me—a man—a tinker—and he'd took the fire with him, and left me wery cold. . . . So fur a I could find, there warn't a soul that see young Abel Magwitch, with as little on him as in him, and either drove him off, or took him up. I was took up, took up, took up, to that extent that I reg'larly grow'd up took up. . . . They always went on agen me about the Devil. But what the Devil was I to do? I must put something into my stomach, mustn't I? (347–47)

Needless to say, this admission verifies that Magwitch, too, was brought up by hand as an orphan (yet another connection to the child Pip). And it explains to some extent how he ended up as Compeyson's not unwitting but also not completely knowledgeable underling—a fact that becomes reiterated in the novel's dominant manual idiom when Magwitch tells Pip that he was "always under [Compeyson's] thumb" (350). Further invocations and narratologically requisite senses of the idiom also have their roots in the novel's opening scenes. Magwitch vows to repay the young Pip's actions with the profits gained from a reformed life of manual work, raising sheep and cattle, in New South Wales by which he can manipulate Pip's London upbringing. Hence the two one-pound notes given to the young Pip "that seemed to be on terms of the warmest intimacy with all the cattle markets in the country" (79). Indeed, as J. Hillis Miller (1958, 250; emphasis original) remarked long ago, "the central motif of *Great Expectations*, the *donnée* with which Dickens began, was the secret manipulation of Pip's life by Magwitch the convict."

As we have seen in each chapter of this study, once Dickens alights on an imaginatively productive idiomatic expression—an idée fixe—to follow Miller's formulation, he (consciously and unconsciously) delights in creating a dynamic array of literal and figurative word playing which extend the idiom's pertinence. À la Wittgentsein (1997, 7), the demarcated "rules" of language are only contextual rules, always awaiting possibility-enhancing creative reformulation through idiomatic wordplay. Such extended wordplay is one of the principal ways idioms become organically absorbed into the novels. In *Great Expectations*, these manual absorptions are legion, such as when Magwitch claims to describe his upbringing (quoted above) "short and handy" (346); when he informs Pip that he made him a gentleman "single-handed" (321); when Joe asks Pip if he will "take [him] in hand in [his] learning" (48); when Pumblechook offers to take Pip "with his own hands to Miss Havisham's" for the first time (52); when Pip is "taken red-handed" to be apprenticed in the forge (104); when Pip suspects Orlick "of having had a hand in that murder-

"BROUGHT UP BY HAND"   143

ous attack" on Mrs. Joe (132); when Herbert renames Pip "Handel" (179); when Pip manages the "whole business" of diverting money to his friend's budding career so "that Herbert had not the least suspicion of [Pip's] hand being in it" (299); when Jaggers tells Pip that his unnamed benefactor will remain a profound secret until "it is the intention of the person to reveal it at first hand by word of mouth" (138); when Wemmick informs Pip that "there's only one Jaggers, and people won't have him at second hand" (199); when we learn that Compeyson "writes [in] fifty hands" (428); and so on. It is as if the text becomes enthralled with its own self-propelling idiomatic energy.

At other times, though, the movement between idiom's literal and figurative registers is much more nuanced. One of the best examples of this kind of idiomatic subtlety centers on Pip's interactions with Joe's comically obnoxious uncle, Pumblechook. Pumblechook exceeds even the indignant Mrs. Joe as the character who most often invokes the "brought up by hand" expression. He uses it eight times, in reference to Pip's upbringing—all but one of which appear in the novel's early chapters. After a litany of reminders of how grateful Pip should be to have been "brought up by hand" and to have had Havisham assume the financial responsibility of apprenticing him to Joe, Pumblechook participates in the physically abusive sense of the original idiom as he violently grabs Pip "by the arm above the elbow," exclaiming that "this boy must be bound, out of hand. . . . Bound out of hand" (104). The repetition here strongly suggests Pumblechook's belief that to be "brought up by hand" is tantamount to being "bound out of hand"—another characteristically brilliant cross-phrasal association that extends the reach of the originating idiom. Indeed, given the barrage of manual idioms that cascade through this scene as Pumblechook expresses his desire to expedite the process of having Pip "bound out of hand" by personally accompanying him to the Magistrates' Hall where the apprenticeship is recorded, Mrs. Joe's sycophantic response seems like another one of Dickens's brilliant inside jokes: "'Goodness knows, Uncle Pumblechook,' said [Mrs. Joe] (*grasping* the money), 'we're deeply *beholden* to you'" (104; emphasis mine).

The comic effect of the idiom becomes physically reembodied later on in the scene when Pumblechook encounters the newly endowed Pip. The former bullying uncle who, just pages earlier, cannot seem to resist an opportunity to remind Pip that he has been "brought up by hand" and therefore must be "bound out of hand," turns suddenly and obsequiously deferential. It is thus comically appropriate that Pumblechook's new state of fawning is embodied in his absurd inability to refrain from shaking Pip's hands:

> "Call it a weakness, if you will," said Mr. Pumblechook, getting up again, "but may I? *may* I—?"

144   **CHAPTER 3**

> It began to be unnecessary to repeat the form of saying he might, so he did it at once. How he ever did it so often without wounding himself with my knife, I don't know.
>
> "And your sister . . . which had the honour of *bringing you up by hand*! It's a sad picter that she's no longer equal to fully understanding the honour. May—" (154; emphasis mine)

Here, the literal and idiomatic movement of the scene recapitulates the narrative movement of the novel. Dickens alternates between, and so conflates, the figurative and the literal dimensions of the novel's principal idiom at the important narrative juncture where Pip's upbringing—"by hand" and "out of hand"—becomes (seemingly) divorced from his new life as a London gentleman. Such alternation between obtrusive and subtle dimensions of the idiomatic register aligns with Bakhtin's (1981, 302) sense of how "common language" operates in prose fiction more generally: "the author exaggerates, now strongly, now weakly, one or another aspect of the 'common language,' sometimes abruptly exposing its inadequacy to its object and sometimes, on the contrary, becoming one with it, maintaining an almost imperceptible distance."

Coming to Grips with Manual Anxieties

No matter how bluntly or subtly *Great Expectations'* dominant idiom appears, however, it is crucial to consider how it partakes of a "common language" in ways that far outstrip its mere familiar linguistic idiomaticity (as an expression of upbringing). The sense of being "brought up by hand," in other words, because of its isolation of a body part that preoccupied ordinary Britons in the 1850s and early 1860s, also had an additional purchase on the collective Victorian conscience that has so far gone unnoticed in critical appraisals of the novel. Dickens was composing *Great Expectations* at a time when readers were transfixed by scientific developments that placed the human hand at the center of urgently interrelated debates about animality, class, race, and gender—all of which have enormous implications for understanding the interconnectedness between nature and nurture invoked by the novel's principal idiomatic formulation. This "socio-verbal intelligibility," contends Bakhtin (1981, 346) in a coincidentally germane formulation, "is very important for coming to grips with the historical life of discourse." Doing so involves thinking about how common language, "the language of everyday life" in Bakhtin's words, "tastes of the context and contexts in which it has lived its socially charged life" (296, 293). Hands, and just about anything relating to them, it turns out, could not have been more socially

"BROUGHT UP BY HAND" 145

charged when Dickens was writing *Great Expectations* in the immediate aftermath of *The Origin of Species'* publication (1859).

Stone's observations concerning Dickens's ability to consolidate seemingly disparate and insignificant resources is as important now for my point about the imaginative richness and timeliness of the "brought up by hand" idiom as they were when he made them over fifty years ago. "Dickens was always a snapper up of unconsidered trifles," Stone (1970, 118) asserted. "His genius made those trifles meaningful, and when an image or association held a special emotional charge for him . . . he unconsciously sifted out every scrap of consonant material scattered through . . . even as a magnet sifts out every scrap of iron scattered through a heap of dust" (118). The body part isolated in the "brought up by hand" idiom did not hold a special emotional charge for Dickens only, though; the entire atmosphere and cultural lexicon of the late 1850s in Britain was disrupted by the magnetic pull of its socially charged life.

It is hardly an overstatement to say that prior historical, philosophical, and religious conceptions of human hands became radically destabilized in the two decades before Dickens composed *Great Expectations*.[17] This is because, with the popularization of new evolutionary theories in the mid-nineteenth century, hands had begun to lose their privileged status as the primary site of physical differentiation between humans and other ("lower") animals. Since time out of mind, philosophical and Western religio-anatomical tradition celebrated the hand as *the* essential feature of human beings. This line of hand privileging among religiously trained anatomists and secular philosophers runs remarkably straight from John Bannister and Charles Bell to Immanuel Kant and Martin Heidegger. Jacques Derrida's (2005a, 185) brilliant coinage of the term *humainisme* (humanualism) aptly locates the importance of this exceptionalized hand to age-old conceptions of human identity. In religious terms, such privileging no doubt stems from the Judeo-Christian Bible's scriptural allusions of divine power that directly connect "the hand of God" to the hands of the Israelites. Think, for instance, of the connection between God ("who created man in His own image" [Genesis 2:27]) "stretching out" His "mighty hand" (Exodus 4:19–20) to Moses's parting of the Red Sea by "stretching out his hand" (Exodus 14:21) over the waters, or "the finger of God" that creates the commandments (Deuteronomy 9:10) and the plagues (Exodus 8:19).[18] The late sixteenth-century work of

---

17. For an analysis of how hands were first radically destabilized from their position as working appendages, see Capuano 2015, especially 1–16.

18. Early prose fiction constantly drew on the power of God's hand. For just a few examples, see *Robinson Crusoe* (1719), where the shipwrecked Crusoe wonders if "the Hand of God" has meted out his punishment; considers whether "the distinguishing goodness of the Hand" saved his life; wavers back to a belief that "the Hand of God [was] against [him]"; and continues to mull over the prospect

CHAPTER 3

FIGURE 16. Contemporary logo for the Royal College of Physicians. Reproduced with permission.

Bannister and the early nineteenth-century work of Bell represent only two salient examples of the long iconographic tendency to link anthropomorphically God and human hands. Bannister's *Historie of Man* (1578) employs the "hand-in-hand" image of God and man, an updated version of which is still used to this day by the Royal College of Physicians (figure 16)—where God's hand emerges from gilded clouds to touch the human hand below. Two hundred and fifty years after Bannister, in 1833, Sir Charles Bell's best-selling Bridgewater Treatise on *The Hand* explored how the "mechanism and vital endowments of the human hand" constituted "the last and best proof of that principle . . . which evinces design in the creation" (38).[19]

Dickens owned a copy of Bell's *Treatise*, which was personally inscribed to him by Bell's widow, Marion.[20] How such an explicitly "design"-oriented text may have influenced Dickens's ideas about hands in *Great Expectations* remains to be seen. For now, it is enough to recognize just how pervasive this overarching sense of anatamo-religious human exceptionalism via God's hand really was through the first part of the nineteenth century. The deeply entrenched, nearly automatic belief in the religio-anatamo-inflected exceptionalism of the human hand began to shift dramatically in the 1840s, however, when a tandem of scientific and fictional work brought anxieties about the relationship between humans and anthropoid apes to a far greater swath of the English public. In 1844, Robert Chambers's *Vestiges of the Natural History of Creation* became one of the first English works to bring a theory of evolu-

---

that "the present Affliction of [his] Circumstances" come from "[God's] Hand" ([1719] 2008, 76–77). At the end of the century, in Fanny Burney's *Evelina* (1778), when Evelina stops Mr. Macartney from committing armed robbery (which she perceives to be a suicide attempt), Macartney proclaims that "the hand of Providence seemed to intervene between me and eternity" ([1788] 2002, 231).

19. For a detailed account of Bell's treatise on *The Hand* in the context of Victorian industrialization, see Capuano 2015, 42–67.

20. See Stonehouse 1935.

tion (known as the development hypothesis) to popular audiences. Because it provided an organic theory for species creation and because it was first published anonymously, *Vestiges* had many detractors. As Adelene Buckland (2021, 430) has shown, though, Dickens was not one of them. He praised the book in an 1848 *Examiner* review for having "created a reading public not exclusively scientific or philosophical" that "awaken[ed] an interest and a spirit of inquiry in many minds" (Dickens 1848, 787). Nonetheless, widespread criticism in other circles seemed only to greater publicize and, hence, to increase the book's popularity. The more *Vestiges* was analyzed at publicly attended scientific meetings and condemned from pulpits and lecture platforms, the more it was borrowed from circulating libraries and read (Secord 2000, 37). A passage from *Vestiges* that would have been alarming to this wider audience was the assertion that human "hands, and other features grounded on by naturalists as characteristic . . . do not differ more from the simidae than bats do from the lemurs" (Chambers [1844] 1994, 266). Chambers's deployment of a double negative here somewhat jumbles the radical controversy of his central point: that the hand may not have been so essentially characteristic of humans after all.

A chilling piece of fiction that appeared at about the same time amplified this uneasy notion that animals, particularly apes, could possess hands. The April 1841 installment of *Graham's Magazine* contained Edgar Allan Poe's ([1841] 1985, 262) story, "The Murders in the Rue Morgue." This new kind of detective tale chronicled a gruesome double murder in the heart of "civilized" Paris, which involved a young woman "strangled to death by manual strength." The detective August Dupin famously solves the mysterious murders only by eventually recognizing that "the dark bruises, and deep indentations of finger nails" (252) match Georges Cuvier's "minute anatomical and generally descriptive account of the large fulvous Ourang-Outang" known for its "gigantic stature . . . prodigious strength and . . . wild ferocity" (264). These narratives featuring what Susan David Bernstein (2001, 255; emphasis original) appropriately calls the *"anxiety of simianation"*—in both their scientific and fictional iterations—reveal that the deep discomfort about the possibility of evolutionary proximity between humans and other primate species was becoming more and more known (and feared) in the decades leading up to the watershed event of Darwin's 1859 *Origin of Species*.[21]

Throughout the 1850s, man's superiority over animals was vehemently debated by what the Victorians referred to as the "development hypothesis." But it

---

21. Since Dickens deeply admired Poe's craft and met him in Philadelphia during his trip to the United States in 1842, it is likely that he would have been aware of this specific strain of manual anxiety before the 1850s. For an exploration of Poe's popularity in England more generally, see Fisher 1999.

148   **CHAPTER 3**

was not until the publication of the *Origin of Species* that a viable mechanism (natural selection) for evolution seriously challenged the notion of a universal law created by a designing and almighty lawgiver. One of the very few passages in the *Origin* containing an explicit reference to human beings discusses, with a similar confidence as Chambers's analogous formulation, how the human hand resembles the extremities of presumably "lower" animals: "the framework of bones [is] the same in the hand of man," Darwin (1996, 387) writes, as in the "wing of a bat, fin of the porpoise, and leg of a horse." Otherwise, Darwin famously excluded human anatomy from his original formulation of natural selection, and yet its conspicuous absence, as Gillian Beer (1983, 59–60) notes, only made the subject more prominent for Victorian readers who considered the *Origin* to be "centrally concerned with man's descent."[22] Theories of racial degeneration multiplied in dizzying fashion as reports of the newly discovered gorilla began to circulate among scientists. A full gorilla skeleton reached the British Zoological Society in 1851 and an entire gorilla body (pickled in alcohol) in 1858. These events, along with the popular African travel books of Paul du Chaillu, helped make gorillas a common topic for the general public in England during the late 1850s. Propelled by Darwin's new theory of evolution, the preoccupation with a "missing link" between the human and the gorilla developed into a full-fledged cultural phenomenon. Virtually every British newspaper and magazine, including Dickens's own, printed stories referencing "man's nearest relation."[23]

---

22. Scholars have continued to interpret the general nineteenth-century "evolution question" similarly. Most recently, for example, Pamela Gilbert (2019, 6) has noted how "the body became the center of an anxious elaboration of the human, from which the consideration of its shadow—the savage, the animal, the irrational—was never far." My point is that this anxiety was never closer than when it involved specific questions about the hand.

23. Because *Great Expectations* has been conspicuously absent from Darwinian criticism (see footnote 28 for specifics), I feel that is important to recall Welsh's (1971, 117) warning not to "underestimate the degree to which Dickens was aware of the intellectual ferment of his time." There is no doubt that the major ferment at the time of *Great Expectations'* composition was the publication of Darwin's *On the Origin of Species*. I call attention to this here because in order to make an evolutionary-based argument about the specific ways the manual idiom operates in this novel, it is necessary to note the many foundational ways that *Great Expectations* is a deeply "Darwinian" text. In November 1859, Charles Darwin had punctuated decades of evolutionary debate with the publication of *On the Origin of Species by Means of Natural Selection, or, the Preservation of Favoured Races in the Struggle for Life*. The inclusion of the full title is relevant because its driving emphasis on *"the Struggle for Life"* (mentioned by Darwin more than fifty times in the first edition) informs the most basic dimensions of *Great Expectations*. On the novel's first page, for instance, Pip refers to his "five little brothers . . . who gave up trying to get a living, exceedingly early in that universal struggle" (3), describes the convicts battling at the bottom of the ditch shortly thereafter as "bleeding and panting and struggling" (36), and refers to his bloody-knuckled fight with the "pale young gentleman" at Satis House as "the late struggle" (94). The sense of strength required in the struggle for dominance also forms the premise of Jaggers's speculation regarding the marriage of Bentley Drummle and Estella. Jaggers frames even their romantic relationship as a struggle for "supremacy" where "the stronger will win in the end" (389, 390). Moreover, the random and chance contingencies necessary for the operation of Darwin's theory of natural selection paradoxically "order" the events in

"BROUGHT UP BY HAND"   149

What propelled the Victorian fascination with gorillas was how much these newly discovered animals resembled humans in various ways. Du Chaillu's (1861, 60) account of his first gorilla sighting confirms the extent to which their general stature invoked comparisons to humans: "they looked fearfully like hairy men," he wrote. Du Chaillu, building on Darwin's interest in the "framework of bones," was even more unsettled to discover how closely gorillas resembled humans from a skeletal perspective. His detailed anatomical comparisons revealed similarities in the cranium, spine, and pelvis, but they repeatedly fixated on the exact same number of bones (twenty-seven) in the human and gorilla hand (418). These comparisons far more explicitly amplified what had been somewhat buried in Chambers's *Vestiges* and Darwin's *Origins*: that the human hand's supposedly divinely ordained ("designed") exceptionality was not so exceptional after all in the larger animal kingdom.[24]

Indeed, the horror for many for many Victorians in the years immediately following Darwin's *Origin* was the possibility that God may have had no hand at all in the order of the natural world. This was clearly a topic in which Dickens took a particular interest, though it is not often remarked upon because of his fierce critiques of overt religiosity in other, mostly secular social contexts.[25] He nonetheless exhibits throughout his fictional career (up to *Great*

Great Expectations more explicitly than in any other Dickensian novel. Pip famously muses on how his life would have unfolded had it not been for that one "memorable day" when he first encounters Miss Havisham and Estella: "Imagine one selected day struck out of it, and think how different its course would have been" (72). But then, of course, there is also "that chance intercourse" with the Magwitch (who later declares "What odds?") which opens the novel (316, 319), the uncertainty Pip feels "exposed to hundreds of chances" in his gentlemanly life (248), and his eventual realization of the "coincidence" that Jaggers just simply happens to be the lawyer of both Miss Havisham and Magwitch (359). Given these alignments with the evolutionary ferment of the 1850s, it is neither coincidental nor surprising that *Great Expectations* configures many of its human characters on a hierarchical scale of animality. Magwitch, so cold and wet on the marshes where he spends the night waiting for assistance, expresses a desire to be better adapted to his environment, exclaiming, "I wish I was a frog. Or a eel!" (6). This establishes a pattern in the text where criminals (and as we shall see, manual workers) are represented "as if they were lower animals" (227), "wild beasts" (36, 93), dogs (19), snakes (320), and so on. Orlick "slouches" (112, 118, way more) "in his stagnant way" (131) from "the mud and ooze" (131, 422), and Pip, after the fight with the pale young gentleman, even "regard[s] [him]self . . . as a species of savage young wolf, or other wild beast" (92–93). Perhaps most tellingly, though, Mrs. Joe "pounce[s] upon [Pip], like an eagle on a lamb" (52). Thus, the character on whom Dickens mostly closely focuses the association of the "brought up by hand" idiom raises Pip not only by the jerks and blows of her hands but by a violent talon clamping associated with a ferocious bird of prey.

24. The Victorian public feared descent even as evolutionary biologists altered their definitions of anatomical species development to, in effect, reassert human supremacy with different rhetoric and body parts. Herbert Spencer (1872, 361; emphasis mine), for example, began to emphasize the "*perfection* of the tactile apparatus*" in human as compared to ape hands while Richard Owen argued for the cerebral primacy of man—a position that would later form the basis of the vituperative public arguments between Samuel Wilberforce and Thomas Huxley.

25. As Dennis Walder (1981) has noted, Dickens had a complex relationship with contemporary religion.

150   **CHAPTER 3**

Expectations) a definitive belief in the designing hand of God and, by extension, the exceptionalism embodied in the human hand. For example, in *The Old Curiosity Shop* (1840–41), "Nature's hand" and "Heaven's work" combine to produce the angelic character of Little Nell, who is often described as "a creature fresh from the hand of God" (389, 401, 538). Even in his most famous novel about "hands," *Hard Times* (1854), Dickens channels Charles Bell in asserting that "the forest of [mechanized] looms" in Coketown are nothing compared to the divinely constructed human hands that operate them. "Never fear, good people of an anxious turn of mind," says the narrator, "that Art will consign Nature to oblivion. Set anywhere, side by side, the work of God and the work of man; and the former, even though it be a troop of Hands of very small account, will gain in dignity from the comparison" ([1854] 2003, 65). Perhaps sentiments like these account for why Dickens received a year later, in 1855, a special sixth edition copy of Sir Charles Bell's Bridgewater Treatise on *The Hand: Its Mechanism and Endowments as Evincing Design* inscribed "with kind regards from Marion Bell" (the author's widow).

But Bell's treatise, which advocated for a perfect, God-given human hand, shared shelf space in Dickens's library at Gad's Hill alongside Chambers's *Vestiges of Creation*, Darwin's *Origin of Species*, and Du Chaillu's *Explorations and Adventures in Equatorial Africa*—inscribed "To Charles Dickens, Esq., with the author's kind remembrances"—and Richard Owen's *Memoir on the Gorilla*.[26] We shall see, then, that if Dickens was not "of an anxious turn of mind" regarding the manufacturing status of human hands while writing *Hard Times*, he was considerably more anxious about their evolutionary status while composing *Great Expectations* six years later.

As I have suggested in discussing Poe's "The Murders in the Rue Morgue," the uneasy Victorian fascination with the gorilla was heightened by the fact that the animal's deadly ferocity was distinctly *not* a matter of redness in tooth and claw. The reports coming back to England in the late 1850s, like Poe's story, dramatized how the gorilla attacked not with its formidable teeth but rather with its bare "hands." Du Chaillu (1861, 62) had described this supposed method of attack in considerable detail: "This animal lies in wait in the lower branches of trees, watching for people to go to and fro; and, when one passes sufficiently near, grasps the luckless fellow with his ["lower hands"], and draws him up into the tree, where he quietly chokes him." Moreover, a prominent piece in *Punch* magazine called "The Missing Link" (1862, 165) bluntly revealed how quickly and readily Britons co-opted contemporary evolutionary theory for colonial purposes in order to help differentiate themselves from their

---

26. See Stonehouse 1935.

"lower" Irish subjects: "A gulf, certainly, does appear to yawn between the Gorilla and the Negro. The woods and wilds of Africa do not exhibit an example of any intermediate animal. But this, as in many other cases, philosophers go vainly searching abroad for that which they would readily find if they sought it at home. A creature manifestly between the Gorilla and the Negro is to be met within some of the lowest districts of London and Liverpool by adventurous explorers. It comes from Ireland, whence it has contrived to migrate; it belongs to a tribe of Irish savages."

L. Perry Curtis, Patrick Brantlinger, and many others have demonstrated that Victorians readily adopted this rhetoric of biological hierarchy to draw connections between the simian and the Irish—a lower "race" regarded as subhuman in the English imagination long before Darwin. Therefore, the idea of an intermediary animal—one that Thomas Carlyle in *Chartism* (1839) believed had "sunk from decent manhood to squalid apehood"—seemed to fit all too well given the supposedly Irish predilection for violence and physical labor (Carlyle 1842, 28). Their status as Europe's only Caucasian "savages" was deeply entrenched by the time Carlyle wrote that the "uncivilized" Irishman "is there to undertake all work that can be done by mere strength of hand . . . for wages that will purchase him potatoes" (28). This description of physically demanding manual labor became literalized shortly thereafter in Richard Beamish's popular work, the *Psychonomy of the Hand* (1843). What many Victorians thought of as a uniquely Irish combination of racial otherness, violence, and capacity for manual labor may be seen in the life-size "tracings of living hands" which accompanied every edition of Beamish's text through the 1850s and 1860s.

These full-page plates appeared at the end of Beamish's *Psychonomy*, and readers were encouraged to trace their own hands on top of them as a means of direct physical comparison. The affiliation between the gorilla and the manual-laboring navvy is implied both by proximity (plate numbers 1 and 3 of 30) and by shape, but also by nationality and race. Beamish (1843, 6) states that "the more the palm dominates over the fingers in the hand of man, the more the character approaches to that of the brute, with instincts low and degrading." Since the discovery of gorillas (figure 17) and the massive influx of Irish navvies (figure 18) into the British workforce occurred more or less simultaneously, large palms and short powerful fingers were interpreted not only as indicators of a "natural" propensity to handle shovels, pickaxes, and barrows but also as signs of a racialized animality itself. The fact that Beamish's hand plates do not include color—as they easily could have at least in terms of darker shading—supports Pamela Gilbert's (2019, 283) recent finding that "color was far less important than skeletal structure to racial distinctions" in England and the Continent (as opposed to the United States).

CHAPTER 3

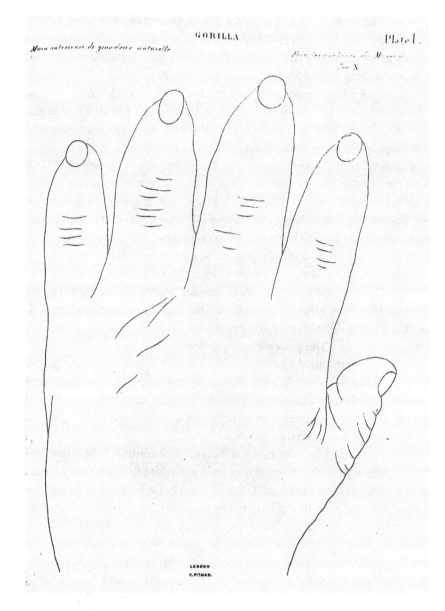

FIGURE 17. Beamish's gorilla hand plate

There is also more than ample evidence that Dickens followed Carlyle in his belief that the Irish were "a racially repellent group" (David 2002, 91). During his visit to America in 1842, Dickens took time out from his denunciation of the racist brutality and injustice of chattel slavery to describe an Irish colony in the Catskill mountains as decidedly "ruinous and filthy," claiming with

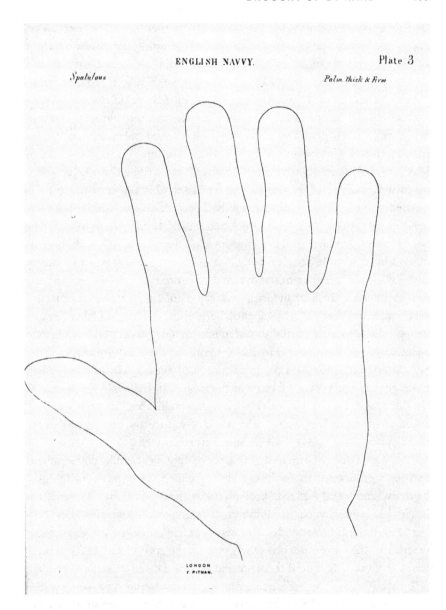

FIGURE 18. Beamish's navy hand plate

a particular deafness to their status as desperate refugees from a famine-ravished Ireland that they were all "wallowing together" in a mess of pigs, dogs, pots, dunghills, refuse, straw, and standing water (91). This disparaging language regarding the Irish reappears when Oliver Twist runs away to London. The young Oliver's first impressions of the outskirts' "wallowing" "filth"

154   CHAPTER 3

are unmistakably connected to the Irish who live there (63). The narrator re-marks that "the lowest orders of Irish (who are generally the lowest orders of anything) were wrangling with might and main"—this last part itself a centuries-old French idiom linking laboring power ("might") to Irish hands ("main"). Dickens's 1853 piece titled "The Noble Savage" in *Household Words* makes similar comparisons. Here, Dickens implies that the "plunging and tear-ing" Zulu "Kaffirs" would be "extremely well received and understood [in the Irish House of Commons] at Cork" (1853, 338–39). Then at the end of May 1859, only four months before Dickens started writing *Great Expectations*, his own magazine (*All the Year Round*) set exactly this aspect of the gorilla's reputed manual savagery against the backdrop of middle-class industrious-ness in a piece titled "Our Nearest Relation" (1859, 114; emphasis mine): "The honey-making, architectural bee, low down on the scale of life, with its insig-nificant head, its little boneless body, and gauzy wing, is our type of industry and skill: while this apex in the pyramid of brute creation [the gorilla], the near approach to the human form, what can it do? *The great hands have no skill but to clutch and strangle.*" Thus apehood, Irishness, and manual labor became biologically constituent in the Victorian imagination just as Dickens began to conceive of the "brought up by hand" idiom for *Great Expectations* in Octo-ber 1860. Commenting on the proliferation of similar articles containing a more general evolutionary focus which appeared in *Household Words* and *All the Year Round*, George Levine (1986, 256) maintains that "Dickens was both aware of what was happening in the world of science and convinced that the new developments had real significance for ordinary life."[27]

My point is that Dickens's interest in contemporary scientific developments and their pertinence to "ordinary life" extended the various meanings—figurative and literal—of the "brought up by hand" idiom he alighted on as he charged himself to begin composing *Great Expectations* so quickly in Octo-ber 1860. Indeed, just months after his magazine published the above piece describing "the portentous power of grasp" in the gorilla hand, Dickens pred-icates an absolutely crucial thematic and narrative detail—Estella's "brought up by hand" status—on her estranged biological relationship to a working-class Irish character (Molly) who murders a rival twice her size by strangling her with her bare hands: "held by the throat at last and choked," as Wemmick tells

---

27. More recently, Laura Peters (2013, 5) has affixed Dickens's "formal" declaration of his avid inter-est in science of his day to his publication of "Review: *The Poetry of Science*" for *The Examiner* in 1848. I would add that Dickens was particularly interested in Darwinian evolutionary ideas in the months *dur-ing* his composition of *Great Expectations*. His journal *All the Year Round* published three anonymous but explicitly Darwin-focused articles more or less immediately after the *Origin* debuted in November 1859: "Species" (June 2, 1860); "Natural Selection" (July 7, 1860); "Transmutation of Species" (March 9, 1861).

Pip (Dickens [1860–61] 2003, 393). Such racialized parallels would be less worthy of identification if Dickens had not committed himself to two things. First, to beginning the novel with an emphasis on the various ramifications resulting from idiomatic and literal nurture "by hand" and second, to conspicuously high-lighting Molly's Irishness throughout the text. In terms of the latter, Molly is known as a traditionally lower-class Irish nickname for the proper name Mary, and Wemmick's early indication to Pip that she has "some gypsy blood in her" is a powerful confirmation of Terry Eagleton's (1995, 3) notion that Gypsy blood in the nineteenth-century novel was "simply an English way of saying that [the character] is quite possibly Irish."

The possibility of Molly's Irishness, as well at its relation to the "brought up by hand" idiom, moves about as close as it can to probability, though, if we consider a piece by William Moy Thomas that Dickens oversaw in a July 1853 edition of *Household Words*. The narrator in the article, titled "Market Gardens," is led through a tour of the agricultural fields outside of London where the crops are (manually) "cultivated by the spade" rather than "by the plough" (Thomas 1853, 409). We learn from the narrator of the only individually named worker in the piece under these circumstances: "A number of women are pull-ing gigantic rhubarb stalks, and loading barrows. I observe a considerable dif-ference in the rapidity with which some do their work; and my conductor conforms my observation. 'That young Irishwoman, yonder,' he says, 'with her gown pinned up behind, and her bare arms, as brown as mahogany, will get through twice as much work in a day as some of our [British] people. We give her two shillings a day; most of them get only a shilling or eighteenpence. *How are you, Molly?*'" (413; emphasis mine). Then, on the next page, the narrator marvels at an exceptional-looking plot where cauliflowers are flourishing. The conductor farmer explains that "each one, I may say, is regularly nursed and *brought up by hand*" (414; emphasis mine). Did Dickens consciously recall the details of this article, right down to the (Irish) name of the female Irish worker, seven years later when he set out to write a story prominently featuring the same idiom and the powerful working hands of a lawyer's housekeeper on which a crucial part of the novel depends? Maybe, maybe not. But the fact that he edited this piece, no matter what he consciously recalled when he was com-posing *Great Expectations*, is potentially important and relevant despite our in-ability to make conclusively determinate claims about it.

What we do know conclusively is that Dickens held prejudicial views toward the Irish, which are evident in his earliest fiction and that, far closer to his be-ginning *Great Expectations*—in late May 1859—he edited a four-page article in *All the Year Round* on "Our Nearest Relation" (1859, 112) in which "the recently discovered Gorilla" shares a kind of wanton predilection for violence with the

156   **CHAPTER 3**

Irish. These specifics should also be situated in the much larger context of how often the English saw rebelliousness and violence "as an Irish character flaw" in general (Brantlinger 2011, 138).

Aviva Briefel (2015, 2, 22) has shown how "racialized hands were vital to literary portrayals of [British] colonial relationships" as they more and more "became productive sites for the Victorian 'desire for race' to be played out." This plays out in *Great Expectations* most vividly through Jaggers's relationship with his Irish housekeeper who is referred to on five occasions as "a wild beast tamed" (Dickens [1860–61] 2003, 202, 392, 394). The convergence of Molly's racialized ethnicity, capacity for rebellion, and violent "nature" reaches its most ideological, subjective, and narratological distillation in the dramatic scene where Jaggers pins her hands to the table for Pip and the other gentlemen in training to view: "'There's power here,' said Mr. Jaggers, coolly tracing out the sinews [of Molly's hand] with his forefinger. 'Very few men have the power . . . this woman has. It's remarkable *what force of grip there is in these hands*. I have had occasion to notice many hands; but I never saw anything stronger in that respect, man's or woman's, than these'" (214; emphasis mine). Jaggers's compulsive and seemingly bizarre admiration of Molly's hands further anatomizes (literalizes) the general association of criminal behavior with animality as we have seen associated with both Magwitch and Pip, but it also establishes a pivotal fulcrum in the novel's tightly plotted narrative. To fulfill the necessities of both theme and plot, Molly *must* be biologically connected to both Magwitch and Estella—but we (readers), like the as-yet unaware Pip, must not be able to predict such a narrative-cinching connection. The "remarkable force of grip" in Molly's hands must be, in the novel's early to late-middle stages, an untraceable allusion to her previous crime *and* the centerpiece to Pip's eventual discovery of Estella's "origins"—her supposedly true "nature" beyond Havisham's nurture. As such, this manual affiliation adds new and refracted meanings to the text's central concern with the relationships between nature and nurture first expressed idiomatically in the various scenarios where so many characters are "brought up by hand."

A significant component of this particular idiom in *Great Expectations* resides in the anxiousness it engenders. Put more specifically, the idiom and its attendant focus on literal hands becomes part and parcel the culture's anxiety regarding the fragility of the barrier between the human and the animal that had been most recently, and most profoundly, destabilized by Darwin's theory of interconnection between species—the recognition of which constitutes an almost inexplicable gap in Dickensian evolutionary criticism.[28] Thus, the "nurture" of being

---

28. Despite the pioneering work of Beer and Levine in the 1980s which broke open the field of Darwinian literary criticism, it is surprising that *Great Expectations* has received almost no evolutionary-

"brought up by hand" is never far away from the violence it represents in Pip's (and Joe's, Magwitch's, and Estella's) upbringing. At the same time the text is concerned with the nature of nurture, it is also preoccupied by the "animalistic" capabilities of the hand that were blurring the heretofore distinct line between human and animal. In this sense, the specter of manual strength and strangulation that becomes explicitly articulated in the story of Molly's crime also haunts the novel in a series of other scenarios involving characters of all classes. Consider, for instance, how Matthew Pocket's sister Camilla's feigned and overwrought concern for Miss Havisham's health manifests itself as a melodramatic weakness in her own throat. "Put[ting] her hand to her throat," Camilla claims to be subject to so many anxious "chokings" that Pip wonders if she will "drop and choke when out of view" (Dickens [1860–61] 2003, 86, 88). Magwitch assures the constables in the opening scenes that had he not been stopped, he would have strangled Compeyson in the ditch: "I'd have held to him with that grip, that you should have found him [dead] in my hold" (37). Later in the narrative when Pip is attacked in the limekiln, the perpetually "slouching" Orlick gloats over his ability destroy Pip at any time by strangling him: "I could have took your weazen [throat] betwixt this finger and thumb and chucked [choked] you away dead" (428). The pervasive specter of strangulation even appears in genteel contexts far removed from immediate physical violence such as when Pip, in conversation with Herbert about their mounting debts, makes an analogy between facing their financial "affairs" and "tak[ing] the foe by the throat" (275).

---

centered attention—especially considering the fact that it is Dickens's first novel after the publication of the *Origin*. As the post-colonic title of Beer's *Darwin's Plots* (1983) indicates, *Evolutionary Narrative in Darwin, George Eliot, and Nineteenth-Century Fiction*, Dickens is not a central concern of this groundbreaking text. When Beer (1983, 42) does discuss Dickens, though, it is in relation to *Bleak House* where "the sense that everything is connected" leads to a realization that all of the characters are "interdependent." Even in her later book *Open Fields: Science in Cultural Encounter*, Beer (1996, 141) does not mention *Great Expectations*—continuing instead to identify *Bleak House* as the novel where "wickedness as well as danger" emerges from the "refus[al]" to recognize that people are connected." Levine's *Darwin and the Novelists* (1988) still stands as the definitive work on Dickens in relation to Darwinian evolutionary thought. However, the chapter in this book titled "Dickens and Darwin" contains only two brief references to *Great Expectations* whereas Levine treats just about every *other* Dickens novel extensively and masterfully in terms of Darwin. Commenting on Dickens's admittedly bizarre defense of Krook's death by "spontaneous combustion" in *Bleak House*, Danny Hack (1999, 134) has maintained that "few critics put much stock in Dickens's scientific sophistication." Jay Clayton (2003, 95) acknowledges that Dickens maintained a keen interest in science throughout his career but believes that this "has been overlooked because none of his concerns figured prominently in evolutionary thinking." Grace Moore (2004) makes no mention of *Great Expectations'* evolutionary context in *Dickens and Empire: Discourses of Class, Race and Colonialism in the Works of Charles Dickens*, nor does Priti Joshi (2011, 292–300) in her chapter on "Race" in *Charles Dickens in Context*. Ivan Kreilkamp's (2007, 81–94) "Dying like a Dog in *Great Expectations*" mentions Darwin only in a single footnote. More recently, Laura Peters (2013), in *Dickens and Race*, entirely excludes *Great Expectations*. For a notable exception to this general critical tendency to bypass the connections between *Great Expectations* and the circulation of contemporary evolutionary ideas, see Morgentaler 1998.

158   CHAPTER 3

It is this emphasis on clutching power—transferred from "animals" to humans—and embedded within the idiomaticity of the text's dominant expression of the relationship between nature and nurture that extends the imaginative horizon by which Dickens composed this novel so quickly, so efficiently, and most importantly, so in sync with his era's evolutionary interests and concerns. As a result, the idiomatic expression of being "brought up by hand" proved wide enough to include the imaginative coordinates around which nearly all of the novel's complicated events and themes could be mapped. Such a fecund and timely linking of idiomatic potential and cultural preoccupation uniquely fits Bakhtin's (1981, 356–57) most Darwinian model for language alteration: "Language in its historical life, in its heteroglot development, is full of such potential dialects: they intersect one another in a multitude of ways; some fail to develop, some die off, but others blossom into authentic languages. We repeat: language is something that is historically real, a process of heteroglot development, a process teeming with future and former languages." The fact that so much of *Great Expectations*' characterizations, themes, and plotting depend on the *actual* hands that are doing the "bringing up" means, in Bakhtinian terms, that Dickens had alighted on "a stage of genius—*a sharpened dialogic relationship to the word*—that in turn uncover[ed] fresh aspects within the word" or idiom (352; emphasis original). No matter how deep Dickens's conscious intention goes in *Great Expectations*, his creation of a sharpened and yet expanded dialogic relationship between actual hands and the novel's governing idiomatic expression reveals his exceptional ability to align idiomaticity with contemporaneity that we have encountered in previous chapters.

One way to calibrate the contemporaneousness of the Victorian concern with both gendered and "wild" hands is to consider the seemingly outré relationship between the real-life Arthur Munby and his servant-cum-wife, Hannah Culliwick. The Cambridge-educated Munby never worked with anything heavier than a pen, yet his diaries are replete with an eccentric attraction to the animalistic features of working female hands. Historians and literary critics have acknowledged the value of Munby's diaries to constructions of mid-nineteenth-century gender and class anxieties but surprisingly not in relation to *Great Expectations* where these concerns surface as a particular form of evolutionary uneasiness in the immediate wake of the publication of *Origin of Species*.[29] Consider the eerie similarity between the dramatic hand-trapping

---

29. The key texts in relation to Munby and Culliwick are Hudson (1972) and Davidoff (1979). More recent studies of this relationship, not in conjunction with *Great Expectations*, include Stanley (1986), Pollock (1993–94), McClintock (1995), and Reay (2002).

scene at Jaggers's house and Munby's diary recollection of an encounter with a servant in 1861:

> I asked her to show me her hand. Staring at me in blank astonishment, she obeyed, and held out her right hand for me to look at. *And certainly, I never saw such a hand as hers, either in man or woman.* They were large and thick & broad, with big rude fingers and bony thumbs—but that was not very remarkable. . . . It was in her palms that she was unrivalled: and such palms! The whole interior of each hand, from the wrist to the finger-tips, was hoofed with a thick sheet of horn. . . . What must be the result to a woman of carrying about her always, instead of a true human hand, such a brutal excrescence at this? (Quoted in Reay 2002, 99–100, 128; emphasis mine)

Since there are no documented links between Dickens and Munby (not to mention the near simultaneousness of Dickens's creation of the Jaggers-Molly relationship), it would be a mistake to dismiss their focus on powerful female hands as isolated instances of bizarre social deviance. Instead, if we view this kind of manual perversion as a culturally central phenomenon, it is possible to recognize the ways in which the deviant hand emerged as an important site of tension between new scientific theories of interconnectedness and a social heterodoxy that assigned innate, unalterable characteristics to gender, class, and animality. In a novel inordinately concerned with the precariousness of so many of these identities, *Great Expectations'* literal and idiomatic attention to hands exposes the disturbingly relational—not immutable—nature of such categories.

Narrative Sleights of Hand

The fact that the novel's most "wild" and violent hands (Molly's) are biologically connected to its most refined hands (Estella's) uncovers fresh aspects latent within the original "brought up by hand" idiom by making the expression's literal body part a prime agent in the novel's plot as well as a site of collapsed social signification. Here, I wish to build on Peter Brooks's (1984, 24) influential claim that plotting is "the central vehicle and armature of meaning" in *Great Expectations* by exploring how the text's aesthetics of embodiment make meaning not only carnal as Brooks notes but, even more specifically, manual. The semioticization of the body idiom eventually converges with the somaticization of the story line in Pip's gradual but then abrupt realization that Molly's "hands [are] Estella's hands" (Dickens [1860–61] 2003, 391).

160   **CHAPTER 3**

This crucial recognition by way of Molly's and Estella's hands is all the more worthy of attention because of its conspicuous departure from a long line of facially based character identifications that prevail in Dickens's previous fiction. Perhaps the earliest example of Dickens's tendency to locate buried filial relationships among characters in terms of faciality occurs in *Oliver Twist* (1837–39), with Mr. Brownlow's linkage of Oliver and his mother through what the narrator calls "the affair of the picture" ([1837–39] 2003, 106). It begins when the gentleman arrives at the jail where Oliver is held for supposedly picking Mr. Brownlow's pocket. Confused by something about Oliver's appearance that jogs his memory, Brownlow says, "'There is something in that boy's face. . . . God bless my soul! where have I seen something like that look before?'" (80). We soon learn that "after musing for some minutes, the old gentleman walked with the same meditative face into a back ante-room opening from the yard; and there, retiring into a corner, called up before his mind's eye a vast amphitheatre of faces over which a dusky curtain had hung for many years" (80). Brownlow believes the dim feeling of recognition he experiences "must be [his] imagination" until he enters a housekeeper's sitting room and encounters Oliver "fix[ing] his eyes most intently on a portrait" with a "look of awe" (80, 90). The painting is, of course, a portrait of Oliver's biological mother, and it is only then that Mr. Brownlow puts the connection together: "he pointed hastily to the picture above Oliver's head, and then to the boy's face. There was its living copy,—the eyes, the head, the mouth: every feature was the same" (93).

A similar process occurs in *Bleak House* (1852–53) when Guppy connects Esther's face with the portrait of Lady Dedlock he encounters on his first visit to Chesney Wold—a connection that spurs his hasty marriage proposal ([1852–53] 2003, 110–12). The resemblance between Lady Dedlock's face and her biological daughter's is also what sends Esther into a state of "unaccountable agitation" on confronting her likeness in a church gathering at the estate: "But why her face should be, in a confused way, like a broken glass to me, in which I saw scraps of old remembrances; and why I should be so fluttered and troubled (for I was still), by having casually met her eyes; I could not think" (292). Throughout the middle sections of the novel, Esther says, "her [Lady Dedlock's] face retained the same influence on me as at first" (366). And in the arresting scene in which Lady Dedlock finally reveals her true identity as Esther's mother, Dickens isolates the face, above all else, as the primary site of identification. Here is Esther's account of the experience: "I was rendered motionless. Not so much by her hurried gesture of entreaty, not so much by her quick advance and outstretched hands, not so much by the great change in

"BROUGHT UP BY HAND" 161

her manner, and the absence of her haughty self-restraint, *as by something in her face* that I had pined for and dreamed of when I was a little child; something I had never seen in any face" (578; emphasis mine). This tendency to connect improbable affiliations among his characters by way of facial features was so prevalent, in fact, that it eventually led G. H. Lewes (1872b, 152) to ascribe the "coincidences" of countenance in Dickens's novels to an overabundance of physiognomy books in his Doughty Street library. As we have already seen, though, by the time Dickens began to compose *Great Expectations* at Gad's Hill, his study's bookshelves were also stocked with many important books by Bell, Chambers, Darwin, Owen, and Du Chaillu, all of which focused to some degree on the natural history of manual appendages.

Dickens builds on the dim but accruing senses of filial identification that appear in *Oliver Twist* and *Bleak House*, but he doubles down on them in *Great Expectations*' hands. And here, the shift in the primary mode of identification between Molly and Estella from faces to hands is essential. Not only is it an extension of the "brought up by hand" idiom that simultaneously adheres to the novel's unfurling narratological and thematic demands, but it is also one whose unique dispersal throughout the text reflects the culture's evolutionary anxieties. The improbability of the biological association between mother and daughter, of course, rests on the putative chasm of difference between what their respective hands mean in the era's symbolic perceptual economy: if Molly's hands connote animality, violence, and lower-class labor, then Estella's signify refinement, beauty, and upper-class leisure.

And yet for much of the novel, Dickens actively abets and even endorses the misinterpretation of these categories as separate, self-contained entities through the depiction of feminine gesture at Satis House. He often figures Miss Havisham's class leverage, for example, as a barely perceptible but consistent combination of verbal *and* manual directive. Over and over again, Miss Havisham's orders for Pip to play, to sing "Old Clem," and to walk her around the decrepit bridal table are accompanied by the same "impatient movement of the fingers of her right hand" (Dickens [1860–61] 2003, 59, 62, 83). What complicates Pip's mistake is the fact that Estella appears to inherit a capacity for similar behavior as she uses her "white," "taunting hand" to reinforce her inaccessibility during Pip's torturous early visits to Satis House (65, 238). Read in retrospect, this extension of and twist on Estella's "bringing up by hand" operates as something of a narrative red herring. It apparently affiliates Satis House with a Ruskinian notion of gentility as an organic sensibility where the "fineness of Nature" is figured as a category of (natural) breeding (Ruskin 1852, iii, 117). Unable to even consider the notion of a less-than-aristocratic Estella,

162   CHAPTER 3

therefore, Pip is blinded by the Victorian ideology that unilaterally tended to convert differences in the acquisition of culture (nurture) into differences of nature.[30]

Dickens intensifies this crucial inability to comprehend the constructed relationships between high and low in Pip's repeated failure to identify the connection between Estella's and Molly's hands. After the dramatic hand-taming scene at Jaggers's dinner party, the text subtly but consistently aligns Molly's animality with Estella's recalcitrance almost exclusively by way of gestural similarity. Estella's insistence that she possesses "no softness, no—sympathy—[no] sentiment," for instance, becomes acutely unsettling to Pip because of how often it is accompanied by "a slight wave of her hand" (Dickens [1860–61] 2003, 237, 238, 264, 269). Her proclamation of insensitivity, combined with the movement of her gesturing hand, on one of these occasions sends Pip into one of his most uncanny and puzzling meditations: "As my eyes followed her white hand, again the same dim suggestion that I could not possibly grasp, crossed me. My involuntary start occasioned her to lay her hand upon my arm. Instantly the ghost passed once more and was gone. What *was* it?" (237–38; emphasis original). After this interaction, the question—"What *was* the nameless shadow?"—revisits Pip each subsequent time he encounters Estella's hands in virtually any capacity (264; emphasis original). And as we have seen with idiomatic expressions in other chapters, Dickens delights in playing with, punning, and reworking idiomaticity into literalizations of which his characters and perhaps even he may not be fully aware. For instance, in the same conversation where Estella reminds Pip that he "was not brought up [by hand] in that strange [Satis] house from a mere baby," she nonetheless tells him that she is "beholden" to him and concludes the very same sentence by saying, "There is my hand upon it" (267). Considering this accrual of manually inflected idiomatic language, it is understandable that hearing and seeing as much in relation to Estella's actual hands during this scene causes Pip "to be all alight and alive with that inexplicable feeling [he] had had before" (269).

The repetition of "that inexplicable feeling" alongside Pip's initial failure to identify the connection between Estella's and Molly's hands plays a significant role in creating the narrative tension necessary for a story told in weekly installments, but it also exposes Pip's crucial misunderstanding of the relationship between nature and nurture which resides at the core of the "brought up by hand" idiom. Estella's beauty and inaccessibility lead Pip to assume that

---

30. My formulation, here, is indebted to Bourdieu 1984, 68.

there is something natural about her class position, an assumption that exemplifies par excellence Bourdieu's notion that social values tend to become invisible as acts of culture. Indeed, Pip suffers from a form of habitus that legitimates (and thus delimits) categories in a society that encourages people to recognize as valid and "truthful" the kinds of everyday ritual, dress, and actions which make people appear to be the flesh-and-blood incarnations of their social environments.

We witness this misperception poignantly in the scene where Pip and Wemmick visit Newgate Prison to kill time before Pip is scheduled to meet Estella at the coach station. Feeling "encompassed by all [Newgate's] taint of prison and crime," Pip believes Estella to be all that is opposite such "taint": "I thought of the beautiful young Estella, proud and refined, coming towards me, and I thought with absolute abhorrence of the contrast between the jail and her" (264). The "contaminat[ion]" Pip feels "from the soiling consciousness of Mr. Wemmick's conservatory" culminates in seeing Estella's "hand waving to [him]" from the coach window as it pulls up (264). The conjunction of what Pip takes to be the opposing markers of lower-class crime—shaking the hands of Newgate prisoners—and genteel refinement—Estella's waving hand from the train window—once again sends Pip into the same bewildering meditation. "What *was* the nameless shadow," he asks, "which again in that one instant had passed?" (264; emphasis original). Pip's reluctance to draw connections at this point in the novel is exhibited perhaps most ironically in his objection to Estella's professed incapacity for feeling by his asseverations that such emotional deficiency from one so beautiful "is not in Nature" (362). Estella's succinct and double-sided riposte more accurately summarizes the interconnectedness between nature and nurture that Pip repeatedly fails to see: "It is in *my* nature," says Estella. "It is in the nature formed within me" (362; emphasis original). The clarification Estella adds in the final sentence, here, correctly but confusingly exhibits her understanding that what Pip assumes is her "nature" is really her nurture by Miss Havisham—the eccentric nurture practiced by the woman who "brought her up by hand."

Dickens is careful, however, to emphasize that Pip's misunderstanding of the relationships between nature and nurture are not unique to him or to his class position. Miss Havisham, the woman who molds the largest portion of Estella's constructed nature, also fails to understand the indiscriminately destructive power of her own nurturing. This misunderstanding reaches its finest narrative consummation when Pip reports what happens "the first time [he] had ever seen them opposed" (303). Utterly nonplussed upon hearing the "pot calling the kettle black" accusation from her "mother by adoption" that

164   **CHAPTER 3**

she has a "cold, cold heart," Estella realizes that she must walk Miss Havisham through the paces of the relationship between one's nurture and one's nature:

> "I begin to think," said Estella, in a musing way, after another moment of calm wonder, "that I almost understand how this [disagreement] comes about. If you had brought up your adopted daughter wholly in the dark confinement of these rooms, and had never let her know that there was such a thing as the daylight by which she has never once seen your face—if you had done that, and then, for a purpose had wanted her to understand the daylight and know all about it, you would have been disappointed and angry?" . . .
>
> "Or," said Estella, "—which is a nearer case—if you had taught her, from the dawn of her intelligence, with your utmost energy and might, that there was such a thing as daylight, but that it was made to be her enemy and destroyer, and she must always turn against it, for it had blighted you and would else blight her; if you had done this, and then, for a purpose, had wanted her to take naturally to the daylight and she could not do it, you would have been disappointed and angry?" (306)

After this bravura articulation of the manner in which Miss Havisham has brought her up by hand, Estella answers her own question with devastating concision: "I must be taken as I have been made" (306).[31]

No matter how self-aware Estella is in terms of how she has "been made" by Miss Havisham's nurture, however, she remains wholly uninformed about her biological kinship with her parents, Molly and Magwitch. Consequently, beneath her genteel aloofness and apparent refinement, there are important parts of Estella's unconscious identity that link her disposition, as well as her hand movements, to Molly's "wild," "untamed," and violent nature. Not only does she exhibit the violent capacity of her mother's hands (and all of those who bring up their children by hand: Mrs. Joe, Pumblechook, Joe's father) as she slaps Pip's face "with such force as she had" while a young girl at Satis House, but she also appears *attracted* to the atmosphere of physical aggression itself. Watching Herbert and Pip's bloody fistfight delights the young Estella so much that she offers Pip her only unsolicited amatory advance in the moments following the altercation: "There was a bright flush upon her face, as though something had happened to delight her. Instead of going straight to the gate, too, she stepped back into the passage, and beckoned me. 'Come here! You may kiss me if you like'" (93). Interestingly, Estella shows her at-

---

31. For an alternate reading of this important scene in relation to Plato's cave and Shakespeare's *King Lear*, see A. Miller (2008, 185–86).

"BROUGHT UP BY HAND" 165

traction to Pip not when he ceases to labor with his "coarse hands" in the forge as he would have thought but after he cuts them on Herbert's teeth and confesses to feeling like a "species of young wolf, or other wild beast" (60, 93). Therefore, Estella's attraction to physical violence—a violence that is apparent also in her seemingly inscrutable decision to marry the horse-beating Drummle—suggests the emergence of a long-buried barbarism that opens deeper, biological connections to her mother, Molly. Yet only in connecting mother and daughter by the appearance of their hands and the "action of their fingers" does Pip register a Darwinian truth that he, along with middle-class culture at large, deeply abhors: that criminality and civilization, violence and refinement, labor and wealth are always inextricably connected.

The Labor of Hand Transformation

This Darwinian model of interconnectedness frames the entire novel in the sense that Pip's *bildung* turns out to be the process by which he learns to comprehend and appreciate his relationship to the social, economic, and emotional value of his own and other previously maligned hands. Such development poses a figurative corollary to the literal transformation of Pip's hands from coarse instruments of apprenticed labor in the forge to bejeweled appendages of leisure in his gentlemanly life. Nowhere does the contrast and connection between laboring and genteel hands appear more starkly than when Magwitch returns to Pip's apartment in London—a plot event in the making since the novel's second page that adds yet another and perhaps most salient dimension to what it means for Pip to be "brought up by hand." In this reunion scene, Magwitch's proclamation that he "lived rough, that [Pip] should live smooth" is not simply highlighted but brilliantly *embodied* by the physical interplay of Magwitch's "heavy brown veinous" hands and Pip's ringed and recoiling hands (319, 315). On seven successive occasions in this brief chapter, Magwitch attempts to embrace "both" of Pip's hands, and Pip at first responds by "recoil[ing] from his touch as if he had been a snake" (320). Pip's horrified withdrawal is a reaction to the realization that, without his knowledge, he has in fact, even as a gentleman, continued to be "brought up by hand." But in this particular refraction of the idiom, his sister's abusive hand is replaced by Magwitch's laboring hand which has been applied so strenuously and profitably to sheep-farming operations after his criminal transportation abroad. This climactic replacement is fittingly underscored with characteristically incisive wordplay connected to the original idiom; not only has Magwitch brought Pip up by hand from another continent, but he assures Pip that his being brought up

166   **CHAPTER 3**

in a leisured, gentlemanly lifestyle has been accomplished entirely "single-handed" (321).

Furthermore, Magwitch's hands appear "large," "heavy," "brown," "veinous," and "knotted" only when he returns from putting them to work in New South Wales (i.e., not in the novel's opening pages when his "work" was criminal). This new characterization seemingly fulfills Friedrich Engels's ([1876] 1968, 253; emphasis original) postulation that "the hand is not only the organ of labour, *it is also the product of labour.*" As we saw with the case of Molly, the size and strength of Magwitch's hands would indicate a combination of wildness, barbarity, and criminality to nineteenth-century readers. In a Marxian sense, though, Dickens's emphasis on the materiality of Magwitch's hands underscores the physiological fact of human labor behind a money commodity that could not have been formerly more abstract to Pip. He admits as much when he confides in Herbert at the height of his confusion, "It has almost made me mad to sit here of a night and see him before me, so bound up with my fortunes and misfortunes, and yet so unknown to me" (Dickens [1860–61] 2003, 344).

This comment is also indicative of Pip's continuing struggle to comprehend the new refraction of the novel's organizing idiom. He assumes that he has been "brought up" to his gentlemanly status by Miss Havisham's hand—a genteel hand so far removed from the labor that guarantees its gentility. Rather than immediately recognize such labor in the hand that has in reality brought him up to his leisured lifestyle, or perhaps *because* he recognizes it, Pip confuses a criminal hand that he speculates is "stained with blood" with a laboring hand that is marked by work (322). His unwillingness to acknowledge a hand so marked engages the more central problem of work's increasing invisibility in the rapidly industrializing and capitalized economy in the decade before *Great Expectations.*[32] Pip confirms his culture's investment in this persistent separation of work and product when he laments early on in the novel that the only thing worse than being a manual laborer is being *seen* in the act of performing such labor: "What I dreaded was, that in some unlucky hour I, being at my grimiest and commonest, should lift up my eyes and see Estella looking in at one of the wooden windows of the forge" (108). In a further ironic twist on Karl Marx, Pip's ignorance of where his fortune comes from is perhaps never so fraught with alienation than on the night when he perceives the hands that actually produced it. The agitation with which Pip receives Magwitch's avowal that "I worked hard, that you should be above

---

32. Although he does not connect their titles' similarities, Richards (1990, 3) has argued that the "Great Exhibition" of 1851 inaugurated an "era of spectacle" where the display of Victorian commodities became physically and semiotically separated from their actual manufacture.

"BROUGHT UP BY HAND"   167

work," therefore, comes not so much because of the convict's former life as a criminal but rather because the producing hand has become literally and, thus, uneasily visible. Pip's rise in class has been so swift and comprehensive (comprehensively associated, he mistakenly believes, with gentility) that the knowledge of being brought up by a laboring hand is at this moment in the novel nearly as rebarbative as being brought up by a physically abusive one.

Up until the point of Magwitch's return, Pip has maintained a state of agitated unawareness regarding the connection between the money that sustains his leisured life and the labor (or not, in Havisham's case) that underwrites it. The "social hieroglyphic" that Marx (1990, 132) sees connecting labor and money, though, becomes immediately decipherable when Magwitch enters Pip's London apartment with his working hands outstretched.[33] The physical features of Magwitch's hands finally materialize the "mystical character" of the commodity that Marx attributes to its ability to embody human labor (240, 132). The size and color of his hands, along with their veins and knots, therefore serve as the text's most important reminder of the Darwinian model of interconnectedness: that the idleness and prosperity of the privileged classes are always interconnected with and dependent on the labor of others—even when the intermediate stages remain unseen.

Indeed, all of the hands in *Great Expectations* end up idiomatically, literally, and thematically conglomerate. Given the novel's early emphasis on the physical implications of being brought up by Mrs. Joe's heavy hand, Pip's time as an idle gentleman ends as aptly as it does abruptly in his attempt to save Miss Havisham from her burning house. The burns he sustains in the attempt to save Havisham render functionally useless the very hands on whose *dis*engagement Pip's Victorian gentility has been predicated since coming into his fortune. The fact that Pip burns his hands also further emphasizes how far his quest for gentlemanly status has taken him since he was "brought up by hand"/"bound out of hand" as an apprentice blacksmith—a vocation that required him to handle fire, burning coals, and molten iron on a daily basis. Regaining "the use of [his] hands" so that he can use them to row Magwitch safely out of the country thus becomes the most important object in Pip's life and one necessary for him to recognize the immediate functionality and value of the burned hands he had earlier so contemptuously disowned as "coarse and common" appendages (404).

Moreover, if Pip's emotional search for Estella's true identity is a displaced search for his own identity, as Carolyn Brown (1987, 71) has usefully suggested,

---

33. Note the difference between Pumblechook's groveling attempts to shake Pip's hands and Magwitch's desire to hold and, presumably, to see the hands his strenuous efforts have kept free from manual labor.

168   CHAPTER 3

then the specific location of the disclosure of Estella's history within the scene where Pip receives treatment for his burned hands is a brilliant masterstroke that merits closer scrutiny. Its brilliance lies in the seamless shift between the idiom's figurative and literal registers even within a single sentence of dialogue. Here, the juxtaposition of Herbert's family's knowledge of Estella—how she was figuratively brought up by hand because of her mother's, Molly's, actions—merges with the literal convalescence of Pip's burned hands: "'It seems,' said Herbert, '—there's a bandage off most charmingly, and now comes the cool one—makes you shrink at first; my poor dear fellow, don't it? but it will be comfortable presently—it seems that the woman [Molly] was a young woman, and a jealous woman, and a revengeful woman; revengeful, Handel, to the last degree'" (405).

Something remarkable happens in this passage's treatment of Pip's "shrinking." The shrinking reaction is at once a physical response to having bandages removed from his blistered hands *and* an emotional flinch from learning of Estella's low, violent, and criminal origins—a scenario that eerily confirms Beer's (1983, 9) notion that "many Victorian rejections of evolutionary ideas register[ed] a physical shudder." Pip shudders from confronting the reality that Molly and Estella, seemingly opposite Victorian social "species," share the closest of biological affiliations.[34] With their "natures" so similar, their only difference is a result of accidental nurture, where Jaggers happens to hold "a trust to find a child for an eccentric rich lady to adopt and bring up" ("by hand") at the same Darwinianly chance time Molly happens to murder her rival (413). Thus, the causes of Pip's physical, intellectual, and emotional pain are the same at this extraordinary moment, and their convergence in the novel's most idiomatically and literally referenced body part draws attention to the ways in which the Victorian anxieties concerning the fragility of the once-impenetrable barrier between human and animal were transferred—often via the hand—to the period's increasingly porous social boundaries.

Dickens eventually mitigates some of these anxieties by having the novel come full circle in terms of its original organizing idiom. Pip, at the novel's conclusion, finally manages to escape the physical and emotional toll of having been brought up by hand (in all its senses) principally by breaking its abusive cycle in Joe-like fashion—participating as he does in "nurturing" Magwitch during his convict benefactor's final days. And as we saw earlier with Joe's nurturing touch—where an altogether new model of bringing Pip up by hand emerges—Dickens channels the lion's share of intense sympathetic feeling between Pip and Magwitch through the hand. In a sequence at the end of the

---

34. A. Miller (2012, 783) discusses the novel's "engagement with types and species" but does not draw any connection to Darwinian influence.

"BROUGHT UP BY HAND" 169

novel that Stone (1979, 330) has referred to as a "secret freemasonry of hands," Pip yearns for contact with the once-criminal hands he so desperately sought to keep separate from his own: "Sometimes [Magwitch] was almost, or quite, unable to speak; then he would answer me with slight pressures in my hand, and I grew to understand their meaning very well. . . . I pressed his hand in silence, for I could not forget that I had once meant to desert him" (Dickens [1860–61] 2003, 459). Many subsequent critics have followed Stone's lead in attempting to decode Dickens's emphasis on hands in *Great Expectations* as part of a "fugitive," "covert," and "textually-established scheme" (Macleod 2002, 127, 129); as the site of "encryption for homosocial desire" (W. Cohen 1993, 221); or simply as "the end point of the novel's metonymic logic" (Woloch 2003, 201). As I have endeavored to show, however, at least one of the meanings behind the pantomime behavior that ends *Great Expectations* is far from secret or "magical" (Stone 1979, 333). Instead, it offers a quite fitting resolution for a novel whose principal idiom is deeply embodied in the unique cultural moment when the hand was diagnostic of biological, social, and moral identity. The events at the end of the novel therefore provide a theater of new possibilities for what it might mean to be "brought up by hand."

Considering Dickens's use of the idiom in the context of contemporary cultural preoccupations also allows us to evaluate how its central body part could become a site where scientists and novelists alike reimagined positive progress and transformation alongside the existential angst often associated with the arrival of radically altered evolutionary paradigms. This is why I think it is important to acknowledge not only Dickens's unnerving parallels between anthropoid apes and humans but also his punning and good-spirited use of Darwinian evolutionary thinking. Specifically, in the world of this novel, those who fail to adapt and to change never truly make any social or moral progress, and Dickens clearly revels in this idea as he concludes. Characters like the smarmy Pumblechook conspicuously ("May I?") offer "the same fat five fingers" (Dickens [1860–61] 2003, 475) at the text's beginning and at its ending. The previously illiterate Joe, over the same course of time, though, develops not only his laboring hand but his writing one as well: "Joe now sat down to his great work, first choosing a pen from the pen-tray as if it were a chest of large tools, and tucking up his sleeves as if he were going to wield a crowbar or sledge-hammer" (464). Likewise, it could hardly be more fitting for a character who is "brought up by hand" to become a man "by hand." Pip's moral development actually becomes manual development; the sensitivity and self-awareness of his character eventually merges with the sensitivity and self-awareness of his hands as he learns to value, among other things, the feel of "pretty eloquence" in Biddy's wedding-ringed hand and the exquisite meaning of the "slight pressures" of

170 **CHAPTER 3**

Magwitch's hand while his benefactor lay on his deathbed (459). Even his ability to thwart Jaggers's "powerful pocket handkerchief" develops concomitantly with his ability to distinguish between criminality and manual labor, between hands that forge bank notes and hands that forge iron, and ultimately, between hands that "work" and hands that work (411). We might even say, in the spirit of Dickens's idiomatic wordplay, that by learning to distinguish between hands that hurt and hands that help, the character nicknamed "Handel" finally manages to come to grips with being brought up by hand.

CHAPTER 4

Sweat Work and Nose Grinding in *Our Mutual Friend*

> Any one reading . . . [*Our Mutual Friend*] might see that the author meant to put forth all his strength and do his very best; and those who have an eye for literary workmanship could discover that never before had Mr. Dickens's workmanship been so elaborate.
>
> —E. S. Dallas (November 29, 1865)

The Emergence of Dual Idiomatic Pillars

The imaginative processes with which Dickens began his last two completed novels were in many ways quite contrary. We have seen how Dickens's reliance on the "brought up by hand" idiom in *Great Expectations* helped him develop a novel in a manner that allowed him to intervene swiftly to boost the slumping sales of *All the Year Round*. Once that fast-paced, weekly serialized novel was finished, though, Dickens began to exhibit significant signs of depletion. He had never toiled so hard or spread himself so thin with writing (both fiction and nonfiction), editing, speechmaking, and performing public readings as he did during this period in his life. Upon finishing *Great Expectations* in the spring of 1861, he confided in William Macready that working such long hours in all these capacities had made him decidedly "worse for the wear" (House et al. 1965–2002, ix, 424). Persistent neuralgic pains in his face, excruciating headaches, and general body fatigue began to incapacitate him for longer periods—especially after his public reading performances started to exhaust him at times to the point of fainting. Thus "trying to plan out [his] new book," *Our Mutual Friend*, amid all the other draws on his time and his battered body proved exceedingly arduous (House et al. 1965–2002, x, 55). In fact, Dickens had more difficulty starting what would turn out to be his final (completed) novel than he did with any other in his career. Harry Stone (1987,

172   CHAPTER 4

331) has characterized *Our Mutual Friend*'s fitful and protracted incubation period as the most "hard, slow, demanding, [and] laborious" that Dickens had ever experienced.

Dickens told John Forster (1892, 740) that he had "leading notions" for his new novel almost immediately after finishing *Great Expectations* in April 1861, but he also found it almost impossible to move past this nebulous initial stage. On several occasions, he tried to begin writing in earnest only to get nowhere. He wrote to W. F. De Cerjat almost a year later, in March 1862, that he was "trying to plan out a new book, but [had] not got beyond trying," and to Forster a month after that, "Alas! I have hit upon nothing for a story. Again and again I have tried" (House et al. 1965–2002, x, 55, 75). "I seize a pen, and resolve to precipitate myself upon [the] story," an exasperated Dickens reports in July 1862, "then I get up again with a forehead as gnarled as the oak tree outside the window, and find all the lines in my face that ought to be on the blank paper" (House et al. 1965–2002, x, 109). As late as the summer of 1863, he complained to Wilkie Collins that he was "always thinking of writing [my] long book and am never beginning to do it" (House et al. 1965–2002, x, 281). The problem, according to Stone (1987, 329), "was how to join [his] scattered themes and images and how to make them live in a larger design"—as he had done so expediently and successfully in *Great Expectations*.

A change of scenery apparently proved to be of enormous help in dislodging Dickens's multiyear imaginative log jam. After "evaporating for a fortnight" in France during August 1863, he wrote Forster to report that he was at last "full of notions . . . for the new twenty numbers" of *Our Mutual Friend*, and this time, the actual writing began to take; he started actively composing the opening chapters within a few weeks (House et al. 1965–2002, x, 283). By January 1864, he had completed the first two numbers (chapters 1–7) and was beginning the third number (chapters 8–10).

What happened during the sojourn in France that helped Dickens finally organize his scattered themes and images into a larger design? To say that we can only speculate would be appropriate on several levels. Dickens's career-long interest in hard, earnest work was becoming a newly urgent "leading notion" for him because of its now heightened contrast with the speculative, get-rich-quick ethos of London's emerging finance capital industry in the early 1860s. The contemporaneousness of these financial concerns is built into the temporality of this new book. Unlike most of his other novels, *Our Mutual Friend* is set in the contemporary present—as the very first words of the novel announce: "In these times of ours . . ." (Dickens [1864–65] 1997, 13). Mary Poovey (1993, 51, 67), among others, has shown how the narrator's vitriolic criticism of "these times" is connected to the ways limited liability legislation

SWEAT WORK AND NOSE GRINDING IN *OUR MUTUAL FRIEND*   173

let loose "a mania for profit" where seemingly everyone inhabited "a giddy world beyond moral restraint."[1] Long a proponent of the secular Victorian "Gospel of Work," Dickens began to heighten his disdain for a culture wherein financial success and social position could be achieved without ever really "working"—as the narrator says in *Our Mutual Friend*—but by speculating in the "mysterious business [of "Shares"] between London and Paris" that "never originated anything, never produced anything" (Dickens [1864–65] 1997, 118). Paradoxically but pertinently, while financial speculators were enriching themselves without actually working or producing anything, Dickens was "having to buckle-to and work [his] hardest" to keep up with the incessant regimes of punishing labor on multiple fronts that he had established for himself by this point in his career (House et al. 1965–2002, ix, 322). Henry James (1865, 786) was probably not far off as he famously observed that was Dickens working to "exhaustion" in *Our Mutual Friend*, laboring (ineffectively in James's opinion) to "d[i]g out" the novel "with a spade and pickaxe."

Considering all of these juxtapositions between London's financially speculating nouveau riche and Dickens's laborious contemporary circumstances, it should be unsurprising (though no critic has yet pointed it out) that Dickens invokes different variants of the idiomatic expression derived from the primeval curse pronounced on the labor of mankind—"by the sweat of the brow shalt thou eat bread"—twenty-four times in *Our Mutual Friend*—and as we have seen with Dickens's other imaginatively governing body idioms, *only* in *Our Mutual Friend* among all of his other fictional works. This would seemingly confirm Robert Douglas-Fairhurst's (2011, 315) belief that Dickens reserved his strongest mockery for the ideas to which he was most strongly attached. A lack of sincerity in and dedication to work was always anathema to Dickens, but it was especially so at this juncture in his life when he was pushing himself to labor on through significant pain and exhaustion. Thus, we will now consider the ways that Dickens brings what could be called *idiomatic mockery* to new heights in his final novel—how he cultivates, hones, and nearly perfects his growing penchant for exploiting an idiom's malleability by way of its direct applications and violations. I agree, in this sense, with Garrett Stewart (2022, 277) who has recently seen *Our Mutual Friend*, contra Henry James and other contemporary reviewers, less as "a depletion of genius than its [genius's] compendium" wherein Dickens's career-long "phrasal habits [become] etched into a sharper new outline." For Stewart *Our Mutual Friend* is the novel where Dickens's "ingrained verbal flourishes" solidify into a "stylistic summa" as the Inimitable's "lexicon

---

1. Poovey 1993, 51, 67. Stewart (1990, 227) has also remarked that central "to the satiric agenda of the novel [is] its attack on the [unearned] money ethic of Victorian society."

174   **CHAPTER 4**

gets emphatically repackaged, [and] labelled with the rhetorical equivalent of 'registered trademark'" (227, 240). The "stylistic summa" of his career-long phrasal habits, the ultimate "registered trademark" we encounter in Dickens's final novel, in my view, though, is distinctly—and doubly—idiomatic.

I say this because the idiomatic intensification Dickens achieves in his last novel involves his imaginative orchestration of not just one but two principal body idioms. We will see how nineteen variants of a second idiom used only in *Our Mutual Friend* and in no other novel—"nose to the grindstone"—links up with the former, first as an expression describing one hard at work and then eventually in terms of the idiom's wider association with coercion, deception, and social mastery. As we have seen, this use and misuse[2] of idiomatic body language has been an accretive and an imaginatively embodied process for Dickens in his mature fiction: the right-hand men and women in *Dombey*, the characters with and without actual shoulders to put to the wheel in *Bleak House*, the nurturing and neglecting ways of being brought up by hand in *Great Expectations* (Bodenheimer 2007, 36). Now we encounter at the end of Dickens's career a showcase of characters who do and do not work "by the sweat of their brows," who do and do not put theirs and others' "noses to the grindstone." Tracing how these unique idioms[3] emerge—and eventually merge—will allow us a new and privileged glimpse into how Dickens imagined the novel that many consider his most self-consciously constructed work.[4] We will see Dickens fulfilling Mikhail Bakhtin's (1981, 292) hypothetical case where "parodic stylizations" of social dialects may "be drawn in by the novelist for the orchestration of his themes and for the refracted (indirect) expression of his intentions and values."

The evaluation of the ways in which these two idioms come to structure *Our Mutual Friend* rhetorically and thematically, however, involves a careful analysis of their appearances over the course of the first five numbers (May through September 1864 installments) as well as an examination of what is

---

2. Bodenheimer (2007, 36) contends that Dickens's "central subject was the use and misuse of language." I agree but argue that his central subject is more precisely a use and misuse of idiomatic body language.

3. These body idioms were not just unique in Dickens's oeuvre; they were extremely rare in nineteenth-century novels more generally: the "sweat of the/my brow" idiom is used three times in one novel, twice in four novels, and a single time in forty-five other novels in my corpus of more than 3,700 nineteenth-century novels. The "nose to the grindstone" idiom is even more rare. Dickens invokes it or its variants nineteen times in *Our Mutual Friend* while it appears only thirteen times (all single instances) in the 3,700-novel corpus.

4. Critics from Knoepflmacher to Poole have seen the novel this way. Knoepflmacher (1971, 137) analyzed it as "the product of a practiced and self-assured craftsman in total command of all the rhetorical skills developed throughout his career." More recently, Poole (2007, xxiii) has called *Our Mutual Friend* the Dickens novel that is "most self-conscious of its own processes."

known about the novel's provenance once *Great Expectations* drew to a close. I mention the first five numbers for a specific reason. Dickens's composition of *Our Mutual Friend* involved a planned return to the monthly number format after almost a decade of writing fiction for weekly publication (*Hard Times, A Tale of Two Cities, Great Expectations*). As Sean Grass (2014, 45) has shown, this return to an elongated publication setup, combined with failing health, the mishandled (and very public) dissolution of his marriage, a concealed new relationship with Ellen Ternan, and declining reputation among contemporary critics, prompted Dickens to make a resolution to Forster that he would not to begin publishing his new long novel with fewer than five numbers completed in advance. Earlier in his career, Dickens had written overlapping novels (*Oliver Twist* and *Nicholas Nickleby, The Old Curiosity Shop* and *Barnaby Rudge*) without any sizable written backlog. However, with his final few novels, he had increasingly wanted a substantial reserve in place before publication began. Partly owing to the complexity of his later art and the difficulty of proceeding rapidly with it while juggling so many other demands on his time but also because a comfortable reserve of writing was now a necessary hedge against illness, distress, and unforeseen interruptions, Dickens conceded to Forster that he was "forced to take more care than [he] once took" (Stone 1997, 331). My overarching argument is that as Dickens took more care in composing his later novels, he also relied more heavily (and often) on his idiomatic imagination to help him organize and execute his novels' plot formulations, characterizations, and themes. Based on what we know about *Great Expectations'* success, the content of early planning documents for *Our Mutual Friend*, and speed and assurance with which he eventually wrote the novel's early sections in late 1863 and early 1864, it is entirely possible that Dickens—after struggling mightily to organize what he called the leading "notions" of his new book—returned from his fortnight in France with relatively definitive ideas of how these two idiomatic phrases, "by the sweat of the brow" and "nose to the grindstone," could productively inform *Our Mutual Friend*'s twenty numbers.

Ridiculing and Relying on the Idiom

It is a likely possibility that Dickens drew on the "sweat of the brow" idiom as an insistence on earnest labor amid his disdain for London's booming but work-bereft finance capital industry. But there is also a deeper relationship between the idiom and its biblical context that helped him imagine some of the novel's core themes. Whereas Dickens's aversion to organized religion is no secret, neither is his firm grasp of the Bible and the Anglican Book of Common Prayer.

176   **CHAPTER 4**

Several scholars have dedicated entire books, or significant portions of books, to Dickens's expansive use of biblical material, though none have analyzed such religiosity in conjunction with the unmistakably Edenic origin of the "sweat of the brow" idiom.[5] This absence is remarkable because the predation, scheming, and deceitfulness by which so many characters pursue money and social dominance without meaningful labor is a major part of what makes the world of *Our Mutual Friend* a decidedly "fallen" world. It is significant, then, that one of its principal idioms directly relates to the original (biblical) fall and the labor that is attendant on that fall in the post-Edenic curse from Genesis. Dickens would have been most familiar with the King James version of the Bible (1997, 3:19), which reads, "In the sweat of thy face shalt thou eat bread, till thou return unto the ground; for out of it wast thou taken: for dust thou art, and unto dust shalt thou return." Because the phrase is used first and foremost by the lower class and illiterate characters, though, Dickens employs the more colloquial (and far more popular) "sweat of the *brow*" idiom throughout *Our Mutual Friend*. The repeated invocation of this universally common idiom allows Dickens to emphasize one of the novel's most supreme and sustained ironies: many characters presented in *Our Mutual Friend* have fallen so far that the novel's greediest "sinners" simultaneously invoke and dodge the divine justification of labor in their elaborate schemes to *avoid* work. Because of the Bible's familiarity to all classes, literate or not—what the popular philologist Richard Chenevix Trench (1852, 30) called its imbricated status in the English "national mind"—this particular idiom needs no historical data visualizations of the kind I have provided in previous chapters to demonstrate its consistent circulation through the British lexicon during this era.[6]

Even so, the context for the relationship between labor and the "sweat of the brow" idiom is not entirely straightforward in *Our Mutual Friend*. This is partly because the representation of work in Dickens in general, and in *Our Mutual Friend* in particular, has long been a flag over notoriously contested ground. Humphry House (1941, 55) believed that Dickens maintained "a passionate interest in what people do for a living and how they make do." George Orwell (1965, 82) argued that Dickens, by and large, failed to present a "realistic" portrait of the working classes. Alexander Welsh (1971, 78) attempted to resolve the discrepancy by claiming that Dickens's novels "espouse work as a value but not

---

5. See Welsh (1971), Walder (1981), Sanders (1982), Larson (1985), and Wheeler (1990). More recently and specifically, Litvack (2008, 434–35) has analyzed the "overt biblical references in *Our Mutual Friend*" but does not mention the "sweat of the brow" idiom.

6. Trench (1852, 30) had written that the Bible "lives on the ear, like music that can never be forgotten. . . . Its felicities often seem to be almost things rather than mere words. It is part of the national [British] mind."

SWEAT WORK AND NOSE GRINDING IN *OUR MUTUAL FRIEND*   177

as an experience." More recently, and more definitively related to the focus of this chapter, Nicola Bradbury (2005, 2) writes that "work . . . proves a powerful key to *Our Mutual Friend*" and Brian Cheadle (2001b, 86) adds specificity to this idea in his assertion that "work enables [*Our Mutual Friend*'s] narrative: it provides 'Secretary Rokesmith' with the pretext to stay at the Boffins', thus initiating the ordering impulse of the main plot, and it calls Mortimer Lightwood out, with Eugene in tow, toward Lizzie and the radical decentering in the subplot." Patrick Brantlinger (1996, 162), on the other hand, has argued that "almost nobody [in *Our Mutual Friend*] does anything that could be called productive labor."[7] My analysis of several working characters will reveal that this is not completely accurate, even as it indexes much of the narrator's indignantly satirical portrayals of characters who resist working. But the sense that very few characters engage in meaningful labor might help explain why the chapter dedicated to Dickensian "Work" in Sally Ledger and Holly Furneaux's (2011) book fails to mention *Our Mutual Friend* at all. For my evaluation of how this particular idiomatic expression pertaining to labor evolves in this novel, though, I would rather not get bogged down in evaluating the "realism" or even the representation (more often the absence) of Dickensian work. It is enough for me, instead, to hew more closely to House's (1941, 55) less controversial idea that "work plays an essential part in the characters' approach to life"—as it did perhaps never more so in Dickens's own life as he began the novel.

In this sense, the opening chapters of *Our Mutual Friend* provide an incredibly detailed glimpse into how each of its characters' approach to life is colored by their various and often opposing relationships to labor. The first chapter, for instance, despite its portrayal of "the awful sort of fishing" in which Gaffer and Lizzie Hexam practice, establishes the father and daughter as an unlikely but dedicated pair of manual laborers (Dickens [1864–65] 1997, 13). We learn that Lizzie unequivocally does not like the work, but she is willing to acknowledge that her labor "pulling a pair of sculls" for her father's boat allows them to survive and for her to set aside money for her brother's education so that he may be freed from having to perform similarly demanding manual work (13). Poovey (1993), Lyn Pykett (2002), and others have demonstrated how Lizzie's reluctant though arduous toil on the river essentially credentializes her for the hardworking roles she later assumes assisting Jenny Wren in the making of doll's dresses and, when she is forced from London, laboring at the paper mill.[8]

---

7. Claire Wood (2015, 132) puts it more precisely: "Only Gaffer's corpse-fishing, Venus's shop, and the dust-heaps are depicted as making money."

8. Poovey (1993, 60) considers Lizzie "a working-class woman." Pykett (2002, 177) describes Lizzie as "hard-working and self-sacrificing from the outset"; "her capacity for hard work" is "demonstrated in her arduous toil at her river trade."

178   CHAPTER 4

Her father, Gaffer, also has several positive qualities associated with his labor despite its indecorousness. Unlike the malingering Rogue Riderhood, "there [is] something business-like in [Gaffer's] steady gaze" on the novel's first page (as he works at what Dickens refers to as his "trade") (House et al. 1965–2002, x, 357). Moreover, another feature differentiating these "waterside characters" is reflected in that part of the body with which the previous chapter has shown the Victorians to be supremely preoccupied: hands. Lizzie, who identifies her rowing hands as "coarse, and cracked, and hard, and brown," tells Charley that their father's laboring hand is "a large hand but never a heavy one when it touches [her]" (Dickens [1864–65] 1997, 519, 37). By contrast, Riderhood's daughter, Pleasant, (understandably) associates her father's hand not with work but with the physical violence that was so prevalent in *Great Expectations*.[9]

Perhaps more noteworthy is how closely Dickens's description of Gaffer resembles Henry Mayhew's (1968, ii, 148) "laborious," "persevering," "steady," and "industrious" characterization of real-life Thames dredgermen. Here is Mayhew describing a dredger and his environs: "There is . . . always the appearance of labour . . . A short stout figure, with *a face soiled and blackened with perspiration* . . . the body habited in a soiled check shirt, with the sleeves turned up at the elbows, and exhibiting a pair of sunburnt brawny arms, is pulling at the sculls, not with the easy and lightness of a waterman, but toiling and tugging away like a galley slave, as he scours the bed of the river with his dredging net in search of some hoped-for prize" (149, emphasis mine). Compare this to Dickens's ([1864–65] 1997, 13, emphasis mine) description of Lizzie and her father in *Our Mutual Friend*'s third paragraph: in their "*sodden* state, this boat and the two figures in it obviously were doing something that they often did, and were seeking what they often sought. Half savage as the man showed . . . with no covering on his [perspiration] matted head, with his brown arms bare to between the elbow and the shoulder . . . still there was business-like usage in his steady gaze." Dickens knew Mayhew well, and it should be clear from the comparison above that he often explicitly borrowed from Mayhew's reporting to produce accurate descriptions of his own working-class characters. My larger point about the comparison is that Dickens, from the very first page of the novel, presents us with working characters who *do* in fact labor by the sweat of their brows before we are introduced to the character—Rogue Riderhood—the notoriously *un*laborious dredgerman who so often hypocritically invokes the idiom.

---

9. "From her infancy [he] had been taken with fits and starts of discharging his duty to her, which duty was always incorporated in the form of a fist or a leathern strap, and being discharged to hurt her" (Dickens [1864–65] 1997, 346).

SWEAT WORK AND NOSE GRINDING IN *OUR MUTUAL FRIEND*   179

Such contrasting conceptions of labor appear to be one of the "leading notions" Dickens had of the novel when it began to take shape in his imagination while he was in France. Dickens never used the "sweat of the brow" idiom in any of his prior fiction and yet it shows up in his earliest plans for *Our Mutual Friend*, which he composed well before the first number was published (May 1864). For example, in his plans for the first number, Dickens has already decided to list the title for chapter 12 as "The Sweat of an Honest Man's Brow," and he notes below the chapter heading that Riderhood will visit the lawyers Wrayburn and Lightwood "To Earn the [Harmon] reward "'by the sweat of his brow'" (Stone 1987, 341). Given the accurate observations of K. J. Fielding, J. Hillis Miller, Juliet McMaster, and others about the way the novel's opening chapters jump from one apparently unconnected part of the story to another, we might even think of Riderhood's favorite idiomatic refrain as the beginning of a consolidating index for those who do and do not "work" in the expansive world of this text.[10]

Even Riderhood's first satirical and ironic uses of the idiom are telling given the context of the novel's opening chapters vis-à-vis work. After all, Riderhood seeks out the lawyers in order to claim a reward for which he has most definitely *not* worked. Despite the fact that it is Gaffer's sodden and perspiring work, not his own, that recovers the body at the outset of the novel, Riderhood boldly asserts that "I am a man as gets my living, and seeks to get my living, by the sweat of my brow. Not to risk being done out of the sweat of my brow, by any chances, I should wish afore going any further to be sworn in" (Dickens [1864–65] 1997, 151). Such clustered repetition suggests Dickens's playful enjoyment with unfurling the parodical contradictions embedded within Riderhood's hypocritical uses of the idiom. Bodenheimer's sense of how parody operates in Dickens is useful, here. According to her, "Parody in Dickens says, 'I simultaneously rely on and ridicule this language'" (Bodenheimer 2007, 36). This is exactly what happens in Riderhood's use of the idiom. For instance, despite Riderhood's plan to avoid work by claiming the reward, he has the gall to assert that he has *earned* the money: "I wouldn't have knowed more, no, not for the sum as I expect to earn from you by the sweat of my brow" (Dickens [1864–65] 1997, 155). When the lawyers balk with suspicion, if only because of the size of the reward (as much as 10,000 pounds), Riderhood doubles down on the premise that a person who has performed the labor of a dredgerman somehow deserves the financial windfall, in part

---

10. Fielding (1958, 185) attests that the outset of the novel can "be enjoyed as a loose collection of pieces." J. Hillis Miller (1958, 284) claims that the opening chapters constitute "the juxtaposition of incomparable fragments in a pattern of disharmony and mutual contradiction." McMaster (1987, 194) says that "In the first number alone we jump between startlingly different scenes and sets of characters."

180 **CHAPTER 4**

to relieve the burden of his "honest" conscience: "It is a pot of money; but is it a sin for a laboring man that moistens every crust of bread he earns. . . . Is it a sin for that man to earn it? . . . So I made up my mind to get my trouble off my mind, and to earn by the sweat of my brow what was held out to me" (157). Here, Dickens relishes parodying Riderhood's ignorance of the connection between Edenic "sin" and its biblical consequences regarding human survival through arduous work. By the hypocritical gymnastics of Riderhood's logic, he [Riderhood] questions whether it is "sinful" for a laborer to "earn" the reward money "by the sweat of [his] brow," not by working—but by simply taking what is "held out to [him]."[11]

For all their hypocrisy, Riderhood's multiple "sweat of the brow" assertions conform to Bourdieu's ideas about how everyday linguistic exchanges operate as a social function of distinction in the relations between classes—and particularly how the struggle for such distinctions is often waged on the terrain of common speech. In *Language and Symbolic Power* (1991), he maintains that the use of everyday expressions, including slang and idioms, is an important way that those with less economic and social capital are able to distinguish themselves. "Language is a body technique," for Bourdieu (1991, 86), "a dimension of bodily hexis in which one's whole relation to the social world, and one's whole socially informed relation to the world, are expressed." Body idioms are therefore "indices of quite general dispositions toward the world and other people. . . . They ai[m] at the very essence of the interlocutor's social identity and self image" (87). This could not be truer of Riderhood's (mis)conception of himself as a laborer. Despite what he really is (a malingering work shirker of the highest order), he seeks to use his "sweat of the brow" assertions to exercise the only "authority" he has when dealing with the genteel lawyers who definitively do not perform their work "by the sweat of [their] brows."[12] Riderhood believes that his membership in the "working" class alone trumps his hypocritical invocation of it by way of the idiom. It is a belief in what Bourdieu (1990, 110) calls "the magical efficacy of [a] performa-

---

11. A similar set of events occurs later in the novel (book 2, chapter 12) when Rokesmith, dressed in seafaring disguise, charges Riderhood with lying about the Harmon murder in order to falsely "earn" the Boffin reward money. Here, Riderhood asserts his honesty ("sweating away at the brow as an honest man ought") and his dedication to physical labor ("I gets my living by the sweat of my brow") only to contradict both when he proposes splitting the reward with Rokesmith (355, 352, 358).

12. Bourdieu is of course building on the theory of speech acts developed by J. L. Austin. Although Austin does considerably more justice to the sociohistorical aspects of language than structural linguists ranging from Ferdinand de Saussure to Noam Chomsky, his (Austin's) account of performative utterances—their social "conditions of felicity"—does not go far enough in Bourdieu's estimation. Within the social conditions of communication, Bourdieu (1991, 107–16) believes that speakers use expressions containing practical strategies that are always adjusted to relations of power.

SWEAT WORK AND NOSE GRINDING IN *OUR MUTUAL FRIEND*   181

tive language which makes what it states"—an efficacy that "does not lie, as some people think, in the language itself, but in the group that authorizes and recognizes it."

Nonetheless, Riderhood's hypocritical ignorance is never greater than when Dickens pivots between the figurative and the literal valences of the idiom. Chapter 12, the chapter in which Riderhood goes to the office of Wrayburn and Lightwood, contains multiple figurative invocations of the idiom, but it becomes literalized only at the moment when Riderhood senses that the lawyers harbor suspicions regarding his claims to "honest" earnings. Riderhood has just pinned the Harmon murder on Gaffer Hexam but in the next breath claims that he "was in reality the man's best friend, and tried to take care of him" (Dickens [1864–65] 1997, 156). Employing what Bourdieu (1991, 68; emphasis original) refers to as *"strategies of [phrasal] condescension"* to maintain social distinctions, Wrayburn uses Riderhood's own words against him as he sardonically asks about whether the dredgerman has tried to take care of his "best" friend "with the sweat of [his] brow?" Riderhood, confident that his laboring status authorizes *him*, rather than condescending lawyers, to use physically laboring language of this kind, ups the idiomatic ante in his response: "Till it poured down like rain," he proclaims (Dickens [1864–65] 1997, 153). But Riderhood's confidence in the expression vanishes as Lightwood uncovers that Gaffer's "best friend" has "merely nothing" besides circumstantial evidence to make his case. Part of the ingeniousness of this important early scene lies in Dickens's orchestration of how the erosion of Riderhood's confidence in the idiomatic expression that he has been repeatedly invoking coincides with the phrase's literalization, as we witness Riderhood "wiping his face with his sleeve" before attempting to justify his increasingly hollow accusations (153). The parodic humor, of course, comes from the fact that Riderhood's brow begins to sweat literally only when he is forced to engage in a kind of laborious truth-twisting "work" in order to try to convince the lawyers of his fabricated story.[13]

Moreover, the manuscript version of this scene reveals a glimpse into how Dickens began simultaneously to both rely on and to ridicule this idiom as he was writing out the novel for the first time. When Eugene asks with mocking derision if Riderhood "tried to take care" of Hexam (his "best friend") "with the sweat of [his] brow?," Dickens had Riderhood's response read, "Exactly that" in the original handwritten manuscript. But then he crossed this out and wrote "Till it poured down like rain"—as if he recognized a chance to exaggerate and

---

13. Although he does not cite this part of the novel in particular, it certainly qualifies as one of the best examples of what Bowles (2019, 151) refers to as Dickens's "technical manipulation of grammar, lexis, and phraseology in his blending of discourse presentation techniques to mock, entertain, and critique individual and collective manners of speech."

182   **CHAPTER 4**

ridicule Riderhood's unearned use of the idiom. There is also an interesting alteration to the lines where Riderhood explains his "deserving" rationale for claiming the reward money. The first written manuscript version of Riderhood's lines read, "So I made up my mind to get my trouble off my mind, and to earn what was held out to me." But Dickens then crossed out "what was held out to me" and wrote in its place, "by the sweat of the brow what was held out to me." Dickens makes a similar alteration in the scene that appears in the next chapter where the Inspector, the lawyers, and Riderhood stake out Gaffer Hexam's house. As Eugene establishes their positions in "the post of watch," he asks, "Mr. Inspector at home?" The Inspector replies, "Here I am, sir." Eugene's next question appears this way in the manuscript: "And our worthy friend is in the far corner?" Dickens later emends the question to, "And our *friend of the perspiring brow* is at the far corner there?" (emphasis mine). He also added—via a caret insertion—the literalized detail where Riderhood appears "wiping his face with his sleeve."[14] These alterations are significant for a number of reasons that link up with my assessment of Dickens's growing reliance on body idioms. In particular, they reveal at close scale (within two successive chapters) and in as "real" a time as we can identify the ways Dickens moves from simply introducing a catch-phrase idiom to refining it and refracting it more thematically at specific junctures in his composition. Focusing our attention on these handwritten manuscript alterations allows us to reflect in a very specific manner on what John Bowen (2021) has termed the small "refinements of thinking and phrasing, refinements of expression" that reveal Dickens's creative process in action.[15]

The refinement of Riderhood's "till it poured down like rain" response to Eugene's mocking question also predicts the original idiom's wider circulation throughout the novel. The fact that Riderhood meets Wrayburn's derision with derision of his own inaugurates a larger pattern wherein he (Riderhood) is not the only butt of the idiomatic joke. John Carey (1973, 63–64) has remarked that Dickens's humor "depends on the detection of falsity, but also on its invention" to the extent that his "hypocrites are the prime beneficiaries of his inventive genius." And this is certainly true of the broader context within which Riderhood first makes his workful assertions. We learn, for example, several chapters before Riderhood comes to claim the reward that Lightwood and Wrayburn are lawyers by training but not in practice, an idleness on which they both openly muse. Eugene remarks that he has been "upon

---

14. These alterations appear in the handwritten manuscript, which is held by the Morgan Library & Museum in New York City. I am indebted to Philip Palmer for arranging my access to the manuscript (and magnifying glass!).

15. From Bowen's introduction to the *Deciphering Dickens* project, which was delivered at the "Dickens in the Digital Age Conference" on February 18, 2021.

SWEAT WORK AND NOSE GRINDING IN *OUR MUTUAL FRIEND* 183

the honourable roll of solicitors of the High Court of Chancery, and attorneys at Common Law" for five years but has "had no scrap of business" (Dickens [1864–65] 1997, 29). Mortimer's description of his own professional unemployment outdoes even his partner's: "I . . . have been 'called' seven years, and have had no business at all, and never shall have any. And if I had, I shouldn't know how to do it" (29). Thus, Dickens's initial presentation of Riderhood's hypocritical boasting could hardly contain more all-around discordancy. The very first paragraph of chapter 12, titled "The Sweat of an Honest Man's Brow," describes the lawyers' formal plan to "establish" their idleness in a more tranquil location: "They had newly agreed to set up a joint establishment together. They had taken a bachelor cottage near Hampton, on the brink of the Thames, with a lawn, and a boat-house, and all things fitting, and were to float the stream through the summer and the Long Vacation" (147). Though the lawyers are at least "honest" about their professional idleness, the comedic element of Riderhood's first appearance is heightened by the fact that he is clearly barking up the wrong tree with his "sweat of the brow" assertions. In fact, Lightwood is so unused to exertions of any kind that the night spent waiting for Gaffer Hexam to return lands him in a state of near complete futility: "the night's work had so exhausted and worn out this actor in it, that he had become a mere somnambulist. He was too tired to rest in his sleep, until he was even tired out of being too tired, and dropped into oblivion" (179).

Even if the lawyers' "friend of the perspiring brow" is the idiom's most obvious (and eventually odious) target, there is evidence that the phrase's repetition by *both* parties has a more subtle effect—at least on Wrayburn—as the lawyers attempt to locate Gaffer at the Six Jolly Fellowship-Porters (168). This public house is frequented almost entirely by the working classes, a point underscored by its owner's (Miss Abbey Potterson's) account of how she has come to the successful management of the place: "It has been hard work to establish order here, and make the Fellowships what it is, and it is daily and nightly hard work to keep it so" (76). Sensing that the idle lawyers would be too conspicuous in such an environment, the Inspector suggests that they feign working in the lime shipping trade as they attempt to learn more about the case of the Harmon murder from the working-class patrons at the Fellowship-Porters (161). Wrayburn is eager to run with the idea of casting off his aristocratic descent and to play the role of one born to a long line of workers, claiming to a working-class customer that his has been "a family immersed to the crowns of their heads in lime during several generations" (162). This would be somewhat eccentric but still perhaps unremarkable were it not for Wrayburn's extended participation in playing this working role well beyond its practical purpose, which is to blend in with the pub's working clientele. For

184   CHAPTER 4

instance, as the lawyers pay their bill, Wrayburn asks "in his careless extravagance" if the potboy, Bob Gliddery, "would like a situation in the lime-trade" (167). Bob respectfully declines, but Wrayburn does not let it go at that; he tells Bob that if he ever changes his mind to "come find me at my *works*, and you'll always find an opening in the lime-kiln" (167; emphasis mine). Bob thanks him, but Wrayburn is still bent on compounding the laboring facade. He introduces Lightwood, saying, "This is my partner . . . who keeps the books and attends to the wages. A fair day's wage for a fair day's work is ever my partner's motto" (167). Even Lightwood is mortified by the unnecessary lengths to which his friend goes, and as they leave the pub, he inquires of Eugene, "How *can* you be so ridiculous?" (167; emphasis original). Although Wrayburn simply chalks this up to being "in a ridiculous humour," it is clear that at some level, the repeated references to working "by the sweat of the brow" induces in the idle lawyer a determined desire to play the part of a man who really does work for his living—a goal for which he explicitly strives at the end of the novel.

Wrayburn may exhibit a momentary desire to associate himself with lower-class manual labor at the Fellowship-Porters, but his interactions with Bradley Headstone reveal his more sustained attraction to earnest middle-class work— even as he gloats over the schoolmaster and denigrates the profession.[16] As we have seen with the case of the Cambridge-educated Arthur Munby, a highly fraught and anxious relationship to the category of middle-class masculinity in relation to lower-class labor began to crest in the 1860s—where positions both above and below the social hierarchy became shot through with conflicting and contradictory desires and behaviors. Wrayburn's seemingly "ridiculous" desire to associate himself with lime-kiln work is actually not so bizarre if we consider it in terms of what James Eli Adams (1995, 1) calls "the energies and anxieties of masculine self-legitimation" at mid-century.

My point as it pertains to the lawyer Wrayburn and the schoolmaster Headstone is not only that we see such complex tensions play out along classed lines but that these same tensions manifest themselves in association with the idiomatic expression pertaining to labor that I have been tracing. Wrayburn mocks Riderhood's claim to working "by the sweat of his brow" partly because his social position allows him to do so. Riderhood offers little threat to his genteel masculinity (as an ostensibly practicing lawyer), and yet his "ridiculous"

---

16. I use the word *attraction* here in acknowledgment of Eve Kosofsky Sedgwick's (1985) pioneering argument in *Between Men* that a complex mapping of homosocial conflicts and affiliations underwrites many of the conflicts and affiliations of economic class in the nineteenth century. One of her strongest arguments culminates in her analysis of the classed and eroticized struggle between Eugene Wrayburn and Bradley Headstone. See Sedgwick 1985, 163–79.

SWEAT WORK AND NOSE GRINDING IN *OUR MUTUAL FRIEND*   185

behavior at the Fellowship-Porters reveals that Riderhood's equally ridiculous assertions of "honest" manual labor *do* hit some kind of uncomfortable mark. That mark gradually becomes something of a bull's-eye when Wrayburn meets Headstone and the latter explicitly asserts that a kind of genuine hard work has "won [him] a station which is considered worth winning" (Dickens [1864–65] 1997, 388).

We will return to Wrayburn's "amiable occupation" of "goading the schoolmaster to madness" on the London streets later on in this chapter, but for now, I want to analyze the subtle but familiar ways in which Dickens registers Headstone's work and his character's deeply vexed relationship to that work. Unlike Bounderby from *Hard Times*, who maintains an arrogant ease as the "bully of humility," Headstone is anxiously proud of the position he has attained. We sense this partly because of the narrator's insistence on his unassailably "decent" appearance but also because of the emphasis on his unsettled physical demeanor. Headstone appears within the first few pages of his entrance into the novel as having "a suspicious manner," a "settled trouble in the face," "a constrained manner," an "uneasy figure," and a "cumbrous and uneasy action" (218, 226, 229). The narrator perhaps sums up the depth of Headstone's conflicted (and repressed) manner best in simply saying, "The schoolmaster was not at his ease. But he never was, quite" (225). This constitutional unease is nevertheless exacerbated by the recognition of his rival suitor's higher class position—especially since it is a position for which Eugene has done no earnest work to achieve. Headstone's uneasiness, for example, spikes on learning of Wrayburn precisely because of the predicament it creates in terms of his own relationship to labor. At one remove, Headstone wants his "pauper lad" origins "to be forgotten" as he vies with a seemingly self-assured aristocratic lawyer for Lizzie's hand, but at another, he feels compelled to emphasize his workful industriousness as a means to assert his moral and ethical superiority over the indolent, aristocratic lawyer (218). This predicament is all the more difficult (and paradoxically cruel) for the schoolmaster to navigate in his first interaction with the razor-witted Wrayburn given Headstone's "naturally slow . . . intellect that had toiled hard to get what it had won" (218).

Part of the complexity of the scene where these two characters first meet lies in the confusion of what constitutes "work" in all of these different scenarios. Eugene's witty and repeatedly arrogant dismissal of "the schoolmaster" creates the embarrassing situation whereby Headstone needs the aid of his pupil, Charley Hexam, to help attempt to establish his respectability: "Mr. Headstone," Charley says in admonishment, is "the most competent authority, as his certificates would easily prove" (288). Realizing that this tack

186   **CHAPTER 4**

only solidifies Eugene's sense of superiority over him, Headstone tries to reframe his professional accomplishments in terms of labor: "You reproach me with my origin," he says. "You cast insinuations at my bringing-up. But I tell you, sir, I have *worked* my way onward, out of both and in spite of both, and have a right to be considered a better man than you, with better reasons for being proud" (291; emphasis mine). Not only has Headstone's "sluggish intelligence" had to toil hard to attain his position, but it is also toiling hard in the moment here to navigate his associations to labor (536). Attempting to do so is tortuously and *literally* hard work for Headstone, a spectacle punctuated by a performance of Riderhood's original idiomatic formulation of labor. "Oh what a misfortune is mine," cries Headstone, "breaking off *to wipe the starting perspiration from his face*" (290; emphasis mine). This idiomatic echo, however melodramatically configured, continues to proliferate in its resemblance to Riderhood's invocation. For example, when Headstone says to Lizzie that seeing him "at [his] work" would convince her that he has "won a station which is considered worth winning," we learn that he again "t[akes] out his handkerchief and wipe[s] his forehead" (340). And still later while recounting for Rokesmith the story of how Lizzie "repels a man of unimpeachable character who has made for himself every step of his way in life," he once again "t[akes] out his handkerchief and wipe[s] his brow" (381). So in Headstone Dickens has created a character who truly embodies the idiom, though not without treacherous complications. As we shall see with more fell implications further on, it is literally and physically hard work for Headstone to repress his "very, very strong feelings" on this topic (381).

Idiomatic Characters and Characteristics

The "sweat of the brow" idiom also poignantly frames the interaction between the two characters who embody the most proximate and yet most contrasting representations of labor in *Our Mutual Friend*: Rogue Riderhood and Betty Higden. The same chapter ("Minders and Re-minders") where we learn that "the death of [Gaffer] Hexam render[s] the sweat of the [Riderhood's] brow unprofitable," and where "the honest man had shufflingly declined to moisten his brow for nothing," we are introduced to the consummately "hard working, and hard living" Betty Hidgen (194, 199). Betty's approach to life and labor could hardly be more opposite to Riderhood's precisely because they are one and the same for her: living and working are inseparable activities. When the Boffins originally ask what they can do for her after losing the orphan baby, Betty's response is refreshingly different not only from Riderhood but from

SWEAT WORK AND NOSE GRINDING IN *OUR MUTUAL FRIEND*   187

the majority of the novel's other scheming characters—Lammle, Silas Wegg, Fascination Fledgeby, the preconversion Bella Wilfer, and so forth—who go to great lengths angling for money rather than working for it. Betty tells the Boffins, "I want for nothing myself, I can work. I am strong. . . . I never did take anything from any one. It ain't that I'm not grateful, but I love to *earn* it better" (202, 203; emphasis mine). She also recognizes that Sloppy, though a hard worker himself, will never achieve independence if she does not leave him, and so she sets out alone to the countryside, providing for herself and repaying a small loan from the Boffins all the while. Contemplating this decision, she thinks, "I'm a good fair knitter, and can make many things to sell. . . . Trudging round the country and tiring myself out, I shall keep the deadness off, and *get my own bread by my own labour*" (376; emphasis mine). Getting her own bread by her own labor, of course, continues to echo the novel's biblical idiom (by the sweat of the brow "shalt thou eat bread") but in an unassuming and selflessly authentic key.

The authenticity she brings to her working life is perhaps the most surprising characteristic of Betty's "surprising spirit" (199). "The poor soul," we learn, "envied no one in bitterness, and grudged no one in anything" (498). This quality certainly sets her apart from the novel's other venal characters in general but from Riderhood most particularly. And it is important for my argument that Dickens renders the starkness of these two characters' differences in repeated references to the idiom we have been tracing. For instance, Riderhood interprets Wrayburn's failure to take up his case and sue for (unearned) compensation after he is nearly drowned by a steamer as a grudge against his so often self-proclaimed "working"-class occupation: "[Wrayburn] always joked his jokes agin me owing, as *I* believe, to my being a honest man as gets my living by the sweat of my brow. Which he ain't, and he don't" (538; emphasis original). Riderhood's hypocritical mantra here and elsewhere heightens the stakes for the scene in which he meets the ungrudgingly workful character of Betty Higden. This is significant because by this point in the novel, Betty has not only proven herself as someone who really *does* earn her living in the manner of Riderhood's favorite invocation, but she has worked herself to the brink of a very real—as opposed to an almost and accidental—death. Betty begrudges no one and wishes only to be left alone to die undegraded without being committed to a parish workhouse. But Riderhood, now "an honest man" who "gets [his] living by the sweat of [his] brow" as the dozing and "indolent" Deputy of Plashwater Weir Mill-Lock, leverages the terrified adamance of Betty's wishes into a bribe in exchange for not turning her in to the parish when he encounters her near the end of her life (501). "Pocketing the coins, one by one," from the person who has worked herself to near death, Riderhood has

188   **CHAPTER 4**

the astounding impertinence to announce that he is "a man as earns his living by the sweat of his brow" (502). Here, though, the narrator acknowledges the despicability of the transaction by once again mockingly literalizing Riderhood's idiomatic calling card: "he drew his sleeve across his forehead, as if this particular portion of his humble gains were the result of sheer hard labour and virtuous industry" (502).

The hypocrisy of Riderhood's extortion (and the narrator's acknowledgment of it) appears even more flagrant given the genuinely "workful" circumstances surrounding Betty's death only a few pages later. Her rugged pilgrimage "toiling away . . . to earn a bare spare living" takes her past laboring poseurs like Riderhood and eventually to the paper mill where she feels comfortable surrounded by earnest industriousness. "When I am found dead," Betty says, "it will be by some of my own sort; some of the *working* people who *work* among the lights yonder" (505; emphasis mine). Betty is correct that she will be found among the workers of the paper mill, but she will not be found dead. Instead, she dies in the arms of Lizzie Hexam, after a solemn and touching exchange—a central part of which confirms her desire to die among "working people who work":

> "Am I not dead?"
>
> "I cannot understand what you say. Your voice is so low and broken that I cannot hear you. Do you hear me?"
>
> "Yes."
>
> "Do you mean Yes?"
>
> "Yes."
>
> "I was coming from my *work* just now, along the path outside (I was up with the night-hands last night), and I heard a groan, and found you lying here."
>
> "What *work*, deary?"
>
> "Did you ask what *work*? At the paper-mill." (505; emphasis mine)

This concentrated prominence of "work" in Betty's death scene helps provide a fitting end for a person who has labored her entire life to stay out of the parish workhouse. Not only does she manage to stay *out* of the workhouse, but her final association with labor is officially instantiated when her remains are brought *in* to an "empty store-room of the mill" to lay among the other workers before her burial (508).

This kind of consistent toggling between scenes of earnest industriousness and hypocritical idleness—often refracted through the "sweat of the brow" idiom—becomes a principal way in which Dickens indexes his characters' central identities. The other important character whose ardent dedication to

SWEAT WORK AND NOSE GRINDING IN *OUR MUTUAL FRIEND* 189

labor authentically aligns with the "sweat of the brow" idiom is the Doll's Dressmaker, Jenny Wren. In an early interaction with the clientless Eugene, this self-described "idlest and least of lawyers" questions why Jenny is *so* industrious (236). Jenny explains to the feckless lawyer that she needs to support not only herself but also her drunken father through her needlework.[17] Indeed, one would be hard-pressed to identify a scene in which Jenny does *not* appear in conjunction with an almost exaggeratedly diligent application to her labor. The narrator's constant association of Jenny with her trade—"work[ing] all night" (223), "sitting alone at her work" (337), "bending over the work" (337), "busy at her work by candle-light" (522), "profoundly meditating over her work" (701), "f[alling] to work at a great rate" (700)—has led some influential critics to reference the Doll's Dressmaker in association with the rhetoric of the brow idiom. Catherine Gallagher (2006, 96), for instance, has recently focused on "the result of all [Jenny's] sweat" in relation to the constancy and industriousness of her labor throughout the novel. This formulation is particularly germane for the "sweat of the brow" expression because it represents yet again a critic's invocation of the idiom where it really *does* belong rather than where it has been hypocritically proclaimed (i.e., with Jenny and not Riderhood). As I have emphasized throughout my study, however, this phenomenon of critical, rather than authorial, acknowledgment of the idiom's explicit applicability to female characters is a troubling and unfortunately deficient component of Dickens's wider idiomatic imagination.

This missed opportunity to acknowledge the sweat of Jenny's brow is even more disappointing if we consider how Gallagher's description of Jenny's working "sweat" could not have been more contemporaneously relevant in the era's lexicon. Her "back's bad" and her "legs are queer" (Dickens [1864–65] 1997, 222) as a result of her need to "work, work, work all day" and also "all night" (223, 713). Here, the triplicated description of Jenny's labor reprises the most oft-repeated lines from Thomas Hood's "The Song of the Shirt" (1843)—the immensely popular poem lamenting the plight of London seamstresses. (Hood's speaker repeats the triplicated rhetoric of "work! work! work!" or "work—work—work" eight times in eleven stanzas.[18]) It is likely that Dickens would have been acutely attuned to the horrors of this so-called "sweated"

---

17. For a discussion of how these circumstances "make Jenny stan[d] for a certain kind of realism" and "sign of a social fact" (contra Henry James's famously harsh assertion of her as unnatural and sentimental), see Schor 1999, 198–202.

18. Hood's poem was a reaction to an 1841 inquiry into the employment and treatment of dressmakers and seamstresses, which revealed shocking reports of women suffering from consumption, starvation, neuralgia, and other developmental problems resulting from long work hours standing or sitting in place. See Ledbetter 2012, 19.

FIGURE 19. The haunted lady, or "the ghost" in the looking glass

trade while he was working up ideas for his new novel in the summer of 1863.[19] In June of that year, at the height of London's fashionable season, the young dressmaker Mary Ann Walkley collapsed and died from heat exhaustion after working twenty-six hours without rest. Just weeks later, *Punch* printed a cartoon by John Tenniel, titled "The Haunted Lady, or 'The Ghost' in the Looking-Glass" (figure 19), that depicted the grim reciprocity between idle aristocratic London women and their immensely overworked dressmakers.[20]

But just as Betty Higden relies on her work to "keep the deadness off," Jenny Wren's sweated labor not only invigorates her, but it paradoxically *mobilizes* her. Talia Schaffer (2018, 201) accurately describes the physically impaired Jenny as "one of the most active figures in the novel, not particularly pitiable in certain

---

19. As McClintock (1995, 98) notes, "subcontracting and undercutting; extremely long hours for miserable pay; and work that was largely manual, repetitive and exhausting, performed in crowded and overheated garrets, gave the name 'sweating' to one of the most appallingly exploitative of the female trades." For a more expansive account of the practice, see Bythell 1978.

20. For an alternate reading of Jenny in terms of her association with Pre-Raphaelite art, see Evernden 2018.

respects."[21] More specifically, she is most active and least pitiable when she is in closest propinquity to her work. She "hobbl[es] up the steps" to Riah's, for example, in order to collect the scraps for her dresses, but once collected, she "trot[s] off to work" quite amiably (and ably) (Dickens [1864–65] 1997, 553, 554).

The various juxtapositions between the hypocritical bluster and the diligent authenticity of the "sweat of the brow" idiom also structures the novel's earliest chapters where the "highest" members of society come in for severe critique. We have seen how the opening chapter, despite its depiction of Gaffer Hexam's unseemly dredging work, identifies his businesslike dedication to the trade that "sodden[s]" his face with sweat (13). Although we are likely to miss it on an initial reading, this sets up another one of Dickens's earliest invocations of the idiom when, at the Veneering dinner party only ten pages into the text, John Podsnap appears (reflected in the magisterial looking-glass scene) with a "dissolving view of red beads on his forehead" (21). The derisive humor lies in the suggestion that sweat-of-the-brow "work" for this section of society is largely comprised of simply mixing among themselves in elaborately pretentious social settings. Such a suggestion culminates in the brilliantly sarcastic chapter "A Piece of Work," where the moneyed group resolves to undertake the supposedly "laborious" task of bringing Veneering in for Parliament. Here, the Veneerings initiate what becomes a refrain that appears on nearly every page of the chapter: "we must work" (244, 246, 248, 249, 251). Podsnap confirms his sense of brow-perspiring work as mingling with fellow socialites (and not with his occupation as a marine insurer) in his response to the working charge: "I have nothing very particular to do to-day . . . and [so] I'll mix with some influential people" (247). Similarly, the charade in which upper-class work effortlessly produces money and notoriety may be seen in Lady Tippins's actions, "for she clatters about town all day, calling upon everyone she knows, and showing her entertaining powers and green fan to immense advantage" (248). And the narrator corroborates that Lady Tippins knows well the name of the game she and the other "hard workers" play to such financial advantage: "that this same working and rallying round is to keep up appearances" because "many vast vague reputations have been made, solely by taking cabs and going about" (249).

Alfred Lammle and Fascination Fledgeby are two characters whose hollow reputations have been made in precisely this way. Although both are despicable characters in relation to their avoidance of work, the circumstances of their despicability are slightly different. Lammle achieves the appearance of a moneyed

---

21. See Schaffer 2018. Schaffer's point extends David's (1981, 122) notion that Jenny Wren "is a million fictive miles away from the passive suffering embodied in Dickens's other diminutive female creatures."

192   CHAPTER 4

gentleman by virtue (or vice) of his association with the 1860s speculative market boom where financial success has no physically traceable derivation beyond the opaqueness of "traffic in Shares" (118). Dickens's unequivocal disgust for this sort of "occupation" manifests itself in the narrator's frustrated attempts to locate anything tangible in Lammle's "achieved success": "Have no antecedents, no established character, no cultivation, no ideas, no manners; have Shares. Have Shares enough to be on Boards of Direction in capital letters, oscillate on mysterious business between London and Paris, and be great. Where does he come from? Shares. Where is he going to? Shares. What are his tastes? Shares. What are his principles? Shares" (118). Of course, we learn soon hereafter that Lammle has no principles (or any money), but he might have maintained the appearance of success in shares if his wife, Sophronia Akershem, had not been similarly deceitful about her own lack of money. The couple's subsequent scheming for unearned money throughout most of the novel crystallizes Dickens's view of the moral dysfunction at the heart of London society.

Whereas the Lammles simply pretend to have money they do not have, Fledgeby compounds his lying, pretending "to be a young gentleman living on his [own] means" at Pubsey and Co.—all while using Riah to deflect the odium for exacting the usurious interest rates that enrich him (269). I bring up Riah in relation to Fledgeby for a particular reason that will provide one final example of the pervasive effect the "sweat of the brow" idiom has on so many characters beyond Riderhood. Consider the scene where Fledgeby forces Riah to play the role of Pubsey's exorbitant and inexorable interest collector most directly (because of an unexpected visit from Lammle). It begins with the two characters (Lammle and Riah) occupying their usual (true) positions. Riah, after making his early morning collection rounds, shows up at the Fledgeby residence to turn over "every sovereign" to the still-comfortably slumbering money lender (419). Fledgeby's hypocrisy and disgracefulness culminates here in "his desire to heighten the contrast between his bed and the streets" where Riah has been toiling on his behalf (418). From the "comfortable rampart" of his fireside bed, Fledgeby experiences "a plunge of enjoyment" thinking about this aspect of his so-called occupation (418). Fascination emerges from his bed only to raise insulting suspicions concerning Jewishness and the money Riah has collected for him in the "chill and bitter" London streets: "'I suppose,' he said, taking [a sovereign] up to eye it closely, 'you haven't been lightening any of these; but it's a trade of your people's, you know. *You* understand what sweating a pound means; don't you?'" (419; emphasis original). Riah meets these insults with a revealing question of his own, asking, "Do you not, sir . . . sometimes mingle the character I fairly *earn* in your employment, with the character which it is your policy that I should bear?" (419; emphasis mine). This measured and ac-

SWEAT WORK AND NOSE GRINDING IN *OUR MUTUAL FRIEND*   193

curate response from Riah effectively turns the tables and makes Fledgeby the unwitting butt of his own insulting insinuation. Far from "sweating a pound," Riah has been sweating it out, fairly *earning* what little money he makes from doing Fledgeby's (dirty) work. And such a prospect is underscored by the narrator's descriptions of Riah's behavior at the opening of the scene where he is shown "drawing out a handkerchief, and wiping the moisture" from his forehead as he awakens Fledgeby (418). There is no question that Riah does so in part because of the scene's physical conditions; he is coming out of the "chill and bitter" London morning and into the warmth of Fledgeby's fireside apartments. But by the often literalized logic of the idiom we have been tracing, Riah's brow-wiping actions also locate him among the novel's very few who genuinely *do* work "by the sweat of the brow."

Deception, Mastery, and Noses to the Grindstone

It is not until the middle of the novel that the second guiding idiom of *Our Mutual Friend* first appears in its most explicit form. Dickens titles the fourteenth chapter of book 3 "Mr Wegg Prepares a Grindstone for Mr Boffin's Nose." This is not to say, however, that the idiom is thematically absent from the text until its midpoint. Following Bakhtin (1981, 346), the play of social dialects in a novel makes it entirely possible for a dialect's "'theme' [to] sound in the text long before the appearance of the actual word." The "sweat of the brow" and "nose to the grindstone" idioms, in this sense, are actually fundamentally linked in compelling ways. God's parting words to Adam in Eden are at least in part a reminder that although he will labor for his food by the sweat of his brow, he will retain nothing from that labor in death: "In the sweat of thy face shalt thou eat bread, till thou return unto the ground; for out of it wast thou taken: for dust thou art, and unto dust shalt thou return" (Genesis 3:19).[22] Claire Wood (2015, 149) and others have observed the ways in which *Our Mutual Friend*'s dust heaps "have clear connotations of the biblical dust that we are returned to by the burial service." Stewart goes even further. He describes the "liturgical formula 'ashes to ashes, dust to dust'" as "the unspoken matrix of the entire novel" (Stewart 1990, 209). Similarly, in an influential critique under the heading "Money, Language and the Body," Steven Connor (1985, 149) maintains that "throughout the novel there is a repeated movement whereby the human body is first stripped of value [and then] reduced to [the] mere dust or detritus" from Genesis. This helps

---

22. This is especially interesting since Dickens had early on considered *The Grindstone* as a title for the novel (Kaplan 1981, 6–7).

194   **CHAPTER 4**

us begin to see how the two principal body idioms in *Our Mutual Friend* are bound up together in a commonly shared biblical imaginary wherein the meanest and most avaricious characters are constantly engaged in venal struggles to grind others down to dust—often in the rhetoric of putting others' "noses to the grindstone"—and crucially, all so that they will *not* have to moisten their brows with work to attain their own bread.

Bradbury does not specifically identify either of the idioms, but she nonetheless hits closest to my sense of how these two salient idiomatic expressions coalesce and operate in the world of the text. The brilliantly concise title of her article, "Working and Being Worked in *Our Mutual Friend*," captures the overlap I see in Dickens's development of the "sweat of the brow" and "nose to the grindstone" idioms because it pinpoints "'Work'—as a noun and a verb; action and object; self-motivated or imposed" (Bradbury 2005, 2). As we have seen, one of the novel's primary themes involves an exploration of how characters either do or do not work; now we will see how this occurs while most of these characters simultaneously *work* each other in efforts to avoid working. For Bradbury, the dual aspect of activity and passivity in the term *work*, noun and verb, epitomizes the most "complex dynamic operating in *Our Mutual Friend*" (2). I agree, but I maintain that the particular way in which this complex dynamic of interpersonal mastery operates depends on the dual idiomatic structure that undergirds an important dimension residing at the novel's imaginative core.

Although Dickens had not specifically used the idiomatic expression "nose to the grindstone" in any of his previous novels, it was hardly a non sequitur for him. His abiding interest in the trope of grinding mastery and literal grindstones has several germane precedents within his oeuvre. We see evidence of this interest very early on in *Pickwick Papers* (1836–37), for instance. Mr. Jackson, the lawyer from Dodson and Fogg who represents the plaintiff in the Bardell case, visits Pickwick to deliver subpoenas to his friends Snodgrass, Tupman, Winkle, and Weller. Jackson's point is to make Pickwick aware of the powerful position such subpoenas afford Dodson and Fogg by incriminating the defendant "upon the testimony of [his] own friends" (Dickens [1836–37] 2003, 377). What is important for our purposes is how the lawyer demonstrates the powerful mastery his firm has over Pickwick via his subpoenaed friends: "Mr. Jackson smiled once more upon the company; and, applying his left thumb to the tip of his nose, worked a visionary . . . mill with his right hand, thereby performing a very graceful piece of pantomime . . . which was familiarly denominated 'taking a grinder'" (378). The ideas associated with noses and grindstones also stay with Dickens through the 1840s. Think, for instance, of how *Barnaby Rudge*'s (1841) Simon Tappertit expresses his frustrated desire to dominate his rival, Joe Willet, by taking to the grindstone in the locksmith's shop:

SWEAT WORK AND NOSE GRINDING IN *OUR MUTUAL FRIEND*   195

"I'll do nothing to-day," said Mr. Tappertit . . . "but grind. I'll grind up
all the tools. Grinding will suit my present humor well. Joe!"

Whirr-r-r-r. The grindstone was soon in motion; the sparks were flying off in showers. This was the occupation for his heated spirit.

Whirr-r-r-r. (Dickens [1841] 1973, 86)

Dickens had also associated the grindstone with oppressive labor, greedy dominance, and social mastery in his depiction of Ebenezer Scrooge in 1843 (1971,
46), describing him as "a tight-fisted hand at the grindstone . . . a squeezing,
wrenching, grasping, scraping, clutching, covetous old sinner! Hard and sharp
as flint, from which no steel had ever struck out generous fire." Similarly, we
learn in *David Copperfield* ([1849–50] 2004, 301) that Rosa Dartle has "brought
everything to a grindstone" in her efforts to master Steerforth's affections—the
futility of which causes her to "w[ear] herself away by constant sharpening."

Dickens takes these individualized characteristics and raises them to far
wider thematic heights in the 1850s and 1860s, though. The list of possible
titles for *Hard Times* (1854), for example, contains a flurry of grindstone references: "The Grindstone," "Mr Gradgrind's grindstone," "The universal general grindstone," "Mr Gradgrind's grindstone facts," and again, "Mr Gradgrind's
grindstone" (Stone, 1987, 251). Of course in the story itself, the stone that the
allegorically named character turns becomes a "mill of knowledge," which is
fitting given the connection between the mechanistic way the Coketown
school churns out facts and the way its factory churns out textiles (Dickens
[1854] 2003, 59). But it seems that by the early 1860s, Dickens was even more
keen on pursuing the imaginative possibilities that literal grindstones afforded.
His *Book of Memoranda* lists the following "Titles for such a notion [of the book
that would eventually become *Our Mutual Friend*]": "The Grindstone," "The
Great Wheel," "Round and Round," "Rokesmith's Forge," and "The Cinder
Heap" (Kaplan 1981, 6–7). Perhaps what Fred Kaplan calls this "notion" can
be traced to Dickens having *actual* grindstones on his mind as he struggled to
get his new book started. Just few years before beginning to compose *Our Mutual Friend*, Dickens had titled a chapter of *A Tale of Two Cities* (1859) "The
Grindstone," wherein he presents a scene of revolutionaries gruesomely working an enormous grindstone to sharpen their blood-stained weapons. It is
important to note that the physical (literal) proximity of one's nose to this kind
of sharpening stone is where the now well-known figurative expression originated. The operator of this type of grindstone was required lie down on a full
body-length plank above the spinning stone so that his or her nose was only
inches away from the actual grindstone in the sharpening process (figure 20).
Such a setup is briefly alluded to in *Little Dorrit* ([1855–57] 2003, 285) when

FIGURE 20. Body-length nineteenth-century grindstone. Finch Foundry, Devon, England

the narrator notes how a "step-ladder" is required in the shop of Doyce and Clennam to access "the large grindstone where tools are sharpened."

As we have seen with his other imaginatively deployed idioms, Dickens's use of the "nose to the grindstone" expression occurs at more or less the time when the idiom was acquiring the figurative meanings that we are so familiar with today. In fact, one of the definitions the *Oxford English Dictionary* lists for

SWEAT WORK AND NOSE GRINDING IN *OUR MUTUAL FRIEND*

the idiom was just beginning to circulate toward the middle of the nineteenth century: "to keep (oneself or another) continually engaged in hard and monotonous labour." The following visualizations from the *British Library Newspapers Digital Archive* (figure 21) and the *British Periodicals* Archive (figure 22) show the growing use of the idiom in wide swaths of the cultural lexicon at mid-century.

So Dickens was once again at the forefront of his era's lexical trends—both in his fiction and in his life. I mention his life because he had drawn on exactly this figurative, "modern" sense of the idiom in describing his own work beginning and completing *Great Expectations* (1860–61)—the novel immediately preceding *Our Mutual Friend*. He told Forster that "the preparations to get ahead of [the publication schedule of *Great Expectations*] . . . will tie me *to the grindstone pretty tightly*" (House et al. 1965–2002, ix, 320, emphasis mine).[23] Barely three weeks later, he characterized his hard work in a letter to Wilkie Collins using a similar formulation: "I must get down to Gad's tonight, and get to work again. Four weekly numbers have been ground off the wheel, and at least another must be turned, afore we meet" (ix, 330).[24] And after Bulwer Lytton had convinced him of the need to alter the novel's ending, he wrote to Collins using the same grindstone rhetoric, reporting "that I have resumed the wheel, and taken another turn at it" (ix, 428).[25] The circumstances that I have enumerated here demonstrate that Dickens had a career-long preoccupation with literal and figurative grindstones and that he associated the hard and sustained labor of writing—what Thomas Carlyle (1842, 194) liked to call "sweat of the brain"—with grindstones at precisely the time he was struggling to develop his ideas about work and mastery that eventually emerge as two of the central idiomatic concerns of his last completed novel.

Nose Abrasions

My claim that the "nose to the grindstone" idiom operates as a second idiomatic pillar of *Our Mutual Friend* requires an analysis of the ways in which the idiom works its way into the imaginative structure of the novel after Dickens lists it in his planning notes but well before its explicit appearance halfway through the novel. This necessarily involves a consideration of how Dickens draws on other literal and figurative parts of the idiom's definition at the time

---

23. October 4, 1860; emphasis mine.
24. October 24, 1860.
25. June 23, 1861.

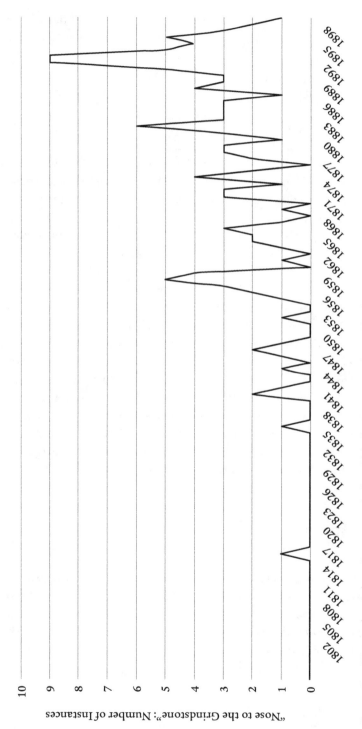

FIGURE 21. "Nose to the grindstone" appearance in the *British Library Newspapers Digital Archive*

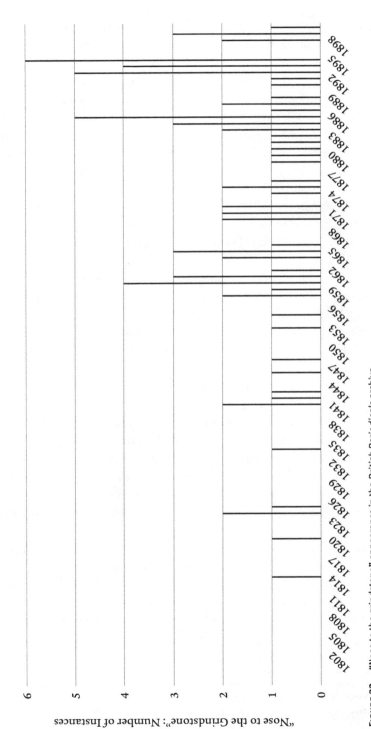

FIGURE 22. "Nose to the grindstone" appearance in the *British Periodicals* archive

200   **CHAPTER 4**

he was composing the novel's early sections. The *Oxford English Dictionary* dates back to the mid-sixteenth century the following usage of the idiom: "to get the mastery over another and treat him with harshness or severity; *to grind down* or oppress" (emphasis mine). The example the *Oxford English Dictionary* cites is from John Heywood's *Proverbs in the English Tongue* (1546): "I shall revenge former hurts, Hold their noses to the grindstone." *Our Mutual Friend*'s theme of just this kind of abrasive oppression in the social sphere is so prevalent, in fact, that it is difficult to locate a critic of the novel who does not specifically acknowledge its "grinding" attributes in some fashion.[26] Nonetheless, the associations between this overarching theme and Dickens's use of the "nose to the grindstone" idiom have been so far critically unexplored.[27]

These repeated idiomatic associations appear at the earliest stages of *Our Mutual Friend*'s composition. The original ending of the second number, the chapter titled "A Marriage Contract" (which Dickens had already composed before the first installment appeared in print), contains several germane connections to the grindstone idiom in this regard.[28] The reference to the Veneering-hosted wedding of Alfred Lammle and Sophronia Akershem as a "contract" in this early chapter is appropriate because both parties agree to marry under the assumption that the other is wealthy. Only during a honeymoon walk on the Isle of Wight do the parties learn that they have married each other "on false pretenses"; neither has any wealth in reality (Dickens [1864–65] 1997, 127). What is important here is how the narrator describes Lammle's angry and embarrassed state on learning of his new wife's lack of money in terms of abrasions that appear on his nose. We learn that its "colour has turned to a livid white, and ominous marks have come to light about his nose" (128). Lammle's shame of confronting the moneyed Veneering circle without the guise of wealth causes "ominous marks" to appear on his nose—as if it has already been pressed to the social grindstone of public em-

---

26. For only a sampling of the phenomenon wherein "grinding" is explicitly used, see Kennedy (1973), Gribble (1975), Romano (1978), Kucich (1985), Brattin (1985), Poovey (1993), Cheadle (2001a, 2001b), Gallagher (2006), Bodenheimer (2007), Ledger (2011), S. James (2012), and Grass (2014).

27. This failure to recognize the imaginative potential of idiomatic language is surprising given that critics such as Kucich (1985,168) have explored how "many of the 'inimitable' characteristics of [Dickens's] prose style" in *Our Mutual Friend* "are dedicated to produce some kind of exchange value in terms of meaning." Although he does not analyze the prevalent idioms to which I have drawn our attention, Kucich maintains that syntax, metaphor, diction, conventions of description, redundancy of phrasing are all devices of "a rhetoric . . . doing some kind of work" (168).

28. Dickens overwrote the second number and was forced to postpone this particular chapter until early in the third number, where it eventually became chapter 10. This does not matter much for my argument, though, since Dickens composed all of this material *before* the novel "began" in print. For the most comprehensive study of the novel's development, see Grass 2014, 37–38.

SWEAT WORK AND NOSE GRINDING IN *OUR MUTUAL FRIEND*   201

barrassment. This phenomenon occurs again on the same page when the Lammles decide to double down in a pact to "pretend to the world" and agree to pursue "any scheme that will bring [them] money" (129). The temporary relief provided by thinking about this ruse is registered in the narrator's affirmation that "those aforesaid marks" on Alfred's nose "have come and gone" (129), a description that suggests reprieve from the grindstone of embarrassing truth.

Moreover, this grinding sense of social mastery and its attendant pressures resurfaces in the Lammles' first moneymaking scheme: their orchestration of an arranged marriage between Georgiana Podsnap and Fascination Fledgeby. Barely three pages after "ominous marks" conspicuously emerge and disappear on Lammle's nose, the weak and impressionable Podsnap daughter is described as possessing a distinctly "rasped surface of nose" in the moments that she is being coerced into a marriage by the designing Lammles (132). Not only does this rasped nose description allude to the grim existence awaiting her as the potential wife of a man (Fascination Fledgeby) whose "youthful fire was all composed of sparks from the grindstone," but it is also representative of the larger "scrunch or be scrunched" world of *Our Mutual Friend* where no one seems to care what happens to others—so long, as the grindstone-associated saying goes, it is no skin (rasped) off *their* nose (266, 470).[29]

Alfred Lammle's nose also continues to be the primary bodily site on which alternating social successes and financial failures manifest themselves. For example, when the ploy to profit from Georgiana Podsnap's marriage runs aground and the "happy pair of swindlers" begin anew their "work together" (i.e., their attempt to make money *without* working), Sophronia pressures her husband, asking, "'Have you no scheme . . . that will bring in anything?'" (545). The desperate prospect of having no scheme while attempting to live in lavish society solely on Alfred's small annuity causes the couple to fret over their ability to "beg money, borrow money, or steal money" successfully (546). Just as when Alfred learns of his wife's lack of money on their honeymoon, this new state of desperation and its attendant loss of leverage in the social sphere is similarly figured in the rhetoric of the grindstone idiom. Pondering the consequences of such a bleak scenario, Lammle once again appears with "a white dint or two about his nose"—as if the pressure to maintain his moneyed persona is, however briefly, embodied in the nicked surface of his nose put to a grindstone (545). This state of desperation, along with the state of Lammle's

---

29. Dickens has previously used this expression in *Hard Times* ([1854] 2003, 103) when Bounderby proclaims that he will "have the skin off [Mrs. Sparsit's Coriolanian] nose."

202   **CHAPTER 4**

nose, however, does not last long. Sophronia hits on the idea to blackmail Boffin by revealing to him their knowledge of Rokesmith's declaration of marriage of Bella. The couple envisions immediate financial profit from this blackmail scheme but also banks on a belief that it will pay further dividends by situating Lammle to replace Rokesmith as Boffin's secretary. The important component of this anticipated turn of events for the purposes of my argument lies in the fact that it, too, is depicted as a relief—figuratively and literally—from the pressures of the grindstone. After the couple evaluates what they take to be the viability and success of their plan to "earn" money by blackmail, Alfred's nose appears no longer in danger of being put to the grindstone: "Mr. Lammle smiled. . . . In his sinister relish of the scheme . . . making it the subject of his cogitations, he seemed to have twice as much nose on his face as he had had in his life" (548).[30]

Indeed, the size and state of noses turns out to matter a great deal in *Our Mutual Friend*. And by this point in his career, Dickens delights in finessing the malleability of idiomatic association throughout the novel. For example, Fledgeby's true disposition as "the meanest cur existing" plays out not in terms we might expect from the narrator's canine reference but in those related to grindstones and noses (266): "Fledgeby . . . maintained a spruce appearance. But his youthful fire was all composed of sparks from the grindstone; and as the sparks flew off, went out, and never warmed anything, be sure that Fledgeby had his tools at the grindstone, and turned it with a wary eye" (266–67). This description, of course, alludes to Fledgeby's "profession" in the bill-brokering line where he uses Riah to keep his clients' noses to the grindstone while collecting exorbitant interest on the money he loans.

The treatment of noses figures prominently in Fledgeby's private life as well, especially in scenarios involving the fluctuations in the atmosphere of interpersonal mastery and social power. One of the most salient examples of this shifting nature of power occurs when Lammle pays a breakfast visit to Fledgeby in order to gauge the status of the proposed marriage he (Lammle) has arranged between Fledgeby and Georgiana Podsnap. Because Lammle is relying on the money that will come to him from the brokered union, he is anxious to push the process along as quickly as possible. But Fledgeby essentially refuses to divulge any information on the scheme's progress and, since he presumably gets to decide on whether the marriage will go forward at all, exercises his position of power over Lammle when he feels uncomfortably pressured. "Don't you on that account," Fledgeby insists, "come talking to me as if I was your doll and puppet, because I am not" (268). Fledgeby's further

---

30. For a distinctly erotic interpretation of Lammle's "palpitating nose," see David 1981, 105–6.

SWEAT WORK AND NOSE GRINDING IN *OUR MUTUAL FRIEND*   203

insinuation that the meek Georgiana (not of the "violent," "pitching-in order") might not answer for his marital liking sends Lammle—"a bully by nature and by usual practice"—into "a violent passion" (270). What follows is an extraordinarily comical tableau of Lammle's nose-centered assertion of social power and mastery:

> "I tell you what, Mr. Fledgeby," said Lammle advancing on him. "Since you presume to contradict me, I'll assert myself a little. Give me your nose!"
>
> Fledgeby covered it with his hand instead, and said, retreating, "I beg you won't!"
>
> "Give me your nose, sir," repeated Lammle.
>
> Still covering that feature and backing, Mr. Fledgeby reiterated . . . "I beg, I beg, you won't."
>
> "And this fellow," exclaimed Lammle, stopping and making the most of his chest—"This fellow presumes on my having selected him out of all the young fellows I know, for an advantageous opportunity! This fellow presumes on my having in my desk around the corner, his dirty note of hand for a wretched sum payable on the occurrence of a certain event, which can only be of my and my wife's bringing about! This fellow, Fledgeby, presumes to be impertinent to me, Lammle. Give me your nose sir!"
>
> "No! Stop! I beg your pardon," said Fledgeby, with humility.
>
> "What do you say, sir?" demanded Lammle, seeming too furious to understand.
>
> "I say," repeated Fledgeby, with laborious and explanatory politeness, "I beg your pardon."
>
> Mr. Lammle paused. "As a man of honour," said he, throwing himself into a chair, "I am disarmed."
>
> Mr. Fledgeby also took a chair, though less demonstratively, and by slow approaches removed his hand from his nose. (271)

I quote this scene at considerable length because it provides an extended example of *Our Mutual Friend*'s preoccupation with mastery by way of noses well before the actual phrase "nose to the grindstone" appears in the text and because it inaugurates a pattern of nose-oriented power shifts that characterize many of the novel's most interesting (and humorous) contests for social dominance.

The end of the scene recounted above also takes on more definitive associations with the grindstone idiom. The narrator tells us that after the humiliating breakfast meeting with Lammle, "Fledgeby did not recover his spirits or

204 **CHAPTER 4**

his usual *temperature* of nose until the afternoon" (272; emphasis mine). This statement suggests that Fledgeby, normally accustomed to sparks flying from putting *others'* noses to the grindstone, experiences a taste of his own nose-burning medicine at the hands of Lammle. Moreover, it demonstrates the ways in which social power is recouped in *Our Mutual Friend* via a repetitive cycle of nasal humiliations and reassertions of mastery. For instance, Fledgeby's experience of nearly having his nose put to the grindstone by Lammle only triggers a truculent desire to reassert himself over someone else who has less power than he. This plays out in the scene directly following Lammle's nose grabbing, as Fledgeby grows impatient when calling on his counting house, Pubsey and Co., where his power and mastery remain unchallenged. "He got out of temper, crossed the narrow street again, and pulled the house-bell as if it were the house's nose, and he were taking a hint from his late experience . . . for he angrily pulled at the house's nose again, and pulled and continued to pull, until a human nose appeared in the dark doorway" (272–73). Of course, the human nose belongs to Riah, the subordinate whom Fledgeby uses as a front to keep his clients' noses to his usurious grindstone.

Shortly hereafter, Fledgeby seizes on an opportunity to exact retribution from Lammle's bullying—and he does so with "a certain remembrance of that feature"—his nose—on which Lammle had previously bullied him (422). Lammle pays an unannounced visit to Pubsey and Co. to inform Fledgeby that Podsnap has been tipped off about the scheme to have his daughter married for money. Podsnap's cancellation of the wedding effectively deprives the Lammles (once again) of the money they expected to receive from their scheme. Never one to miss a glimpse of weakness or to pass up an occasion to exercise power over another, Fledgeby realizes the likelihood that Lammle will need a loan from his firm and, therefore, levels a dire threat from behind a charade that Riah is the real owner of Pubsey and Co. "'You have sustained a loss here. . . . But whatever you do, Lammle, don't—don't—don't, I beg of you—ever fall into the hands of Pubsey and Co. in the next room, for they are *grinders*. Regular flayers and *grinders*, my dear Lammle,' repeated Fledgeby with a peculiar relish, 'and they'll skin you . . . and *grind* every inch of your skin to tooth-powder. You have seen what Mr. Riah is. Never fall into his hands, Lammle, I beg of you as a friend!'" (423; emphasis mine). The narrator's comments on Lammle's physical reaction to this most recent threat only strengthen the linkages to the theme of noses and grindstones: "The brooding Lammle," the narrator tells us, appears at this vulnerable moment "with certain white dints coming and going in his palpitating nose" (423). The real grinder, of course, is not Riah but Fledgeby. And this is fitting since the character who revels in his ability "to work a lot of power over you" is "all composed of sparks from

SWEAT WORK AND NOSE GRINDING IN *OUR MUTUAL FRIEND*   205

the grindstone" (427–28, 266). Fledgeby might well be what the narrator calls "the meanest cur existing," but his actions and those around him who jockey for money and power reveal that *Our Mutual Friend*'s social atmosphere is idiomatically less "dog-eat-dog," as Ledger (2011, 266) has characterized it, than it is "nose-grind-nose."[31]

The experience of having his nose on and off the grindstone continues to index Lammle's fortunes and misfortunes all the way through to his exit from the novel. After his scheming with his wife fails and they are forced to sell their possessions at auction, the Lammles pay an urgent visit to the Boffins in a last-ditch effort to procure Alfred a position as the Golden Dustman's new secretary. The Lammles waste no time insinuating Alfred's willingness and competence for the position, but they are met by a double rampart of Boffin silence: "here had been several lures thrown out, and neither of [the Boffins] had uttered a word" (629). Wondering if the Boffins' untutored social graces account for their silence but also sensing the urgency of the moment, Mrs. Lammle decides to make a more direct appeal, declaring that her husband is "burning to serve" Mr. Boffin (630). When again "neither Mr nor Mrs Boffin s[ay] a word" in response to this explicit appeal, the Lammles begin to perceive the gravity of their powerless and ruined state, but important for my argument, this perception becomes registered in the now familiar sense that Lammle's nose is being put to a grindstone: "several white dints began to come and go about Mr. Lammle's nose, as he observed that Mrs. Boffin merely looked up from the teapot for a moment with an embarrassed smile, which was no smile" (630). The desperation rapidly grows for the Lammles and their decision "try 'em again" eventually, though reluctantly, moves the Boffins to reveal their knowledge of the couple's deceitful ways. This disclosure, and all the opportunities it shuts down in terms of the Lammles' survival by scheming, yet again manifests itself as an even more grinding pressure on Alfred's nose: "the coming and going dints got almost as large, the while, as . . . the teaspoon" (631). However, the Boffins' keenest desire is to be rid of the Lammles altogether, and they know that providing them money is the most expedient way to ensure their swift departure. Thus, Boffin provides a bank note for one hundred pounds under the pretense that the Lammles have done "a very great service" by informing them of Rokesmith's pursuit of Bella. But it is telling that the narrator frames even this development as one in which Lammle's nose is lifted from the grindstone of having either to find other schemes or, heaven forbid, work for his survival. Almost immediately after Mrs. Lammle takes possession of the money packet, we learn that Alfred "had the appearance of feeling

---

31. Ledger (2011, 366, 373) maintains that the novel "exhaustively anatomizes" the "dog-eat-dog mentality."

206   **CHAPTER 4**

relieved, and breathing more freely" flashes "a glittering smile and *a great deal of nose*" (632; emphasis mine).

Without question, Dickens's most psychologically complex exploration of this kind of grinding mastery occurs in the antagonistic relationship between Bradley Headstone and Eugene Wrayburn. Money still matters here but only in relation to broader class antagonism and, eventually, to romantic rivalry. The class antagonism is on full display when the pair first meet in the lawyer's offices and Wrayburn acts "as if there were nothing where [Headstone] stood" while he pejoratively asks, "And who might this other person be?" (285). Headstone unwittingly makes the mistake of responding to the question not with his name but with his professional position as a "schoolmaster"—a mistake that Wrayburn leverages throughout the duration of their first meeting by reducing Headstone to his respectable but undeniably lower social occupation.[32] And unwitting is the right word for Headstone in comparison to Wrayburn. The schoolmaster's paradoxically "sluggish intelligence" is no match for the lawyer's quick wit at every turn of their initial conversation (536). Wrayburn's aggressively condescending and dismissive treatment of Headstone in this first meeting, because it is performed for no evident reason (the romantic rivalry for Lizzie not yet established), is perhaps the best reflection of the unmitigated social cruelty that *Our Mutual Friend* repeatedly exposes. The "consummate[ly] indolen[t]" lawyer's quick wittedness seeks no larger fulfillment at this point in the novel than demeaning his intellectual and social inferior for his own enjoyment (285).[33]

Audrey Jaffe identifies this impulse toward social mastery for its own sake as one of the defining features of the novel. "More than any other of Dickens's novels," she argues, "*Our Mutual Friend* traces a pattern of epistemological one-upsmanship: characters not only busy themselves finding out all they can about one another, but they invent their own plots, entrapping others in schemes of which the point is often merely to entrap" (Jaffe 1991, 157). This

---

32. For an analysis of how the possession or use of people's names becomes a means of exercising power more broadly, see Connor 1985, 150–53.

33. There is also something more sinister in Wrayburn's intellectual bullying of Headstone. To think about it in terms of the novel's preoccupation with work (by the sweat of the brow or otherwise), the Headstone-Wrayburn antagonism represents something of a Dickensian anomaly. As Ledger (2011, 372) has noted, Dickens "repudiates, here as rarely before . . . the hard-working respectable school teacher with whom one might have expected Dickens to sympathize." As despicable and destructive as his ungovernable passions become, Headstone works diligently at his profession and Wrayburn conspicuously does not. This anomalous depiction of Headstone reflects Bodenheimer's (2007, 207) sense of Dickens's own paradoxical relationship to class: "His views about social class were deeply ambivalent, alternating in an inchoate way between a paternalism that looked down and a resentment that looked up; these oscillations were conditioned by a personal experience of class instability that he could neither discuss outright nor stop representing."

SWEAT WORK AND NOSE GRINDING IN *OUR MUTUAL FRIEND* 207

assessment certainly applies to both sides of the Headstone-Wrayburn relationship: Headstone uses various methods to gather information about the status of Lizzie Hexam's romantic life. And Wrayburn, for his part, enjoys a perverse satisfaction from "goad[ing] the schoolmaster to madness" by leading him on through cat-and-mouse night chases all over London (Dickens [1864–65] 1997, 533). Since Wrayburn derives "inexpressible comfort" from this cruel endeavor, it is worth recounting at length the detailed way in which he describes the process to Lightwood that leads to the infliction of "grinding torments" on Headstone (533):

> I do it thus: I stroll out after dark, stroll a little way, look in at a window and furtively look out for the schoolmaster. Sooner or later, I perceive the schoolmaster on the watch. . . . Having made sure of his watching me, I tempt him on all over London. One night I go east, another night north, in a few nights I go all around the compass. Sometimes, I walk; sometimes, I proceed in cabs, draining the pocket of the schoolmaster who then follows in cabs. I study and get up abstruse No Thoroughfares in the course of the day. With Venetian mystery I seek those No Thoroughfares at night, glide into them by means of dark courts, tempt the schoolmaster to follow, turn suddenly, and catch him before he can retreat. Then we face one another, and I pass him as unaware of his existence, and he undergoes *grinding torments*. Similarly, I walk at a great pace down a short street, rapidly turn the corner, and, getting out of his view, as rapidly turn back. I catch him coming on post, again pass him as unaware of his existence, and again he undergoes *grinding torments*. (533; emphases mine)

On both of the above occasions I emphasize with italics, Dickens revised in the manuscript from what had originally been simply "torments" to "*grinding torments*" (156; emphasis mine). Joel Brattin (1985, 340) surmises that Dickens made these changes "perhaps looking back to the mill metaphor" from book 2 where Headstone, in conversation with Lizzie, labors with his words "as though they came from a rusty mill." This explanation is possible, of course, but Dickens's alterations here resonate more plausibly with a particular kind of physically abrasive mastery which he has repeatedly associated with having one's nose put to the grindstone. For instance, Wrayburn gloats that his night rambles make "the schoolmaster so ridiculous, and aware of being made ridiculous, that [he] see[s] him *chafe* and fret at every pore when [they] cross one another" (Dickens [1864–65] 1997, 533; emphasis mine).

At one point shortly hereafter, the two lawyers pass Headstone on their way back to their chambers, and Wrayburn appeals to Lightwood to notice the

208   CHAPTER 4

accuracy of his descriptions: "you see as I was saying—undergoing grinding torments" (534). As we have now seen Dickens do so often, he relishes extending the figurative to a partial literalization of the idiom in the narrator's description of the passing schoolmaster: "It [grinding torment] was not too strong a phrase for the occasion. . . . [Headstone] went by them in the dark, like a haggard head suspended in the air" (534). Moreover, in the subsequent pages, the narrator continues to describe the schoolmaster's apparently severed head on multiple other occasions: "the haggard head suspended in the air flitted across the road," "The haggard head floated up the dark staircase," "The head arose to its former height from the ground, floated down the staircase again" (536–37). This is surely Dickens at his grotesquely but thematically punning best. The character on whose name he eventually settles as *"Headstone"*[34] endures such grinding mastery at the hands of Wrayburn that his "head" repeatedly appears as if it has been *entirely* ground off at the (grind) "stone"! He becomes a character, like Captain Cuttle, in whose very name Dickens (dis)embodies one of the central idiomatic themes of the novel.

The finest literalization and inscription of this theme on Headstone's body, however, occurs after he has been ground down to his physical breaking point in staying up all night following Wrayburn around the city while also attending to his regular teaching duties in the daytime. It culminates in the confirmation of Headstone's most humiliating fear as he witnesses Wrayburn and Lizzie "walking side by side" during one of his ragged night vigils (625). Here, Headstone's resigned acceptance of Wrayburn's mastery over him may be seen in his recounting of the event to Riderhood. "What did you do?" asks Riderhood to which Headstone responds, "Nothing" (625). Riderhood's next question, "What are you going to do?" though, elicits a bodily response that not only locates but literalizes in excelsis Headstone's vulnerability as a consequence of enduring such "grinding torments":

> [Headstone] dropped into a chair, and laughed. Immediately afterwards, a great spirt of blood burst from his nose.
>
> "How does that happen?" asked Riderhood.
>
> "I don't know. I can't keep it back. It has happened twice—three times—four times—I don't know how many times—since last night. I taste it, smell it, see it, it chokes me, and then it breaks out like this." (625)

---

34. According to Dickens's number plans (No. 6), the following is the whittled list of possible names: Amos Deadstone, Amos Headstone, Bradley Deadstone, and then finally (underlined) Bradley Headstone (Stone 1987, 345). For an alternate interpretation of Headstone's name, see David 1981, 81.

SWEAT WORK AND NOSE GRINDING IN *OUR MUTUAL FRIEND*

Critics have long remained as baffled to explain this event as Headstone himself. Stephen James's (2012, 226) description of Headstone's "unaccountable and repeated nosebleeds" is representative of the larger critical inability to make sense of Headstone's seemingly bizarre nose bleeding. Thinking about this scene, though, in relation to the novel's overarching preoccupation with mastery and its grinding effects on noses allows us to access perhaps one of the greatest but as-yet-unremarked-on Dickensian in-jokes. Headstone, as we have seen, is the character in whose very name Dickens embeds the elements of his own demise. Just as he puts his head to its own stone (all but grinding it off in his nightly pursuits of Wrayburn), his ungovernable passion to torture himself in confirming Lizzie's romantic choice after his rejection has the effect of putting his nose so thoroughly to the grindstone that beyond the sparks and white dints of the novel's earlier proboscis pressures, we encounter a nose ground down to a bloody pulp. Headstone's *defacement* is thus ingeniously fulfilled in virtually every sense of the idiom.[35]

Idiom Convergence

Thus by the time the "nose to the grindstone" idiom first appears explicitly in *Our Mutual Friend* (in book 3, chapter 14: "Mr Wegg Prepares a Grindstone for Mr Boffin's Nose"), it not only officially names a thematic pattern of grinding mastery that has been structuring the novel from the start, but it also emerges organically in conjunction with issues of work and labor heralded by the "sweat of the brow" idiom. In fact, the "nose to the grindstone" idiom could not fulfill its narrative purpose of exposing frauds and keeping the Harmon property intact without a direct relationship to the ways in which those involved—Boffin, Wegg, and Venus—do and do not work. We know from very early on that Mr. and Mrs. Boffin's "religious sense of duty" and "moral straightness" make it difficult for them to *stop* working even when they inherit the Bower (Dickens [1864–65] 1997, 105). The newly wealthy dustman who confounds the idle lawyer Wrayburn by cheerfully asserting that "there's nothing like work" even goes so far as to consult his wife about "beginning work again" despite their newly inherited fortune (98, 104). In contrast, Wegg, the "wily" character who speaks in the "nose to the grindstone" idiom most has a "mercenary mind" that is constantly focused on exacting the greatest amount of money out of Boffin with the least possible work (186, 64).

---

35. For the historical and emblematic quality of the nose in the drama of defacement, see Groebner 2009, 76.

210   CHAPTER 4

The difference in these two characters' dispositions reaches its highest and most comical pitch in the chapter where the semiliterate Wegg frets that Boffin's hiring of Rokesmith as his secretary will jeopardize his cushy "job" as a ballad and book reader. Boffin assures Wegg that this is not the case because it would mean "that [he, Wegg] were not going to do anything to deserve [his] money" (188). But the changing hands of this undeserved money is exactly what comes to pass in the final page of the chapter. The narrator tells us that Wegg, "being something drowsy after his plentiful repast, and constitutionally of a shirking temperament, was well enough pleased to stump away, without doing what he had come to do, and what he was paid for doing" (191–92). It is ultimately this Rogue-like, work-shirking aspect of Wegg's constitution that leads him to attempt "to put [Boffin's] nose to the grindstone" by blackmailing him into paying for the right to retain the Harmon estate (570).

Although Venus at first joins in the blackmailing plan, his earnest dedication to his work as a taxidermist precipitates his decision to withdraw from it and to inform Boffin of Wegg's untoward designs. Dickens makes it clear in his first descriptions that Venus "take[s] a pride and a pleasure" in his trade, describing himself as "a workman" who has improved his knowledge of anatomy "by sticking to it until one or two in the morning" (89, 90). It takes some digging around in the dust heaps with Wegg and searching for treasures and later-dated wills that would deprive Boffin of his inheritance to remind Venus of his (Higden-like) preference for honest work over easy money. He tells Boffin as much when he makes the decision to reveal Wegg's nose-grinding plans: "All I know is this: I am proud of my calling after all. . . . Putting the same meaning into other words, I do not mean to turn a single dishonest penny by this affair" (565). Venus's wording here is an inverted echo of the narrator's description of Riderhood: "It had been the calling of his life to slink and dog and waylay" (689).

As with Riderhood, Fledgeby, Lammle, and the novel's other rapacious schemers, Wegg has no regard for work, honesty, or fellow feeling. All he (thinks he) knows of the world is the one of grinding social mastery that comes in for heaviest indictment. Wegg's view of the world is limited to Bradbury's notion of work as a verb: work or *be worked*. Interestingly but not surprisingly, the chapter wherein Wegg proclaims his intentions to put the Dustman's "nose to the grindstone" on seven different occasions, he first assumes Boffin has similar intentions: "Boffin. Dusty Boffin. That foxey old grunter and *grinder*, sir, turns into the yard this morning, to meddle with our property" (568; emphasis mine). This is the climactic chapter (book 3, chapter 14) that finds Boffin listening to the conversation between Wegg and Venus from behind the alligator in the taxidermist's shop. Dickens heightens the comedy of this scene,

SWEAT WORK AND NOSE GRINDING IN *OUR MUTUAL FRIEND* 211

though, as we have seen him do so many times before, by alternating between the literal and figurative dimensions of the idiom. Wegg considers Boffin's appointment of Sloppy as a foreman of the dustheaps to be "an act of sneaking and *sniffing*" and in the same sentence declares, "his nose shall be put to the grindstone for it" (568; emphasis mine). Such idiomatic rhetoric only becomes more and more comically visceral as Wegg promises that he "shall not neglect bringing the grindstone to bear, nor yet bringing Dusty Boffin's nose to it. His nose once brought to it, shall be held to it by these hands . . . till the sparks fly out in showers" (571). Moreover, the repetition of Wegg's idiomatic threats become fully somatic for Boffin several chapters later. When Venus informs Boffin, who has yet to find the later-dated will, that the blackmail scheme is imminent, and that he supposes Wegg will "turn to at the grindstone" at his next chance, the narrator describes how "Mr. Boffin took his nose in his hand, as if it were greatly excoriated, and the sparks were beginning to fly out of that feature" (638).

Fittingly, the two guiding idioms that I have been tracing converge most definitively near the end of the novel in the plot sequence that resolves *Our Mutual Friend*'s principal problem of deciding who will inherit the old Harmon estate. For Wegg, the "great exertion" of "turning an imaginary grindstone" becomes real "sweat of the brow" labor when he is forced to keep pace with Boffin and Sloppy sifting the dust mounds day after day (643, 646). Dickens marks this transformation with a literal fulfillment of the first idiom, using the creative power of idiomatic language to make the phrase do several things at once. Working "by the sweat of his brow" for perhaps the first time in his life, Wegg appears "panting and mopping his head with his pockethandkerchief" (643). But Boffin's discovery of an even-later-dated will in which he, not the Crown, is the beneficiary allows him to counter Wegg's "newly-asserted power" (646). The Golden Dustman, however, exercises his power over "the ligneous sharper" by forcing Wegg to do precisely what he (Wegg), like so many others, spends the novel trying to avoid: work (60). The combined idiomatic irony, of course, is that the "sweat of the brow" work Wegg must now undertake in the dustheaps to "sharpen fine" Boffin's nose "w[ears] Mr. Wegg down" to a state of reversed literal and figurative mastery. We learn that working the mounds has so "worn Mr. Wegg down to skin and bone" that "the grindstone did undoubtedly appear to have been whirling at his own nose, rather than Boffin's" (759, 760)—an exquisitely deserved reversal that Dickens had been aiming to achieve based on his planning notes from the novel's earliest compositional stages which ask, "Mr Wegg's Grindstone sharpens the wrong nose?" (Stone 1987, 371).

212   **CHAPTER 4**

Like so much of his later fiction, Dickens's final novel ends not by offering a solution to society's systemic ills but by emphasizing traits and characteristics that can make living in such a society more bearable. And it is crucial for the argument I have been making that these traits and characteristics are deeply aligned with the two idiomatic phrases that appear only in *Our Mutual Friend*. Those who dedicate themselves to work (by the sweat of their brows or otherwise), like Sloppy and Jenny Wren, gravitate toward each other and remain in London while those who do not, like the Lammles and the Veneerings, are exiled abroad. Even the lawyers, a professional group normally skewered by Dickens throughout his career, come off relatively well because of their newly acquired appreciation for work at the end of the novel. Mortimer Lightwood, in addition to now *working* as the solicitor for the Harmons, "applie[s] himself with infinite zest to attacking and harassing Mr. Fledgeby" and to "disentangle[ing]" Twemlow from "the sublime Snigsworth's wrath" (Dickens [1864–65] 1997, 782, 783). Lightwood's embrace of work is so thoroughgoing that Dickens actually describes it with rhetoric associated with Jenny Wren's sweated profession: Lightwood acts "professionally with such unwonted dispatch and intention, that a piece of work was vigorously pursued as soon as it was cut out" (782). The lawyers' changed attitudes regarding work also invoke the "nose to the grindstone" idiom's sense of diligent labor. Just as Dickens described his own diligence "turning to the wheel" in order to compose and revise his fiction, Lightwood regrets that he allowed his inheritance to "preven[t] [him] from *turning to* at Anything" for so much of his life (790; emphasis mine). What is more, Wrayburn not only develops the capacity to understand his friend's regret but also the ability to transform it into a hopeful future defined by similarly meaningful labor. "In turning to at last, we turn to in earnest," Wrayburn says as he envisions a life in the colonies, "*working* at [his] vocation there" (791; emphasis mine).

Idiomaticity and Intentionality

The concern most central to this study—the generative impulses of the Dickens's creative imagination—comes to a fitting and quite explicit climax with the material Dickens appended to the final completed piece of fiction he ever wrote. In his "Postscript, In Lieu of Preface" that appeared at the conclusion of the last double number of *Our Mutual Friend* in November 1865, Dickens attempted to beat "a class of readers and commentators" to the critical punch by anticipating their objections to his treatment of the novel's "leading incident": the Harmon-Rokesmith murder/survival plot (798). Here, he defends

SWEAT WORK AND NOSE GRINDING IN *OUR MUTUAL FRIEND*   213

his efforts to maintain a delicate balance between what he was required to reveal and what to conceal over the course of the story's nineteen-month publication, finally declaring "that an artist (of whatever denomination) may perhaps be trusted to know what he is about in his vocation":

> To keep for a long time unsuspected, yet always working itself out, another purpose originating in that leading incident, and turning it to a pleasant and useful account at last, was at once the most interesting and the most difficult part of my design. Its difficulty was much enhanced by the mode of publication; for, it would be very unreasonable to expect that many readers, pursuing a story in portions from month to month through nineteen months will, until they have them complete, perceive the relations of its finer threads to the whole pattern which is always before the eyes of the story-weaver at his loom. (798)

As anyone might expect, Dickens's bald and public attempt to outflank criticism of the novel's construction at its conclusion only made the target more conspicuous to his contemporary detractors. The *Saturday Review*, for example, directly criticized the "story weaver at his loom" control that Dickens had so confidently described: "The execution is coarse and clumsy, and the whole picture is redolent of ill-temper and fractiousness. . . . Even Mr. Dickens has seldom written a book in which there is so little uniformity of plot, so few signs of any care to make the parts fit in with one another in some kind of proportion"[36] (Grass 2014, 612–13). Writing for the *Westminster Review* in October 1864, Justin McCarthy reached conclusions that similarly contested Dickens's postscripted declaration of his awareness (and control) of "the finer threads to the whole pattern." Because "his mind [was] in fragments," according to McCarthy ([1864] 1965, 438), Dickens began the book "without having formed clear notions of it as a whole" (419), "abandons himself to the guidance of fancy, and makes a point of giving complete liberty to his Spirit at the very commencement of his task," which necessarily in McCarthy's view reveals "the absence of controlling power" (420).

Not surprisingly, then, especially given the confident pronouncement of retrospective control Dickens makes in the postscript, a significant portion of twentieth- and twenty-first-century criticism of *Our Mutual Friend* has also been preoccupied with the nature and degree of Dickens's organization and intent— even as the novel's critical esteem rose far beyond the purview of its first reviewers. As Grass (2014, 5) has commented, this makes sense for reasons that heighten the importance of Dickens's appended postscript: "[*Our Mutual*

---

36. November 11, 1865.

214   **CHAPTER 4**

Friend] simply came last, and it will always therefore remain the final example of Dickens's habits of writing and revision, his final striving after long-held artistic aims." The questions Ernest Boll asks at the outset of a 1944 article in *Modern Philology* test the claims of Dickens's postscript (using Dickens's own story-weaver trope) and set the agenda for those interested in probing the novel's imaginative "design": "What were the headline images that sprang up before Dickens's mind when the inspiration began to work in him? What gropings did his imagination evolve in its reach after interest and plausibility? How consciously did Dickens work at his craft, that is, how responsible an artist was he? To what detail did he keep his hand upon the design he wove month after month?" (96). It speaks to the immense and sprawling complexity of *Our Mutual Friend* that critics have taken up far-ranging (and widely opposing) positions on these important questions regarding the novel's construction. At one end of the spectrum, there are those who recognize it as Dickens's culminating artistic achievement but who see its incohesive disjointedness as its highest artistic merit. J. Hillis Miller's pioneering assessment from the 1950s, for instance, maintains that "*Our Mutual Friend* might be compared to a cubist collage. Its structure is formed by the juxtaposition of incompatible fragments in a pattern of disharmony and mutual contradiction."[37] Robert Kiely (1983) and Jaffe (1987) have extended this view by noting the ways in which the novel's fragmentation and confusion make it Dickens's most modernist work. McMaster (1987, 194) likewise sees "the fragmented world" of *Our Mutual Friend* as a notable departure from Dickens's more tightly "designed" novels. "No previous novel," she attests, "had been so atomic in its structure, or required more in the way of leaps, on the part of the reader, from one apparently unconnected part of the story to another" (194). Most recently, Anna Gibson (2015, 66) has argued compellingly that Dickens's return to the monthly serial format allowed him to embrace an unknowing openness to multiple narrative possibilities where the fictional world appears "always being made, dismantled, updated, and remade" by characters who "act, react, and adapt to one another" in a free and open distributive network.

There are also many critics who occupy various positions at the other end of the spectrum, drawing either directly or indirectly on Dickens's pronouncement in his postscript. More than half a century ago, U. C. Knoepflmacher (1971, 137) saw *Our Mutual Friend* as "the product of a practiced and self-assured craftsman in total command of all the rhetorical skills developed throughout his career." Even more influential for generations of later critics, Knoepflm-

---

37. J. Hillis Miller 1958, 284. In the same year, K. J. Fielding (1958, 185) suggests that the novel "can be well enjoyed as a loose collection of pieces that might have appeared in the pages of a magazine."

SWEAT WORK AND NOSE GRINDING IN *OUR MUTUAL FRIEND*

acher introduced the notion that the novel consists of "a gigantic jigsaw puzzle" in which the reader "eventually learns to recombine the jagged pieces that Dickens has so meticulously cut asunder" (143). Gregg Hecimovich (1995, 964, 960), for example, extends the interpretive conceit of Knoepflmacher's giant jigsaw puzzle by asserting that Dickens's "semantic trickery" is structured by an elaborate series of riddles wherein the reader becomes conscripted into "trying to find meaning in the accretion of clues." Similarly putting full faith in Dickens's ability to craft and conceal simultaneously (and intentionally), Kathleen Pacious (2016, 348; emphasis mine) views Dickens as "a master of trickery"—"plant[ing] the clues and applaud[ing] the savvy reader who is able to unearth them" as s/he/they "piece[s] together the separate strands of the plot to reveal *the* concealed meaning of the whole." I emphasize Pacious's identification of a singularity of meaning because of the way it restricts critics in the "Dickens as (conscious) designer" camp. For instance, John Reed (2011, 85) claims that Dickens "was in full command of his narrative [in *Our Mutual Friend*], so much so that he wanted to assist his readers in interpreting it correctly and to retain command of the mode of that interpretation." This means identifying redundant passages that "constitute instructions for the proper deciphering" of information—Dickensian redundancies that Reed believes "convey *the* central meaning" of the novel and that "make as certain as possible that [the] text will not be misread" (97, 118; emphasis mine).

My point in surveying some of the opposing critical landscape related to Dickens's construction of *Our Mutual Friend* is to think more deeply about the Inimitable's creative energies both within his final novel and within his oeuvre more generally. At one level, the sheer number of the two idiomatic expressions we have been tracing in *Our Mutual Friend*, especially considering their appearance in *only* this one novel, suggests what Gallagher (2006, 115), discussing a different concern with the text's bioeconomics, has termed "continuity too consistent to be accidental." Given Dickens's growing incorporation of unique idiomatic expressions to help in the imaginative construction of his mature fiction, his use of these two interconnected body idioms throughout *Our Mutual Friend* is indeed no accident by the time we come to his final novel. But I have no interest in attempting to prove Knoepflmacher's sense that Dickens, in *Our Mutual Friend*, is in "total command of *all* the rhetorical skills developed throughout his career." I do, however, submit that Dickens is at his "idiomatic best" in *Our Mutual Friend* where the "sweat of the brow" and "nose to the grindstone" idioms become braided together to make up at least one of the "finer threads to the whole pattern" in the Inimitable "story weaver's" last novel. The combination of these two idioms is indeed the specific "stylistic summa" that Stewart (2022, 227) ascribes more generally to Dickens's "ingrained

216   **CHAPTER 4**

verbal flourishes" and "phrasal habits etched into a sharper new outline." I have argued that his reliance on these two particular idioms not only helped him to get started on the novel during a period of extreme physical and intellectual exhaustion, but they also helped him establish and execute many of the book's major thematic developments. That said, the *extent* of Dickens's awareness at every step of his composition and what that extent might mean in terms of authorial intention remains, thankfully, indeterminate. As Edward Casey (1976, 39) says in his phenomenological study *Imagining*, the imagination seldom produces even two acts of intention that work in exactly the same way. In my analysis of this last novel, as with Dickens's others, I would never want to limit meaning to what the author supposedly intended by his reliance on certain idiomatic expressions (even if it were possible to determine such a thing irrefutably).

I realize that my position is partly at odds with what Dickens explicitly states at the end of his career in *Our Mutual Friend*'s postscript: that the artist must always understand what he is "about" better than the critic. This is patently not true, though. If it were, a writer, painter, sculptor, or artist of any kind would be the only competent judge of the merit and meaning of their own work. My entire study, in its most concentrated sense, is a response to Ernest Boll's (1944, 96) question in *Modern Philology*—a question in which the author is in some ways paradoxically *un*qualified to answer: "What were the headline images that sprang up before Dickens's mind when the inspiration began to work in him?" I have argued that the headline images that sprang up in Dickens's mature imagination were idiomatic and that these idioms were at once bodily, lexically, formally, and conceptually thematic. In short, Dickens drew more and more from an embodied idiomatic inspiration—on varying levels of conscious and unconscious intent—as his career developed. It turns out, as George Levine has recently put it in a discussion of the intentional fallacy, "with Dickens, an almost terrifying creative energy unleashes forces of which he himself (like us on the psychiatrist's couch babbling away) might not have been aware."[38] We can learn from Dickens's idiomatic imagination—at whatever level of consciousness—important new dimensions of his fiction that the Inimitable himself may not ever have been able to articulate.

---

38. This quotation comes from an email forum of the *Geezer Gazette*, an informal but nonetheless intellectually rigorous outlet for conversations about life and literature started by the late Gerhard Joseph, James Kincaid, and George Levine. March 9, 2021.

Conclusion
The Afterlife of Idiomatic Absorption
Among Novelists and Critics

> When language is in a state of energy, there is a
> continuous reciprocal influence of colloquial speech
> on writing, and of writing on colloquial speech.
>
> —T. S. Eliot, "The Writer as Artist" (1940)

The Idiomatic Body in James, Joyce, and Woolf

In December 1865, hardly before the ink was dry on the final monthly installment of *Our Mutual Friend*, the twenty-two-year-old Henry James penned a withering and now-famous review in *The Nation*. The first sentence of the review declares *Our Mutual Friend* "the poorest of Mr. Dickens's works" mainly because of its supposed failure in character development: "every character here put before us is a mere bundle of eccentricities, animated by no principle of nature whatever" (James 1865, 786). After objecting to nearly every character in *Our Mutual Friend*, James expands his critique to Dickens's work more generally. He concludes that Dickens "is not serious reading," that Dickens "is nothing of a philosopher," and that it would be "an offence against humanity to place Mr. Dickens among the greatest novelists."[1] The evolving reality behind his early dismissals of Dickens was far more complicated, however. As the biographer R. W. B. Lewis (1991, 89) has pointed out, "Dickens was always a special novelistic case" for Henry James.

Just two years after his review in *The Nation*, in 1867, James ([1914] 2011b, 205) met Dickens in America and remembered "how tremendously it had been

---

1. James's assessment (and his language) is remarkably similar to George Henry Lewes's (1872a, 152) appraisal of Dickens as a sentimental writer, not cerebral or educated, with "no interest in philosophy, science, and the higher literature."

218   CONCLUSION

laid upon young persons of our generation to feel Dickens, down to the soles of our shoes." And feel Dickens deeply he certainly did. Some of the earliest memories that James recounts in his autobiography (2011a) near the end of his life are explicitly Dickensian.[2] The family's eccentric New York dentist, Dr. Parkhurst, becomes an embodiment of "Joey Bagstock" (57); their acquaintance, Miss Cushman, is "the Nancy of Oliver Twist" (98); his cousin Henry "was more or less another Mr. Dick" (120); his cousin Helen was "another Miss Trotwood" (120). These last two associations emerge from James's account of how, as a young boy, he hid under a tablecloth to listen to his grandmother read *David Copperfield* to his older cousins: "I held my breath and listened, I listened long and drank deep while the wondrous picture grew, but the tense cord at last snapped under the strain of the Murdstones and I broke into the sobs of sympathy that disclosed my subterfuge" (102). After this memorable outburst of feeling, James recalls how additional Dickens novels were read aloud in his own household; the James family "breathed heavily through Hard Times, Bleak House and Little Dorrit . . . Chuzzlewit and Dombey and Son" (102–3).

The bodily rhetoric that the older James uses to describe these recollections is also quite revealing. He describes his experiences of reading individual Dickens novels where he "held [his] breath," he "drank deep," he "breathed heavily." It is interesting to note the compelling relationship between the body and the idiom in James's most profound memories. Consider how he continued to frame the importance of Dickens's impact on not only his own but also on his entire generation's consciousness by way of distinctly idiomatic body language:

> The force of the Dickens imprint, however applied, in the soft clay of our generation. . . . To be brought up thus against the author of it, or to speak at all of the dawn of one's consciousness of it and of his presence and power, is to begin *to trod ground* at once sacred and boundless, the associations of which, looming large, warn us off even *as they hold*. He did too much for us surely ever to leave us free—free of judgment, free of reaction, even should we care to be, which heaven forbid: he *laid his hand on us* in a way to undermine as in no other case the power of detached appraisement. (James [1913] 2011a, 101; emphasis mine)

The older James goes on to say that "criticism, roundabout [Dickens], is somehow futile and tasteless," acknowledging that, although Dickens's "own taste is easily impugned," the Inimitable nonetheless "entered so early into *the*

---

2. It is quite possible that James is the "very distinguished man" Lewes (1872a, 143) discusses in "Dickens in Relation to Criticism": "It is not long since I heard a very distinguished man express measureless contempt for Dickens, and . . . afterwards . . . admit that he had 'entered into his life.'"

CONCLUSION   219

blood and bone of our intelligence that it always remained better than the taste of overhauling him" (101; emphasis mine). This sentiment held up, too. Never again did James "overhaul" Dickens as rebarbatively as he did in his career-opening review of *Our Mutual Friend*. Writing from the perspective that age grants in "The Art of Fiction" (*Longman's Magazine* 1884), the forty-one-year-old James eventually included Dickens among the "talents" of Miguel Cervantes, Alexandre Dumas, Jane Austen, Gustave Flaubert, and Émile Zola—all of whom, according to James, "have worked in [novel-writing] with equal glory" ([1884] 1999).[3]

And then shortly before his death in 1916, James ([1913] 2011a, 103) called Dickens "the great actuality of the current imagination." This assessment aligns with the remarkable concessions of another early and unequivocal Dickens detractor, Justin McCarthy, whose 1864 *Westminster Review* essay confidently held that Dickens's literary legacy would never survive: "We cannot think that he will live as an English classic" is the verdict McCarthy ([1864] 1965, 415) delivers in his review's final paragraph. Despite this harsh (and dead wrong) overall verdict, however, McCarthy acknowledges the popular contemporaneous impact of Dickensian language at the start of his review: "[he] has entered our every-day life in a manner which no other author has done," McCarthy concedes. "Much of his phraseology has become common property. Allusions to his works and quotations from them are made by everybody, and in all places" (415). But by the end of the review twenty-five pages later, McCarthy is convinced that "the influence of [Dickens's] style" will not last (415). "Before long his language will have passed away . . . only [to] be found in a Dictionary of Antiquities" (441). As we shall see in fiction and beyond, McCarthy could not have been more mistaken, especially in terms of idiomatic "phraseology" pertaining to the body.

The use of such idiomatic phraseology becomes more and more a part of Henry James's common fictional property throughout his career. Just as his general regard for Dickens grows over time, so too does James's employment of body idioms in his own fiction. For example, a major work from his early period, *The Portrait of a Lady* (1881), averages about one body idiom per three pages of text (233 in 647 pages [285,300 words[4]]). *The American* (1887) utilizes significantly more body idioms: 393 in 350 pages (154,330 words) for an average of more than one per page. Even *The Golden Bowl* (1904), from James's mature late stage, averages about 1.5 idioms per page (572 in 374 pages [102,850

---

    3. From *Longman's Magazine*, September 1884.

    4. For the remainder of this section, the word counts I offer of books and chapters are similarly approximate.

220   CONCLUSION

words]). I cite these numbers not because I want to suggest that there is a simple and causal connection between Dickens's and James's use of body idioms in their fiction. I do so instead to draw our attention to one of the paradoxical and surprising through lines of my study. As we have seen, Dickens's use of idiomatic language was early and often held up as evidence of his "vulgarity" and of his predilection for the ostensibly low, unsophisticated ideas contained in his fiction. No one, to my knowledge, has ever raised such objections about Henry James's work, and yet he, too, becomes a relatively high user of bodily idioms. I am also not claiming that James uses body idioms in the same way that I have argued Dickens does; nowhere in James do body idioms become absorbed into the themes, characterizations, or structures of his novels. This, as I have argued, is one of the dimensions that makes Dickens's imagination inimitable. It is enough to point out that Dickens helps pave the way for late-Victorian and modernist novelists to write about "serious" and "sophisticated" topics using everyday idiomatic language even if critics have never tracked their usages in this specific manner. A summative section from the end of Garrett Stewart's (1974, 225) first book, *Dickens and the Trials of Imagination*, comes closest to the spirit of how I see Dickens's imaginative influence working more generally: "Without his whole-hearted, brilliantly driven experiments in language, the extremist vistas of twentieth-century fiction might have settled for nearer horizons, safer terrain." The previous chapters of this book, I hope, demonstrate that no one experimented with idiomatic language as much as Dickens. And his career-long idiomatic experimentation had real-world effects. In an ironic but fitting reversal of Samuel Johnson's eighteenth-century warning to avoid the use of "licentious idioms," the late and eminently distinguished German-born critic Edgar Rosenberg (2019, 221) recounted how after arriving in the United States in 1940 at age fourteen not knowing "a word of English," he learned to use "correct idiomatic English" principally by reading Dickens.

A different case altogether, Dickens's status as a writer supposedly repudiated by the modernists is perhaps never so inaccurate as it is when considering the case of James Joyce's experimental use of language. I am not alone, of course, in this assessment. Anny Sadrin (1999, xiii) has called Dickens "a great precursor to Modernity," and Barbara Hardy (2008, 69) sees him as a "model" for the general "creative informality of language celebrated by the Modernists." Hardy (2008, 166) even recounts a story from early in Joyce's life when, as he was training to become a teacher in Zurich, he submitted an essay arguing that Dickens had "entered the English Language" more than any writer since Shakespeare. Data culled from the OED would have corroborated Joyce's statement regarding Dickens as a lexically innovative writer on par with the

CONCLUSION   221

Bard: the dictionary cites Dickens 9,218 times—far more than any author in the last three hundred years.[5] Indeed, one of the most specific ways that Dickens entered Joyce's artistic language was through the creation of an urban, informal, and modernist vernacular.[6] Much of what scholars have to say about Joyce's language could easily be said and, in fact as we saw in the introduction, *was* said of Dickens. Derek Attridge (1988, 158, 174) highlights Joyce's extensive use of language "that good writers were supposed to avoid": "deviations from the norms of what traditionally constitute[d] 'good' style . . . that one finds in such handbooks as Hodgson's *Errors in the Use of English* (1882) and Fowler's *Modern English Usage* (1926)." Katie Wales (1992, 78) focuses on "Joyce's ear for the idioms and the tone of ordinary informal Dublin speech" and the ingenious way his characters "tend to think in the idiom of their speech, and speak in the idiom of their thoughts." Wales traces Joyce's felicity in achieving this level of ingenuity to his deep fascination with "the whole relationship between literal and figurative meanings," where the supreme "fertility of [his] imagination" depends on "colloquialisms and idioms [that] spring to new life" (121–22). This deep fascination with and integration of the "whole" imaginative play between literal and figurative meanings of idiomatic language is a uniquely Dickensian influence.

We see this influence from the earliest points in Joyce's career. The very first sentence of "The Dead" (*Dubliners*, 1914) hinges on the extended use of one particular body idiom: "Lily, the caretaker's daughter, was literally run off her feet" (James [1914] 1991, 119). As Hugh Kenner (1978, 15–16) has pointed out in *Joyce's Voices*, "whatever Lily was literally . . . she was not literally run off her feet. . . . That first sentence was written, as it were, from Lily's point of view, and though it looks like 'objective' narration it is tinged with her idiom." This is because the story begins with Lily trying to cope with putting away too many simultaneously arriving visitors' jackets amid the cramped quarters of the Morkan household as the group convenes for their annual Christmas dance. Speaking in a fitting tangential idiom of his own, Kenner asserts that "Joyce is at his subtle game of specifying what pretensions to elegance are *afoot* on this occasion" (15; emphasis mine). And Kenner is correct to invoke this idiom; there is a sense of physical crowdedness in the Morkan house throughout the story, and therefore, many of Joyce's idioms in this famous story are derivative from the one used in the first sentence. In the cramped dancing space, for example, Aunt Kate often comes "close on [others'] heels," while moving around the dinner

---

5. Bowles (2019, 160) arrives at a similar conclusion.
6. See Gibbons 2013.

222   **CONCLUSION**

table she and her sister (Aunt Julia) appear "walking on each other's heels, getting in each other's way," contributing to the sense that people are often "underfoot" and "after [their] heels" (125, 134, 145, 146).

Like Dickens, much of Joyce's most imaginative language emerges from bodily wordplay that constantly shifts between the literal and the figurative. Merve Emre (2022, 71) has commented that "life, in *Ulysses*, is the experience of the body . . . as it wanders through the world. It is sensation mediated by language, and is language mediated by sensation." Although the entirety of *Ulysses* (1922) is suffused with idiomatic wordplay predicated on bodily observation and sensation, a single but otherwise unremarkable scene from *Ulysses* will demonstrate the point. Stephen Bloom contemplates a man eating in a Burton restaurant and thinks, "Gums: no teeth to chewchewchew it. Chump chop from the grill . . . bitten off more than he can chew. . . . Hungry man is an angry man. Working tooth and jaw. . . . Couldn't swallow it all however" (Joyce [1922] 2008, 161). Then, watching another man eating cabbage with a knife: "Tear it limb from limb. Second nature to him. Born with a silver knife in his mouth" (162). It is important, here, to emphasize Wales's (1992, 121; emphasis mine) contention that Joyce was fascinated by "the *whole* relationship between literal and figurative meanings." We see this on display in the examples above where Joyce is not content simply to use familiar body idioms. Instead, he anticipates the reader's familiarity with them ("bitten off more than he can chew," "tear from limb to limb") and then alters others in ways that defamiliarize and, hence, create surprising new associations. The man in the restaurant bites off more than he can chew but then works on his food not "tooth and nail," as the familiar idiom goes, but "tooth and jaw." Similarly, the other man's aggressiveness emerges from the way he tears his cabbage from limb to limb and also from the description of his being "born with a silver knife," rather than "a silver spoon in his mouth." This is one specific area where it is difficult not to agree with Barbara Hardy's (2008, 66) claim that "you can't imagine Joyce's word-play without [Dickens's] model." We have seen over and over again throughout this study how Dickens's use of body idioms exploits the *whole* relationship between literal and figurative meanings as he constantly tinkers with and twists them, abstracts them, stretches them, reliteralizes them, and presses them into all manner of slight and even outright violation—the full ("whole") range of which allow him to reach extraordinary creative heights by way of ordinary everyday language.

Unlike Joyce, no one is likely to consider Virginia Woolf a "bodily" writer, including herself. Woolf went on record early and often to state her explicit disaffection for her Victorian predecessors, and her critical hostility toward them was frequently based on the view that they focused inordinately on the physiological at the expense of the psychological. In perhaps the best known

CONCLUSION 223

of all her essays, "Modern Fiction," Woolf ([1919] 1984, 285) bristles against the materialist interests of earlier (Victorian) fiction—saying "it is because [it is] concerned not with the spirit but with the body that [it has] disappointed us." Mary Jean Corbett (2020, 27) has recently written that Woolf's Victorian "predecessors are unevenly acknowledged at best, yet their presence in that past can be felt and at times heard in her work." Woolf did not have much (good) to say about Dickens,[7] but interestingly, one of the ways that he *can* be felt and heard in what she says nonetheless comes by way of idiomatic body language. As it turns out, she was oddly sympatico with Dickens on at least one score: Dickens's favorite of all his novels—the "favourite child" in his "heart of hearts"—was *David Copperfield* (Tambling 1996, 10.) It was Woolf's favorite as well. The only one of her hundreds of essays dedicated solely to Dickens was "*David Copperfield*," a short piece in which she writes this "most perfect of all the Dickens novels" achieves "an atmosphere of beauty" (Woolf [1925] 1966, 195). Apparently, the beauty of *David Copperfield*'s atmosphere even had the power to heal her frequently debilitating headaches. She wrote in her diary for February 25, 1936, "I've had headaches. Vanquish them by lying still & binding books and reading D. Copperfield" (Woolf 1985, 5:13).

The point I wish to make about Woolf's ([1925] 1966, 194) essay on *David Copperfield* does not necessarily depend on her deeply held belief that life's "youth, gaiety, hope" "flows into every creek and cranny" of the novel. Instead, I want to draw our attention to how an inordinate number of body idioms seep into so many nooks and crannies of Woolf's own language *about David Copperfield*.[8] On fifteen different occasions in only four pages of text (1,600 words), Woolf uses body idioms such as when "stories [are] communicated by word of mouth" (191); "Dickens talking" would "make us blush to the roots of our hair" (192); "where the foot sinks deep into the mud" (193); "people are branded upon our eyeballs" (194); "the penetrating glance [is] . . . itself pierced to the bone" (194). This is not characteristically Woolfian language either. Consider her essay "George Eliot" (1919) where she uses three times fewer body idioms (5) in more than double the pages (13) and words (3,600) of her *Copperfield* piece. The same is true of her six-page (2,600-word) essay on "Charlotte Brontë" (Woolf 1998) where she uses only a single body idiom.

---

7. She generally objected to what she saw as the (lower- and middle-)class-bound limitations of his fiction. In "Dickens by a Disciple," which ran in the *Times Literary Supplement*, Woolf ([1919] 1998, 25–28) pans W. Walter Crotch for what she takes to be a blind and unreflective enthusiasm of Dickens by his admirers.

8. It is important to note that when I count critics' use of body idioms in their writing about Dickens, I do not count any body idioms that the critics use while quoting Dickens's prose. In other words, the only body idioms I count are those of the critic her-/himself.

224   CONCLUSION

The Critic's Hand, Subdued to What It Works In

The inordinately high number of body idioms we encounter in Woolf's single piece of criticism on Dickens represents an early instantiation of a phenomenon that becomes uncannily consistent in twentieth- and twenty-first-century critical practice. In short, a sample of influential critics reveals that they, too, incorporate disproportionately high incidences of body idioms into their work on Dickens—and only on Dickens (i.e., not when they write on other Victorian novelists). Paul de Man (1983, 85), assessing the Geneva school critics, describes such a phenomenon as one in which "the creative impulse itself" begins to converge with the critical apparatus surrounding it. J. Hillis Miller (1991a, 35) later identifies how one particular Geneva school critic, Georges Poulet, is fundamental to the theorization of how "the critic's language" becomes inflected with "the style and vocabulary of the author [criticized]." In "The Phenomenology of Reading," which appeared in the inaugural issue of *New Literary History*, Poulet (1968, 54) describes his experience of what can happen while reading a novel: he notices that he starts, "with an unheard-of licence [*sic*], to think what it thinks and feel what it feels." The "remarkable *complicity* . . . of this relationship—between criticizing subject and criticized object" initiates a "participation by the critic in the powers active in the [author's] use of language" (63, 60, 66; emphasis original). For Poulet, "the language of the critic *signifies* the language of the literary work" precisely because, "on the level of indistinct thought, of sensations, emotions, images, and obsessions of preconscious life, it is possible for the critic to repeat, within himself, that life of which the work affords a first version, inexhaustibly revealing and suggestive" (61; emphasis original). Poulet characterizes this process as one that entirely "absorbs" the critic by way of a "vital inbreathing inspired [in] the act of reading" a particular author (58, 59).

I have argued throughout this study that body idioms become absorbed into the structures, themes, characters, and language of the imaginative worlds Dickens creates in his most mature and complex fiction. We have even seen how individual critics sometimes adopt the language of a particular novel's unique idiom in their critiques of that novel (such as when Terry Eagleton, Karen Chase, and Michael Levenson discuss the "shouldering" of responsibility in *Bleak House*). But it is eerily consistent to consider how the bodily *idiom absorption* that I have analyzed in Dickens's creative imagination also extends more generally to the language used by many of his most prominent critics. D. A. Miller's (1988) *The Novel and the Police* will serve as a first example. In his forty-five-page (approximately 16,100-word[9])

---

9. I do not include Miller's footnotes in this approximate word count. It is also important to note that these idiom counts used by critics were manually tallied. I want to thank my graduate students

CONCLUSION   225

chapter on Dickens's *Bleak House*, "Discipline in Different Voices," Miller uses nineteen body idioms whereas he uses only four body idioms in his forty-five-page (16,300-word) chapter on Anthony Trollope's *Barchester Towers* ("The Novel as Usual"), and only three body idioms in his forty-six-page (16,500-word) chapter on Wilkie Collins's *The Woman in White* ("*Cage aux folles*"). A similar pattern emerges in Mary Poovey's (1988) *Uneven Developments*. She uses twenty-three body idioms in her thirty-five-page (15,200-word) chapter on Dickens's *David Copperfield* and only four such idioms in her thirty-seven-page (16,000-word) chapter on Charlotte Brontë's *Jane Eyre*.

This discrepancy of between four and five times the use of body idioms in the criticism of Dickens's fiction as opposed to that of his peers holds up even in the more recent work of critics such as Catherine Gallagher, Garrett Stewart, and Terry Eagleton. In *The Body Economic*, Gallagher (2008) uses twenty-eight body idioms in her thirty-one-page (15,300-word) chapter on *Our Mutual Friend*, only seven in her thirty-eight-page (19,100-word) chapter on George Eliot's *Daniel Deronda*, and three in her thirty-six-page (19,200-word) chapter on Eliot's *Scenes of Clerical Life*. Garrett Stewart, perhaps the foremost analyst of Dickens's language, may very well be in a category all his own when it comes to Poulet's sense of linguistic "*complicity*" that can exist between critic and author. Stewart's (2018) *The One, Other, and Only Dickens* contains a whopping 332 body idioms in 191 pages (96,600 words), many of which are by far the most playfully clever I have ever encountered in serious scholarly criticism. A sampling of Stewart's body idioms in relation to Dickens include language "spoken under one's breath and in the ear of uptake" (xii), the "biting of a lexical tongue" (13), "prose thinking on its feet" and "keeping us on our toes" (17), "the tongue-twisting hinge of hyphenated epithet" (76), turning "the serviceable breather of the comma into something closer to quietly breathtaking" (85), "knock-kneed" associations (103), "comic phrasing that has, quite deliberately, either two legs or none to stand on" (107), the "bowlegged grammar of syllepsis" (110), a character who "*lie[s] through his teeth* (132, emphasis original), "passing by him almost shoulder to shoulder" (165), and so on. Despite Stewart's prolific critical output, however, he has not yet written a monograph solely dedicated to a different Victorian author, and so we are left to compare his extremely high incidence of scintillating body idioms in *The One, the Other, and Only Dickens* to chapters of his other books. *Dear Reader* (1996), for instance, contains a chapter subtitled "Relays of Desire in *Wuthering Heights, Jane Eyre,* and *Villette*." In this thirty-nine-page (18,200-word) chapter,

---

Caitlin Mathies, Luke Folk, Will Turner, Jonathan Cheng, and Trevor Bleick for helping to check and recheck my manual counts.

226   **CONCLUSION**

Stewart uses only eight body idioms in his criticism of the Brontës. Similarly, in his twenty-eight-page (13,100-word) chapter on the "Afterlives of Interpretation in *Daniel Deronda*," he uses just four body idioms when discussing George Eliot. Terry Eagleton's (2005) *The English Novel* provides a slightly different, though no less congruous, example because it is comprised of chapters that consider not just a single work by a given author but that author's whole oeuvre (a practice for which the Geneva critics advocated). In his twenty-page (8,900-word) chapter on "Charles Dickens," Eagleton employs forty-three body idioms, whereas his twenty-page (8,700-word) chapter on "The Brontës" contains just ten body idioms. The phenomenon I enumerate in these instances would not have surprised Poulet (1969, 63) because he believed in a process of "verbal mimesis which transposes into the critic's language . . . the style and vocabulary of the author" (J. H. Miller 19991a, 35). The best criticism, according to Poulet, "is not possible unless the thought of the critic *becomes* the thought of the author criticized, unless it succeeds in re-feeling, in re-thinking, in re-imagining the author's thought from the inside" (J. H. Miller 1991a, 15; emphasis original). It appears that if Dickens imagined in the language of bodily idiom, many of his critics reimagine their criticism of him in the same idiom.

As J. Hillis Miller (1991a, 21; emphasis mine) has said, "Poulet thinks of criticism as beginning and ending in a *coincidence* of the mind of the critic and the mind of the author." Miller (1991a, 15) obviously uses "coincidence" here in a Pouletian sense where there is a coinciding or correspondence between the critic and the author, where there is a "transposition of the mental universe of an author into the interior space of a critic's mind."[10] But in an effort to probe the extent to which this curious phenomenon of "verbal mimesis" among critics might be merely that *other* kind of coincidence—just chance—I turn to the evidence culled from two of the best twenty-first-century literary biographers in the profession: Rosemarie Bodenheimer and Robert Douglas-Fairhurst. Measuring the varying levels of bodily idiom usage in the cases of these two biographers may provide the best test cases yet for several reasons.

---

10. I am very lucky to be indebted to Miller for my thinking about the "coincidental" in these terms. I am even luckier to have had conversations with Hillis regarding the possible gradations of conscious intent—both in terms of Dickens's predilections and those of the critics. In terms of the latter, he once wondered aloud about contacting the critics to ask if they were conscious of an intent to use so many body idioms when writing about Dickens. We eventually decided that doing so would be tantamount to asking Dickens if he was aware that one of the most interesting parts of his imagination was structured by certain bodily idioms. I have since taken consolation not only in a Keatsian sense of negative capability but also in the position on authorial meaning described by Garrett Stewart (2015, 231): "it doesn't matter, doesn't matter ultimately, what the writer had in mind, because the only mind in which those thoughts are now to be had, in which they happen, is the reader's own, guyed and guided by the filaments of a written syntax."

CONCLUSION   227

First, both Bodenheimer and Douglas-Fairhurst have produced major, full-length literary biographies of Dickens and of another Victorian author: Bodenheimer has written one book on George Eliot and another on Dickens; Douglas-Fairhurst one on Dickens and one on Lewis Carroll. And both authors have published their biographies with the same presses—Cornell University Press and Harvard University Press, respectively. I mention the fact that both biographies by both authors were published by the same press because it gives a more accurate sense of the relationship between pagination and word count. In *The Real Life of Mary Ann Evans*, Bodenheimer (1994) uses a total of just eleven body idioms in 267 pages (120,100 words). In *Knowing Dickens* (2007), she uses 119 body idioms in 208 pages (98,100 words). Even without adjusting for word length, Bodenheimer uses over ten times the body idioms when writing about Dickens than she does when writing about Eliot. The proportional case with Douglas-Fairhurst is only slightly less astounding. In *Becoming Dickens* (2011), he uses 264 body idioms in 336 pages (133,700 words). In *The Story of Alice* (2015), he uses only thirty-nine body idioms in 415 pages (164,300 words). These lopsided proportions, combined with what we know about Dickens as far and away the highest user of body idioms among nineteenth-century novelists, make it very likely that there is some kind of Pouletian "coincidence" between the mind of the critic and the mind of the author. Put another way, Dickens's body idioms are contagious: they have a strong tendency to subdue the critic's nature to the stuff it works in, like the dyer's hand. Throughout this book, I have referred to Dickens as the "Inimitable," and yet, paradoxically, the sharpest register of his genius turns out to be its absorptive influence, carried across to produce lexical imitation in his critics. Like no other Victorian author, we speak of Dickens using the vernacular language that his novels have put within our earshot, the idioms he has pressed into currency by putting them in our mouths and at the ends of our fingertips. Ultimately, what could be more inimitable?

APPENDIX A

List of 100 Commonly Used Idioms [*Without Dickens's Unique Idioms]

1. Afoot
2. Arm in arm
3. At arm's length
4. At hand
5. At the hands of
6. At the foot of
7. At her/his heels
8. Bad blood
9. Behind-hand
10. Black in the face
11. Break his/her heart
12. Broken-hearted
13. Body and mind
14. By heart
15. Clean hands
16. Cold blooded
17. Cold shoulder
18. Deaf ear
19. Down at heel
20. Ear for
21. Eye for

APPENDIX A

22. Eyes for
23. Eyes wide open
24. Face to face
25. Fingers to the bone
26. Flesh and blood
27. Footing
28. From ear to ear
29. From head to foot
30. From his/her/your lips
31. From limb to limb
32. From mouth to mouth
33. Full in the face
34. Hair-breadth
35. Hair's-breadth
36. Half a mind
37. Hand in hand
38. Hard-hearted
39. Hat in hand
40. Head and ears
41. Head for detail
42. Head-first
43. Head over ears
44. Head to foot
45. Headlong
46. Heart of hearts
47. Heart's content
48. Heart and soul
49. Heavy hand
50. Her/his tongue
51. Hold your tongue
52. In the flesh
53. In the same breath
54. Knee-deep
55. Light-hearted
56. Might and main
57. Mind and matter
58. Neck and crop
59. Neck and heels
60. No eye(s) for
61. Off-hand

APPENDIX A   231

62. On her/his heel
63. On her/his lips
64. On my lips
65. On her/his mind
66. On this head
67. On that head
68. On tiptoe
69. One bone and one flesh
70. Out at elbows
71. Out of hand
72. Out of joint
73. Peace of mind
74. Presence of mind
75. Same breath
76. Set foot
77. Sharp eye
78. Sharp-eyed
79. Single-handed
80. Single-handedly
81. Skin and bone
82. Slip of the tongue
83. State of mind
84. Teeth on edge
85. The same mind
86. Ties of blood
87. Time out of mind
88. To the bone
89. Took to their heels
90. Tooth and nail
91. Top to toe
92. Touched to the quick
93. Of two minds
94. Under foot
95. Under her/his breath
96. Upon his/her heel
97. Upon this/that head
98. With open arms
99. Without heart
100. Word of mouth

Appendix B

Nineteenth-Century British Novel Corpus for Idiom Usage Comparison

(124 novels by 11 novelists)

Jane Austen

Lady Susan (1794)
The Watson's (1805)
Sense and Sensibility (1811)
Pride and Prejudice (1813)
Mansfield Park (1814)
Emma (1816)
Sandition (1817)
Northanger Abbey (1817)
Persuasion (1817)

Charlotte Brontë

Jane Eyre (1847)
Shirley (1849)
Villette (1853)
The Professor (1857)

234   **APPENDIX B**

Anne Brontë

Agnes Grey (1847)

The Tenant of Wildfell Hall (1848)

Emily Brontë

Wuthering Heights (1847)

Charles Dickens

Sketches by Boz (1833–36)

Pickwick Papers (1836–37)

Oliver Twist (1837–39)

Nicholas Nickleby (1838–39)

The Old Curiosity Shop (1840–41)

Barnaby Rudge (1841)

A Christmas Carol (1843)

Martin Chuzzlewit (1843–44)

Dombey and Son (1846–48)

David Copperfield (1849–50)

Bleak House (1852–53)

Hard Times (1854)

Little Dorrit (1855–57)

A Tale of Two Cities (1859)

Great Expectations (1860–61)

Our Mutual Friend (1864–65)

The Mystery of Edwin Drood (1870)

George Eliot

Scenes of Clerical Life (1857)

Adam Bede (1859)

The Mill on the Floss (1860)

Silas Marner (1861)

Romola (1862–63)

Felix Holt (1866)

Middlemarch (1871–72)

Daniel Deronda (1876)

Thomas Hardy

Under the Greenwood Tree (1872)

A Pair of Blue Eyes (1872–73)

Far from the Madding Crowd (1874)

APPENDIX B   235

The Return of the Native (1878)
The Trumpet Major (1880)
The Mayor of Casterbridge (1886)
The Woodlanders (1886–87)
Tess of the D'Urbervilles (1891)
The Well-Beloved (1892)
Jude the Obscure (1894–95)

William Thackeray
Catherine (1839–40)
A Shabby Genteel Story (1840)
Samuel Titmarsh and the Hogarty Diamond (1843)
Barry Lyndon (1844)
Vanity Fair (1847–48)
Pendennis (1848–50)
Henry Esmond (1852)
The Newcomes (1855)
The Virginians (1857–59)
Dennis Duval (1864)

Margaret Oliphant
Merkland (1850)
Adam Graeme (1852)
Harry Muir (1853)
Zaidee (1855)
Lilliesleaf (1855)
The House on the Moor (1861)
A Son of the Soil (1863)
In Trust (1881)
Miss Marjoribanks (1865–66)
Agnes (1866)
John (1870)
At His Gates (1872)
Innocent (1873)
A Rose in June (1874)
For Love and Life (1874)
Phoebe Junior (1876)
Harry Joscelyn (1881)
Hester (1883)
A House Divided Against Itself (1886)

236   **APPENDIX B**

A Poor Gentleman (1886)
A House in Bloomsbury (1894)

Walter Scott
Waverly (1814)
Guy Mannering (1815)
Old Mortality (1816)
The Antiquary (1816)
The Black Dwarf (1816)
Rob Roy (1817)
The Heart of Midlothian (1818)
The Bride of Lammermoor (1819)
A Legend of Montrose (1919)
Ivanhoe (1820)
Kenilworth (1821)
The Fortunes of Nigel (1822)
Peveril of the Peak (1822)
Quentin Durward (1823)
Redgauntlet (1824)
St. Ronan's Well (1824)
Anne of Geierstein (1829)

Anthony Trollope
The Warden (1855)
The Three Clerks (1857)
Barchester Towers (1857)
Doctor Thorne (1858)
Framley Parsonage (1860)
The Small House at Allington (1862)
Can You Forgive Her? (1864–65)
The Last Chronicle at Barset (1867)
Phineas Finn (1867–68)
The Eustace Diamonds (1871)
Phineas Redux (1873)
The Way We Live Now (1875)
The Prime Minister (1876)
The Duke's Children (1879)

APPENDIX B 237

Charlotte Yonge

The Heir of Redclyffe (1853)
The Daisy Chain (1856)
Dynevor Terrace (1857)
Hopes and Fears (1860)
The Young Step-Mother (1861)
Magnum Bonum (1879)
Nuttie's Father (1885)
The Two Sides of the Shield (1885)
Chantry House (1886)
Beechcroft at Rockstone (1888)
Grisley Grisell (1893)

Appendix C

Full Code Used for Data Comparisons

```
# Main Script for Identifying the ngrams (aka idioms)
Sys.setenv(
   RETICULATE_PYTHON =
"/Library/Frameworks/Python.framework/Versions/3.7/bin/python3"
)
library(tidyverse)
library(readxl)
library(cleanNLP)
cleanNLP::cnlp_init_spacy()
idioms <- sort(read_excel("More.idioms.xlsx")$idioms)
novels <- read_excel(path = "CAPUANO_CORPUS.xlsx") %>%
   filter(Capuano == 1) %>%
   mutate(path = gsub(":", "_", `#filename`))
get_all_ngrams <- function(text_string, ngrams){
   message("CHECKING FOR NGRAMS")
   padded <- paste(" ", ngrams, " ", sep="") # white space padding for regex
   x <- trimws(
      unlist(
         str_match_all(ngram::preprocess(text_string), padded)
      )
   )
```

240   APPENDIX C

```
    return(x)
}
idioms_in_books <- tibble()
for(i in 1:lenght(novels)){
    raw_ms <- readtext::readtext(novels$path[i])$text
    normalized_text <- tolower(clean_manuscript(raw_ms, "British English"))
    annotation <- get_annotation(tibble::tibble(doc_id = novels$id[i], text =
    normalized_text))
    just_words <- filter(annotation$token,!upos == "PUNCT")
    total_words <- nrow(just_words)
    found_idioms <- get_all_ngrams(normalized_text, idioms)
    new_rows <- bind_cols(author = novels$author_sort[i], title = novels$title[i],
    word_count = total_words, idioms = found_idioms)
    idioms_in_books <- bind_rows(idioms_in_books, new_rows)
    cat(i, "\n")
}
idioms_in_books$idioms <- gsub("'", "'", idioms_in_books$idioms)
write_csv(idioms_in_books, "idioms_in_books.csv")
x <- group_by(idioms_in_books, author, title, idioms) %>%
    summarise(count = n(), word_count) %>%
        mutate(count_per_100k = (100000 * (count / word_count))) %>%
    select(-count, -word_count) %>%
    ungroup() %>%
    distinct()
wide1 <- pivot_wider(x, names_from = idioms, values_from = count_
per_100k, values_fill = 0)
write_csv(wide1, "book_x_idiom_frequencies.csv")
y <- group_by(idioms_in_books, author, title, idioms) %>%
    summarise(count = n(), word_count) %>%
    ungroup() %>%
    distinct() %>%
    select(-word_count)
wide2 <- pivot_wider(y, names_from = idioms, values_from = count, values_
fill = 0)
write_csv(wide2, "book_x_idiom_count.csv")
# Post processing code for merging the data into one file with metadata

novels <- read_excel(path = "CAPUANO_CORPUS.xlsx") %>%
    filter(Capuano == 1) %>%
    mutate(path = gsub(":", "_", `#filename`))
```

APPENDIX C   241

```
counts <- read_csv("book_x_idiom_count.csv") %>%
   full_join(novels, by = "title") %>%
   select(-id, -Capuano, -`#filename`,-`#formats`,-`path`, -authors) %>%
   relocate(`#pubyear`, .before = author) %>%
   relocate(author_sort, .before = title) %>%
   mutate(idiom_count = rowSums(select(., -`#pubyear`, -author, -title,
   -author_sort)!= 0)) %>%
   select(-author) %>%
   relocate(idiom_count, .after = title) %>%
   replace(is.na(.), 0) %>%
   select(title, idiom_count)

freqs <- read_csv("book_x_idiom_frequencies.csv") %>%
   full_join(novels, by="title") %>%
   select(-id, -Capuano, -`#filename`,-`#formats`,-`path`, -authors) %>%
   relocate(`#pubyear`, .before = author) %>%
   relocate(author_sort, .before = title) %>%
   mutate(idiom_sum = rowSums(select(., -`#pubyear`, -author, -title, -author
   _sort))) %>%
   select(-author) %>%
   relocate(idiom_sum, .after = title) %>%
   replace(is.na(.), 0) %>%
   full_join(counts, by = "title") %>%
   relocate(idiom_count, .after = idiom_sum)

write_csv(freqs, "book_x_idiom_freqs_with_dates.csv")
```

BIBLIOGRAPHY

Aarsleff, Hans. 1967. *The Study of Language in England, 1780–1860*. Princeton, NJ: Princeton University Press.

Aarsleff, Hans. 1981. *From Locke to Saussure*. Minneapolis: University of Minnesota Press.

Abberly, Will. 2015. *English Fiction and the Evolution of Language, 1850–1914*. Cambridge: Cambridge University Press.

Adams, James Eli. 1995. *Dandies and Desert Saints*. Ithaca, NY: Cornell University Press.

Adams, James Eli. 2005. "'The Boundaries of Social Intercourse': Class and the Victorian Novel." In *A Concise Companion to the Victorian Novel*, edited by Francis O'Gorman, 47–70. Hoboken, NJ: Blackwell.

Adams, James Eli. 2012. *A History of Victorian Literature*. Oxford: Wiley-Blackwell.

Addison, Joseph. 1712. *The Spectator*, No. 285 (January 26). In *The Spectator* (1965), edited by Donald F. Bond. Volume III. Oxford: Clarendon Press, 9–15.

Aesop. 1926. *The Fables of Aesop*. Edited by Joseph Jacobs. London: Macmillan.

Agamben, Giorgio. 1999. *Potentialities*. Edited and translated by Daniel Heller-Roazen. Stanford, CA: Stanford University Press.

Ahl, Fredrick. 1985. "Ars Est Artem (Art in Puns and Anagrams Engraved)." In *On Puns: The Foundation of Letters*, edited by Jonathan Culler, 17–43. Ithaca, NY: Cornell University Press.

Allard, James. 2007. *Romanticism, Medicine, and the Poet's Body*. Burlington, VT: Ashgate.

Allison, Sarah. 2018. *Reductive Reading: A Syntax of Victorian Reading*. Baltimore: Johns Hopkins University Press.

Alter, Robert. 1996. "Reading Style in Dickens." *Philosophy and Literature* 20 (1): 130–37.

Altick, Richard D. 1980. "*Bleak House*: The Reach of Chapter One." *Dickens Studies Annual* 8:73–104.

Altieri, Charles. 2015. *Reckoning with the Imagination*. Ithaca, NY: Cornell University Press.

Andrews, Malcolm. 2006. *Charles Dickens and His Performing Selves*. Oxford: Oxford University Press.

Andrews, Malcolm. 2013. *Dickensian Laughter: Essays on Dickens and Humour*. Oxford: Oxford University Press.

Aristotle. 1986. *De Anima*. Edited by Hugh Lawson-Tancred. New York: Penguin.

Armstrong, Nancy. 1987. *Desire and Domestic Fiction*. Oxford: Oxford University Press.

Armstrong, Nancy. 2005. *How Novels Think*. New York: Columbia University Press.

Armstrong, Nancy, and Warren Montag. 2017. "The Figure in the Carpet." *PMLA* 132, no. 3 (May): 613–19.

244 BIBLIOGRAPHY

Attridge, Derek. 1988. *Peculiar Language: Literature as Difference from the Renaissance to James Joyce*. London: Methuen.

Attridge, Derek. 1989. "Language as History/History as Language: Saussure and the Romance of Etymology." In *Post-structuralism and the Question of History*, edited by Derek Attridge, Geoff Bennington, and Robert Young, 183–211. Cambridge: Cambridge University Press.

Attridge, Derek. 2000. *Joyce Effects: On Language, Theory, and History*. Cambridge: Cambridge University Press.

Auerbach, Nina. 1982. *The Woman and the Demon: The Life of a Victorian Myth*. Cambridge, MA: Harvard University Press.

Austin, J. L. 1979. *Philosophical Papers*. Edited by J. O. Urmson and G. J. Warnok. Oxford: Oxford University Press.

Ayto, John, ed. 2009. *Oxford Dictionary of English Idioms*. Oxford: Oxford University Press.

Bakhtin, Mikhail. 1968. *Rabelais and His World*. Translated by Helene Iswolsky. Cambridge, MA: MIT Press.

Bakhtin, Mikhail. 1981. *The Dialogic Imagination: Four Essays*. Translated by Caryl Emerson and Michael Holquist. Austin: University of Texas Press.

Barringer, Tim. 2005. *Men at Work: Art and Labour in Victorian Britain*. New Haven, CT: Yale University Press.

Barthes, Roland. 1982. "The Plates of the *Encyclopedia*." In *A Barthes Reader*, edited by Susan Sontag, 218–34. New York: Hill & Wang.

Barthes, Roland. 1988. "The Death of the Author." In *Image Text Music*, translated by Stephen Heath, 142–48. New York: Noonday Press.

Beamish, Richard. 1843. *Psychonomy of the Hand*. London: Pitman.

Beer, Gillian. 1983. *Darwin's Plots*. Cambridge: Cambridge University Press.

Beer, Gillian. 1996. *Open Fields: Science in Cultural Encounter*. Oxford: Oxford University Press.

Beeton, Isabella. 1861. *Book of Household Management*. London: S. O. Beeton.

Beirderwell, Bruce. 1985. "The Coherence of *Our Mutual Friend*." *Journal of Narrative Theory* 15 (3): 234–43.

Bell, Charles. 1833. *The Hand: Its Mechanism and Endowments as Evincing Design*. London: Pickering and Chatto.

Benston, Alice. 2002. "The Smallweeds and Trooper George: The Autochthony Theme in *Bleak House*." *Mosaic* 21 (4): 99–110.

"The Bentinck Bubble." 1847. *The Examiner*, February 13, 1847.

Bernstein, Susan David. 2001. "Ape Anxiety: Sensation Fiction, Evolution, and the Genre Question." *Journal of Victorian Culture* 6, no. 2 (Autumn): 250–71.

Best, Stephen, and Sharon Marcus. 2009. "Surface Reading: An Introduction." *Representations* 108, no. 1 (Fall): 1–21.

The Bible: Authorized King James Version with Apocrypha. 1997. Oxford: Oxford University Press.

Black, Max. 1962. *Models and Metaphors: Studies in Language and Philosophy*. Ithaca, NY: Cornell University Press.

Bode, Katherine. 2018. *A World of Fiction: Digital Collections and the Future of Literary Study*. Ann Arbor: University of Michigan Press.

Bodenheimer, Rosemarie. 1991. *The Politics of Story in Victorian Social Fiction*. Ithaca, NY: Cornell University Press.

Bodenheimer, Rosemarie. 1994. *The Real Life of Mary Ann Evans*. Ithaca, NY: Cornell University Press.

Bodenheimer, Rosemarie. 2002. "Dickens and the Identical Man: *Our Mutual Friend* Doubled." *Dickens Studies Annual* 31:159–74.

Bodenheimer, Rosemarie. 2007. *Knowing Dickens*. Ithaca, NY: Cornell University Press.

Boileau, Nicolas. 2014. "Trauma and 'Ordinary Words': Virginia Woolf's Play on Words." In *The Edges of Trauma*, edited by Tomás Bényei and Alexandra Stara, 48–60. Newcastle upon Tyne, UK: Cambridge Scholars.

Boll, Ernest. 1944. "The Plotting of *Our Mutual Friend*." *Modern Philology* 42 (2): 96–122.

Booth, Alison. 2017. "Mid-range Reading: Not a Manifesto." *PMLA* 132, no. 3 (May): 620–27.

Bourdieu, Pierre. 1984. *Distinction*. Translated by Richard Nice. Cambridge, MA: Harvard University Press.

Bourdieu, Pierre. 1990. *The Logic of Practice*. Translated by Richard Nice. Stanford, CA: Stanford University Press.

Bourdieu, Pierre. 1991. *Language and Symbolic Power*. Edited by John B. Thompson. Translated by Gino Raymond and Matthew Adamson. Cambridge, MA: Harvard University Press.

Bourrier, Karen. 2015. *The Measure of Manliness: Disability and Masculinity in the Mid-Victorian Novel*. Ann Arbor: University of Michigan Press.

Bowen, John. 2000. *Other Dickens: Pickwick to Chuzzlewit*. Oxford: Oxford University Press.

Bowen, John. 2013. "Dickens's Umbrellas." In *Dickens's Style*, edited by Daniel Tyler, 26–45. Oxford: Oxford University Press.

Bowen, John, and Robert Patten. 2006. *Palgrave Advances in Charles Dickens Studies*. London: Palgrave Macmillan.

Bowles, Hugo. 2019. *Dickens and the Stenographic Mind*. Oxford: Oxford University Press.

Bradbury, Nicola. 2003. Introduction to *Bleak House*, xix–xxxv. New York: Penguin.

Bradbury, Nicola. 2005. "Working and Being Worked in *Our Mutual Friend*." *Australasian Victorian Studies Journal* 1 (1): 1–7.

Bradshaw, David, and Suzanne Ozment, eds. 2000. *The Voice of Toil: Nineteenth-Century Writings about Work*. Athens: Ohio University Press.

Brantlinger, Patrick. 1996. *Fictions of State: Culture and Credit in Britain, 1694–1994*. Ithaca, NY: Cornell University Press.

Brantlinger, Patrick. 2011. *Taming Cannibals: Race and the Victorians*. Ithaca, NY: Cornell University Press.

Brattin, Joel. 1985. "Dickens' Creation of Bradley Headstone." *Dickens Studies Annual* 14:147–65.

Breton, Rob. 2005. *Gospels and Grit: Work and Labor in Carlyle, Conrad, and Orwell*. Toronto: University of Toronto Press.

Briefel, Aviva. 2015. *The Racial Hand in the Victorian Imagination*. Cambridge: Cambridge University Press.

246 BIBLIOGRAPHY

British Library Newspapers. 2008. Gale. https://www.gale.com/c/british-library-newspapers.

British Periodicals. 2007. ProQuest. https://proquest.com/en/products-services/british_periodicals.

Bromwich, David. 2019. *How Words Make Things Happen.* Oxford: Oxford University Press.

Brontë, Charlotte. 2019. *Jane Eyre.* Oxford:: Oxford World's Classics.

Brooks, G. L. 1970. *The Language of Dickens.* London: Deutsch.

Brooks, Peter. 1984. *Reading for the Plot.* New York: Knopf.

Brooks, Peter. 1993. *Body Work: Objects of Desire in Modern Narrative.* Cambridge, MA: Harvard University Press.

Brooks, Peter. 2005. *Realist Vision.* New Haven, CT: Yale University Press.

Brorby, Joshua. 2020. "Our Mutable Inheritance: Testing Victorian Philology in *Our Mutual Friend.*" *Dickens Quarterly* 37, no. 1 (March): 47–66.

Brown, Carolyn. 1987. "*Great Expectations*: Masculinity and Modernity." In *Broadening the Cultural Context*, edited by Michael Green, 60–74. London: Murray.

Buckland, Adelene. 2021. "Charles Dickens, Man of Science." *Victorian Literature and Culture* 49 (3): 423–455.

Burke, Peter, and Roy Porter, eds. 1987. *The Social History of Language.* Cambridge: Cambridge University Press.

Burney, Frances. (1788) 2002. *Evelina.* Oxford: Oxford University Press.

Butler, Judith. 1993. *Bodies That Matter: On the Discursive Limits of Sex.* New York: Routledge.

Butt, John, and Kathleen Tillotson. 1957. *Dickens at Work.* London: Methuen.

Buzard, James. 2005. *Disorienting Fiction.* Princeton, NJ: Princeton University Press.

Bythell, Duncan. 1978. *The Sweated Trades: Outwork in Nineteenth-Century Britain.* New York: St. Martin's.

Callow, Simon. 2012. *Dickens and the Great Theatre of the World.* New York: Vintage.

Capuano, Peter J. 2015. *Changing Hands: Industry, Evolution, and the Reconfiguration of the Victorian Body.* Ann Arbor: University of Michigan Press.

Carey, John. 1973. *The Violent Effigy: A Study of Dickens' Imagination.* London: Faber & Faber.

Carlyle, Thomas. 1842. *Chartism.* London: Chapman & Hall.

Carlyle, Thomas. 1919. *Past and Present.* London: Dent.

Carlyle, Thomas. 1974. *Sartor Resartus, Heroes, and Past and Present.* Edinburgh: Edinburgh University Press.

Casey, Edward S. 1976. *Imagining: A Phenomenological Study.* Bloomington: Indiana University Press.

Cavell, Stanley. 1969. *Must We Mean What We Say?* New York: Scribner's.

Cavell, Stanley. 1979. *The Claim of Reason.* Oxford: Oxford University Press.

Cavell, Stanley. 2005. *Philosophy the Day after Tomorrow.* Cambridge, MA: Harvard University Press.

Chambers, Robert. (1844) 1994. *Vestiges of the Natural History of Creation and Other Evolutionary Writings.* Edited by James A. Secord. Chicago: University of Chicago Press.

Chapple, J. A. V. 1986. *Science and Literature in the Nineteenth Century*. London: Macmillan.

Chase, Karen. 1984. *Eros and Psyche: The Representation of Personality in Charlotte Brontë, Charles Dickens, and George Eliot*. London: Methuen.

Chase, Karen, and Michael Levenson. 2017. "*Bleak House*, Liquid City: Climate to Climax in Dickens." In *A Global History of Literature and the Environment*, edited by John Parham and Louise Westling, 201–17. Cambridge: Cambridge University Press.

Cheadle, Brian. 2001a. "The Late Novels: *Great Expectations* and *Our Mutual Friend*." In *The Cambridge Companion to Charles Dickens*, edited by John O. Jordan, 78–91. Cambridge: Cambridge University Press.

Cheadle, Brian. 2001b. "Work in *Our Mutual Friend*." *Essays in Criticism* 51 (3): 308–29.

Chenier, Natasha Rose. 2014. "'And Words. They Are Not in My Dictionary': A Lexicographical Study of James Joyce and the *Oxford English Dictionary*." *James Joyce Quarterly* 51, no. 2–3 (Winter–Spring): 419–36.

Chesterton, G. K. 1911. *Appreciations and Criticisms of the Works of Charles Dickens*. London: Dent.

Chittick, Kathryn. 1990. *Dickens and the 1830s*. Cambridge: Cambridge University Press.

Christie, John, and Sally Shuttleworth, eds. 1989. *Nature Transfigured: Science and Literature: 1700–1900*. Manchester, UK: Manchester University Press.

Clayton, Jay. 2003. *Charles Dickens in Cyberspace: The Afterlife of the Nineteenth Century in Postmodern Culture*. Oxford: Oxford University Press.

Cockshut, A. O. J. 1962. *The Imagination of Charles Dickens*. New York: New York University Press.

Cohen, Jane R. 1980. *Charles Dickens and His Original Illustrators*. Columbus: Ohio State University Press.

Cohen, William A. 1993. "Manual Conduct in *Great Expectations*." *ELH* 60 (1): 217–59.

Cohen, William A. 1996. *Sex Scandal*. Durham, NC: Duke University Press.

Cohen, William A. 2009. *Embodied: Victorian Literature and the Senses*. Minneapolis: University of Minnesota Press.

Coleman, Rosemary. 2014. "How *Dombey and Son* Thinks about Masculinities." *Dickens Studies Annual* 45:125–45.

Collins, Philip. 1963. *Dickens and Education*. London: Macmillan.

Collins, Philip, ed. 1971. *Dickens: The Critical Heritage*. New York: Barnes & Noble.

Connor, Steven. 1985. *Charles Dickens*. London: Basil Blackwell.

Connor, Steven. 2000. "Consequential Ground: The Foot Passengers of *Bleak House*." Lecture at the Birkbeck College Dickens Day, September 30, 2000. http://stevenconnor.com/foot.

Corbett, Mary Jean. 2020. *Behind the Times: Virginia Woolf in Late Victorian Contexts*. Ithaca, NY: Cornell University Press.

Cowie, A. P., and R. Mackin, eds. 1975. *Oxford Dictionary of Current Idiomatic English*. Volume 1. Oxford: Oxford University Press.

Cowie, A. P., R. Mackin, and I. R. McCaig, eds. 1983. *Oxford Dictionary of Current Idiomatic English*. Volume 2. Oxford: Oxford University Press.

248 **BIBLIOGRAPHY**

Cox, G. W. 1862. "Max Müller on the Science of Language." *Edinburgh Review* 115 (January): 67–103.

Culler, Jonathan. 1985. "The Call of the Phoneme: Introduction." In *On Puns: The Foundation of Letters*, 1–16. Ithaca, NY: Cornell University Press.

Culler, Jonathan. 2010. "The Closeness of Close Reading." *ADE Bulletin* 149 (1): 20–25.

Curtis, L. Perry. 1979. *Apes and Angels: The Irishman in Victorian Caricature*. Washington, DC: Smithsonian Institution Press.

Da, Nan Z. 2019. "The Computational Case against Computational Literary Studies." *Critical Inquiry* 25, no. 2 (Spring): 601–39.

Daleski, H. M. 1970. *Dickens and the Art of Analogy*. New York: Schocken.

Dalgano, Emily. 2012. *Virginia Woolf and the Migrations of Language*. Cambridge: Cambridge University Press.

Dames, Nicholas. 2007. *The Physiology of the Novel: Reading, Neural Science, and the Form of Victorian Fiction*. Oxford: Oxford University Press.

Danahay, Martin. 2005. *Gender at Work in Victorian Culture*. Burlington, VT: Ashgate.

Danahay, Martin. 2011. "Work." In *Charles Dickens in Context*, edited by Sally Ledger and Holly Furneaux, 194–202. Cambridge: Cambridge University Press.

Darwin, Charles. 1996. *On the Origin of Species*. Edited by Gillian Beer. Oxford: Oxford University Press.

David, Deirdre. 1981. *Fictions of Resolution in Three Victorian Novels*. New York: Columbia University Press.

David, Deirdre. 2002. "Empire, Race, and the Victorian Novel." In *A Companion to the Victorian Novel*, edited by Patrick Brantlinger and William B. Thesing, 84–100. London: Blackwell.

David, Deirdre. 2011. "Review of *Supposing* Bleak House." *Review 19*, September 17, 2011. http://www.review19.org.

Davidoff, Leonore. 1979. "Class and Gender in Victorian England: The Diaries of Arthur J. Munby and Hannah Culliwick." *Feminist Studies* 5 (1): 86–141.

Davis, Lennard. 1995. *Enforcing Normalcy: Disability, Deafness, and the Body*. New York: Verso.

Davis, Lennard. 2012. "Seeing the Object as in Itself It Really Is: Beyond the Metaphor of Disability." In *The Madwoman and the Blindman:* Jane Eyre, *Discourse, Disability*, edited by David Bolt, Julia Miele Rodas, and Elizabeth J. Donaldson, ix–xii. Columbus: Ohio State University Press.

Davis, Lennard. 2013. "The End of Identity Politics: On Disability as an Unstable Category." In *The Disabilities Reader*, edited by Lennard Davis, 263–67. New York: Routledge.

Davison, Sarah. 2014. "Trenchant Criticism: Joyce's Use of Richard Chenevix Trench's Philological Studies in 'Oxen of the Sun.'" *Joyce Studies Annual* 24 (1): 164–95.

de Certeau, Michel. 1984. *The Practice of Everyday Life*. Translated by Steven Randall. Berkeley: University of California Press.

de Man, Paul. 1983. *Blindness and Insight*. Minneapolis: University of Minnesota Press.

Deering, Dorothy. 1977. "Dickens's Armory for the Mind: The English Language Studies in *Household Words* and *All the Year Round*." *Dickens Studies Newsletter* 8:11–17.

BIBLIOGRAPHY 249

Defoe, Daniel. (1719) 2008. *Robinson Crusoe*. Edited by Thomas Keymer. Oxford: Oxford University Press.

Derenzy, George Webb. 1822. *Enchiridion: Or A Hand for the One-Handed*. London: Underwood.

Derrida, Jacques. 2005a. *On Touching—Jean-Luc Nancy*. Translated by Christine Irizarry. Stanford, CA: Stanford University Press.

Derrida, Jacques. 2005b. *Paper Machine*. Translated by Rachel Bowlby. Stanford, CA: Stanford University Press.

Derrida, Jacques. 2007. "Heidegger's Hand (Geschlecht II)." Translated by John P. Leavey Jr. In *Psyche: Inventions of the Other*, edited by Peggy Kamuf and Elizabeth Rottenberg. Stanford, CA: Stanford University Press.

Detloff, Madelyn. 2016. *The Value of Virginia Woolf*. Cambridge: Cambridge University Press.

DiBattista, Maria. 2000. "Virginia Woolf and the Language of Authorship." In *The Cambridge Companion to Virginia Woolf*, edited by Sue Roe and Susan Sellers, 127–45. Cambridge: Cambridge University Press.

Dickens, Charles. (1836) 1995. *Sketches by Boz*. New York: Penguin.

Dickens, Charles. (1836–37) 2003. *The Pickwick Papers*. New York: Penguin.

Dickens, Charles. 1837. "The Pantomime of Life." *Bentley's Miscellany* 1, no. 1 (January): 291–97.

Dickens, Charles. (1837–39) 2003. *Oliver Twist*. New York: Penguin.

Dickens, Charles. (1840–41) 2000. *The Old Curiosity Shop*. New York: Penguin.

Dickens, Charles. (1841) 1973. *Barnaby Rudge*. New York: Penguin.

Dickens, Charles. (1843) 1971. *A Christmas Carol / The Chimes*. New York: Penguin.

Dickens, Charles. 1848. "The Poetry of Science, or Studies of the Physical Phenomena of Nature." *The Examiner*, no. 2132: 787–88. London: George Lapham.

Dickens, Charles. (1848) 2002. *Dombey and Son*. New York: Penguin.

Dickens, Charles. (1849–50) 2004. *David Copperfield*. New York: Penguin.

Dickens, Charles. 1850. "Supposing!" *Household Words* 1, no. 4: 96.

Dickens, Charles. (1852–53) 2003. *Bleak House*. New York: Penguin.

Dickens, Charles. 1853. "The Noble Savage." *Household Words* 7 (168): 337–39.

Dickens, Charles. (1854) 2003. *Hard Times*. New York: Penguin.

Dickens, Charles. (1855–57) 2003. *Little Dorrit*. New York: Penguin.

Dickens, Charles. (1859) 1988. *A Tale of Two Cities*. Oxford: Oxford University Press.

Dickens, Charles. (1860–61) 2003. *Great Expectations*. New York: Penguin.

Dickens, Charles. (1864–65) 1997. *Our Mutual Friend*. New York: Penguin.

Dickens, Charles. (1865) 1997. "Postscript, In Lieu of Preface." In *Our Mutual Friend*, 798–800. New York: Penguin.

Dickens, Charles. 1999. *Great Expectations*. Edited by Edgar Rosenberg. New York: Norton.

Dickens, Charles. 2003. *The Mystery of Edwin Drood*. New York: Penguin.

Dickens, Charles. 2006. *A Christmas Carol and Other Christmas Books*. Oxford: Oxford University Press.

Dickens, Mamie. 1896. *My Father as I Recall Him*. London: Roxburghe.

Dixon, Edmund Saul. 1853. "The Mind of Brutes." *Household Words* 7 (177): 564–69.

Douglas-Fairhurst, Robert. 2006. Introduction to *A Christmas Carol and Other Christmas Books*, vii–xxix. Oxford: Oxford University Press.

Douglas-Fairhurst, Robert. 2011. *Becoming Dickens: The Invention of a Novelist*. Cambridge, MA: Harvard University Press.

Douglas-Fairhurst, Robert. 2013. "Dickens's Rhythms." In *Dickens's Style*, edited by Daniel Tyler, 73–92. Cambridge: Cambridge University Press.

Douglas-Fairhurst, Robert. 2022. *The Turning Point: 1851—A Year that Changed Charles Dickens and the World*. New York: Knopf.

Dowling, Linda. 1982. "Victorian Oxford and the Science of Language." *PMLA* 97 (2): 160–78.

Dowling, Linda. 1986. *Language and Decadence in the Victorian Fin de Siècle*. Princeton, NJ: Princeton University Press.

Downing, Gregory M. 1998. "Richard Chenevix Trench and Joyce's Historical Study of Words." *Joyce Studies Annual* 9 (1): 937–68.

Dramatic Dickens. 1989. Edited by Carol Hanberry MacKay. London: Macmillan.

Drucker, Johanna. 2017. "Why Distant Reading Isn't." *PMLA* 132, no. 3 (May): 628–35.

Du Chaillu, Paul. 1861. *Explorations and Adventures in Equatorial Africa*. London: John Murray.

Dyson, A. E. 1970. *The Inimitable Dickens*. London: Macmillan.

Eagleton, Terry. 1995. *Heathcliff and the Great Hunger*. New York: Verso.

Eagleton, Terry. 2003. Preface to *Bleak House*, vii–xii. Edited by Nicola Bradbury. New York: Penguin.

Eagleton, Terry. 2005. *The English Novel*. London: Wiley-Blackwell.

Eigner, Edward. 1989. *The Dickens Pantomime*. Berkeley: University of California Press.

Elfenbein, Andrew. 1995. "Managing the House in *Dombey and Son*: Dickens and the Uses of Analogy." *Studies in Philology* 92 (3): 361–82.

Elfenbein, Andrew. 2018. *The Gist of Reading*. Stanford, CA: Stanford University Press.

Eliot, T. S. 1927. "Wilkie Collins and Dickens." *Times Literary Supplement*, August 4, 1927, 525–26.

Emre, Merve. 2022. "Getting to Yes: The Making of *Ulysses*." *The New Yorker*. February 14 and 21, 68–73.

Emre, Merve. 2023. "The Return to Philology." *PMLA* 138 (1): 171–177.

Engels, Friedrich. (1845) 1993. *The Condition of the Working Class in England*. Edited by David McLellan. Oxford: Oxford University Press.

Engels, Friedrich. (1876) 1968. "The Part Played by Labour in the Transition from Ape to Man." In *Karl Marx and Frederick Engels, Selected Works*, 358–73. New York: Progress.

Eve, Martin Paul. 2019. *Close Reading with Computers*. Stanford, CA: Stanford University Press.

Evernden, Tamsin. 2018. "Crooked Antics: The Visions of Jenny Wren in Dickens's *Our Mutual Friend*." *Working Papers in the Humanities* 12 (1): 11–19.

Fahnstock, Jeanne. 2011. *Rhetorical Style: The Uses of Language in Persuasion*. Oxford: Oxford University Press.

Felski, Rita. 2000. *Doing Time: Feminist Theory and Postmodern Culture*. New York: New York University Press.

BIBLIOGRAPHY 251

Felski, Rita. 2009. "After Suspicion." *Profession* 33 (1): 28–35.

Felski, Rita. 2011. "Context Stinks." *New Literary History* 42 (4): 573–91.

Felski, Rita. 2015. *The Limits of Critique*. Chicago: University of Chicago Press.

Ferguson, Frances. 2013. "Philology, Literature, Style." *ELH* 80 (2): 323–41.

Fernando, Chitra, and Roger Flavell. 1981. *On Idiom*. Exeter, UK: University of Exeter Press.

Fielding, K. J. 1958. *Charles Dickens: A Critical Introduction*. London: Longman's and Green.

Fielding, K. J., ed. 1960. *The Speeches of Charles Dickens*. Oxford: Oxford University Press.

Fielding, K. J. 1961. "The Critical Autonomy of *Great Expectations*." *Review of English Literature* 2 (1): 75–88.

Fisher, Benjamin. 1999. "Poe in Great Britain." In *Poe Abroad: Influence, Reputation, Affinities*, edited by Lois Davis Vines, 52–61. Iowa City: University of Iowa Press.

Flanders, Julia. 2013. "The Literary, the Humanistic, the Digital: Toward a Research Agenda for Literary Studies." In *Literary Studies in the Digital Age*, edited by Ken Price and Ray Siemens. New York: Modern Language Association.

Flint, Kate. 1986. *Dickens*. London: Harvester.

Flint, Kate. 2001. "The Middle Novels: *Chuzzlewit, Dombey,* and *Copperfield*." In *The Cambridge Companion to Charles Dickens*, edited by John O. Jordan, 34–48. Cambridge: Cambridge University Press.

Flint, Kate. 2018. "*Bleak House*." In *The Oxford Handbook of Charles Dickens*, edited by Robert L. Patten, John O. Jordan, and Catherine Waters, 220–32. Oxford: Oxford University Press.

Ford, George H. 1955. *Dickens and His Readers*. Princeton, NJ: Princeton University Press.

Ford, George H. 1958. "Self-Help and the Helpless." In *From Jane Austen to Joseph Conrad*, edited by Robert C. Rathburn and Martin Stienmann Jr., 92–105. Minneapolis: University of Minnesota Press.

Ford, George H., and Lauriat Lane Jr., eds. 1961. *The Dickens Critics*. Ithaca, NY: Cornell University Press.

Forker, Charles. 1961–62. "The Language of Hands in *Great Expectations*." *Texas Studies in Literature and Language* 3 (1): 280–93.

Forster, John. 1892. *The Life of Charles Dickens*. 3 Vols. London: Chapman & Hall.

Foucault, Michel. 1973. *The Order of Things*. New York: Vintage.

Foucault, Michel. 1977. *Discipline and Punish*. Translated by Alan Sheridan. New York: Vintage.

Foucault, Michel. 1979. "What Is an Author?" In *Textual Strategies: Perspectives in Post-structuralist Criticism*, edited by Josué V. Havari, 141–60. Ithaca, NY: Cornell University Press.

Free, Melissa. 2008. "Freaks That Matter: The Doll's Dressmaker, the Doctor's Assistant, and the Limits of Difference." In *Victorian Freaks*, edited by Marlene Tromp, 259–82. Columbus: Ohio State University Press.

Furneaux, Holly. 2009. *Queer Dickens: Erotics, Families, Masculinities*. Oxford: Oxford University Press.

Gager, Valerie L. 1996. *Shakespeare and Dickens: The Dynamics of Influence*. Cambridge: Cambridge University Press.

Gailey, Amanda. 2016. "Some Problems with Big Data." *American Periodicals* 26 (1): 22–24.

Gallagher, Catherine. 2008. *The Body Economic*. Princeton, NJ: Princeton University Press.

Gallop, Jane. 1988. *Thinking through the Body*. New York: Columbia University Press.

Gane, Gillian. 1996. "The Hat, the Hook, the Eyes, the Teeth: Captain Cuttle and Mr. Carker." *Dickens Studies Annual* 25:91–126.

Garis, Robert. 1965. *The Dickens Theatre*. Oxford: Oxford University Press.

Garland-Thomson, Rosemarie. 1997. *Extraordinary Bodies: Figuring Physical Disability in American Literature and Culture*. New York: Columbia University Press.

Garland-Thomson, Rosemarie. 2002. "The Politics of Staring: Visual Rhetorics of Disability in Popular Photography." In *Disability Studies: Enabling the Humanities*, edited by Sharon L. Snyder, Brenda Jo Brueggeman, and Rosemarie Garland-Thomson, 56–75. New York: Modern Language Association.

Garland-Thomson, Rosemarie. 2009. *Staring: How We Look*. Oxford: Oxford University Press.

Genette, Gérard. 1997. *Paratexts*. Translated by Jane E. Lewin. Cambridge: Cambridge University Press.

Gerschick, Thomas, and Adam Stephen Miller. 1995. "Coming to Terms: Masculinity and Physical Disability." In *Men's Lives*, edited by Michael S. Kimmel and Michael A. Messner, 262–75. Boston: Allyn & Bacon.

Gibbons, Luke. 2013. "'He Says No, Your Worship': Joyce, Free Indirect Discourse and Vernacular Modernism." In *James Joyce in the Nineteenth Century*, edited by John Nash, 31–45. Cambridge: Cambridge University Press.

Gibson, Anna. 2015. "*Our Mutual Friend* and Network Form." *Novel: A Forum on Fiction* 48 (1): 63–84.

Gibson, Anna, Adam Grener, and Frankie Goodenough. 2022a. "General Introduction: Dickens and Serial Form." Anna Gibson and Adam Grener, Directors. Digital Dickens Notes Project. http://dickensnotes.com/introduction/general.

Gibson, Anna, Adam Grener, and Frankie Goodenough. 2022b. "Scholarly Introduction: Rethinking Dickens's Serial Form with the *Digital Dickens Notes Project*." Anna Gibson and Adam Grener, Directors. *Digital Dickens Notes Project*. http://dickensnotes.com/introduction/scholarly.

Gilbert, Pamela K. 2019. *Victorian Skin: Surface, Self, History*. Ithaca, NY: Cornell University Press.

Gillooly, Eileen, and Deirdre David, eds. 2009. *Contemporary Dickens*. Columbus: Ohio State University Press.

Gitleman, Lisa. 2013. "*Raw Data" Is an Oxymoron*. Cambridge, MA: MIT Press.

Gitter, Elisabeth. 2004. "Dickens's *Dombey and Son* and the Anatomy of Coldness." *Dickens Studies Annual* 34:99–116.

Glass, Montague. 1911. *Abe and Mawruss*. New York: Doubleday.

Goffman, Erving. 1963. *Behavior in Public Places*. New York: Free Press.

Goldberg, Michael. 1972. *Carlyle and Dickens*. Athens: University of Georgia Press.

Golding, Robert. 1985. *Idiolects in Dickens*. London: Macmillan.

Goodlad, Lauren M. E. 2003. "Is There a Pastor in the *House*? Sanitary Reform, Professionalism, and Philanthropy in Dickens's Mid-century Fiction." *Victorian Literature and Culture* 31 (2): 525–53.

Goodrich, Peter. 2017. "Proboscations: Excavations in Comedy and Law." *Critical Inquiry* 43 (1): 361–88.

Gore, Clare Walker. 2021. *Plotting Disability in the Nineteenth-Century Novel*. Edinburgh: Edinburgh University Press.

Görlach, Manfred. 1999. *English in Nineteenth-Century England*. Oxford: Oxford University Press.

Grass, Sean. 2014. *Charles Dickens's* Our Mutual Friend: *A Publishing History*. Burlington, VT: Ashgate.

Greenberg, Kenneth S. 1990. "The Nose, the Lie, and the Duel in the Antebellum South." *American Historical Review* 95 (1): 57–74.

Grève, Sebastian, and Jakub Mácha, eds. 2016. *Wittgenstein and the Creativity of Language*. London: Palgrave.

Gribble, Jennifer. 1975. "Depth and Surface in *Our Mutual Friend.*" *Essays in Criticism* 25 (2): 197–214.

Gribble, Jennifer. 2013. "Compound Interest: Dickens's Figurative Style." In *Dickens's Style*, edited by Daniel Tyler, 195–213. Cambridge: Cambridge University Press.

Groebner, Valentin. 2009. *Defaced: The Visual Culture of Violence in the Late Middle Ages*. New York: Zone.

Hack, Danny. 1999. "'Sublimation Strange': Allegory and Authority in *Bleak House.*" *ELH* 66 (1): 129–56.

Hack, Danny. 2005. *The Material Concerns of the Victorian Novel*. Charlotteville: University of Virginia Press.

Hack, Danny. 2016. *Reaping Something New*. Princeton, NJ: Princeton University Press.

Hager, Kelly. 2010. *Dickens and the Rise of Divorce*. Burlington, VT: Ashgate.

Hansard Parliamentary Debates Archive. Nineteenth-Century Collections Online (NCCO). Gale-Cengage.

Hardy, Barbara. 1970. *The Moral Art of Dickens*. Oxford: Oxford University Press.

Hardy, Barbara. 2008. *Dickens and Creativity*. New York: Continuum.

Harpham, Geoffrey. 2009. "Roots, Races, and the Return to Philology." *Representations* 106 (1): 34–62.

Hartley, Jenny. 2016. *Charles Dickens: An Introduction*. Oxford: Oxford University Press.

Hawes, Donald. 1972. "Marryat and Dickens: A Personal and Literary Relationship." *Dickens Studies Annual* 2:39–68.

Hayles, N. Katherine. 2010. "How We Read: Close, Hyper, Machine." *ADE Bulletin* 150 (1): 62–79.

Hazlitt, William. 1810. *A New and Improved Grammar of the English Tongue*. London: M. J. Godwin.

Hazlitt, William. 1905. *Table-Talk: Essays on Men and Manners*. London: Henry Frowde.

Hecimovich, Gregg A. 1995. "The Cup and the Lip and the Riddle of *Our Mutual Friend.*" *ELH* 62 (4): 955–77.

Heidegger, Martin. 1968. *What Is Called Thinking?* Translated by Fred D. Wieck and J. Glenn Gray. New York: Harper & Row.

Heywood, John. 1546. *Proverbs in the English Tongue*. London: Thomas Berthelet.

Hingston, Kylee-Anne. 2019. *Articulating Bodies: The Narrative Form of Disability and Illness in Victorian Fiction*. Liverpool: Liverpool University Press.

254 BIBLIOGRAPHY

Hockett, Charles F. 1956. "Idiom Formation." In *For Roman Jakobson*, edited by Morris Halle, 222–29. London: Mouton.

Holmes, Martha Stoddard. 2004. *Fictions of Affliction: Disability in Victorian Culture*. Ann Arbor: University of Michigan Press.

Holquist, Michael. 2002. "Why We Should Remember Philology." *Profession* 25 (1): 72–79.

Hori, M. 2004. *Investigating Dickens' Style: A Collocational Analysis*. London: Palgrave.

Horne, Philip. 2013. "Style and the Making of Character in Dickens." In *Dickens's Style*, edited by Daniel Tyler, 155–75. Cambridge: Cambridge University Press.

Horne, Richard. 1852. "Strings of Proverbs." *Household Words* 4 (101): 538–40.

Horsman, Alan. 1974. Introduction to *Dombey and Son* by Charles Dickens, xiii–xlvi. Edited by Alan Horsman. Oxford: Oxford University Press.

Houghton, Walter. (1857) 1963. *The Victorian Frame of Mind, 1830–1870*. New Haven, CT: Yale University Press.

House, Humphry. 1941. *The Dickens World*. Oxford: Oxford University Press.

House, Madeline, Graham Storey, Kathleen Tillotson, and Margaret Brown, eds. 1965–2002. *The Letters of Charles Dickens*. 12 vols. Oxford: Clarendon.

Houston, Gail Turley. 1994. *Consuming Fictions: Gender, Class, and Hunger in Dickens's Novels*. Carbondale: Southern Illinois University Press.

Hudson, Derek. 1972. *Munby, Man of Two Worlds: The Life and Diaries of Arthur J. Munby 1828–1910*. Cambridge: Cambridge University Press.

Hughes, Kathryn. 2018. *Victorians Undone: Tales of the Flesh in the Age of Decorum*. Baltimore: Johns Hopkins University Press.

Hui, Andrew. 2019. *A Theory of the Aphorism: From Confucius to Twitter*. Princeton, NJ: Princeton University Press.

Hullah, John. 1837. "A Visit to the Madrigal Society." *Bentley's Miscellany* 1:465–68.

Hunt, Leigh. 1842. "The Tories on Peace with China." *The Examiner*, no. 1817:753.

Hunt, Leigh. 1846. "The Faintest Ministry." *The Examiner*, no. 1995:257.

Husserl, Edmund. 1973. *Experience and Judgement*. Evanston, IL: Northwestern University Press.

Husserl, Edmund. 1989. *Ideas Pertaining to a Pure Phenomenology and to a Phenomenological Philosophy* (Second Book). Philadelphia: Kluwer.

Igarashi, Yohei. 2015. "Statistical Analysis at the Birth of Close Reading." *New Literary History* 46, no. 3 (Summer): 485–504.

Ingham, Patricia. 1992. *Dickens, Women and Language*. Toronto: University of Toronto Press.

Ingham, Patricia. 2008. "The Language of Dickens." In *A Companion to Charles Dickens*, edited by David Paroissien, 126–41. Hoboken, NJ: Blackwell.

Jaffe, Audrey. 1987. "Omniscience in *Our Mutual Friend*: On Taking the Reader by Surprise." *Journal of Narrative Technique* 17, no. 1 (Winter): 91–101.

Jaffe, Audrey. 1991. *Vanishing Points: Dickens, Narrative and the Subject of Omniscience*. Berkeley, CA: University of California Press.

Jakobson, Roman. 1987. *Language in Literature*. Edited by Krystyna Pomorska and Stephen Rudy. Cambridge, MA: Harvard University Press.

James, Henry. 1865. "Our Mutual Friend." *The Nation*, December 21, 1865, 786–87.

James, Henry. (1877) 1999. *The American*. New York: Oxford World Classics.

BIBLIOGRAPHY 255

James, Henry. (1881) 1999. *The Portrait of a Lady*. New York: Oxford World Classics.

James, Henry. (1884) 1999. "The Art of Fiction." In *Henry James: Major Stories and Essays*, edited by Leon Edel et al., 572–93. New York: Library of America.

James, Henry. (1904) 1952. *The Golden Bowl*. New York: Grove Press.

James, Henry. (1913) 2011a. *A Small Boy and Others: A Critical Edition*. Edited by Peter Collister. Charlottesville: University of Virginia Press.

James, Henry. (1914) 2011b. *Notes of a Son and Brother*. Edited by Peter Collister. Charlottesville: University of Virginia Press.

James, Henry. (1921) 2011c. "Preface to *The Tragic Muse*." In *The Art of the Novel: Critical Prefaces*. Edited by Colm Tóibín, 79–97. Chicago: University of Chicago Press.

James, Stephen. 2012. "Repetition, Rumination, and Superstition: The Rituals of *Our Mutual Friend*." *English* 61 (234): 214–33.

Jameson, Fredric. 1982. *The Political Unconscious*. Ithaca, NY: Cornell University Press.

Janechek, Jennifer. 2015. "'This Curious Association of Objects': Dickens's Treatment of Chair-Transported Characters in *Dombey and Son* and *Bleak House*." *Dickens Studies Annual* 46:147–65.

Jerdan, William. 1857. "The Gift of Tongues." *Household Words* 15 (355): 41–43.

John, Juliet. 2001. *Dickens's Villains: Melodrama, Character, Popular Culture*. Oxford: Oxford University Press.

John, Juliet. 2010. *Dickens and Mass Culture*. Oxford: Oxford University Press.

Johnson, Mark. 1987. *The Body in the Mind: The Bodily Basis of Meaning, Imagination, and Reason*. Chicago: University of Chicago Press.

Johnson, Samuel. 1984a. "The Lives of the Poets: Abraham Cowley." In *Samuel Johnson: The Major Works*, edited by Donald Greene, 677–97. Oxford: Oxford University Press.

Johnson, Samuel. 1984b. Preface to *A Dictionary of the English Language*. In *Samuel Johnson: The Major Works*, edited by Donald Greene, 307–28. Oxford: Oxford University Press.

Johnson, Samuel. 2018. *Samuel Johnson*. Edited by David Womersley, 411–14. *The Rambler*, no. 208 [1752]. Oxford: Oxford University Press.

Jordan, John O. 2010. *Supposing Bleak House*. Charlottesville: University of Virginia Press.

Jordan, John O. 2011. "Response to Review by Deirdre David." *Review* 19, September 29, 2011. www.review19.org.

Joshi, Priti. 2011. "Race." In *Charles Dickens in Context*, edited by Sally Ledger and Holly Furneaux, 292–300. Cambridge: Cambridge University Press.

Joyce, Simon. 2002. "Inspector Bucket versus Tom-all-Alone's, Literary Theory, and the Condition-of-England in the 1850s." *Dickens Studies Annual* 32:129–49.

Kant, Immanuel. 1950. *Critique of Pure Reason*. Translated by Norman Kemp Smith. New York: Humanities Press.

Kaplan, Fred. 1975. *Dickens and Mesmerism: The Hidden Springs of Fiction*. Princeton, NJ: Princeton University Press.

Kaplan, Fred. 1981. *Dickens's Book of Memoranda*. New York: New York Public Library Publications.

256 BIBLIOGRAPHY

Keatley, Paula. 2017. "'It's about a Will': Liberal Protestant Theology in Dickens's *Bleak House." Nineteenth-Century Contexts* 39 (2): 77–86.

Kelty, Jean McClure. 1961. "The Modern Tone of Charles Dickens." *The Dickensian* 57 (335): 160–65.

Kennedy, G. W. 1973. "Naming and Language in *Our Mutual Friend." Nineteenth-Century Fiction* 28 (2): 165–78.

Kenner, Hugh. 1978. *Joyce's Voices*. Berkeley CA: University of California Press.

Keyes, Ralph. 2021. *The Hidden History of Coined Words*. Oxford: Oxford University Press.

Kiely, Robert. 1983. "Plotting and Scheming: The Design of Design in *Our Mutual Friend." Dickens Studies Annual* 12:267–83.

Kincaid, James. 1971. *Dickens and the Rhetoric of Laughter*. Oxford: Oxford University Press.

Kincaid, James, ed. 2018. *The Daily Charles Dickens: A Year of Quotes*. Chicago: University of Chicago Press.

Kittay, Eva Feder. 1987. *Metaphor: Its Cognitive Force and Linguistic Structure*. Oxford: Oxford University Press.

Kitton, F. G. 1890. *Charles Dickens by Pen and Pencil*. 2 Vols. London: Sabin and Dexter.

Kitton, F. G. 1899. *Dickens and His Illustrators*. London: George Redway.

Knoepflmacher, U. C. 1971. *Laughter and Despair: Readings in Ten Novels of the Victorian Era*. Berkeley: University of California Press.

Knoepflmacher, U. C. 1988. "From Outrage to Rage: Dickens's Bruised Femininity." In *Dickens and Other Victorians*, edited by Joanne Shattock, 75–96. London: Macmillan.

Kopec, Andrew. 2016. "The Digital Humanities, Inc.: Literary Criticism and the Fate of a Profession." *PMLA* 131, no. 2 (March): 324–39.

Korte, Barbara. 1997. *Body Language in Literature*. Toronto: University of Toronto Press.

Kreilkamp, Ivan. 2007. "Dying like a Dog in *Great Expectations." In Victorian Animal Dreams*, edited by Martin Danahay and Deborah Morse, 81–94. Burlington, VT: Ashgate.

Kreilkamp, Ivan. 2009. *Voice and the Victorian Storyteller*. Cambridge: Cambridge University Press.

Kucich, John. 1981. *Excess and Restraint in the Novels of Charles Dickens*. Athens: University of Georgia Press.

Kucich, John. 1985. "Dickens's Fantastic Rhetoric: The Semantics of Reality and Unreality in *Our Mutual Friend." Dickens Studies Annual* 14:167–89.

Lakoff, George, and Mark Johnson. 1980. *Metaphors We Live By*. Chicago: University of Chicago Press.

Lakoff, George, and Mark Johnson. 1999. *Philosophy in the Flesh*. New York: Basic Books.

Lambert, Mark. 1981. *Dickens and the Suspended Quotation*. New Haven, CT: Yale University Press.

Larson, Janet. 1985. *Dickens and the Broken Scripture*. Athens: University of Georgia Press.

Law, Jules. 2010. *The Social Life of Fluids: Blood, Milk, and Water in the Victorian Novel*. Ithaca, NY: Cornell University Press.

BIBLIOGRAPHY 257

Leavis, F. R., and Q. D. Leavis. 1970. *Dickens the Novelist*. London: Chatto & Windus.

Ledbetter, Kathryn. 2012. *Victorian Needlework*. Santa Barbara, CA: Praeger.

Ledger, Sally. 2007. *Dickens and the Radical Popular Imagination*. Cambridge: Cambridge University Press.

Ledger, Sally. 2011. "Dickens, Natural History, and *Our Mutual Friend*." *Partial Answers* 9 (2): 363–78.

Ledger, Sally, and Holly Furneaux, eds. 2011. *Charles Dickens in Context*. Cambridge: Cambridge University Press.Lefebvre, Henri. 1984. *Everyday Life in the Modern World*. Translated by Sacha Rabinovitch. New York: Transaction.

Lefebvre, Henri. 1991. *Critique of Everyday Life*. Translated by John Moore. New York: Verso.

Lesjak, Carolyn. 2006. *Working Fictions*. Durham, NC: Duke University Press.

Levine, George. 1986. "Dickens and Darwin, Science and Narrative Form." *Texas Studies in Literature and Language* 28 (3): 250–81.

Levine, George. 1988. *Darwin and the Novelists*. Cambridge, MA: Harvard University Press.

Levine, George. 2021. "The Intentional Fallacy." *The Geezer Gazette*. [Email March 9, 2021]

Lewes, George Henry. 1872a. "Dickens and the Art of the Novel." *Fortnightly Review* 17:143–51.

Lewes, George Henry. 1872b. "Dickens in Relation to Criticism." *Fortnightly Review* 11, no. 62 (February): 141–54.

Lewis, R. W. B. 1991. *The Jameses: A Family Narrative*. New York: Farrar, Straus and Giroux.

Lightman, Bernard. 1997. "'The Voices of Nature': Popularizing Victorian Science." In *Victorian Science in Context*, edited by Bernard Lightman, 187–211. Chicago: University of Chicago Press.

Litvack, Leon. 2008. "*Our Mutual Friend*." In *A Companion to Charles Dickens*, edited by David Paroissien, 433–43. Hoboken, NJ: Wiley-Blackwell, 2008.

Long, Hoyt, and Richard Jean So. 2016. "Literary Pattern Recognition: Modernism between Close Reading and Machine Learning." *Critical Inquiry* 42, no. 1 (Winter): 235–67.

Lougy, Robert. 2018. "Entangled Paths and Ghostly Resonances: *Bleak House* and *Oedipus Rex*." *Dickens Studies Annual* 49 (1): 378–401.

Louttit, Chris. 2009. *Dickens's Secular Gospel*. New York: Routledge.

Love, Brigid. 2008. "*Dombey and Son*." In *A Companion to Charles Dickens*, edited by David Paroissien, 358–68. Hoboken, NJ: Blackwell.

MacKay, Carol Hanbery, ed. 1981. *Dramatic Dickens*. New York: St. Martin's.

Macleod, Norman. 2002. "Which Hand? Reading *Great Expectations* as a Guessing Game." *Dickens Studies Annual* 31:127–57.

Mahlberg, Michaela. 2013. *Corpus Stylistics and Dickens's Fiction*. New York: Routledge.

Mahlberg, M., Stockwell, P., Wiegand, V., and Lentin, J. 2020. CLiC 2.1. Corpus Linguistics in Context. clic.bham.ac.uk.

Marcus, Stephen. 1965. *Dickens: from Pickwick to Dombey*. New York: Basic Books.

Marcus, Stephen. 1972. "Language into Structure: *Pickwick* Revisited." *Daedalus* 101, no. 1 (Winter): 183–202.

BIBLIOGRAPHY

Marryat, Florence. 1869. *Véronique*. London: Richard Bentley.

Marryat, Frederick. 1834. *Peter Simple*. London: Saunders and Otley.

Marryat, Frederick. 1836. *Rattlin the Reefer*. London: Richard Bentley.

Marryat, Frederick. 1841. *Joseph Rushbrook*. Philadelphia: Carey and Hart.

Marryat, Frederick. 1842. *Percival Keene*. London: Henry Colburn.

Marx, Karl. 1990. *Capital*. Vol. 1. Edited by Ernest Mandel. Translated by Ben Fowkes. New York: Penguin.

Masson, David. 1859. *British Novelists and Their Styles*. London: Macmillan.

Mayhew, Henry. 1968. *London Labour and the London Poor*. Vols. 1–4. New York: Dover.

McCarthy, Justin. (1864) 1965. "Modern Novelists: Charles Dickens." *Westminster Review* 26:415–41.

McClintock, Anne. 1995. *Imperial Leather*. New York: Routledge.

McMaster, Juliet. 1987. *Dickens the Designer*. London: Macmillan.

Melisi, Laurent. 2003. *James Joyce and the Difference of Language*. Cambridge: Cambridge University Press.

Merleau-Ponty, Maurice. 1962. *The Phenomenology of Perception*. New York: Routledge.

Michie, Helena. 1987. *The Flesh Made Word: Female Figures and Women's Bodies*. Oxford: Oxford University Press.

Michie, Helena. 2018. "Extra Man: Dining Out beyond the Marriage Plot in *Our Mutual Friend*." In *Replotting Marriage in Nineteenth-Century British Literature*, edited by Jill Galvan and Elsie Michie, 211–28. Columbus: Ohio State University Press.

Miller, Andrew. 2008. *The Burdens of Perfection*. Ithaca, NY: Cornell University Press.

Miller, Andrew. 2012. "'A Case of Metaphysics': Counterfactuals, Realism, *Great Expectations*." *ELH* 79 (3): 773–96.

Miller, D. A. 1988. *The Novel and the Police*. Berkeley: University of California Press.

Miller, D. A. 2003. *Jane Austen, or The Secret of Style*. Princeton, NJ: Princeton University Press.

Miller, J. Hillis. 1958. *Charles Dickens: The World of His Novels*. Cambridge, MA: Harvard University Press.

Miller, J. Hillis. 1971. Introduction to *Bleak House* by Charles Dickens, 11–34. Edited by Norman Page and J. Hillis Miller. New York: Penguin.

Miller, J. Hillis. 1982. *Fiction and Repetition*. Cambridge, MA: Harvard University Press.

Miller, J. Hillis. 1991a. *Theory Then and Now*. Durham, NC: Duke University Press.

Miller, J. Hillis. 1991b. *Victorian Subjects*. Durham, NC: Duke University Press.

"The Missing Link." 1862. *Punch* 43:165.

Mitchell, Charlotte. 1996. Ed and Notes to *Great Expectations*. New York: Penguin.

Mitchell, David T. 2002. "Narrative Prosthesis and the Materiality of Metaphor." In *Disability Studies: Enabling the Humanities*, edited by Sharon L. Snyder, Brenda Jo Brueggemann, and Rosemarie Garland-Thomson, 15–30. New York: Modern Language Association.

Mitchell, David T., and Sharon L. Snyder. 2000. *Narrative Prosthesis: Disability and Dependencies of Discourse*. Ann Arbor: University of Michigan Press.

Mitchell, Sally. 1981. *The Fallen Angel*. Bowling Green, OH: Bowling Green State University Press.

Moore, Grace. 2004. *Dickens and Empire: Discourses of Class, Race and Colonialism in the Works of Charles Dickens*. Burlington, VT: Ashgate.

Moore, Jack. 1965. "Hearts and Hands in *Great Expectations*." *Dickensian* 61:52–56.

Moran, Patricia. 1996. *Word of Mouth: Body Language in Katherine Mansfield and Virginia Woolf*. Charlottesville: University of Virginia Press.

Morgentaler, Goldie. 1998. "Mediating on the Low: A Darwinian Reading of *Great Expectations*." *SEL* 38 (4): 707–21.

Moretti, Franco. 2005. *Graphs, Maps, Trees: Abstract Models for a Literary History*. New York: Verso.

Moretti, Franco. 2013. *Distant Reading*. New York: Verso.

Morley, Henry, and William Lowes Rushton. 1858. "Saxon-English." *Household Words* 18 (433): 89–92.

Morris, Pam. 1991. *Dickens's Class Consciousness*. New York: St. Martin's.

Mufti, Nasser. 2016. "Walking in *Bleak House*." *Novel* 49 (1): 65–81.

Mugglestone, Lynda. 2005. *Lost for Words: The Hidden History of the Oxford English Dictionary*. New Haven, CT: Yale University Press.

Mugglestone, Lynda. 2011. "'Life-Writing': The Lexicographer as Biographer in the *Oxford English Dictionary*." In *New Approaches to Historical Lexis*, edited by R. W. McConchie et al., 14–26. Sommerville, MA: Cascadilla Proceedings Project.

Müller, Friedrich Max. 1899. *Lectures on the Science of Language*. London: Longmans, Green.

Müller, Max. 1861. *Lectures on the Science of Language*. 2 Vols. London: Scribner.

Murray, K. M. Elisabeth. 1977. *Caught in the Web of Words: James A. H. Murray and the Oxford English Dictionary*. New Haven, CT: Yale University Press.

Nash, John, ed. 2013. *James Joyce in the Nineteenth Century*. Cambridge: Cambridge University Press.

"Natural Selection." 1860. *All the Year Round*. (July 7) 3:293–99.

Nayder, Lillian. 2012a. Introduction to *Dickens, Sexuality and Gender*, edited by Lillian Nayder, xxi–xxviii. Burlington, VT: Ashgate.

Nayder, Lillian. 2012b. *The Other Dickens: A Life of Catherine Hogarth*. Ithaca, NY: Cornell University Press.

Newsom, Robert. 1977. *Dickens on the Romantic Side of Familiar Things*. New York: Columbia University Press.

Newsom, Robert. 1989. "Embodying *Dombey*: Whole and in Part." *Dickens Studies Annual* 18:197–219.

Nineteenth-Century Fiction. 2000. Chadwyck-Healey Literature Collections. ProQuest.

"O'Connell." 1847. *The Examiner*, no. 2052:337.

OED Online. 2000–. Edited by John Simpson et al. Oxford: Oxford University Press. http://oed.com.

O'Farrell, Mary Ann. 1997. *Telling Complexions*. Durham, NC: Duke University Press.

Oliphant, Margaret. 1897. *William Blackwood and His Sons*. Edinburgh: Blackwood.

"Oliver Twist." 1839. *Quarterly Review* 64:83–102.

Orwell, George. 1965. *The Decline of the English Murder*. New York: Penguin.

O'Sullivan, Michael. 2008. *The Incarnation of Language: Joyce, Proust and a Philosophy of the Flesh*. New York: Continuum.

"Our Nearest Relation." 1859. *All the Year Round* 1 (5): 112–15.

Pacious, Kathleen. 2016. "Misdirections, Delayed Disclosures, and the Ethics of Telling in Charles Dickens's *Our Mutual Friend*." *Narrative* 24 (3): 330–50.

260 BIBLIOGRAPHY

Parish, Charles. 1962. "A Boy Brought Up 'By Hand.'" *Nineteenth-Century Fiction* 17 (3): 286–88.

Partlow, Robert B. Jr., ed. 1970. *Dickens the Craftsman: Strategies of Presentation*. Carbondale: Southern Illinois University Press.

Pasanek, Bradley M. 2015. *Metaphors of Mind: An Eighteenth-Century Dictionary*. Baltimore: Johns Hopkins University Press.

Pasanek, Bradley M., and D. Sculley. 2008. "Meaning and Mining: The Impact of Implicit Assumptions in Data Mining for the Humanities." *Literary and Linguistic Computing* 43 (4): 409–24.

Patten, Robert L. 1978. *Charles Dickens and His Publishers*. Oxford: Oxford University Press.

Patten, Robert L. 2002. "Serial Illustration and Storytelling in *David Copperfield*." In *The Victorian Illustrated Book*, edited by Richard Maxwell, 91–128. Charlottesville: University of Virginia Press.

Patten, Robert L. 2012a. *Charles Dickens and "Boz": The Birth of the Industrial-Age Author*. Cambridge: Cambridge University Press.

Patten, Robert L. 2012b. *Dickens and Victorian Print Cultures*. Burlington, VT: Ashgate.

Patten, Robert L., John O. Jordan, and Catherine Waters, eds. 2018. *Oxford Handbook of Charles Dickens*. Oxford: Oxford University Press.

Peters, Laura. 2013. *Dickens and Race*. Manchester, UK: Manchester University Press.

Perloff, Marjorie. 2004. *Differentials: Poetry, Poetics, Pedagogy*. Tuscaloosa: University of Alabama Press.

Pettitt, Clare. 2004. *Patent Inventions: Intellectual Property and the Victorian Novel*. Oxford: Oxford University Press.

Philip, Alex. 1906. "Blunders of Dickens and His Illustrators." *Dickensian* 2 (11): 294–96.

Philpotts, Trey. 2014. *The Companion to* Dombey and Son. Liverpool: Liverpool University Press.

Piper, Andrew. 2018. *Enumerations: Data and Literary Study*. Chicago: University of Chicago Press.

Piper, Andrew. 2020. *Can We Be Wrong? The Problem of Textual Evidence in a Time of Data*. Cambridge: Cambridge University Press.

"Plain English." 1868. *All the Year Round* 20 (485): 205–8.

Poe, Edgar Allan. (1841) 1985. "The Murders in the Rue Morgue." In *The Works of Edgar Allan Poe*. New York: Random House.

Pollock, G. 1993–94. "The Dangers of Proximity: The Spaces of Sexuality and Surveillance in Word and Image." *Discourse* 16 (1): 3–50.

Poole, Adrian. 1997. Introduction to *Our Mutual Friend* by Charles Dickens, ix–xxiv. Edited by Adrian Poole. New York: Penguin.

Poovey, Mary. 1988. *Uneven Developments*. Chicago: University of Chicago Press.

Poovey, Mary. 1993. "Reading History in Literature: Speculation and Virtue in *Our Mutual Friend*." In *Historical Criticism and the Challenge of Theory*, edited by Janet Levarie Smarr, 42–80. Urbana-Champaign: University of Illinois Press.

Poovey, Mary. 1995. *Making a Social Body*. Chicago: University of Chicago Press.

"The Posthumous Papers of the Pickwick Club." 1837. *Quarterly Review* 59:484–518.

Poulet, Georges. 1969. "Phenomenology of Reading." *New Literary History* 1, no.1 (October): 53–68.

Price, Janet, and Margrit Shildrick. 2002. "Bodies Together: Touch, Ethics and Disability." In *Disability/Postmodernity: Embodying Disability Theory*, edited by Marian Corker and Tom Shakespeare, 62–75. New York: Continuum.

Purton, Valerie. 2000. "Work." In *The Oxford Reader's Companion to Dickens*, edited by Paul Schlicke, 593–96. Oxford: Oxford University Press.

Pykett, Lyn. 2002. *Charles Dickens*. London: Palgrave.

Qualls, Barry. 1992. *The Secular Pilgrims of Victorian Fiction*. Cambridge: Cambridge University Press.

Rancière, Jacques. 2004. *The Flesh of Words*. Stanford, CA: Stanford University Press.

Reay, Barry. 2002. *Watching Hannah: Sexuality, Horror and Bodily Deformation in Victorian England*. New York: Reaktion.

Reé, Jonathan. 2019. *Witcraft: The Invention of Philosophy in English*. New York: Penguin.

Reed, John R. 2011. *Dickens's Hyperrealism*. Columbus: Ohio State University Press.

Richards, Thomas. 1990. *The Commodity Culture of Victorian England*. Stanford, CA: Stanford University Press.

Risam, Roopika, and Alex Gil. 2022. "Introduction: The Questions of Minimal Computing." *Digital Humanities Quarterly* 16 (2): 1–10.

Robbins, Bruce. 1990. "Telescopic Philanthropy: Professionalism and Responsibility in *Bleak House*." In *Nation and Narration*, edited by Homi Bhabha, 213–30. New York: Routledge.

Robson, Catherine. 2006. "Historicizing Dickens." In *Palgrave Advances in Charles Dickens Studies*, edited by John Bowen and Robert Patten, 234–54. London: Palgrave.

Rockwell, Geoffrey, and Stefan Sinclair. 2016. *Hermeneutica: Computer-Assisted Interpretation in the Humanities*. Cambridge, MA: MIT Press.

Rodas, Julia Miele. 2004. "Tiny Tim, Blind Bertha, and the Resistance of Miss Mowcher: Charles Dickens and the Uses of Disability." *Dickens Studies Annual* 34:51–97.

Rodas, Julia Miele. 2006. "Mainstreaming Disability Studies." *Victorian Literature and Culture* 34 (1): 371–84.

Romaine, Suzanne, ed. 1992. *The Cambridge History of the English Language*. Vol. 4, 1776–1997. Cambridge: Cambridge University Press.

Romano, John. 1978. *Dickens and Reality*. New York: Columbia University Press.

Rosenberg, Edgar. 1972. "The Pale Usher Dusts His Lexicons." *Dickens Studies Annual* 2:294–335, 374–78.

Rosenberg, Edgar. 1999. "A Note on Dickens's Working Plans." In *Great Expectations* by Charles Dickens, 469–88. Edited by Edgar Rosenberg. New York: Norton.

Rosenberg, Edgar. 2019. "How to Read Dickens in English: A Last Retrospect." In *Charles Dickens as an Agent of Change*, edited by Joachim Frenk and Lena Steveker. Ithaca, NY: Cornell University Press.

Ruskin, John. 1852. *Modern Painters*. London: Smith, Elder.

Ruskin, John. 1903. *The Collected Works of John Ruskin*. Edited by E. T. Cook and Alexander Wedderburn. London: George Allen.

262 BIBLIOGRAPHY

Sadrin, Anny, ed. 1999. *Dickens, Europe and the New Worlds*. London: Macmillan.

Said, Edward. 2004. *Humanism and Democratic Criticism*. New York: Columbia University Press.

Sala, George Augustus. 1853a. "Legal Houses of Call." *Household Words* 7 (164): 253–57.

Sala, George Augustus. 1853b. "Slang." *Household Words* 7 (183): 73–78.

Sanders, Andrew. 1982. *Charles Dickens: Resurrectionist*. London: Macmillan.

Sanders, Andrew. 1999. *Dickens and the Spirit of the Age*. Oxford: Oxford University Press.

The Saturday Review, November 11, 1865.

Scarry, Elaine. 1994. *Resisting Representation*. Oxford: Oxford University Press.

Schad, John, ed. 1996. *Dickens Refigured: Bodies, Desires, and Other Histories*. Manchester, UK: Manchester University Press.

Schaffer, Talia. 2016. *Romance's Rival: Familiar Marriage in Victorian Fiction*. Oxford: Oxford University Press.

Schaffer, Talia. 2018. "Disabling Marriage: Communities of Care in *Our Mutual Friend*." In *Replotting Marriage in Nineteenth-Century British Literature*, edited by Elsie Michie and Jill Galvan, 192–210. Columbus: Ohio State University Press.

Schaffer, Talia. 2021. *Communities of Care: The Social Ethics of Victorian Fiction*. Princeton, NJ: Princeton University Press.

Schalk, Sami. 2016. "Reevaluating the Supercrip." *Journal of Literary and Cultural Disabilities Studies* 10 (1): 71–86.

Schlicke, Paul, ed. 1999. *The Oxford Reader's Companion to Dickens*. Oxford: Oxford University Press.

Schor, Hillary. 1999. *Dickens and the Daughter of the House*. Cambridge: Cambridge University Press.

Schor, Hillary. 2006. "Dickens and Plot." In *Palgrave Advances in Charles Dickens Studies*, edited by John Bowen and Robert L. Patten, 90–110. London: Palgrave.

Searle, John R. 1979. *Expression and Meaning: Studies in the Theory of Speech Acts*. Cambridge: Cambridge University Press.

Secord, James A. 2000. *Victorian Sensation: The Extraordinary Publication, Reception, and Secret Authorship of* Vestiges of the Natural History of Creation. Chicago: University of Chicago Press.

Sedgwick, Eve Kosofsky. 1985. *Between Men: English Literature and Male Homosocial Desire*. New York: Columbia University Press.

Shattock, Joanne, ed. 1988. *Dickens and Other Victorians: Essays in Honor of Philip Collins*. London: Macmillan.

Shoaf, R. A. 1985. "The Play of Puns in Late Middle English Poetry: Concerning Juxtology." In *On Puns: The Foundation of Letters*, edited by Jonathan Culler, 44–61. Ithaca, NY: Cornell University Press.

Shore, Daniel. 2018. *Cyberformalism: Histories of Linguistic Forms in the Digital Archive*. Baltimore: Johns Hopkins University Press.

Schröder, Leena. 2000. "Virginia Woolf and the Body: Corporeality, Metaphor, and the In-Between." *Virginia Woolf Bulletin* 3 (1): 15–20.

Shusterman, Richard. 2012. *Thinking through the Body: Essays in Somaesthetics*. Cambridge: Cambridge University Press.

BIBLIOGRAPHY 263

Shuttleworth, Russell. 2004. "Disabled Masculinity: Expanding the Masculine Repertoire." In *Gendering Disability*, edited by Bonnie G. Smith and Beth Hutchinson, 166–78. New Brunswick, NJ: Rutgers University Press.

Siebers, Tobin. 2008. *Disability Theory*. Ann Arbor: University of Michigan Press.

Silverman, Kaja. 1992. *Male Subjectivity at the Margins*. New York: Routledge.

Smith, L. P. 1925. *Words and Idioms: Studies in the English Language*. Boston: Houghton Mifflin.

Smith, Olivia. 1986. *The Politics of Language, 1791–1819*. Oxford: Oxford University Press.

Sobchak, Vivian. 2006. "A Leg to Stand On: Prosthetics, Metaphor, and Materiality." In *The Prosthetic Impulse: From a Posthuman Present to a Biocultural Future*, edited by Marquad Smith and Joanne Morra, 17–41. Cambridge, MA: MIT Press.

Solberg, Sarah. 1980. "Dickens and Illustration: A Matter of Perspective." *Journal of Narrative Technique* 10 (1): 128–37.

"Species." 1860. *All the Year Round*. (June 2) 3:174–78.

Spencer, Herbert. 1872. *The Principles of Psychology*. New York: Appleton.

Spitzer, Leo. 1948. *Linguistics and Literary History*. Princeton, NJ: Princeton University Press.

Spivak, Gayatri. 2003. *Death of a Discipline*. New York: Columbia University Press.

Stanley, L. 1986. "Biography as Microscope or Kaleidoscope? The Case of Hannah Culliwick's Relationship with Arthur Munby." *Studies in Sexual Politics* 13/14 (1): 28–46.

Steig, Michael. 1978. *Dickens and Phiz*. Bloomington: Indiana University Press.

Stephen, Leslie, ed. 1988. *Dictionary of National Biography*. Vol. 15. London: Smith, Elder.

Stern, Alexander. 2019. *The Fall of Language*. Cambridge, MA: Harvard University Press.

Stewart, Garrett. 1974. *Dickens and the Trials of Imagination*. Cambridge, MA: Harvard University Press.

Stewart, Garrett. 1990. *Reading Voices: Literature and the Phonotext*. Berkeley: University of California Press.

Stewart, Garrett. 1996. *Dear Reader: The Conscripted Audience in Nineteenth-Century Fiction*. Baltimore, MD: Johns Hopkins University Press.

Stewart, Garrett. 2001a. "Dickens and Language." In *Cambridge Companion to Charles Dickens*, edited by John O. Jordan, 136–51. Cambridge: Cambridge University Press.

Stewart, Garrett. 2001b. "Narrative Economies in *The Tenant of Wildfell Hall*." In *New Approaches to the Literary Art of Anne Brontë*, edited by Julie Nash and Barbara A. Suess, 75–102. Burlington, VT: Ashgate.

Stewart, Garrett. 2010a. "The Ethical Tempo of Narrative Syntax: Sylleptic Recognitions in *Our Mutual Friend*." *Partial Answers* 8 (1): 119–45.

Stewart, Garrett. 2010b. "Reading Feeling and the 'Transferred Life': *The Mill on the Floss*." In *The Feeling of Reading: Affective Experience and Victorian Literature*, edited by Rachel Ablow, 179–206. Ann Arbor: University of Michigan Press.

Stewart, Garrett. 2015. *The Deed of Reading: Literature, Writing, Philosophy*. Ithaca, NY: Cornell University Press.

264   BIBLIOGRAPHY

Stewart, Garrett. 2018. *The One, the Other, and Only Dickens.* Ithaca, NY: Cornell University Press.

Stewart, Garrett. 2022. "The Late Great Dickens: Style Distilled." In *On Style in Victorian Fiction*, edited by Daniel Tyler, 227–43. Cambridge: Cambridge University Press.

Stitt, Megan. 1998. *Metaphors of Change in the Language of Nineteenth-Century Fiction.* Oxford: Oxford University Press.

Stone, Harry. 1970. "The Genesis of a Novel: *Great Expectations.*" In *Charles Dickens, 1812–1870: A Centennial Volume*, edited by E. W. F. Tomlin, 110–31. New York: Simon & Schuster, 1969.

Stone, Harry. 1979. *Dickens and the Invisible World.* Bloomington: Indiana University Press.

Stone, Harry. 1985. "What's in a Name: Fantasy and Calculation in Dickens." *Dickens Studies Annual* 14:191–204.

Stone, Harry. 1987. *Dickens' Working Notes for His Novels.* Chicago: University of Chicago Press.

Stone, Harry. 1994. *The Night Side of Dickens: Cannibalism, Passion, Necessity.* Columbus: Ohio State University Press.

Stonehouse, J. H., ed. 1935. *Catalogue of the Library of Charles Dickens from Gadshill.* London: Piccadilly Fountain Press.

Storey, Gladys. 1939. *Dickens and Daughter.* London: Frederick Muller.

Sucksmith, H. P. 1970. *The Narrative Art of Charles Dickens.* Oxford: Oxford University Press.

Sussman, Herbert. 1995. *Victorian Masculinities.* Cambridge: Cambridge University Press.

Sussman, Herbert, and Gerhard Joseph. 2004. "Prefiguring the Posthuman: Dickens and Prosthesis." *Victorian Literature and Culture* 32 (2): 617–28.

Tambling, Jeremy. 1996. "Preface to the Charles Dickens Edition (1867)." In *David Copperfield* by Charles Dickens, xi–xli. Edited by Jeremy Tambling. New York: Penguin.

Taylor, Dennis. 1993. *Hardy's Literary Language and Victorian Philology.* Oxford: Oxford University Press.

Tenniel, John. 1863. "The Haunted Lady, or 'The Ghost' in the Looking-Glass." *Punch*, July 4, 1863.

Thackeray, William Makepeace. 1963. *Vanity Fair.* Edited by Geoffrey Tillotson and Kathleen Tillotson. Boston: Houghton Mifflin.

Thomas, William Moy. 1853. "Market Gardens." *Household Words* 7 (171): 409–14.

Thomson, David Croal. 1884. *The Life and Labours of Hablot Knight Brown, "Phiz."* London: Chapman & Hall.

Tillotson, Kathleen. 1956. *Novels of the Eighteen-Forties.* Oxford: Clarendon.

Times Digital Archive, 1785–1985. Gale.

Tomalin, Claire. 2011. *Charles Dickens: A Life.* New York: Penguin.

Tomalin, Marcus. 2007. "'Vulgarisms and Broken English': The Familiar Perspicuity of William Hazlitt." *Romanticism* 13 (1): 28–52.

Tooke, John Horne. 1860. *Diversions of Purley.* London: William Tegg.

"Transmutation of Species." 1861. *All the Year Round.* (March 9) 4:519–21.

BIBLIOGRAPHY

Trench, Richard Chenevix. 1852. *On the Study of Words*. London: Macmillan.

Tromp, Marlene. 2000. *The Private Rod*. Charlottesville: University of Virginia Press.

Turner, James. 2014. *Philology: The Forgotten Origins of the Modern Humanities*. Princeton, NJ: Princeton University Press.

Tyler, Daniel. 2011. "Feeling for the Future: The Crisis of Anticipation in *Great Expectations*." *19: Interdisciplinary Studies in the Long Nineteenth Century* 14. https://doi.org/10.16995/ntn.607.

Tyler, Daniel, ed. 2013. *Dickens's Style*. Cambridge: Cambridge University Press.

Underwood, Michael. 1784. *A Treatise on the Diseases of Children, with Directions for the Management of Infants from the Birth; Especially Such as Are Brought Up by Hand*. London: J. Matthews.

Underwood, Ted. 2019. *Distant Horizons: Digital Evidence and Literary Change*. Chicago: University of Chicago Press.

Vlock, Deborah. 1998. *Dickens, Novel Reading, and the Victorian Theatre*. Cambridge: Cambridge University Press.

Walder, Dennis. 1981. *Dickens and Religion*. London: Allen & Unwin.

Walder, Dennis. 1995. Introduction to *Sketches by Boz* by Charles Dickens, ix–xxxiv. New York: Penguin.

Wales, Katie. 1992. *The Language of James Joyce*. New York: St. Martin's.

Waters, Catherine. 1997. *Dickens and the Politics of Family*. Cambridge: Cambridge University Press.

Welsh, Alexander. 1971. *The City of Dickens*. Oxford: Oxford University Press.

Welsh, Alexander. 2000. *The Art of* Bleak House *and* Hard Times. New Haven, CT: Yale University Press.

"*Western Himalaya and Tibet* Review." 1852. *The Examiner*, no. 2326:548–49.

Wheeler, Michael. 1990. *Death and the Future Life in Victorian Literature and Theology*. Cambridge: Cambridge University Press.

Wider, Kathleen. 1997. *The Bodily Nature of Consciousness*. Ithaca, NY: Cornell University Press.

Williams, Raymond. 1964. "Social Criticism in Dickens." *Critical Quarterly* 6 (4): 214–27.

Williams, Raymond. 1970. "Dickens and Social Ideas." *Dickens 1970*, edited by Michael Slater, 77–98. London: Stein and Day.

Williams, Raymond. 1975. *The Country and the City*. Oxford: Oxford University Press.

Williams, Raymond. 1979. *Politics and Letters*. New York: New Left Books.

Wills, David. 1995. *Prosthesis*. Stanford, CA: Stanford University Press.

Wilson, Angus. 1961. "Charles Dickens: A Haunting." In *The Dickens Critics*, edited by George H. Ford and Lauriat Lane, 374–85. Ithaca, NY: Cornell University Press.

Wittgenstein, Ludwig. 1997. *Philosophical Investigations*. Translated by G. E. M. Anscombe. Hoboken, NJ: Blackwell.

Woloch, Alex. 2003. *The One vs. the Many: Minor Characters and the Space of the Protagonist in the Novel*. Princeton, NJ: Princeton University Press.

Wood, Claire. 2015. *Dickens and the Business of Death*. Cambridge: Cambridge University Press.

Woolf, Virginia. (1919) 1984. "Modern Fiction." In *The Virginia Woolf Reader*, edited by Michael A. Leaska, 283–91. New York: Harcourt, Brace, Jovanovich.

266   **BIBLIOGRAPHY**

Woolf, Virginia. (1919) 1925. "George Eliot." In *The Common Reader*, 229–42. New York: Harcourt Brace.

Woolf, Virginia. (1919) 1998. "Dickens by a Disciple." In *The Essays of Virginia Woolf*, edited by Andrew McNellie, 3:25–28. London: Hogarth.

Woolf, Virginia. (1925) 1966. "*David Copperfield*." In *Collected Essays of Virginia Woolf*, edited by Leonard Woolf, 1:191–95. New York: Harcourt, Brace and World.

Woolf, Virginia. (1930) 1967. "Street Haunting." In *Collected Essays of Virginia Woolf*, edited by Leonard Woolf, 4:155–56. New York: Harcourt, Brace, and World.

Woolf, Virginia. 1985. [February 25, 1936 entry]. In *The Diary of Virginia Woolf*, edited by Anne Olivier Bell, 5:12–13. London: Harvest Press.

Woolf, Virginia. 1998. "Charlotte Brontë." In *The Essays of Virginia Woolf*, edited by Andrew McNellie, 2:26–31. London: Hogarth.

Wordsworth, William. (1802) 1991. Preface to *Lyrical Ballads* by William Wordsworth and Samuel Taylor Coleridge, 241–72. Edited by R. L. Brett and A. R. Jones. New York: Routledge.

"Writings of Charles Dickens." 1845. *North British Review* 3 (May): 65–87.

Yaeger, Patricia. 2007. "Editor's Column: The Polyphony Issue." *PMLA* 122 (2): 433–48.

Zemka, Sue. 2015. "1822, 1845, 1869, and 1917: Artificial Hands." *BRANCH: Britain, Representation and Nineteenth-Century History*, edited by Dino Felluga. Extension of *Romanticism and Victorianism on the Net*.

Zirker, Angelika. 2011. "Physiognomy and the Reading of Character in *Our Mutual Friend*." *Partial Answers* 9 (2): 379–90.

Index

Note: page numbers in italics refer to figures.

Ada, 82, 97, 101, 103; Esther and, 106; Richard and, 96, 106, 110
Addison, Joseph, 7, 10, 12, 23, 32
Aesop, 84, 90n8, 92, 96, 122, 123; "shoulder to the wheel" and, 90
aesthetics, 11, 17, 38, 159; physiological, 23
affectionate lunacy, 117
Akershem, Sophronia, 192, 200, 201, 202
Alford, Henry, 15
All the Year Round, 13, 46, 46n19, 127, 131n11, 132, 154, 154n27, 155; body idiom titles in, 16; sales of, 171
Allard, James: hypersensible body and, 23n39
Allison, Sarah, 5–6, 12
Altick, Richard, 103, 123
American, The (James), body idioms in, 219
Andrews, Malcolm, 9, 98, 100
Angelou, Maya: "hurt people hurt people" and, 139n16
Anglican Book of Common Prayer, 175
animality, 144, 149n23, 156, 159, 161, 162; racialized, 151
Armstrong, Nancy, 69, 105, 106n14
"Attorney and client, fortitude and impatience," *112*
Attridge, Derek, 221
Austen, James, 219
Austin, J. L.: theory of speech acts of, 180n12

Badger, Bayham, 106
Bagnet, Mrs., 116, 117, 117n20
Bagstock, Joey, 218
Bagstock, Major, 39, 40, *40*, 42, 43, 49, 52, 62, *77*; Dombey and, 41; "right-hand man" and, 41, 47, 103
Bakhtin, Mikhail, 35, 36, 42n13, 43, 47, 47n20, 103, 131, 158, 193; on grotesque

style, 120n23; heteroglossic discourse and, 39; on language/historical life, 130; parodic stylizations and, 174; socio-verbal intelligibility and, 144; sociological stylistics of, 17; speech diversity and, 22
Bannister, John, 145, 146
barbarism, 8, 11, 165
Barchester Towers (Trollope), 225
Barley, George, 19
Barnaby Rudge (Dickens), 6n10, 31n1, 91, 149, 175
Barthes, Roland, 126
"Beadle—The Parish Engine—The Schoolmaster, The" (Dickens), body idiom in, 24
Beadnell, Maria, 29
Beamish, Richard, 151
"Beamish's gorilla hand plate," *152*
"Beamish's navy hand plate," *153*
Becoming Dickens (Douglas-Fairhurst), body idioms in, 227
Beer, Gillian, 148, 156–57n28, 168
Beeton, Isabella, 132, 135
Bell, Charles, 145, 146, 150, 161, 146n19
Bell, Marion, 146, 150
Bentinck, George, 85
Bentley's Miscellany, 16, 21, 35, 46n19
Bernstein, Susan David, 147
Best, Stephen, 4–5, 6
Bible, 2, 145, 175, 176, 176n6
Biddy, 28n43, 130, 169–70
Blackwood's, 16, 46n19
Blake, William, 23
Bleak House, stay at, 121, 124
Bleak House (Dickens), 6, 13, 28, 79, 96–97, 111, 114, 119–20, 122–23; body idioms in, 10, 13n21; cohesive effect of, 80–81; *Dombey and Son* and, 82; filial identification in, 161; idiomatic humor of, 98–101;

267

268 **INDEX**

Bleak House (Dickens) (*continued*)
imagery/theme of, 103; length of, 83;
plans for, 92–93; praise for, 80; prospective titles for, 81; puns in, 108; representations of work in, 107; responsibility in,
116, 224; "shoulder to the wheel" and, 17,
84, 85, 88, 89, 90, 91, 92, 103, 107, 125;
working titles for, 127n6
Blimber, Doctor, 62, 69, 70
Bloom, Stephen, 222
"Blunders of Dickens and His Illustrators"
(Philip), 77
Bodenheimer, Rosemarie, 89, 206n33; body
idiom and, 226–27; mysterious interplay
and, 79; on parody, 179; on self-creation,
17–18; on use/misuse of language, 174n2
Bodily Nature of Consciousness, The
(Wider), 21
Body Economic, The (Gallagher), 225
body idioms: body behind, 18–23; (in)
visibility of, 12–14; measuring, 226–27;
number of, 22, 25, 224; relying on,
175–86; tinkering with, 11–12; using, 2–3,
5, 7–12, 24, 30, 46, 174, 220, 225;
workaday, 135
Body Idioms Used per 100,000 Words, 3
(table)
body language: early Dickensian, 2327;
idiomatic, 11, 218, 223; use/misuse of,
174n2
*Body in the Mind: The Bodily Basis of Meaning,
Imagination, and Reasoning, The*
(Johnson), 21
Boffin, Dusty, 202, 209; "nose to the
grindstone" and, 210, 211; Wegg and, 211
Boffin, Mr. and Mrs., 177, 186, 187, 205, 209
Boll, Ernest, 214, 216
Bolo, Miss, 25, 26
Book of Household Management (Beeton), 132
Book of Memoranda (Dickens), 126n2, 195
Booth, Alison: "mid-range" reading and, 6
"bound out of hand," 143, 167
Bounderby, Josiah, 49, 185, 201n29
Bourdieu, Pierre, 181; on language/body
technique, 180; linguistic exchanges and,
180; social values and, 163; theory of
speech acts and, 180n12
Bowen, John, 48, 89, 182
Bowles, Hugo, 10n19, 181n13
Bradbury, Nicola, 92, 119, 122–23, 210; work
and, 177, 194
Bradbury and Evans, 74, 89
Brantlinger, Patrick, 151, 177

Brass, Sampson, 27
Brattin, Joel, 207
Breen, Henry, 15
Bridgewater Treatise, 146, 146n19, 150
Briefel, Aviva: on racialized hands, 156
British Library Newspapers Digital Archive, 35,
35n5, 47, 85, 135, 197; "brought up by
hand" appearances in, *133*; "nose to the
grindstone" appearances in, *198*;
"right-hand man" appearances in, *33*;
"shoulder to the wheel" appearances
in, 86
British Periodicals Archive, 35, 35n5, 47, 85,
135, 197; "brought up by hand"
appearances in, *134*; "nose to the
grindstone" appearances in, *199*;
"right-hand man" appearances in, *34*;
"shoulder to the wheel" appearances in,
87
British Zoological Society, 148
Bromwich, David, 78
Brontë, Charlotte, 3, 63n34, 225, 226; body
idioms and, 1
Brooks, Peter, 49, 159, 137n12
"brought up by hand," 3, 135, 136, 137, 139,
140, 141, 144, 145; appearances of, *133*,
134; breastfeeding and, 13, 28n43; nature/
nurture and, 162–63; uniqueness of, 129;
using, 6, 17, 130, 132, 155, 167, 169, 170,
171; variations of, 131
Brown, Carolyn, 167–68
Brown, Margaret, 129
Browne, Hablôt K., 50, 51, 52
Buckland, Adelene, 147
Bunsby, Jack, 36, 49
Bunyan, John, 90
Burnett, Henry, 20
Butler, Judith, 103
Butt, John, 25n42, 37, 90, 90n8, 126n1,
127n6; on *Bleak House*, 80; *Great
Expectations* and, 126
Buzard, Jim, 82

Captain Cuttle (play), 50n22
"Captain Cuttle consoles his friend," *50*
Carey, John, 98, 182
Carker, Harriet, 45
Carker, James, 39, 41, 42, 43, 47, 53, 57, 68,
98; characterizations of, 67n38; Cuttle
and, 60, 99; Dombey and, 67; Edith and,
69; as "right-hand man," 45, 49, 50, 62, 63,
65, 66, 74
Carker, John, 4

INDEX

Carlyle, Thomas, 88, 92, 151, 197; Dickens and, 88n5, 152; *Hard Times* and, 88n5
Carroll, Lewis, 227
Carstone, Richard, 82, 83, 95, 104, 105, 108, 111, 118, 122, 123; Ada and, 96, 106, 110; Chancery suit and, 125; character of, 96, 98, 109; death of, 113, 122; downfall of, 107; Ixion and, 124; Jarndyce and, 101; "shoulder to the wheel" and, 97, 98, 107; Vholes and, 114
Casey, Edward: on imagination, 216
Cervantes, Miguel, 219
Chadwyck-Healey Nineteenth-Century Fiction, 4, 46, 46n16, 89n7
Chambers, Robert, 146, 147, 148, 149, 150, 161
characteristics / characters, idiomatic, 186–93
Charles Dickens: The World of His Novels (Miller), 17
Charles Dickens and "Boz" (Patten), 17
"Charlotte Brontë" (Woolf), body idioms in, 223
Chartism (Carlyle), 151
Chase, Karen, 104, 105, 224
Cheadle, Brian: on work, 177
Chesterton, G. K., 125
Chick, Miss, 38, 65
Christmas Carol, A (Dickens), 6n10, 22, 31n1
circularity, idiom of, 80–84
Coavinses, 101–2
Coleman, Rosemary, 60
Coleridge, Samuel Taylor: Dickens and, 23
Collins, Wilkie, 127, 172, 197, 225
Compeyson, 126n2, 142, 143, 157
Connor, Steven, 81, 193
context, intertext and, 84–85, 88–92
Copperfield, David, 10, 18, 82, 122n27, 124, 129, 191n21; industriousness of, 83
Corbett, Mary Jean: on Woolf, 223
Cornhill, 16, 46n19
Country and the City, The (Williams), 80
Coutts, Angela Burdett, 88
criminality, 165; manual labor and, 170
Culler, Jonathan, 61, 61n32, 61n33; close reading and, 6
Culliwick, Hannah, 158, 158n29
Curtis, L. Perry, 151
Cushman, Miss, 218
Cuttle, Edward, 17, 36, 37, 41, 43, 45, 48, *50*, 89, 208; appearance of, 52; Carker and, 60, 99; critical treatment of, 60; disability for, 53, 54, 55, 58, 60, 61; Dombey and, 51, 72; Edith and, 71; Florence and, 60,

61, 62, 69; illustrations of, *50*; as major character, 78n42; motility and, 59n31; planning, 39; prosthesis of, 49, 59, 60, 62, 74; resourcefulness of, 56; as "right-hand man," 38, 52–53, 55, 57, 59–60, 62–63, 78, 98; title page placement of, 78
Cuvier, Georges, 147
Cyberformalism (Shore), 5

Daily News, 35, 85
Dallas, E. S., 171
Dames, Nicholas, 20
Daniel Deronda (Eliot), 225
Dartle, Rosa: grindstone and, 195
Darwin, Charles, 145, 147, 148n23, 149, 151, 161; interconnection and, 156; theory of evolution and, 148; theory of natural selection and, 148–49n23
data mining, 4, 5, 6, 46n18
David Copperfield (Dickens), 6n10, 10, 31n1, 52n25, 79, 79n44, 125, 129, 195, 225; character initials in, 92; as Dickens's favorite, 223; physical abuse in, 135; publication of, 88, 88n5; rereading, 130, 154
Davis, Lennard: disability and, 54, 62, 71; normalcy and, 53n26
Day's Ride, A (Lever), 127
De Cerjat, W. F., 172
De Certeau, Michel, 22
De Man, Paul, 224
De Saussure, Ferdinand, 180n12
Dear Reader (Stewart), 225
deception, 129, 174, 193–97
Dedlock, Lady, 123, 160
Dedlock family, 93, 94
Deering, Dorothy, 16, 46n19
Derenzy, George Webb: Cuttle and, 57
Derrida, Jacques, 145
Dickens, Catherine, 88
Dickens, Charles: compulsive exercise of, 20; education of, 2; imaginative life of, 29; OED citations of, 220–21; organizational process of, 80–81; physical energy of, 19
Dickens, Kate: on father / women, 28n44
Dickens, Mamie: on father's writing, 19
Dickens and His Illustrations (Kitton), 77
"Dickens and Illustration: A Matter of Perspective" (Solberg), 77
Dickens and the Trials of Imagination (Stewart), 9n18, 17, 220
Dickens at Work (Butt and Tillotson), 37
Dickens Theatre, The (Garis), 19

270 **INDEX**

"Dickens's Figurative Style" (Gribbles), 48
"Dickens's Rhythms" (Douglas-Fairhurst), 48
Dickens's Style (Tyler), 48
Dictionary of the English Language, A (Johnson), 8, 11
Dictionary of National Biography (Stephen), 9
Digital Dickens Notes Project, 98
Digital Textual Studies, 1
disability, 51–62, 71–72, 74
discourse, 35, 39, 135, 144; double-voiced, 43, 103; everyday, 24; popular, 47
Dodson and Fogg, 25, 194
"dog-eat-dog," 205, 205n31
Dombey, as anagram, 56
Dombey, Edith, 41, 43, 47, 48, 48n21, 64, 65, 99; Carker and, 69; Cuttle and, 71; defiance by, 69n40; endurance of, 67; feminine solidarity with, 66; Florence and, 66
Dombey, Fanny, 48n21
Dombey, Florence, 38, 50, 53, 57, 59, 65, 71, 72, 73, 99; Cuttle and, 56, 60, 61, 62, 69; feminine solidarity with, 66; marriage of, 70; Polly and, 48; "right-hand man" and, 55; as "right-hand woman," 62, 70
Dombey, Mr., 38, 39, 45; appearance of, 52; autonomy/superiority and, 53; Bagstock and, 41; Carker and, 67; Cuttle and, 51, 72; disability and, 62, 74; Edith and, 41, 65, 66; Florence and, 66–67, 69–73; inspection by, 65; milk kinship and, 64; party by, 43–44; "right-hand man" for, 40–41, 42, 43, 44, 49, 63; "right-hand women" and, 64
Dombey, Paul, 38, 48, 64, 69; death of, 72; education of, 70
Dombey and Son (Dickens), 6, 17, 27, 49, 91, 98, 99, 105, 127, 130; *Bleak House* and, 82; body idioms in, 13n21, 46; commercial/domestic contexts of, 13; criticism of, 60; (dis)ability and, 51–62; embodied rhetoric of, 38–47; end of, 73–74, 77–79; feminine competence and, 63; framing themes in, 55; idiomatic beginning in, 73–74, 77–79; idiomatic expressions and, 30, 31, 38, 50, 79; illustrations for, 74; length of, 83; Marryat influence on, 37n10; masculinity and, 60; new title-page vignette for, 76; planning of, 30–32, 35–38, 72, 78, 80; puns in, 108; "right-hand man" and, 28, 32, 36, 37, 38–47, 48, 51, 59–60, 84, 103; "right-hand manness" in, 49; "right-hand

women" in, 62–67, 69; serial number cover design, 75; stage adaptations of, 50n22; themes of, 37–38; writing, 35, 38, 74, 79
Douglas-Fairhurst, Robert, 20, 22, 22n16, 48, 89, 173; body idiom and, 226–27; on Dickens's vocabulary, 63
Dowling, Linda, 15
Doyce and Clennam, 196
Drucker, Johanna: digital tools and, 4
Drummle, Bentley, 148n23, 165
Du Chaillu, Paul, 148, 149, 150, 161
Dumas, Alexandre, 219
Dupin, August, 147

Eagleton, Terry, 92, 103, 105, 155, 224, 225, 226; on *Bleak House*, 91
Edinburgh Review, 15, 16, 46n19
Elfenbein, Andrew, 63, 70
Eliot, George, 3, 8, 225, 227; body idioms and, 2, 226
Eliot, T. S., 80, 217
Emre, Merve: on *Ulysses*, 222
Enchiridion: or A Hand for the One-Handed (Derenzy), 57
Engels, Friedrich, 166
English in Nineteenth-Century England (Görlach), 32
English Novel, The (Eagleton), 226
Errors in the Use of English (Hodgson), 221
Estella, 127, 129, 130, 136, 139, 154, 157, 159, 161–66; "brought up by hand" and, 163; fate of, 138; hands of, 159, 160, 162; Havisham and, 137, 137n13, 138, 149n23, 163–64; identity of, 167; Molly and, 156, 161; origins of, 156, 168; physical violence and, 165; Pip and, 138, 156, 162, 163, 164–65; sociodemographic assessment of, 138
Evelina (Burney), 146n18
Examiner, The, 35n6, 85, 147
Explorations and Adventures in Equatorial Africa (du Chaillu), 150
Eyre, Jane: disparagements of, 1

Feenix, Cousin, 43
Ferguson, Frances, 31
Fiction and Repetition (Miller), 30
Fielding, K. J., 179, 179n10, 214n37
finance capital industry, 172, 175
Firth, William: on Dickens, 20
Flanders, Judith: phraseological peculiarity and, 46

INDEX   271

Flaubert, Gustave, 219
Fledgeby, Fascination, 187, 192, 202, 210, 212; described, 205; Lammle and, 203–4; marriage of, 201; reputation of, 191; "sweat of the brow" and, 193
Flint, Kate, 80, 82, 92
Ford, George, 9, 90
Forster, John, 18, 85, 91, 92, 127, 128, 129, 130, 175, 197; on Dickens, 20–21; on *Our Mutual Friend*, 172
Forster, Robert, 9
Foucault, Michel, 117n21, 138n14, 139; *energeia* and, 21; philology and, 16–17
Fowler, H. W., 221
Fraser's, 16, 46n19
Furneaux, Holly, 61, 140, 177

Gad's Hill, 36, 150, 161
Gallagher, Catherine, 189, 215, 225
Gane, Gillian, 60
Gargery, Joe, 129, 130, 132, 139n16, 157, 164, 169; nature of, 141; nurture of, 168; Pip and, 139, 140, 143; restorative touch of, 140
Gargery, Mrs. Joe, 129, 132, 135, 137, 141, 164; "brought up by hand" and, 143; physical abuse by, 139, 140; Pip and, 139, 140, 167
Garis, Robert, 19
Garland-Thomson, Rosemarie, 54, 54n27
Gay, Walter, 36, 39, 45, 56, 57, 66, 70, 73; "right-hand man" for, 52–53, 55
General Theatrical Fund, 88, 89, 93
"George Eliot" (Woolf), body idioms in, 223
George, Trooper, 116, 117, 125; Phil and, 118–19, 120
Gershick, Thomas, 61
Gibson, Anna, 97, 98
Gilbert, Pamela, 148n22, 151
Gills, Solomon, 36, 39, 45, 48, 57, 72, 74
Gitleman, Lisa, 4
Gliddery, Bob, 184
Golden Bowl, The (James), body idioms in, 219–20
Goodlad, Lauren, 82, 92, 95
Gore, Clare Walker: on Cuttle, 78n42
Gorilla, 155; manual savagery of, 154; Negro and, 151
Görlach, Manfred, 32, 35, 85
"Gospel of Work," 82–83, 88, 173
Gradgrind, Mr., 195
Graham's Magazine, 147
Granger, Edith, 40, 62

Grass, Sean, 175, 213
Great Expectations (Dickens), 6, 13, 127, 129, 131, 146, 149–50, 166–67, 169, 172; "brought up by hand" and, 17, 28n43, 135, 142, 144, 154, 156, 156–57n28, 158, 171; character names for, 126n2; complexity of, 128; conscious repetitions in, 130; Darwinian criticism and, 148n23; filial identification in, 161; hands in, 131n10, 158, 159; idiomatic dimension for, 128; "nose to the grindstone" and, 197; nurture and, 135–36; publication of, 132; violence in, 178; writing, 139, 145, 154, 155, 156, 161, 171
Grener, Adam, 97–98
Gribbles, Jennifer, 48
grinding, 200n26, 207, 208, 210
grindstone, 207; body-length, 196; figurative, 197; social, 200–201
Guppy, 114, 160

"Hackney-Coach Stands" (Dickens), 24
hand, 148, 178; clutching power of, 157, 158; conceptions of, 145; critic's, 224–27; idiomatic, 126–31; mechanism/vital endowments of, 146; narrative sleight of, 159–65; preponderance of, 131; racialized, 156; secret freemasonry of, 169; transformation of, 165–70; wild/violent, 159. *See also* "brought up by hand"
Hand, The (Bell), 146, 146n19
Hand: Its Mechanism and Endowments as Evincing Design, The (Bell), 150
"hand of God," 145, 145n18
Handel, 143, 168; "brought up by hand" and, 170
Hansard Corpus, 32
Hard Times (Dickens), 6n10, 31n1, 49, 150, 175, 185, 218; Carlyle and, 88n5; "nose to the grindstone" and, 195, 201n29
Hardy, Barbara, 69, 220, 222
Hardy, Thomas, 3, 42n13
Harmon estate, 179, 210, 211, 212
Harmon murder, 180n11, 181, 183, 212
Hartley, Jenny, 25n42, 69n40, 101
"haunted lady, or 'the ghost' in the looking glass, The," 190
Havisham, Miss, 28n43, 127, 129, 130, 142, 157, 166, 167; Estella and, 137, 137n13, 138, 149n23, 163; nurture of, 164; Pip and, 161
Hawes, Donald, 36n7
Hayles, Katherine: hyper-reading and, 6
Hazlitt, William, 23, 23n38, 24

272 **INDEX**

Headstone, Bradley, 186; defacement of, 209; nose bleeding of, 209; Wrayburn and, 184, 184n16, 185, 206, 206n33, 207–8
Hecimovich, Gregg, 215
Heidegger, Martin, 145
Hercules, 84–85
"Hercules and the Wagoner" (Aesop), 84–85
heteroglossia, 43, 103, 104
Hexam, Charley, 185
Hexam, Gaffer, 177, 177n7, 179, 182, 183, 186; description of, 178; Harmon murder and, 181; work of, 191
Hexam, Lizzie, 28, 185, 186, 206, 207, 208, 209; Betty's death and, 188; hands of, 178; work and, 177, 177n8
Heywood, John, 200
Higden, Betty, 28, 186, 187, 188, 190, 210
High Court of Chancery, 81, 83, 88, 97, 106, 113, 121, 122, 183
Historie of Man (Bannister), 146
Histories of Linguistic Forms (Shore), 5
Hodgson, William Ballentyne, 221
Hogarth, Georgina, 63
Hogarth, Mary, 29
Holmes, Martha Stoddard, 54, 55
Holofernes, Judith and, 69, 69n39
Hood, Thomas: poem by, 189, 189n18
Horne, Richard, 88
House, Humphry: on Dickens, 176
House, Madeline, 129
Household Words, 2, 16, 21, 46n19, 88, 113, 114, 154, 155
Houston, Gail Turley: on Esther's hand, 104
Humanism and Democratic Criticism (Said), 17
humor, idiomatic, 98–101
Humphrey, Master, 26

Ideas to a Pure Phenomenology (Husserl), 19n28
identity, 120n26, 137n12, 145, 160, 164, 167; biological, 169; masculine, 61, 61n33; moral, 169; social, 69, 180; spectrum of, 56
idiom absorption, 13, 49, 91, 104, 224
idiom convergence, 209–12
idiomatic expressions, 12–13, 18, 22, 26, 37, 78, 98, 131, 135, 162; affinity for, 27; emergence of, 171–75; as linguistic burrs, 47; origins of, 11, 23; using, 10, 24
idiomatic language, 11, 16, 30, 162; experimenting with, 220; literal and figurative meanings of, 221; using, 1, 2, 2n1, 7, 110
idiomatic narrative contingency, handling, 131–32, 135–44

idiomaticity, 144, 158; intentionality and, 212–16; masculinized, 28; nasal, 49
idioms: at full circle, 123–25; class-defining, 92–98; contextualizing, 6; dominant, 104; embryonic, 23–27; expansion of, 106–17; foot-related, 25; identifying, 6; isolating, 13; licentious, 8, 11, 220; manners and, 8; origins of, 30–32, 35–38; rhetorical variations of, 29; term, 7–8; using, 1, 7n12, 196
imagination, 5, 61, 171, 189, 216, 220; creative, 212; development of, 17, 29, 31; fictional, 3; idiomatic, 5, 26–29, 69, 73, 79, 91, 98, 103, 114–15, 119; mature, 216
Imagining, phenomenological study of, 216
Ingham, Patricia, 42
Inimitable, 3, 10–11, 110, 216, 218, 220, 227
intention, philology and, 14–18
intentionality, idiomaticity and, 212–16
interconnectedness, 144, 156, 158, 159, 166, 167, 215
intertext, context and, 84–85, 88–92
Irish Railway Bill, 85
Ixion, 109, 109n16, 124

Jaffe, Audrey, 206, 214
Jaggers, Mr., 138, 141, 143, 156, 170; Molly and, 159
Jakobson, Roman, 61n32, 61n33
James, Henry, 173; body idioms and, 217–23; Dickens and, 219, 220
James, Stephen, 209
Jane Eyre (Brontë), 63n34, 225
Jarndyce, John, 81–82, 83, 95, 100, 102, 104, 106–7, 110, 114, 122; Richard's character and, 96, 98, 101
Jarndyce, Tom, 81–82, 95, 109
Jarndyce suit, 81–82, 97, 107, 108, 114
Jellyby, Caddy, 98, 99, 119n22, 124, 125
Jellyby, Mr., 119, 119n22
Jellyby, Mrs., 119, 125
Jo, 82, 120, 123; death of, 122; Phil and, 121; Turveydrop and, 121
Jobling, Tony, 114
Joe B., 42, 44
"Joe B. is sly, sir, devilishly sly," 44
Johnson, Mark, 21, 21n33, 23
Johnson, Samuel, 10, 11, 12; idiomatic phrasing and, 8; licentious idioms and, 220
Jordan, John O., 89, 89n6
Joseph, Gerhard, 57, 216n38
Joseph Rushbrook (Marryat), 36n8

INDEX 273

Joyce, James: artistic language of, 221; Dickens and, 220–21; idiomatic body in, 217–23; imaginative language of, 222; literal/figurative meanings and, 222; wordplay by, 222
Joyce, Simon, 90
Joyce's Voices (Kenner), 221
Judith, Holofernes and, 69, 69n39

Kant, Immanuel, 18n26, 145
Kaplan, Fred: notion and, 195
Kemble, Charles, 19
Kemble, John Mitchell, 14, 15
Kenner, Hugh, 221
Kent, Duke, 42
Kiely, Robert, 214
King Lear (Shakespeare), 164n31
Kitton, Frederic, 77
Knoepflmacher, U. C., 98, 174n4; on "nonnurturant" upbringing, 136; on *Our Mutual Friend*, 214–15
Knowing Dickens (Bodenheimer), 17
Kreilkamp, Ivan, 9n17, 50n22, 157n28
Krook, 114, 115, 116, 157n28

labor, 165, 181, 182, 185, 186, 188, 193; conceptions of, 178–79; criminality and, 170; lower-class, 161; manual, 170; relationships to, 177; of writing, 197. *See also* work
Lakoff, George, 21, 21n33
Lammle, Alfred, 187, 200, 201–2, 210; Fledgeby and, 203–4; nose of, 202n30, 203, 205; "nose to the grindstone" and, 205; reputation of, 191–92; Riah and, 192
language: colloquial, 7, 9, 32; common, 2, 15, 32, 39, 144; creative informality of, 220; doodling, 25; English, 11, 15, 46n19; "familiar style," 23; figurative, 38; literary, 15; physiological theories of, 21; popular, 15; purity, 16; social history of, 46; "vulgar," 15, 32. *See also* idiomatic language; vernacular language
language alteration, 7, 46, 158, 182
Language and Symbolic Power (Bourdieu), 180
Law, Jules, 64, 65
Lectures on the Science of Language (Müller), 15n24
Ledger, Sally, 85, 177, 205, 205n31
Leicester, Sir, 93, 94, 95, 96, 106
Letters of Charles Dickens (House, Storey, Tillotson, and Brown), 129
Levenson, Michael, 104, 105, 224

Lever, Charles, 127, 131n11
Levine, George, 154, 156n28, 216, 216n38
Lewes, George Henry, 8, 91, 98, 161
Life and Labours of Hablot Knight Browne, "Phiz" (Thomson), 77
Lightwood, Mortimer, 28, 177, 179, 181, 182, 184, 207–8, 212; "sweat of the brow" and, 183
listening, walking and, 22n36, 23
listening narrator, 42, 42n13, 43, 103, 110
literacy, rise of, 32, 85
Little Dorrit (Dickens), 6n10, 31n1, 45n15, 127n6, 195–96, 218
Little Nell, 54, 150
Lougy, Robert, 90
Lyrical Ballads (Wordsworth), 23
Lytton, Bulwer, 197

Magwitch, Abel, 128, 130, 149n23, 157, 170; "brought up by hand" and, 141, 142; hands of, 166, 167n33; Molly and, 156, 164; Pip and, 141, 142, 156, 165–66, 166–67, 168–69
Mahlberg, Michaela, 5n6, 5n8
"Major Bagstock is delighted to have that opportunity," *40*, 77
manual anxieties, coming to grips with, 144–59
Marcus, Sharon, 4–5, 6
Marcus, Steven, 22, 25, 25n42
"Market Gardens" (Dickens), 155
Marryat, Frederick, 36, 37n10, 46, 57; novels by, 36n8
Martin Chuzzlewit (Dickens), 6n10, 31n1, 218
Marx, Karl, 166, 167
Masson, David, 7
Mayhew, Henry: description of, 178
McCarthy, Justin, 213, 219
McMaster, Juliet, 179, 179n10, 214
Memoir on the Gorilla (Owen), 150
Merleau-Ponty, Maurice: motility and, 59n31
metaphors, 55, 116, 122, 207; complicated, 37; proliferation of, 80
methodologies, 12; Bakhtinian, 7; digital, 4–7
Michie, Helena, 106, 106n14
milk kinship, 37n9, 64
Mill-Lock, Weir, 187
Miller, Andrew, 36n9, 61, 138n15; on *Dombey*, 48, 48n21; on Florence, 73
Miller, D. A., 117n21, 224–25; body idioms by, 225

274 INDEX

Miller, J. Hillis, 30, 123, 128, 142, 179, 179n10, 214, 224; on *Bleak House*, 80; on *Dombey*, 37n11; on imagining mind, 19; on Poulet, 226; "right-hand man" and, 31; writing of, 17
"Mind of Brutes, The" (*Household Words*), 113
"Missing Link, The" (*Punch*), 150–51
"Mr. Carker in his hour of triumph," 68
Mitchell, Charlotte, 132
Mitchell, David: disability and, 71–72
Mitchell, Sally, 106, 106n14
Modern English Literature: Its Blemishes and Defects (Breen), 15
Modern English Usage (Fowler), 221
"Modern Fiction" (Woolf), 223
Modern Philology, 214, 216
Molly, 28n43, 130, 154, 165, 168; Estella and, 156, 161; hands of, 156, 159, 160, 161, 162, 166; Irishness of, 155; Jaggers and, 159; Magwitch and, 156, 164; Pip and, 159; racialized ethnicity of, 156
Mouths of the Vulgar, 8, 10
Müller, Friedrich Max, 15, 15n24, 16
Munby, Arthur, 158, 158n29, 159, 184
"Murders in the Rue Morgue, The" (Poe), 147, 150
Mystery of Edwin Drood, The (Dickens), 6n10, 31n1

National Humanities Center, 1
Native, as "right-hand man," 40, 41
nature, 161; nurture and, 138, 158, 162–63
Nayder, Lillian, 28, 89
Neckett, Charley, 28, 83, 95n9, 101–2, 111, 124, 125; death of, 102; hands of, 178; responsibility/industry and, 102–3; "shoulder to the wheel" and, 105
New English Dictionary on Historical Principles, 14
New and Improved Grammar of the English Tongue (Hazlitt), 23
New Literary History, 224
Newgate Prison, 138, 163
Newsom, Robert, 60
Nicholas Nickleby (Dickens), 6n10, 31n1, 38, 175
Nipper, Susan, 65, 66, 69
"Noble Savage, The" (Dickens), 154
North British Review, 8
"nose to the grindstone," 3, 6, 12, 13, 17, 174n3, 193–97, 200, 209; appearances of, 198, 199; development of, 194; rhetoric of, 201; using, 175, 196, 202, 203–4, 205

Not So Bad as We Seem (play), 88
Novel and the Police, The (Miller), 224
nurture, 156–57, 164; nature and, 138, 158, 162–63

O'Connell, Daniel, 85, 88
Oedipus Rex (Sophocles), 90
O'Farrell, Mary Ann, 28
Old Curiosity Shop, The (Dickens), 6n10, 26, 31n1, 150; success of, 38; writing, 175
Oliphant, Margaret, 3, 8
Oliver Twist (Dickens), 6n10, 8, 26, 31n1, 91, 106n14, 128, 129, 135, 160; filial identification in, 161; success of, 38; writing, 175
On the Origin of Species (Darwin), 147, 148, 149, 154n27, 157n28, 158; publication of, 145
On the Study of Words (Trench), 15
One, Other, and Only, The (Stewart), body idioms in, 225
orientation: body, 21, 22; errors in, 77; gendered, 63; idiomatic, 89, 117; philological, 15, 17; psychological, 19; social, 14
Orlick, 126n2, 142, 149n23, 157
Orwell, George, 105, 176
Our Mutual Friend (Dickens), 6, 6n10, 13, 31n1, 200, 211, 225; body idioms in, 13n21, 174, 194, 212; criticism of, 213, 214; development of, 171–72, 179; idiomatic imagination and, 27; James review of, 219; labor in, 186; "nose to the grindstone" and, 17, 174n3, 193, 195, 197, 201, 202, 203, 204, 209; prose style in, 200n27; reading, 171; setting of, 172; social atmosphere of, 205; social cruelty in, 206; structure of, 214; "sweat of the brow" and, 176, 176n5; work and, 177; writing, 173, 175, 214–15
"Our Nearest Relation," 154, 155
Owen, Richard, 149n24, 150, 161
Oxford Dictionary of English Idioms, 2
Oxford English Dictionary (OED), 7, 14, 15, 32, 35, 57, 85, 100, 114, 116

Pacious, Kathleen, 215
"Pantomime of Life, The" (Dickens), 21
parody, 101, 179, 180
Past and Present (Carlyle), 88, 92
Patten, Robert, 8, 17, 48, 111, 128
Pearsall, Logan, 10
Peel, Robert, 35n6, 85

INDEX 275

Percival Keene (Marryat), 36n8, 46
Perker, Mr.: Pickwick and, 25
perseverance, 54, 72, 83, 93, 96, 117, 119;
    empty rhetoric of, 123; personal/
    professional, 109
Peter Simple (Marryat), 36
Peters, Laura, 154n27, 157n28
"Phenomenology of Reading" (Poulet), 224
Philip, Alex, 77
Philological Society of London, 14
philology: English, 14, 14n23; German,
    14n21, 15; intention and, 14–18;
    participatory, 14
Phineas Redux (Trollope), 46
physicality, 18–19, 21, 56, 105, 106n14
Physiology of the Novel, The (Dames), 20
Pickwick, Mr., 25, 26, 194
Pickwick Papers, The (Dickens), 6n10, 25,
    25n42, 31n1, 37n11, 38, 194
Pilgrim's Progress (Bunyan), 90
Pip, 127, 128, 129, 130, 132, 135, 137,
    148–49n23, 155; "brought up by hand"
    and, 140, 141, 167; Estella and, 138, 156,
    162, 163, 164–65; hands of, 165, 167n33,
    168, 169; Havisham and, 161; Herbert
    and, 143, 164, 166; Joe and, 139, 140, 143;
    Magwitch and, 141, 142, 156, 165–66,
    166–67, 168–69; Molly and, 159; moral
    development of, 169; Mrs. Joe and, 139,
    140, 167; nature/nurture and, 163;
    physical abuse of, 140; upbringing of, 136,
    140–41, 142, 144, 157; Wemmick and,
    143, 163
Piper, Andrew, 4, 4n4, 5n7
"Plates of the *Encyclopedia*, The" (Barthes),
    126
Pocket, Camilla, 157
Pocket, Herbert, 136, 137n13, 157, 165, 168;
    Pip and, 143, 164, 166
Pocket, Matthew, 157
Podsnap, Georgiana, 201, 202, 203, 204
Podsnap, John, 191
Poe, Edgar Allan, 61n33, 147, 150
Politics and Letters (Williams), 1
Poovey, Mary, 177, 225; on *Our Mutual
    Friend*, 172–73
Portrait of a Lady, The (James), body idioms
    in, 219
Potterson, Abbey, 183
Poulet, Georges, 91, 104, 224, 226
Price, Janet, 53
Project Gutenberg, 46n16, 89n7
Proverbs in the English Tongue (Heywood), 200

Pscyhotomy of the Hand (Beamish), 151
Pumblechook, 129, 142, 143, 164, 167n33, 169
Punch, 150
puns, 61, 61n33, 108
Pykett, Lyn: on work, 177, 177n8

Qualls, Barry, 90
Quarterly Review, 8, 9
Queen's English, The (Alford), 15
Quilp, Daniel, 27, 54

Rabelais and His World (Bakhtin), grotesque
    body in, 120
racial degeneration, theories of, 148
rarity, 30–32, 35–38, 35n5, 45, 46, 84, 132;
    extreme, 73, 89
Rattlin the Reefer (Marryat), 36n8
"Raven, The" (Poe), 61n33
"Raw Data" Is an Oxymoron (Gitleman), 4
Real Life of Mary Ann Evans, The (Boden-
    heimer), 227
realism, 120n23, 177, 189n17
Reductive Reading (Allison), 5, 12
Reed, John: on *Our Mutual Friend*, 215
repetitions, 84, 110, 143, 162, 179, 183, 211;
    conscious/unconscious, 129–30; ebbs/
    flows in, 10; isolated, 30–31
responsibility, 80, 120, 125; personal, 92, 97;
    shirking, 119; shouldering, 91, 103, 224
Riah, Mr., 191, 202, 204; Lammle and, 192;
    "sweat of the brow" and, 193
Richards, Thomas: Great Exhibition and,
    166n32
Riderhood, Pleasant, 178
Riderhood, Rogue, 28, 178, 179, 180n11,
    189, 208; behavior of, 184–85; description
    of, 210; extortion by, 188; labor and, 181,
    182, 185, 186; parody of, 180; "sweat of
    the brow" and, 181, 187–88; working
    class and, 180; Wrayburn and, 182, 187
"right-hand": feminine solidarity, 105; status,
    70, 73
"right-hand man," 3, 6, 12, 13, 28, 38–47, 56,
    62, 84–85; appearances of, 33, 34; being,
    59–60, 63, 65, 73; idiomatic orientation of,
    89; instances of, 35, 35n5; lack of, 64;
    using, 31, 32, 36–37, 39, 43, 45, 47, 51, 70,
    72–73
"right-hand manness," 37, 46, 49, 62–63
"right-hand mistress," 67, 69
"right-hand wife," 67
"right-hand woman," 28, 62, 65, 66, 67, 69,
    70, 72; possibilities of, 63; using, 73

276 **INDEX**

"right-hand womanness," 28, 37, 46, 69
Risam, Roopika, 5, 5n8
Robson, Catherine, 24
Rodas, Julia Miele, 52, 52n25
Rokesmith, Secretary, 177, 180n11, 202, 205, 210
Rosenberg, Edgar, 126, 128, 139, 220
Rouncewell, Mr., 96, 97, 105, 106, 107, 110; "shoulder the wheel" and, 94, 98
Rouncewell, Mrs., 93, 95, 116
Royal College of Physicians, logo for, 146, 146
"Ruined Mill House, The," Bleak House and, 81

Said, Edward: aesthetic hypothesis of, 17
Sala, George, 88
Salem House, 129
Satis House, 127, 137n12, 138, 148n23, 162, 164; Pip at, 137, 161
Saturday Review, 85, 213
savages, 15, 141, 148n22, 149n23, 154, 178; Irish, 151
Scenes of Clerical Life (Eliot), 225
Schaffer, Talia, 71, 191n21, 120
Schlicke, Paul, 139
Schor, Hilary, 37, 54, 82, 105, 123
Scrooge, Ebenezer, 195
sensitivity, 23n39, 62, 136–37, 137–38, 169
"shadow in the little parlor, The," 58
Shakespeare, William, 7n12, 164n31, 220
Sharp, Becky: depiction of, 67n38
Shildrick, Margrit, 53
Shore, Daniel, 5
"shoulder to the wheel," 3, 6, 12, 13, 17, 81, 98, 99, 119, 123; appearances of, 86, 87; personal responsibility and, 92; using, 83, 84, 91, 93–95, 101, 105, 106, 107, 109–10, 125; variations of, 90
shouldering, 91, 110, 113, 116, 117, 118, 121, 224
Shuttleworth, Russell: on disability, 60–61
Siebers, Tobin, 59
Sisyphus, 107, 109n16
Sketches by Boz, Illustrative of Everyday Life and Every-day People (Dickens), 6n10, 24, 31n1
Skewton, Mrs., 40, 41, 42, 44, 47, 52, 74; as "right-hand woman," 62
Skimpole, Harold, 90, 102, 114, 122, 125; "shoulder to the wheel" and, 101
"Slang" (Dickens), 21
slangular, 11
Sloppy, 187, 211, 212

Smallweed, Grandfather, 118
Smallweed, Mr., 105, 115, 116, 117n20
Smallweed family, 115, 115, 116
"Smallweed family, The," 115
Smith, L. P., 11, 23
Smith, Olivia, 32
Snuphanuph, Lady, 25
Snyder, Sharon: disability and, 71–72
Sobchak, Vivian, 55
social contexts, 72, 149
social dominance, 176, 204
social mastery, 174, 206
social power, 202, 203, 204
Solberg, Sarah, 77
"Song of the Shirt, The" (Hood), 189
Sparsit, Mrs.: nosiness of, 49
Spectator, The (Addison), 7
Spenlow and Jorkins, 83
"spinning one's wheels," 107, 108
Spitzer, Leo, 13, 49
Spivak, Gayatri: on digital methodologies, 4n2
Squod, Phil, 83, 104, 105, 125; deformation of, 120n26; described, 117–18; George and, 118–19, 120; Jo and, 121; perseverance of, 119
Steig, Michael, 67, 69n39
Stephen, Leslie: on Dickens, 9
Stewart, Garrett, 9n18, 10, 17, 62, 78n43, 91, 108, 120n24, 173n1, 220; body idioms and, 26, 225; Dickensian "style" and, 47, 215–16; figures and, 26; liturgical formula and, 193; on Our Mutual Friend, 173–74; Vholes and, 112n18
Stone, Harry, 126n3, 128n8, 145, 169; on Dickens, 130n9; on Dombey, 79; on Our Mutual Friend, 172
Storey, Graham, 129
Story of Alice, The (Douglas-Fairhurst), body idioms in, 227
"Street Haunting" (Woolf), 22
substitution, 36, 36n9, 39, 42, 73, 78; thematic of, 63
Summerson, Esther, 82, 96, 99, 101, 102, 108, 111, 114, 119, 123; Ada and, 106; appraisal of, 104, 105; Bleak House and, 124; hand of, 104; moral resolution of, 125; "shoulder to the wheel" and, 28, 83, 105, 110; work ethic of, 104, 106
Summerson, Tom, 124
surface reading, 6
surrogacy: "right-handed," 73, 79; thematic of, 63

INDEX

Sussman, Herbert, 57
"sweat of the brow," 3, 6, 180, 181, 183, 187–88, 193, 292; development of, 194; using, 175, 176, 176n5, 182
Swiveller, Dick, 27

Tale of Two Cities, A (Dickens), 6n10, 31n1, 175; "nose to the grindstone" and, 195
Tappertit, Simon, 194, 195
Ternan, Ellen, 175
Thackeray, William, 3, 46; body idioms and, 1; Sharp and, 67n38; social satires of, 2
thematics, 12, 37, 48, 63, 130, 131, 135; imaginative, 103; structural, 103
theory of evolution, 131, 148, 148n22, 150, 156–57
Thomas, William Moy, 155
Thomson, David Croal, 77
Thomson, Thomas: "shoulder to the wheel" and, 88
Thorpe, Benjamin: philology and, 14
Tillotson, Kathleen, 25n42, 37, 51, 90, 90n8, 126n1, 127n6, 129; on *Bleak House*, 80; on *Dombey*, 51; *Great Expectations* and, 126
Tiny Tim, 54
Tippins, Lady, 191
Tom-all-Alone, 82, 92, 113, 114, 121, 122, 124
Tomalin, Claire, 20, 64n35, 98
"tongue-in-cheek," 1
Toodle, Polly, 38, 48, 64n35, 64n36; examination of, 65; as "right-hand woman," 62, 64
Tox, Miss, 39, 48, 54, 65, 72, 73; on Cuttle, 59
Treatise (Bell), 146, 146n19, 150
Treatise on the Diseases of Children, A (Underwood), 132
Trench, Richard Chenevix, 15, 16, 176, 176n6
Trollope, Anthony, 3, 8, 46, 225
Tromp, Marlene, 106, 106n14
Turveydrop, Mr., 100, 105, 111, 118, 125; characterization of, 98, 99; Jo and, 121; as "model of Deportment," 98, 99; "shoulder to the wheel" and, 101
Turveydrop, Prince, 98–99
Turveydrop Dancing Academy, 99, 100, 102
Twist, Oliver, 26, 129, 153–54, 160
Tyler, Daniel, 24, 48, 128; on Dickens/style, 47–48

Ulysses, wordplay in, 222
Underwood, Michael, 132
Underwood, Ted, 6

Uneven Development (Poovey), 225
Unique Body Idioms Used per Novel, 3 (table)

Vale of Taunton, 107, 125
Vanity Fair (Thackeray), 2, 46, 67n38
Veneerings, 191, 200, 212
Venus, 177n7, 209; Wegg and, 210–11
vernacular language, 10, 47, 78, 227; bodily, 48; proliferation of, 13
Vestiges of the Natural History of Creation (Chambers), 146, 147, 149, 150
Vholes, Mr., 105, 107, 108, 111, 112–13, 112n18, 115, 116, 122; living arrangements of, 114; professional mantra and, 113; Richard and, 114; "shoulder to the wheel" and, 109, 109n16, 110; Vale of Taunton and, 125
Victoria & Albert Museum, 41, 93
Victorians, 28, 46n17, 135, 147, 149, 151; hands and, 178
Villette (Brontë), 225
violence, 106n14, 151, 155–56, 161; physical, 135, 140, 157, 165, 178
Vlock, Deborah, 98

Walder, Dennis, 22, 149n25; everyday and, 24n40
Wales, Katie, on Joyce, 221, 222
walking: listening and, 22n36, 23; rhetoric of, 22
Warren's Blacking Factory, 2, 9, 22
Waters, Catherine, 36n9, 48, 55n28
Weevle, Mr., 114, 115
Wegg, Silas, 28, 54, 187, 209; Boffin and, 211; grindstone and, 211; Venus and, 210–11
Welsh, Alexander, 148n23, 176
Wemmick, 154–55; Pip and, 143, 163
Westminster Review, 213, 219
Wider, Kathleen, 21
Wilberforce, Samuel, 149n24
Wilfer, Bella, 187, 202, 205
Willet, Joe, 194, 195
Williams, Raymond, 1, 13, 39, 73–74, 80, 81, 84
Wittgenstein, Ludwig, 108, 142
Wold, Chesney, 93–94, 95, 116
Woman in White, The (Collins), 225
Wood, Claire, 177n7, 193
Woodcourt, Allan, 83, 107, 121, 125
Woolf, Virginia, 22; body idioms and, 224; *David Copperfield* and, 223; idiomatic body in, 217–23; Victorian predecessors of, 223

278 INDEX

word count, 219n4, 224n9; pagination and, 227

wordplay, 56; idiomatic, 170, 222; literal/figurative and, 222

Wordsworth, William, 23

work, 176, 177, 184, 189, 191; Dickensian, 177; representation of, 107; term, 194. *See also* labor

working class, 176, 180, 183, 187

Wrayburn, Eugene, 28, 177, 179, 183, 186, 189, 209, 212; goading by, 185; Headstone and, 184, 184n16, 185, 206, 206n33, 207–8; Riderhood and, 182, 187; work and, 184

Wrayburn and Lightwood (firm), 180, 181

Wren, Jenny, 28, 177, 189n17, 191n21, 212; "sweat of the brow" and, 189

"Writer as Artist, The" (Eliot), 217

writing: labor of, 197; styles/Dickensian, 12; as theatrical acting, 19, 20

Wuthering Heights (Brontë), 225

Yaeger, Patricia, 90

York, Duke of, 42

Young, Robert, 74

Younquist, Paul: physiological aesthetics and, 23

Zemka, Sue: on Derenzy, 57, 58

Zola, Émile, 219

Printed in the USA
CPSIA information can be obtained
at www.ICGtesting.com
LVHW081810021123
762854LV00003B/388